THE PHILOSOPHY OF SPINOZA

VOLUME I

THE PHILOSOPHY
OF SPINOZA

UNFOLDING THE LATENT PROCESSES
OF HIS REASONING

HARRY AUSTRYN WOLFSON

VOLUME I

SCHOCKEN BOOKS • NEW YORK

First SCHOCKEN PAPERBACK edition 1969

Copyright © 1934 by the President and Fellows of Harvard College
Copyright © renewed 1961 by Harry Austryn Wolfson
Library of Congress Catalog Card No. 70-83674
Published by arrangement with Harvard University Press
Manufactured in the United States of America

PREFACE

To the trained observer the simplest thing in nature has a structure and a history; to the naïve mind the most complicated product of human device appears simple and spontaneous. Imagine a primitive man, brought up in natural surroundings and without ever having witnessed human art in its making. Placed suddenly in one of the canyon-like streets of a modern metropolis, such a primitive man would undoubtedly think of the flanking sky-soaring structures of intricate design and workmanship as something which grew out of the soil like trees and grass. Similarly, imagine a student of philosophy, trained in some miraculous manner in the usages of philosophic concepts and vocabulary of the present day, without any inkling of their past history. Confronted suddenly with the *Ethics* of Spinoza, such a trained student would undoubtedly think of it as something which sprang forth full-grown and completely armored, like Minerva, from the brain of its author, and he would quite naturally try to interpret it in the light of whatever associations it evoked in his mind. Of course, there is no such preposterously trained student of philosophy, any more than there is such a naïve-minded primitive man as he to whom we have compared him. But, still, many a student of Spinoza comes very near treating his *Ethics* in the fantastic fashion which we have described. Like the Bible, the *Ethics* of Spinoza has often been the subject of homiletical interpretations. It has been treated like an amorphous mass of floating clouds in which one's fancy may cut whatever figures it pleases.

Now, I will not deny that we must allow for philosophic license as we allow for poetic license, and that the cutting of imaginary figures in Spinoza's *Ethics* is not without its uses. When Goethe confesses that he cannot tell what he got out of the *Ethics* and what he may himself have put into it, we can only say that we are grateful to Spinoza for having served as a stimulus to the thought of Goethe. In the same way, many a worthy thought of men less distinguished — and perhaps also less frank — than Goethe has had its birth in a misinterpretation of Spinoza or else has received due attention by its having been mounted, gratuitously, on Spinoza's writings. But it would be carrying the analogy of the license too far if we should say that the philosopher in his interpretation is to be as little bound by the truth of scholarship as the poet in his imagery is by the truth of science. It is certainly no compliment to a philosopher of the past who is prominent enough for us to study him to say that only by being misunderstood does he become philosophically important. Indeed, the entire field of the history of philosophy would be placed outside the bounds of exact disciplined study if we should maintain that its study is of philosophical importance only when we superciliously disregard its objective meaning as established by research, or indolently make no effort to acquaint ourselves with it, or blissfully keep ourselves in ignorance of it. The fact is, what is often called subjective interpretation in philosophy is nothing but the explanation of a text in terms of the haphazard knowledge that one happens to possess, just as what is called popularization means nothing but the explanation of a text in terms of the ignorance supposed to be possessed by the readers for whom it is intended. In either of these cases, whatever merit the particular form of presentation possesses is derived from the fact that it helps to give currency to the results of historical

scholarship, which in its proper sense means the interpretation of a text in terms of everything that can be known about
it, for which a systematic search must be made. The first
step, the basic step, in the understanding of any philosopher,
one upon which any subjective form of interpretation or
any literary form of presentation must rest, is the determination by the method of historical criticism of what the
philosopher meant by what he said, how he came to say
what he said, and why he said it in the manner in which he
happened to say it.

It is this threefold task that we have set ourselves in the
present study of Spinoza. Now, the historico-critical method
really means the presupposition that in any text treated by
it there is a sort of dual authorship — an explicit author,
who expresses himself in certain conventional symbols and
patterns, and an implicit author, whose unuttered thoughts
furnish us with the material for grasping the full significance
of those symbols and patterns. In the case of the *Ethics* of
Spinoza, there is, on the one hand, an explicit Spinoza,
whom we shall call Benedictus. It is he who speaks in definitions, axioms, and propositions; it is he, too, who reasons
according to the rigid method of the geometer. Then there
is, on the other hand, the implicit Spinoza, who lurks behind
these definitions, axioms, and propositions, only occasionally revealing himself in the scholia; his mind is crammed
with traditional philosophic lore and his thought turns along
the beaten logical paths of mediaeval reasoning. Him we
shall call Baruch. Benedictus is the first of the moderns;
Baruch is the last of the mediaevals. It is our contention
that we cannot get the full meaning of what Benedictus says
unless we know what has passed through the mind of Baruch.
Starting with the assumption that the *Ethics* is primarily
a criticism of fundamental problems of philosophy as they

presented themselves to Spinoza, we proceed to analyze these problems, to set forth their salient features, to construct hypothetically the arguments which constitute the criticism, and to show how these arguments and criticism underlie the statements which we have before us in the *Ethics*. As a result of this procedure, the *Ethics* emerges as a logically constructed work throughout which there is order and sequence and continuity: propositions, apparently disconnected, group themselves into unified and coherent chapters; words, phrases, and passages, apparently meaningless or commonplace, assume meaning and significance; and the philosophy of Spinoza, as a systematic whole and in all its fulness of detail, appears in a new light and in a new setting and perspective. Into the fabric of this work, which in form follows the order of the *Ethics*, we have also woven relevant passages from the other writings of Spinoza, so that the study of his philosophy herein presented is based upon his *Ethics* as well as upon all his other writings in so far as they are related to the *Ethics*.

This work can be read as a self-explanatory systematic presentation of the philosophy of Spinoza. It can be read with greater profit as a companion volume to the *Ethics* and a running commentary on it. It can be read with still greater profit together with some standard works or special studies on Spinoza, for, with the exception of general references to the literature on Spinoza whenever they were necessary either for the bibliographical guidance of the reader or as an acknowledgment of indebtedness on certain points, and with the further exception of an occasional expression of disagreement, we have refrained from entering upon an examination and comparison or criticism of the various extant interpretations of Spinoza — a subject which, if dealt with at all, is deserving of a study by itself. Independently of

Spinoza, this work can be read as a study of the development
of certain fundamental problems in the history of philosophy,
or of the understanding of certain points in the teachings of
the authors brought into the discussion and of certain significant texts in their writings. Students who are interested in
the relation of Spinoza to other philosophers will find in
this work an abundance of undreamed-of new material, culled
from the writings of various philosophers ranging from Aristotle to Descartes, though we do not say that every author
whom we have found it useful or necessary to quote is to be
considered a forerunner of Spinoza or as having had a dominant influence upon his philosophy. The principles on which
the selection of this material was made, the manner in which
it was used in the interpretation of Spinoza, and the method
by which its direct literary relationship to Spinoza and its
influence upon him can be determined, are discussed in the
opening chapter. The analytical table of contents at the beginning of each volume and the several Indexes at the end of
the second volume will serve as guides to the reader in these
various uses to which the book may be put.

Chapters III, IV, V, and VIII were published in *Chronicon
Spinozanum*, Vols. I (1921), pp. 101–112, II (1922), pp. 92–
117, III (1923), pp. 142–178, and IV (1924–1926), pp. 79–
103, respectively. Chapter VI appeared in Italian translation in *Ricerche Religiose*, Vol. IX (1933), pp. 193–236. All
these chapters are reprinted here with some revisions. The
original title and description of this work were announced
in the *Chronicon Spinozanum* as "Spinoza the Last of the
Mediaevals: a Study of the *Ethica Ordine Geometrico Demonstrata* in the light of a hypothetically constructed *Ethica
More Scholastico Rabbinicoque Demonstrata*." This title had
to be abandoned, as it did not seem advisable to have the
title begin with the word "Spinoza."

The protracted delay in the completion of the work was amply made up for by the promptness with which its publication was undertaken when the manuscript was finished. This was made possible by the Fund for the Support of the Humanities at Harvard University provided by the General Education Board. For this I am profoundly grateful. I am also deeply indebted to Miss Christabel Garner, of the Harvard University Press, for her searching reading of the proofs and for valuable suggestions.

HARRY AUSTRYN WOLFSON

CAMBRIDGE, MASSACHUSETTS
    May, 1933

CONTENTS

VOLUME I

CHAPTER I

CHAPTER II

CONTENTS

CHAPTER V

CHAPTER VI

CHAPTER VII

CHAPTER IX

CHAPTER X

CHAPTER XI

CHAPTER XII

VOLUME II

(ETHICS, II)

CHAPTER XIII

CHAPTER XIV

CHAPTER XV

CHAPTER XVI

CHAPTER XVII

(ETHICS, III)

CHAPTER XVIII

(ETHICS, IV)

CHAPTER XIX

(ETHICS, V)

CHAPTER XX

CHAPTER XXI

CHAPTER I

BEHIND THE GEOMETRICAL METHOD

IN DISCUSSING once with a group of friends the importance of philology and of bookish learning in general for the study of the history of philosophy, I happened to remark that philosophers, after all, see the universe which they try to explain as already interpreted to them in books, with the only possible exception, perhaps, of the first recorded philosopher, and all he could see was water. "How about Spinoza?" challenged one of the listeners. "Was he also a bookish philosopher?" Without stopping to think, I took up the challenge. "As for Spinoza," I said, "if we could cut up all the philosophic literature available to him into slips of paper, toss them up into the air, and let them fall back to the ground, then out of these scattered slips of paper we could reconstruct his *Ethics*."

Not long after that I found myself reconstructing the *Ethics* out of scattered slips of paper figuratively cut out of the philosophic literature available to Spinoza. The problem before us, as I discovered, was like that of a jig-saw puzzle. Suppose we have a box of pieces out of which we are to construct a certain picture. But the pieces contained in the box are more than can be used, and from among them we have to select those which are needed for our purpose. Furthermore, the pieces do not fit together, and they have to be reshaped. Finally, many necessary pieces are missing, and we have to supply them ourselves. But to offset all these difficulties, we have an outline of the picture which we are to construct.

The picture which we have to construct in our own jig-saw puzzle is the *Ethics* as it was originally formed in the mind of

Spinoza, of which the present *Ethics* in its geometrical form is only a bare outline.[1] Since, however, we do not know nor can we ascertain exactly what books Spinoza had actually read, what quotations he had come across in the course of his readings, or what casual information he had gathered from conversations with friends, we must take as our box of pieces the entire philosophic literature available at the time of Spinoza and out of this make our necessary selections. Furthermore, since philosophic texts and ideas are the most plastic of material, capable of assuming a variety of meanings with different philosophers, we must reshape our pieces in the form which we have reason to believe they assumed in the mind of Spinoza. Finally, since the *Ethics* before us is not the result of a syncretism of traditional philosophy but rather the result of criticism, and since this criticism, though implied, is not explicitly expressed, we shall have to supply it ourselves.

In our study of the *Ethics* we must try to follow the same method that Spinoza followed in writing it. Spinoza did not start out with classified lists of bibliographies, outlines, abstracts, quotations, and all the elaborate equipment with which methodical scholarship of today prepares itself for the writing of an informative work of reference. He started out with a certain fund of knowledge acquired through miscellaneous reading which in his mind formed itself into a composite picture of the salient features of traditional philosophy. In this composite mental picture, we may assume, the problems of philosophy presented themselves in a certain order, each problem modelled after a certain pattern and expressed in a certain terminology. Tagged on to this picture, underneath its surface, and deep down into the recesses of Spinoza's consciousness, we may further assume, there was an

[1] Cf. below, p. 59.

aggregation of notes swarming with references to sources of texts, to parentages of ideas, to conflicts of opinions, and to diversities of interpretations, all of them ready to come up to the surface, whenever the occasion arose, and take their place in the picture. In our endeavor to retrace the steps of Spinoza's reasoning, we must, therefore, first of all, equip ourselves with a similar fund of knowledge, or philosophical mass of apperception, as it may be called.

With such an apperceptive mass as our equipment we begin to read the *Ethics*. Without forcing ourselves to understand the book, we let its propositions penetrate into our amassed fund of knowledge and by the natural process of association and attraction become encrusted with terms, phrases, and ideas out of the storehouse of our memory. At first these encrustations are indistinguishable and shapeless clumps, clinging to the propositions as bits of scrap-iron cling to a magnet. But then we let our mind play upon them — to scrutinize them and to study them. By the catalytic action of the mind these indistinguishable and shapeless clumps begin to dissolve; they begin to group themselves, to solidify themselves into larger units, to become differentiated from each other, to assume form, and ultimately to crystallize themselves into distinct topics of recognizable historical problems of philosophy. Thus at the very outset of the *Ethics*, Proposition I, together with Definitions III and V and Axioms I and II upon which it is based, emerges as a distinct topic by itself, which we label the definition of substance and mode. The next five propositions, II–VI, crystallize themselves into a discussion of the unity of substance, made up of two historical problems, the unity of God and creation. Propositions VII–X and XII–XIII shape themselves into a discussion of three closely related topics under the general heading of the Simplicity of Substance, and wedged in be-

tween them is Proposition XI, where the term "substance"
gives way to the term "God"; this is easily recognized as a
discussion of the traditional proofs of the existence of God.
Next follow two propositions, XIV and XV, which deal with
the attributes of extension and thought, and a Scholium,
which deals with the infinity of extension. The remaining
propositions of the First Part of the *Ethics* readily group
themselves into discussions of the various meanings of the
causality of God, among which Spinoza dwells especially
upon the immanence, freedom, necessity, and purposelessness
of God's causality. In the Second Part of the *Ethics* the propositions fall into the traditional outline of the discussion of
the soul, dealing in the conventional order and manner with
the definition of the soul, its relation to the body, and the
classification of its faculties. The last three parts of the
Ethics deal with what is traditionally known as practical
philosophy as contrasted with the theoretical philosophy of
the first two parts, dealing successively with the problems of
the emotions, virtues, and the final happiness of man. As our
mind scrutinizes still further these groups of propositions it
discovers that they follow one upon the other according
to a certain order of sequence, which is at once intrinsically
logical and extrinsically in conformity with historical patterns. With this, the first stage in our study of the *Ethics*
comes to an end.

Then the next stage in our investigation is to find a certain
coherence within each group of propositions. The data upon
which we have to work are twofold. On the one hand, there
are the problems of philosophy as they unfold themselves before us in all their variety of forms in the vast literature that
was available to Spinoza. On the other hand, there are the
utterances of Spinoza in the *Ethics*, elliptical, fragmentary,
disjointed, and oftentimes, if we are to admit the truth to

ourselves, enigmatic and unintelligible. Between these two extremes we expect to find the problems as they must have formulated themselves in the mind of Spinoza, the doubts which he must have raised against accepted views, and his own solutions of these doubts which he must have meant to express in his uttered statements in the *Ethics*. The task before us, then, is to reconstruct the process of Spinoza's reasoning in all its dialectical niceties and in all its fulness of detail so that it will lead us to a thorough understanding of the statements which confront us in the *Ethics*. By the method of trial and error we experiment with one conjecture after another, until we finally arrive at a result which seems to us satisfactory. Thus, for instance, at the very outset of the *Ethics*, in Proposition I and its underlying Definitions III and V and Axioms I and II, which we have already set apart as a topic by itself, dealing with definition of substance and mode, we reconstruct out of the material scattered in the literature of philosophy the problem as we assume it presented itself to the mind of Spinoza — the division of being, the definition of substance and accident, the classification of substances, and so on. Again, out of direct internal discussions of these problems which occur in the philosophic literature of the past, or indirectly out of certain suggestions and hints, and sometimes even without these direct or indirect aids, we reconstruct a criticism of these traditional definitions as we assume it formulated itself in the mind of Spinoza. As a result we are enabled to integrate these Axioms, Definitions, and Proposition I into a coherent chapter, containing a logically formed argument.[1] We follow the same method in our study of the next group of propositions, Propositions II–VI, which we have found to reflect two historical problems, the unity of God and creation, and which we have subsumed

[1] Cf. below, pp. 61 ff.

under the heading of the Unity of Substance. Here our task
is somewhat more difficult, for we have to deal here not with
one single proposition, as is the case in Proposition I, but
with five propositions, each of which is followed by a demonstration, and between which there seems to be no unity and
transition. Again, by the method of trial and error we ultimately succeed in reconstructing the thought of Spinoza so
that in the light of it these five propositions form a connected
logical syllogism.[1] And so we go through the entire *Ethics*,
and by the use of different devices we succeed in bringing
unity, coherence, and harmony within each group of propositions. With this, the second stage of our investigation
comes to an end.

Then we take up the third and last stage of our investigation, that of documenting our findings so that we may con-
vince others of the truth of our statements and reasoning.
Here, too, we must follow the same method that Spinoza
would have followed, had he documented his *Ethics*. We feel
that it would not be enough to quote from books which we
happen to know, or which happen to be generally known. We
must ask ourselves what works Spinoza himself would have
used if he had chosen to document his writings. To answer
this question we must determine, even though only in a general way, the extent and variety of the philosophic literature
available to Spinoza.

Two philosophic literatures were open to Spinoza, the
Hebrew and the Latin. His knowledge of Hebrew he had
acquired in a school where he had studied it systematically
under the guidance of competent teachers probably from the
age of seven to the age of eighteen (1639–1650).[2] Latin he

---

[1] Cf. below, pp. 85 ff.

[2] As for the years of Spinoza's entering and leaving the Hebrew School '*Eẓ
Hayyim*, see Dunin-Borkowski, *Der junge De Spinoza* (1910), p. 103, and Freudenthal, *Spinoza Leben und Lehre* (ed. Gebhardt, 1927), I, p. 31.

began to study later, at first not in a school but privately.
His systematic study of that language under the tutorage of
Francis van den Enden did not begin until 1652, when he was
already twenty years old. Though he had also a knowledge
of several modern languages, Spanish, Portuguese, Dutch,
French, and possibly also Italian, German, and Flemish,[1] the
philosophic material in these languages was negligible. Hebrew made accessible to him not only the works of Jewish
philosophers but also the works of Arabic philosophers, the
works of Aristotle, mostly as incorporated in the commentaries of Averroes, the works of some of the Greek commentators on Aristotle, and also the works of some of the Latin
scholastic philosophers. Latin similarly opened to him not
only the original Latin writings of the philosophers of the
Roman period, of mediaeval scholasticism, and of the Renaissance, but also translations from the Greek, Arabic, and
Hebrew. In Hebrew the most important works of Jewish
philosophers, whether those translated from the Arabic or
those written originally in Hebrew, were already accessible
to him in printed form, some of them in several editions; but
the translations from non-Jewish authors, with but a few
slight exceptions, were accessible to him only in manuscript
form. Manuscripts, however, at that time were not yet
gathered up and stored away in a few closely guarded central
libraries; they were still widely scattered among individual
owners and freely circulated, especially in Amsterdam, where
Hebrew scholarship and Hebrew printing presses flourished
and where privately owned collections of Hebrew manuscripts must have existed. Furthermore, the student of
Hebrew philosophic texts could gain a thorough knowledge

---

[1] As for Spinoza's knowledge of languages, see Epistola 19 (*Opera*, IV, p. 95,
ll. 12–15); Epistola 26 (p. 159, l. 16); Lucas' *La Vie de feu Monsieur de Spinoza* in
A. Wolf, *The Oldest Biography of Spinoza*, pp. 51–52 and 104.

of the contents of the unpublished Hebrew translations of Arabic and Greek authors through the numerous and extensive quotations from their works as well as through the elaborate discussions of their views which were to be found in Hebrew works already published. In Latin the proportion of printed works in philosophy was greater than in Hebrew, even of works which were translated into Latin from the Hebrew. Thus, for instance, the bulk of Averroes' commentaries on Aristotle, which were translated into Latin from the Hebrew, existed in many printed editions in Latin, whereas in Hebrew they existed only in manuscript form.

To Spinoza these three literatures, Hebrew, Latin, and Arabic, represented a common tradition. Whatever differences he noticed between them, they concerned only problems of a purely theological and dogmatic nature; the philosophic basis of all such problems, and especially the discussion of problems of a purely philosophic nature, he could not fail to see, were all of a common origin. They were all based upon Greek philosophy, at the centre of which stood Aristotle. The same Greek terminology lay behind the Arabic, Hebrew, and Latin terminology, and the same scientific and philosophic conceptions formed the intellectual background of all those who philosophized in Arabic, Hebrew, or Latin. The three philosophic literatures were in fact one philosophy expressed in different languages, translatable almost literally into one another. And within each of these philosophic literatures numerous works existed which were encyclopaedic in nature, covering as they did the entire range of philosophy, containing the same roster of problems, the same analyses of those problems, the same definitions of terms, the same metaphysical brocards, the same clash of contrasting views, the same arguments in support or in refutation of each view, and, barring certain individual differences of emphasis or of interpretation, arriving also at the same conclusions. A reader who had mastered any of these books in one of these three languages found himself treading upon familiar ground when he came to read any book in the other languages.

We do not know exactly in what language Spinoza would have written his books had the choice of language been determined by him on the basis of the ease with which he could express himself in it rather than on the basis of the linguistic equipment of the readers whom he wished to reach. Had Spinoza lived in the land of his forefathers, Spain or Portugal, before the expulsion, or in any other European country where Jewish philosophy was cultivated, such as Southern France or Italy, he would have undoubtedly written in Hebrew, for Hebrew had been the exclusive medium of expression of Jewish philosophers and scientists throughout Europe ever since the disappearance of Jewish life in Southern Spain under Moslem rule with the coming of the Almohades in the twelfth century. The particular attitude of an author toward the problems of religion was no deterrent to his use of Hebrew, for every shade of opinion, from extreme adherence to tradition to the most daring adventures into freedom of thought, found expression in Hebrew literature. In the intellectual autonomy which the Jews enjoyed during the Middle Ages, with the systematic pursuit of the study of philosophy and the sciences in Jewish schools out of Hebrew books, Jewish thinkers were always assured of appreciative as well as critical readers among their own people of whatever views they chose to express in Hebrew. But toward the end of the fifteenth century there appeared Jewish philosophers who, though brought up on Hebrew philosophic literature and themselves writing in Hebrew, wrote books in non-Jewish languages for non-Jewish readers. Elijah Delmedigo, better known as Helias Hebraeus Cretensis (1460–1497), wrote his

Quaestiones Tres and his *Adnotationes in Dictis Averrois super Libros Physicorum* [1] in Latin, and Judah Abrabanel, better known as Leo Hebraeus (d. 1535), wrote his *Dialoghi d'Amore* in Italian.[2]   In Spinoza's own time and in the community in which he was born, Hebrew was still used extensively by his own teachers and schoolmates in their literary works, but use was also made by some of them of Spanish and Latin.   His teacher Manasseh ben Israel wrote on theological problems in Hebrew, Latin, Spanish, and Portuguese.   Under these circumstances, what language Spinoza would have used if he had chosen that in which self-expression was the easiest for him can be only conjectured.   That it would not have been Latin or Dutch, in which his books happen to be written, is quite evident by his own confession.   At the time of the publication of his *Principia Philosophiae Cartesianae* and *Cogitata Metaphysica* (1663) he still felt the deficiency of his Latin, and before allowing his friends to publish these works he stipulated that one of them should, in his presence, "clothe them in more elegant style." [3]   In 1665, in one of his letters to Blyenbergh,[4] he intimates that he could express his thoughts in Spanish, "the language in which I was brought up," better than in Dutch.   Whether Hebrew was with him, as it was with many Jewish authors of his time and place, a more natural vehicle of literary expression is uncertain.

But it is quite certain that Hebrew literature was the primary source of his knowledge of philosophy and the main stock upon which all the other philosophic knowledge which

---

[1] These two works are printed together with Joannes de Janduno's *Quaestiones in Libros Physicorum*, 1501, and other editions.

[2] It is quite possible, however, that the *Dialoghi d'Amore* was written originally in Hebrew.   Cf. I. Sonne, *Lishe'elat ha-Lashon ha-Mekorit shel Wikkuhe ha-Ahahab li-Yehudah Abarbanel*, in *Ziyyunim* (Berlin, 1929), pp. 142–148.   For new evidence that it was originally written in Hebrew, see below, vol. II, p. 14.

[3] Epistola 13 (*Opera*, IV, p. 63, ll. 20–22).   [4] Epistola 19 (p. 95, ll. 12–15).

he later acquired was grafted. He had become familiar with Hebrew philosophic literature before he began to read philosophy in Latin. His nascent philosophic doubt arose as a reaction against the philosophy which he read in Hebrew. With the exception of the new sciences, his readings in Latin supplied him merely with a new vocabulary for old ideas. Throughout his discussions of philosophical problems, especially those bordering upon theology, Hebrew sources appear as the matrix in which the general outline of ideas was formed. Other sources appear as insets. It is Hebrew sources, too, upon which he draws for his casual illustrations. An outstanding example of this is to be found in his discussion in Chapter XV of the *Tractatus Theologico-Politicus* of the two contrasting attitudes shown by philosophers towards the problem of the relation of faith to philosophy or of theology to reason. The problem was an old one, and it had been discussed in Mohammedanism, Christianity, and Judaism alike. In each of these three religions, the two contrasting attitudes had their exponents. In Mohammedanism, such exponents, to mention but two, were Algazali and Averroes. In Christianity, two typical exponents of these attitudes could be found in Bernard of Clairvaux and Abelard. Spinoza, however, mentions none of these. He takes Alpakhar and Maimonides as his examples of typical representatives of these two contrasting views, and he does so simply because these were the two men through whose works he first became acquainted with the nature of the problem. He did not even feel the need, writing as he did in Latin for non-Jewish readers, to substitute two corresponding Christian authors for these two Jewish authors, for in Spinoza's time Jewish philosophy had not yet been eliminated from European philosophy and relegated to the esoteric field of oriental wisdom. From the thirteenth century down through the seventeenth

century it was quite fashionable for theologians and philosophers to quote Hebrew authorities by the side of Greek
authorities, and those who followed the habit of quoting
Greek sources in the original Greek also quoted Hebrew
sources in the original Hebrew. The only concession that
Spinoza seems to have made to his non-Jewish readers is that
he referred to his Hebrew authorities with the aloofness of an
outsider.

Following this principle, we go first to Hebrew philosophic
literature for our documents. It is not any particular author
that we go to, but the field of literature as a whole. If one
particular author, Maimonides for instance, happens to be
resorted to more often than others, it is not because he has
been especially selected for our purpose, but because Spinoza
himself would have selected him, for his work is the most excellent depository of mediaeval philosophic lore, where one
can find the most incisive analyses of philosophic problems,
the most complete summaries of philosophic opinions, the
clearest definitions of terms, and all these couched in happy and
quotable phrases. But we always try to give sufficient parallels from other Hebrew authors so as not to create the erroneous impression that we are trying to draw parallels between
one single Hebrew author and Spinoza. In like manner, in
order not to create the erroneous impression that the material
drawn upon is unique in Hebrew philosophic literature, we
quote, or refer to, similar passages in the works of Arabic or
scholastic authors. When the occasion demands, scholastic
sources are resorted to in preference to the Hebrew. Furthermore, in order not to create the erroneous impression that
there is something peculiarly "mediaeval" about the views
we quote from the various mediaeval sources, we trace their
origin to Aristotle's works. Frequently we string together
a list of names from the various linguistic groups of philos-

ophy in order to indicate that the views under discussion are a common philosophic heritage. Before quoting a passage from a certain book we do not stop to ask ourselves whether that book was known to Spinoza. In several instances we rather suspect that the book in question was unknown to him. But that makes no difference to us. Provided the idea expressed in the passage under consideration is not uncommon, we assume that it was known to Spinoza, even though for the time being we do not know exactly the immediate literary source of his knowledge. In such instances, only one who would arrogate to himself divine omniscience could assert with certainty that the idea could not be found in any source available to Spinoza. The burden of proof is always upon the negative.

But very often certain passages are identified as being the direct and immediate sources of Spinoza. As a rule Spinoza does not quote sources literally, even when he mentions them. In a letter to Meyer, for instance, he introduces his reproduction of Crescas' proof of the existence of God by the words "it reads as follows" (*sic sonat*),[1] and yet the passage which follows is not an exact quotation. But in many instances the evidence points to certain passages as directly underlying the utterances of Spinoza. In determining these direct sources it is not the similarity of single terms or even of single phrases that guides us, for in the history of philosophy terms and phrases, no less than the ideas which they express, have a certain persistency about them and they survive intact throughout their winding transmigrations. It is always a term or a phrase as imbedded in a certain context, and that context by its internal structure and by a combination of enveloping circumstances, that help us to determine direct literary relationships. When we feel that we are in a position,

[1] Epistola 12 (*Opera*, IV, p. 61, l. 18).

for instance, to affirm with reasonable certainty that it is
Thomas Aquinas from whom Spinoza has taken over in the
Scholium to Proposition XXIX of *Ethics*, I, the distinction
of *natura naturans* and *natura naturata* it is not because these
phrases happen to occur in his works, for as phrases they
happen to occur also in the works of other authors; it is only
because Spinoza's description of these two phrases seems
to be a modification of the description given by Thomas
Aquinas, and also because the reason for the modification of
the description by Spinoza can be adequately accounted for.[1]
When, again, we are in a position to affirm with reasonable
certainty that it is Crescas from whom Spinoza has taken
over in the Scholium to Proposition XV of *Ethics*, I, the
three "examples" by which his "opponents" prove the impossibility of an infinite extension and in refutation of them
the three "distinctions" which he mentions in Epistola XII
to Meyer, it is not because these "examples" and "distinctions" are to be found in Crescas, for as individual "examples" and "distinctions" they are to be found also in other
authors; it is only because these three "distinctions" are
used by Crescas as refutations of three arguments which
correspond respectively to the three "examples" of Spinoza.[2]
Finally, to take but one more example, when we are in a
position to affirm with reasonable certainty that Spinoza's
discussion of the highest good, of human society, and of the
virtues in Propositions XIX–LXXIII of *Ethics*, IV, is based
upon Aristotle's *Nicomachean Ethics* it is not because we discover in them certain similarities in individual terms or
phrases; it is only because we discover in them definite literary similarities in the construction of the arguments.[3] It is
by such methods that direct literary relationship has been

[1] Cf. below, pp. 254 f.   [2] Cf. below, pp. 264 ff.
[3] Cf. below, Vol. II, pp. 233 ff.

established between Spinoza and many of the authors quoted in this work.

A list of passages quoted or referred to in this work from various authors will be found in the Index of References, and an analysis of topics of each of these authors will be found in the Index of Subjects and Names. The works quoted or referred to, it will be noticed, are drawn indiscriminately from the various linguistic groups of philosophic literature — Greek, Latin, Hebrew, and Arabic. Conspicuously absent among them, with the exception of a few references, mostly of ancillary importance, to Meir ibn Gabbai, Moses Cordovero, and Abraham Herrera,[1] is the Cabalistic literature, which from earliest time has been considered a source of Spinoza's philosophy. This exclusion was unintentional; it merely happened that in our search for documentation we had no occasion to resort to the Cabalistic literature for source material. Not that the Cabalistic literature could not have furnished us with apt illustrative material, but there is nothing in the Cabalistic literature which could be used for our purpose the like of which we did not find in philosophic literature, for, as has been said by one of the leading Cabalists, Moses Cordovero: "Know that in matters metaphysical oftentimes the true masters of Cabala will be found to agree with the philosophers."[2] "To follow" would perhaps have been a more accurate term than "to agree."

The list of passages is by no means exhaustive. Had we thought it necessary, we could have added innumerable parallels to every passage quoted; but our purpose was not to compile a complete catena of parallel passages. A complete Index of mediaeval philosophy, Latin, Hebrew, and

---

[1] Two of the references to Herrera, however, seem to point to a direct literary connection and are of special significance. Cf. below, pp. 245 and 314.

[2] *Elimah Rabbati*, I, 16.

Arabic, is indeed one of the desiderata of scholarship, but that will have to be done independently of any study of Spinoza. Nor are the passages quoted or referred to by us irreplaceable by similar passages from other works, though we have always tried to select passages which are most suitable for our purpose. It would be quite possible to rewrite considerable portions of this work by substituting other quotations for those used by us, without necessarily changing our present analysis and interpretation of the *Ethics*, for the passages quoted are only representative of common views which were current in the philosophic literature of the past. Had we thought it desirable, then instead of writing one single book on the *Ethics*, we could have written a series of papers bearing such titles as "Aristotle and Spinoza," "Seneca and Spinoza," "Averroes and Spinoza," "Maimonides and Spinoza," "Thomas Aquinas and Spinoza," "Leo Hebraeus and Spinoza," "Descartes and Spinoza," and many other correlations of Spinoza with names of authors who are quoted in this work or who could have been quoted. But our purpose was only to draw upon these authors for material in building up our interpretation of Spinoza and not to establish analogies, and we were especially careful to avoid the extension of analogies beyond the limits of what the actual facts warranted, and also to avoid the suggestion of influences when no direct literary relationship could be established. Had we thought it advisable we could have eliminated all the quotations from our texts, either by omitting them altogether or by giving them in paraphrase form. But the interpretation of texts is an essential part of our work, and since texts had to be used, no paraphrase, however felicitous, could take the place of an exact quotation. Probably the most logical literary form for this work would have been that of a commentary upon the *Ethics* preceded by a few general chapters of introduction. But we chose our present method because our purpose was not to comment upon single and isolated passages of the *Ethics*, but to show the unity, continuity, and logical order that runs throughout the work, and withal to present the philosophy of Spinoza as a systematic whole. Of all the authors quoted or referred to in this work, it is only Maimonides and Descartes, and indirectly through them, and quite as often directly through his own works, also Aristotle,[1] that can be said to have had a dominant influence upon the philosophic training of Spinoza and to have guided him in the formation of his own philosophy. It would indeed have been possible, within certain limits, to depict the philosophy of Spinoza against the simple background of any one of these three philosophers, except for the fact that that would not have been a true presentation of the genesis of his thought, for it had a more complex origin. All the other authors quoted in this work, however helpful they may have been in our reconstruction of the *Ethics*, can be said to have had a direct influence only upon single passages in the *Ethics*, or upon single propositions, or at most upon certain groups of propositions. To go beyond that and to attempt to build up an extended analogy between the philosophic systems of any of these authors and Spinoza, on the mere basis of such isolated parallels of expressions or passages, even when a direct literary relationship between them could be established, would only mean the inflation of footnotes into essays or monographs.

---

[1] For lists of authors in relation to whom Spinoza has been studied, see Ueberweg–Frischeisen-Köhler–Moog, *Die Philosophie der Neuzeit bis zum Ende des XVIII. Jahrhunderts* (12th ed., 1924), pp. 668 ff.; R. McKeon, *The Philosophy of Spinoza* (1928), pp. 322 ff. Among all the studies listed, no less than five on Spinoza and Maimonides and no less than sixteen on Spinoza and Descartes, there is only the following one which deals with Spinoza's relation to Aristotle: Julius Guttmann, "Spinozas Zusammenhang mit dem Aristotelismus," in *Judaica, Festschrift zu Hermann Cohens siebzigstem Geburtstage* (Berlin, 1912), pp. 515–534.

But whether direct or indirect, the sources of Spinoza are more important for us as a means of establishing the meaning of his text and philosophy than as a means of establishing an analogy or priority of doctrine. The text of his *Ethics* is not a mosaic of quoted or paraphrased passages. Nor has his philosophy developed as a rash out of the infection of certain heretical or mystical phrases. It has grown out of the very philosophy which he discards, and this by his relentless driving of its own internal criticism of itself to its ultimate logical conclusion. In our endeavor to reconstruct the processes of Spinoza's reasoning, therefore, it is not phrases that we are to deal with but the thought and the history that lie behind them and the use that he makes of them. When he says, for instance, that God is the immanent cause of all things, it is not enough for us to find some one who had called God an immanent cause. We have to study the meaning of the term "immanent" in its complicated historical development and the particular use made of it by Spinoza throughout his writings. We shall then discover that he means by it something quite different from what we should ordinarily take it to mean.[1] Not that we are to assume that Spinoza had actually gone through all the steps of the investigation which we are to trudge through in discovering the meaning of such terms — for that was not necessary for him. He lived in an age when the traditions of philosophy were still alive, and what we nowadays have to discover by the painstaking methods of research came to him naturally as the heritage of a living tradition.

Studied against the rich background of tradition, even the most colorless of terms and expressions may become invested with technical significance of the utmost importance. A case in point is the special significance which may be discovered in

[1] Cf. below, pp. 323 ff.

Spinoza's choice of the terms "attribute," "created things," and "actuality" in his definition of duration,[1] and of the terms "first thing," "actual," "human mind," "idea," "individual thing," and "actually existing" in his definition of mind.[2] Even when Spinoza is obviously merely restating well-known sources our task is not completed by merely supplying the perfunctory references. We must again study the meaning of the sources quoted and their implications and all the possible uses he could have made of them. We shall often find that what at first sight appears merely as a repetition of what others have said is in reality a criticism of what they have said. For despite Spinoza's expressed aversion toward openly criticizing his opponents,[3] and perhaps because of it, his *Ethics* is primarily an implied criticism of his opponents. Thus, for instance, when he enumerates the various meanings of cause and asserts that God is a universal, efficient, essential, and first cause, it is not enough merely to identify the immediate source of his statement. We must study the implications of these terms, and we shall then find that instead of merely repeating what his predecessors have said, Spinoza is really challenging their right of saying what they have said and of applying to their God the term "cause" in all these senses.[4] And so throughout the *Ethics*, from his opening definition of substance to his concluding description of the religion of reason, we shall find that behind every positive statement there is lurking a negative criticism. With every one of his positive assertions we seem to hear Spinoza's challenge to his opponents: I accept your own definitions of terms, but I use them with greater consistency than you. I am not unwilling to use your own descriptions of God, but

[1] Cf. below, pp. 347 ff.   [2] Cf. below, Vol. II, pp. 42 ff.
[3] Cf. below, p. 58.
[4] Cf. below, pp. 304 ff.

they are logically more applicable to my God than to yours. I see no reason why I should not use your own formulae, but I must give them an interpretation of my own. It is quite possible for me to adopt with some reservation one of your views, but I must reject all the others which you consider of equal probability.

That the *Ethics* in its literary form is a peculiar piece of writing is quite apparent. But its peculiarity does not consist in the obvious fact that it is divided into propositions and demonstrations instead of chapters and sections. It consists in the fact, which becomes obvious only after a careful study of the work, that the manner in which it makes use of language is rather peculiar. It uses language not as a means of expression but as a system of mnemonic symbols. Words do not stand for simple ideas but for complicated trains of thought. Arguments are not fully unfolded but are merely hinted at by suggestion. Statements are not significant for what they actually affirm but for the denials which they imply. Now, the mere use of the geometrical method cannot explain that, for even within the geometrical method Spinoza could have been clearer and more expatiative. To some extent it may be explained, perhaps, by the cloistered atmosphere in which the *Ethics* was conceived and written. No challenging questions of inquiring students or friends guided Spinoza in the manner of its exposition or goaded him into a fuller expansion of its statements. Despite the fact that he allowed himself to enter into the discussion of problems which troubled the minds of his correspondents, he never communicated to them the fulness of his own thought or discussed with them the philosophic problems which troubled his own mind. The congenial group of merchants, booksellers, medical students, and holders of public office which formed the immediate circle of Spinoza's friends had a layman's interest in the general prob-

lems of philosophy, but they could hardly serve as effective
sounding-boards for his views during the experimental stages
of his thinking. They seem to have had a more vigorous
grasp of the problems of theology, in which they were the
liberals of their day, but with all the adventuresomeness of
their spirit they were just beginning to approach the liberal-
ism of the mediaeval writings of Jewish rationalists read by
Spinoza in his early youth, which he had long outgrown.
Spinoza was welcomed by them as an exotic genius to whose
occasional expression of shocking views they could listen in-
dulgently because they could dismiss them from their minds
as a sort of outlandish heresy. In this strange environment,
to which externally he seems to have fully adjusted himself,
Spinoza never felt himself quite free to speak his mind; and
he who among his own people never hesitated to speak out
with boldness became cautious, hesitant, and reserved. It
was a caution which sprang not from fear but from an inner
sense of decorum which inevitably enforces itself on one in
the presence of strangers, especially strangers who are kind.
Quite early in his new career among his newly found friends
he showed evidence of this cautious and guarded attitude,
and when on one occasion he became conscious of it, in the
case of Casearius, he deluded himself into the belief that it
was due to the faults of the latter arising from his youth and
immaturity.[1] Little did he understand the real cause of his
own behavior, and little did he know to what extent it
stamped his general attitude towards all the others who had
not the faults of youth and immaturity. So long had the
thoughts of this book been simmering in his uncommu-
nicative mind that it was boiled down to a concentrated
essence, and it is this concentrated essence that we are
served in the form of propositions. The *Ethics* is not a

[1] Epistola 9 (*Opera*, IV, p. 42, ll. 19–26).

communication to the world; it is Spinoza's communication with himself.

In its concentrated form of exposition and in the baffling allusiveness and ellipticalness of its style, the *Ethics* may be compared to the Talmudic and rabbinic writings upon which Spinoza was brought up, and it is in that spirit in which the old rabbinic scholars approach the study of their standard texts that we must approach the study of the *Ethics*. We must assume that the *Ethics* is a carefully written book, in which there is order and sequence and continuity, and in which every term and expression is chosen with care and used with precision. We must try to find out not only what is within it, but also what is behind it. We must try to understand not only what the author says, but also what he omits to say, and why he omits it. We must constantly ask ourselves, with regard to every statement he makes, what is the reason? What does he intend to let us hear? What is his authority? Does he reproduce his authority correctly or not? If not, why does he depart from it? What are the differences between certain statements, and can such differences be reduced to other differences, so as to discover in them a common underlying principle? In order to understand Spinoza in full and to understand him well, we must familiarize ourselves with his entire literary background. We must place ourselves in the position of students, who, having done the reading assigned in advance, come to sit at his feet and listen to his comments thereon. Every nod and wink and allusion of his will then become intelligible. Words previously quite unimportant will become charged with meaning. Abrupt transitions will receive an adequate explanation; repetitions will be accounted for. We shall know more of Spinoza's thought than what is merely expressed in his utterances. We shall know what he wished to say and what he would have said had we been able to question him and elicit further information.

But a question may now naturally come up. How do we know that our interpretation is correct? After all, what we have done is to construct an imaginary setting to fit the *Ethics*. How do we know, then, that the setting is not a mere figment of the imagination? Even if it is admitted that the setting is constructed out of historical material and that the *Ethics* seems to fit snugly in it, still it may be argued that the plot of a historical novel may be similarly constructed out of historical material, the individual incidents may be all historically authenticated, and the personages of the novel may all act in their true historical character, and yet the work as a whole be nothing but an artificial and fictitious production.

In answer to this question we may say, in the first place, that the validity of our interpretation of the *Ethics* rests upon its workability and universal applicability. If there is anything arbitrary in our interpretation it is the initial assumption that Spinoza thought out his philosophy in a logical, orderly, and coherent manner, and that he wrote it down in a work which is logical, orderly, and coherent, and in a language which is self-explanatory. But having started out with this assumption and finding that the *Ethics* is far from being a book which is logical, orderly, and coherent, and that the language in which it is written is far from being self-explanatory, we have a right to believe that any interpretation, historically substantiated, that will help to explain the entire *Ethics* as a logically, orderly, coherently, and intelligibly written book is not fictitious like the plot of a historical novel. It is more like the plot of a work of true historical research in which a meagre and sketchy account of certain historical events preserved in a single fragmentary document is presented in a new reconstructed form by the filling in of gaps, by the supplying of details, and by the explaining of causes and motives, all on the basis of other authentic records. Historical research in philosophy, no less than in literature or politics, is justified in claiming the same test of certainty as the hypotheses of the natural scientists, namely, the test of workability and of universal applicability as a description of all the phenomena that come under observation.

The analogy of our study of the *Ethics* to the scientific method of research holds true in still another respect — in the employment of a method which may be considered as a modified form of what is called in science control-experiment. Invariably in the writings of Spinoza several texts are to be found in which the same problems are dealt with. In our study of Spinoza we have always treated these parallel texts as the scientific experimenter would treat his guinea-pigs, performing our experimental interpretation on some of them and using the others as a control. Thus in working on any problem, instead of collecting at once all the parallel texts and ancillary material in the writings of Spinoza and working on all of them at the same time, we confined our investigations to some particular texts, and then tested our conclusions by the other texts. Thus, for instance, in the problem of the unity of substance,[1] for which Propositions II–VI of *Ethics*, I, Chapter II of *Short Treatise*, I, and Appendix I of the *Short Treatise* are parallel texts, or in the problem of the relation of mind and body,[2] for which Proposition X of *Ethics*, II, Preface to *Short Treatise*, II, and Appendix II of the *Short Treatise* are parallel texts, the problem was fully worked out first in connection with one of these sets of texts and then tested and checked up by the others.

[1] Cf. below, pp. 79 ff.
[2] Cf. below, Vol. II, pp. 33 ff.

Then also, again in analogy to the method of research in the sciences, our investigation was not merely a matter of classifying data; it consisted mainly in discovering problems, stating them, and solving them; and the solution, as a rule, started with a conjecture which was afterwards verified by a method which in scholarship may be said to correspond to the method of experiment and prediction in science. One problem with which to start our investigation always presented itself to us, and that was the problem of linking together apparently disconnected propositions into a coherent argument. To solve this problem it was required to find the missing links which in the original form in which the *Ethics* was conceived in the mind of Spinoza and before it was broken up into geometric propositions supplied a logical transition between the disconnected statements which we now have before us. Now sometimes these missing links could be forged out of material which we happened already to have at our disposal, but most often they had to be invented imaginatively out of material which we only assumed to exist and the corroborative evidence was to be discovered afterwards. And, as a rule, it was discovered. But problems of still greater difficulty presented themselves to us on frequent occasions, such, for instance, as apparent misuse of terms on the part of Spinoza, or apparent contradictions in his own statements, or apparent misrepresentations of the views of others. Invariably in the solution of such problems we set up some distinction in the use of the term which Spinoza seemed to misuse, or we discerned some new aspect in the statement of the idea in which Spinoza seemed to contradict himself, or we assumed the possibility of some new interpretation of the view in which Spinoza seemed to misrepresent others. Here, again, most often these new distinctions, aspects, and interpretations were invented *ad hoc*, merely for the purpose of solving a certain difficulty, and the evidence corroborating them was discovered afterwards. This is the method which we have followed throughout our investigation, though it is not the method which we have adopted in the presentation of the results. In the final form which this work has assumed, for the sake of clearness and brevity, the order of exposition has had to be the reverse of the order of discovery, and sources, which in the actual process of investigation were evidence by which *a priori* conjectures were corroborated, have had to be presented as data from which conclusions were drawn. The material dealt with in this work did not seem to us to possess sufficient elements of human interest to justify our attempting to intrigue the reader by presenting each problem in the form of a mystery story.

A typical illustration of this kind of proof by experiment or prediction may be found in Spinoza's discussion of the problem of infinite extension. This is one of the discussions in which Spinoza makes reference to his opponents, restating their views and criticizing them. He finds that one of the reasons why his opponents denied the existence of an infinite extension was their belief in the divisibility of extension, and therefore concludes that inasmuch as matter is not divisible an infinite extension does exist. From the context of his discussion it appears that by divisibility he means divisibility into indivisible parts or atoms and that by indivisibility he means indivisibility in the same sense as a point is said to be indivisible. Having identified his opponents, we found that that kind of divisibility of extension which he seems to ascribe to them is explicitly denied by them. Furthermore, we found that Spinoza, in maintaining the existence of an infinite extension which is indivisible, uses the term "infinite" in a sense which is explicitly rejected by his opponents. Spinoza thus seems to misrepresent his opponents and to commit the fallacy of equivocation. This was the difficulty which confronted us. Now, of course, we could have dismissed this difficulty by assuming either that Spinoza purposely misrepresented his opponents in order to be able to refute them, or that out of sheer ignorance he attributed to them views of which they did not approve. But we preferred to believe that Spinoza was both intellectually honest and accurately informed. We therefore tried to find whether it would not be possible for us to interpret his utterances in such a way as would remove our difficulty. We made several vain attempts, until we finally hit upon a possible distinction in the use of the term "indivisible" and correspondingly in that of the term "divisible." By assuming that Spinoza had used these terms according to this new distinction which we invented *ad hoc*, we were able to explain his statements about his opponents in a fully satisfactory manner. We therefore adopted this as a tentative hypothesis, for the truth of which we had no evidence except the internal criterion of its workability. But then, after we had satisfied ourselves as to the workability of our hypothesis, we began to ask ourselves whether it would not be possible to find some external corroboration of it in the form of a statement by some author, mediaeval or ancient, where that distinction in the use of the terms "indivisible" and "divisible" was made. After some search, we found that this distinction in the use of the term "indivisible" is made by Aristotle and Thomas Aquinas.[1]

Or, to take another illustration. In Spinoza's classification of the stages of knowledge, we traced the history of the classification itself as well as of the terms used in it to Aristotle. Then when Spinoza evaluates these orders of knowledge and

[1] Cf. below, pp. 270, 282 ff.

says that "knowledge of the first kind alone is the cause of falsity; knowledge of the second and third orders is necessarily true" (*Ethics*, II, Prop. XLI), we likewise traced this evaluation to Aristotle. But here we were faced with a difficulty. Aristotle makes use of four terms, naturally in Greek. Two of these terms correspond exactly to the two terms which Spinoza describes elsewhere as the second and third kinds of knowledge, but the other two terms used by Aristotle usually mean in Greek just the opposite of the two Latin terms which are used by Spinoza in his first kind of knowledge. But inasmuch as all the evidence pointed to this Aristotelian origin of Spinoza's evaluation of knowledge, we assumed that somewhere in the history of the transmission of Aristotle's writings from the Greek into Latin the two terms in question were somehow translated or interpreted in a sense corresponding to the two terms used by Spinoza. Then, after we had completed the chapter on the Stages of Knowledge, we began to ask ourselves whether it would not be possible for us to find some work accessible to Spinoza where that unusual translation or interpretation of the two Aristotelian terms in question actually occurred. After some search, we found that in two Latin translations made from the Hebrew of Averroes' Arabic Long Commentary on Aristotle's *Analytica Posteriora* these two Aristotelian terms are translated exactly as they are found in Spinoza.[1]

And so in innumerable instances external corroborative evidence was found for previously conceived conjectures. This gave us a sense of assurance that it was not merely an artificial structure that we were setting up for the *Ethics*, but that to some extent we had succeeded in penetrating into the mind of Spinoza and were able to see its workings, to sense its

[1] Cf. below, Vol. II, pp. 146, 151.

direction, to anticipate its movements, and to be guided to its goal. In order to understand another we must completely identify ourselves with that other, living through imaginatively his experience and thinking through rationally his thoughts. There must be a union of minds, like the union of our mind with the Active Intellect which the mediaevals discuss as a possibility and of which Spinoza speaks as a certainty.

CHAPTER II

THE GEOMETRICAL METHOD

OF THE eleven works which bear the name of Spinoza as author, two, the *Ethics* and the *Tractatus Theologico-Politicus*, present his entire philosophy in its definitive form. The *Ethics* treats of the philosophy of nature — of God as the whole of nature, and of man as a part of nature. The *Tractatus Theologico-Politicus* treats of human society — of organized religion with its beliefs and traditions as embodied in Scripture, and of organized government with its powers and authority as embodied in established institutions. All his other works, to the student of Spinoza's philosophy as distinguished from the student of Spinoza's writings, are only ancillary material, not to be studied by themselves but in connection with his two major works. The *Short Treatise on God, Man, and His Well-Being* (*Korte Verhandeling van God, de Mensch en des zelfs Welstand*) is nothing but a tentative draft of that phase of Spinoza's philosophy which was later completed and perfected in the *Ethics*. The *Cogitata Metaphysica* is a summary of certain philosophic views of scholastic origin, just as his *Principia Philosophiae Cartesianae* is, as described by Lodewijk Meyer and by Spinoza himself, a summary of "the first and second parts of Descartes' *Principia Philosophiae*, together with a fragment of the third," [1] and if these two works are not to be altogether disregarded by the student of the *Ethics*, they may be considered only as introductory to it. The *Tractatus de Intellec-*

[1] *Principia Philosophiae Cartesianae*, Praef. (*Opera*, I, p. 131, l. 24). Cf. Epistola 13 (*Opera*, IV, ll. 13–17). In his letter Spinoza does not mention the fragment of the third part.

tus Emendatione in its present unfinished form may be considered as supplementary to the discussion of the problems of knowledge and truth which occurs in Part II of the *Ethics*, though from the outline of its plan which appears at the beginning of this treatise it may be assumed that it was originally intended to deal also with the problem of the highest good which is discussed at length in Parts IV and V of the *Ethics*. The *Compendium Grammatices Linguae Hebraeae* was probably intended for the use of those who would undertake the study of the Hebrew Bible along the lines suggested by Spinoza in his *Tractatus Theologico-Politicus*, and the *Tractatus Politicus* is nothing but an extension of the latter part of the *Tractatus Theologico-Politicus*. His *Epistolae*, of course, do not constitute an independent work; and as for his treatises on the Rainbow (*Stelkonstige Reeckening van den Regenboog*) and the calculation of chances (*Reeckening van Kanssen*), they have as much or as little to do with his main philosophy as the woolens, linen, furniture, and silver which were left by him at his death.[1]

All these works of Spinoza, the writing of which, from the first dated letter to the end of his life, cover a period of over sixteen years,[2] are in pursuit of one purpose — to bring to its logical conclusion the reasoning of philosophers throughout history in their effort to reduce the universe to a unified and uniform whole governed by universal and unchangeable laws.[3] That philosophers before him had fallen short of the attainment of this purpose — that they had broken up the universe into discontinuous parts by positing a spiritual

[1] For a list of these, see "Inventaire des biens et des meubles délaissés par feu le Seigneur Bénédict de Spinoza," in A. J. Servaas van Rooijen, *Inventaire des Livres formant la Bibliothèque de Bénédict Spinoza* (La Haye, 1889), pp. 111–116.

[2] $\frac{16}{26}$ August, 1661–21 February, 1677. His *Short Treatise*, however, may have been written before that.

[3] Cf. below, Vol. II, Chapter XXI.

God as distinct from a material world, and correspondingly in man a spiritual soul as distinct from a material body, with the resulting beliefs of design in nature and free will in man — was in his opinion due to a logical inconsistency in their thinking. Already in his youth, when he first came out in opposition to traditional belief, he had revealed the main trends of his philosophic thinking. The heresies of which he was accused are said to have been three — that God is corporeal, that angels do not exist, that the soul is identical with life.[1] Interpreted, these heresies meant a denial of the existence of an immaterial God as distinct from the material world, of purely spiritual beings as distinct from material beings, and of a soul as distinct from body, which in maturer years gave expression to the principles that extension and thought are attributes of God, that infinite modes — which in his philosophy were the successors of the Intelligences or angels in mediaeval philosophy [2] — are both of extension and of thought, and that the soul is inseparable from the body. As corollaries to these views he denied also design in nature and freedom of will in man. These are the central ideas which run through all his works and to establish which he fights against his opponents with their own weapons, using their own arguments and their own terminology and confronting them with conclusions drawn from their own premises. Whatever differences may be found between his various works, they are only in the use of terminology, or in the restatement of the views of others, or in the arguments employed against those views. In his essential doctrines no change or even development is to be noticed in all these works.

[1] Cf. A. Wolf, *The Oldest Biography of Spinoza* (Lucas' *La Vie de feu Monsieur de Spinoza*), pp. 45–46 and 97–98.
[2] Cf. below, pp. 218 ff.

The titles which Spinoza gives his works are all descriptive of their contents, and some of them are borrowed from, or modelled after, the titles of well-known books. Such terms as *Opusculum*, by which Spinoza refers to what we call the *Short Treatise*,[1] and *Tractatus*, by which he refers to two of his other books, and such a combination as *Theologico-Politicus*, were in common use. Thus, for instance, the short treatises of Thomas Aquinas are each described as *Opusculum*, and the younger Buxtorf calls two of his works *Tractatus de Punctorum . . . Origine . . .* and *Dissertationes Philologico-Theologicae*. His *Principia Philosophiae Cartesianae*[2] retains, of course, the title of Descartes' work upon which it is based. The *Cogitata Metaphysica* is modelled after such titles as the *Disputationes Metaphysicae* of Suarez and the *Institutiones Metaphysicae* of Burgersdijck. The word "compendium" in his *Compendium Grammatices Linguae Hebraeae* may have been suggested by the word "epitome" in the elder Buxtorf's *Epitome Grammaticae Hebraeae*, though in the latter case there was an obvious justification for the use of the term "epitome," for the book was an abridgement of his larger work entitled *Thesaurus Grammaticus Linguae Sanctae Hebraeae*. The title of the *Tractatus de Intellectus Emendatione* is evidently a paraphrase of Ibn Gabirol's ethical work which translated into Latin would read *Tractatus de Animae Virtutum Emendatione*.[3] The title *Ethics* naturally goes back to Aristotle's *Nicomachean Ethics*. Still, its use by Spinoza as the title of his chief work needs some explanation.

According to its contents the *Ethics* may be divided into three parts, corresponding to the three parts into which the

---

[1] Epistola 6 (*Opera*, IV, p. 36, l. 13).
[2] Or, more accurately, *Renati Des Cartes Principiorum Philosophiae Pars I, et II*.
[3] *Sefer Tikkun Middot ha-Nefesh*.

Short Treatise is divided and which, according to a statement by Meyer, must have been described by Spinoza himself as *De Deo, Anima rationali, summa hominis felicitate.*[1] In fact the original division of the *Ethics* into three parts, in which the present Parts III, IV, and V are combined into one, corresponded to this threefold division of the *Short Treatise*. Now, in this original division of the *Ethics*, the term "ethics" in its historical usage describes only the Third Part, or rather the present last three parts, dealing as they do with the emotions of the soul (Part III), virtue and vice (Part IV), and human happiness (Part V). These are exactly the topics which are dealt with in the Aristotelian work called the *Nicomachean Ethics*. The Second Part of Spinoza's *Ethics*, dealing with mind or the rational soul, is historically to be described as psychology, and the First Part, dealing with God, is historically to be described as theology, metaphysics, or first philosophy. Furthermore, these three disciplines — metaphysics, psychology, and ethics — which form the subject-matter of Spinoza's *Ethics* fall, in the traditional classification of the sciences, under different headings. Ethics is contrasted with both psychology and metaphysics as practical science with theoretical science. Again, psychology and metaphysics, though belonging to the same type of science called theoretical, are contrasted with each other in that psychology is a subdivision of physics which differs from metaphysics in its subject-matter.[2] The term "ethics," therefore, would seem not to be used quite accurately by Spinoza as a description of the contents of his work called by that name.

Spinoza, however, had ample justification for the use of

[1] Cf. quotation from the *Epilogus* to his *Philosophia S. Scripturae Interpres; Exercitatio Paradoxa*, in *Spinoza Opera*, I, *Textgestaltung*, p. 408.

[2] Cf. *Metaphysics*, VI, 1, 1026a, 6–16. See below, Vol. II, p. 3.

the term "ethics" as the title of a book of which the greater part consisted of metaphysics and psychology. The inclusion of psychology under ethics was recommended by Aristotle himself in his statement that the student of politics — and for that matter, we may say, also the student of ethics — must be a psychologist.[1] Furthermore, in mediaeval philosophy, psychology, or at least the treatment of the higher functions of the soul, was removed from physics and placed under metaphysics. Thus the Iḥwan al-Ṣafa,[2] Baḥya Ibn Paḳuda,[3] Judah ha-Levi,[4] Abraham Ibn Ezra,[5] and Shem-Ṭob Falaquera,[6] in their enumeration of the topics of metaphysics, include under it the science of the soul and the intellect. Thus psychology, which originally was a branch of physics, could very well be treated either under ethics or under metaphysics.

But then metaphysics, too, during the Middle Ages, had changed its position in the classification of the sciences. As the first and the highest of the three branches of theoretical science, it stood, in the original Aristotelian classification, contrasted with ethics, which was the first of the three practical sciences, and, in accordance with the Aristotelian conception of the superiority of the contemplative life to the active life, it was superior to ethics. In the Middle Ages, however, when the ethical writings of the pagan authors were supplemented, and sometimes supplanted, by the revealed

[1] Cf. *Nicomachean Ethics*, I, 13, 1102a, 18–19. See below, Vol. II, pp. 181–182.

[2] Cf. Fr. Dieterici, *Die Logik und Psychologie der Araber*, p. 15; Arabic text: *Die Abhandlungen der Ichwân Es-Safâ*, p. 251.

[3] Cf. *Ḥobot ha-Lebabot*, Introduction.

[4] Cf. *Cuzari*, V, 12.

[5] Cf. *Yesod Mora*, I.

[6] Cf. M. Steinschneider, *Die hebraeischen Uebersetzungen des Mittelalters*, § 2, quoting from *De'ot ha-Pilosofim*.

Cf. my "The Classification of Sciences in Mediaeval Jewish Philosophy," in *Hebrew Union College Jubilee Volume* (1925), pp. 290 ff.

writings of religion, ethics sometimes becomes a part of
theology or metaphysics. Ethics is thus treated as a part of
theology by the Iḫwan al-Ṣafa,[1] al-Mukammas,[2] and Baḥya
Ibn Paḳuda.[3] Furthermore, the relative importance of ethics
and metaphysics is sometimes also changed. Instead of
ethics being a prelude to metaphysics, metaphysics becomes
a prelude to ethics. Baḥya Ibn Paḳuda is especially explicit
on this point: "All the divisions of philosophy as determined
by the difference of their subject-matter are gates which
God has opened to rational beings through which they may
attain a knowledge of the Law and the world. . . . The
science which is more particularly necessary for the Law
is that which is regarded as the highest science, namely,
theology." [4] In his own ethical work, "The Duties of the
Heart" (*Ḥobot ha-Lebabot*), Baḥya gives a concrete example
of this view by placing his treatment of theological problems
at the beginning of his book as a sort of preamble to his subsequent treatment of ethical problems.

It is thus not without precedent that Spinoza gives the
book in which he treats of metaphysics, psychology, and
ethics the general title of *Ethics*. By precedent he was quite
justified in subsuming psychology either under ethics or
under metaphysics, and to treat of metaphysics as merely a
prelude to ethics. That that was his purpose is quite evident
from the structure of the *Ethics*, the last part of which, he
says, "concerns the method or way which leads to liberty" [5]
— "liberty" being one of the terms which Spinoza uses as
synonymous with "blessedness." [6]

---

[1] Cf. Fr. Dieterici, *op. cit.*, pp. 16–17; Arabic text, *op. cit.*, pp. 252–253.
[2] *Perush Sefer Yeẓirah le-Rabbi Judah ben Barzilai* (Berlin, 1885), p. 65.
[3] *Ḥobot ha-Lebabot*, Introduction.
[4] *Ibid.*
[5] *Ethics*, V, Praef. (*Opera*, II, p. 277, ll. 7–8).
[6] Cf. below, Vol. II, p. 311.

As in the titles of his works, so also in the form in which they are written Spinoza follows traditional patterns. With the notable exception of the poetical form, in which such philosophers as Parmenides, Cleanthes, Lucretius, Solomon Ibn Gabirol, Dante, and Bruno expounded their philosophy, Spinoza experimented with every literary form in which philosophy throughout its history had been written. The gnomic saying with which the philosophy of the Greeks and the wisdom of Israel had made their beginning is represented in many of Spinoza's propositions, especially those which deal with human conduct, some of which read like verses from the Book of Proverbs or like sayings from the Seven Wise Men. The dialogue form used by Plato and the author of the Book of Job and favored by such authors as Erigena, Abelard, Solomon Ibn Gabirol, Judah ha-Levi, Leo Hebraeus, Galileo, and Bruno is represented in the two Dialogues which are inserted between the second and third chapters of Part I of the *Short Treatise*. Philosophy in the form of exegeses of Scriptural passages which appears alike in the Agadic Midrashim of the rabbis and in the writings of Philo, from whom it passed on to the Christian Church Fathers, and was used by Jews as well as by Christians throughout the Middle Ages, and even up to the very time of Spinoza, is the characteristic literary form of the theological part of the *Tractatus Theologico-Politicus*. The autobiographical method of philosophic writing such as we find in Descartes' *Discours de la Méthode* and in some of the works of other philosophers before him is attempted by Spinoza at the beginning of his *Tractatus de Intellectus Emendatione*. The discussion of problems of philosophy in letters to correspondents such as we find, for instance, in the writings of Cicero, Seneca, Maimonides, and Descartes is represented in his *Epistolae*. In addition to all these forms, Spinoza makes use of the geometrical method in the *Principia Philosophiae Cartesianae*, in the Appendix to the *Short Treatise*, and in the *Ethics*. This method, too, had its precedents.

What the external form of this literary method is may be ascertained by a study of the form of Euclid's *Elements*, which served as a model to all those who used the geometrical method of demonstration in philosophy. The geometrical method may be said to consist of the following parts: First, the primary truths which form the premises in the demonstrations are grouped together and placed apart from the demonstrations as the first principles upon which the demonstrations rest, and are divided into definitions, postulates, and axioms or common notions. Second, that which is sought to be demonstrated, that is, the conclusion which is to be established by the demonstration, is summarized apart from the demonstration in the form of a proposition. Third, the demonstration itself reasons from the known, that is, the first principles, to the unknown, that is, the conclusion. Fourth, supplementary deductions, explanations, and propositions are given in the form of corollaries, scholia, and lemmas.

Now this method of demonstration, which is called geometrical, because it is employed by Euclid in his work on geometry, was also used in part or in whole in philosophy.

An example of one kind of partial application of the geometrical method to philosophy is the reduction of philosophic views to the form of propositions, which may be either followed or not followed by demonstrations. This is to be found in Porphyry's *Sententiae ad Intelligibilia Ducentes* (Ἀφορμαὶ πρὸς τὰ νοητὰ) and in Proclus' *Institutio Theologica* (Στοιχείωσις θεολογική). It is also to be found in almost every mediaeval compendium of philosophy. Duns Scotus in his *Theoremata* and Burgersdijck in his *Institutiones Logicae* even designate these propositions by the Euclidian term "theorem." An imitation of this partial form of the geometrical method is also to be discerned in Bruno, when he summarizes the conclusions of his doctrine of the unity and simplicity of God's being in a series of propositions.[1] In Jewish philosophy, the twenty-six propositions at the beginning of Part II of Maimonides' *Moreh Nebukim*, which summarize some of Aristotle's physical and metaphysical principles and to which commentators later added demonstrations, belong to the same type of literary composition. Outside of the field of philosophy and quite independently of Euclid's *Elements*, propositions which may be described as geometrical are to be found in various literatures. In Hebrew literature, this form of proposition is characteristic of the Mishnah, which contains a digest of the teachings of the Tannaim, legal as well as ethical. So impressed was an anonymous early Hebrew author with the similarity between the Mishnaic form and the form of geometrical propositions, with which he must have become acquainted through Euclid, that his geometric work written not later than the tenth century and perhaps as early as the second century, consisting of a series of definitions, constructions, and propositions without demonstrations, is called by him the Mishnah of Geometry (*Mishnat ha-Middot*).

An example of another kind of partial application of the geometrical method to philosophy may be found in the identification of the syllogistic form of demonstration with the Euclidian geometrical form or the transformation of one into the other. Thus Aristotle's first argument against the existence of a vacuum,[2] which is syllogistic in nature and is restated by Crescas in the form of a hypothetico-disjunctive

---

[1] *De Immenso*, I, Ch. 11 (*Opera Latina*, Vol. I, Pars I, Neapoli, 1879, pp. 242 ff.). Cf. J. L. McIntyre, *Giordano Bruno*, pp. 192 f.

[2] *Physics*, IV, 8, 214b, 28–215a, 24.

syllogism,[1] is concluded by both Averroes and Crescas [2] with the equivalent of the phrase *quod erat demonstrandum* with which Euclid concludes his geometrical demonstrations. The same Euclidian phrase is also used by Avicenna at the conclusion of some of his own syllogistic arguments.[3] Conversely, too, Aristotle's arguments against the existence of a circularly moving infinite body in *De Caelo*, I, 5–7, which are obviously written in the form of geometrical demonstrations and are restated by Averroes in the form of geometrical demonstrations, are reduced by Crescas to the syllogistic form.[4] The identification of the syllogistic method of reasoning with the geometrical method is clearly indicated by Saadia, who in his plea for the validity of logical inference as a source of knowledge and for its application to matters religious describes the conclusion arrived at by demonstrative reasoning as that which is "geometrically demonstrated." [5]

Finally, in evident imitation of Euclid, we sometimes find in philosophic demonstrations that the first principles upon which the demonstration hinges are grouped together and put apart from the demonstration itself in the form of a series of propositions sometimes even called by the Euclidian terms, definitions, postulates, and axioms or common notions. Thus Maimonides introduces his restatement of the Aristotelian proofs of the existence of God by a series of twenty-six propositions upon which the proofs rest. Though

[1] Cf. my *Crescas' Critique of Aristotle*, pp. 141–143.

[2] Cf. *ibid.*, p. 339, n. 24.

[3] Cf. Avicenna's treatise on the soul published by S. Landauer under the title of "Die Psychologie des Ibn Sînâ" in *Zeitschrift der Deutschen Morgenländischen Gesellschaft*, 29 (1875), at the end of Chs. 1, 2, 3, and 9.

[4] Cf. my *Crescas' Critique of Aristotle*, pp. 175 ff.

[5] *Emunot we-De'ot*, Introduction: כפי מה שיתבררו (p. 20), على ما تتهندس במלאכת השעור. Cf. D. Neumark, "Saadya's Philosophy," in *Essays in Jewish Philosophy*, p. 183, where the phrase used by Saadia is aptly translated by "in so far as they are deduced *more geometrico*."

these twenty-six propositions, unlike Euclid's "first principles," are themselves subject to demonstration, still they
are used in these proofs of the existence of God as the "first
principles" are used by Euclid. Prior to Maimonides,
Baḥya Ibn Pakuda, in his un-Aristotelian proof for the existence of God, similarly lays down three propositions,
which are again subject to proof but are used by him as first
principles, and then says: "And when these three propositions have been established, the conclusion will follow, to
him who knows how to use them and to join them together,
that the world has a creator." [1] To "join them together" [2]
may be taken here as a technical term meaning "to syl-
logize" (συλλογίζεσθαι). A contemporary of Maimonides,
Alanus de Insulis or Nicolaus of Amiens, follows the same
method and gives still clearer indication that he is consciously
following the geometrical method. In his *De Arte seu Arti-
culis Catholicae Fidei*, before starting upon his main work,
which consists of a series of propositions, each followed by a
demonstration in syllogistic form, he lays down in the pro-
logue a number of definitions (*descriptiones*),[3] postulates
(*petitiones*), and axioms (*communes animi conceptiones*),[4] so
that the whole book assumes the geometrical form in its
completeness. A complete geometrical form is also used in
Liber de Trinitate, which is falsely ascribed to Alanus.[5]
Boethius in the preface to his *Liber de Hebdomadibus* definitely recommends the mathematical method as the method
to be followed also in other branches of learning.[6]

---

[1] *Ḥobot ha-Lebabot*, I, 5. [2] و تاليفها (p. 43), ‏ולחברן‎.

[3] Cf. below, p. 160, n. 1.

[4] Cf. Migne, *Patrologia Latina*, Vol. 210, Col. 597.

[5] Cf. Cl. Baeumker, "Handschriften zu den Werken des Alanus," in *Philosophisches Jahrbuch*, VI (1893), pp. 428–429.

[6] Cf. M. Baumgartner, *Die Philosophie des Alanus de Insulis* (Münster, 1896),
pp. 27–32; Ueberweg-Baumgartner, *Grundriss der Geschichte der Philosophie der*

It was not without precedent, therefore, that one of Descartes' objectors suggested to him to present his *Meditationes* in the geometrical form, that Descartes himself made an attempt at it, and that Spinoza attempted it in the Appendix to the *Short Treatise*, carried it out in full in his *Principia Philosophiae Cartesianae* and *Ethics*, and wanted to use it in his Hebrew Grammar.[1]

Still, the geometrical method which with all his predecessors was only a casual attempt, and which Descartes himself, who attempted it, explicitly characterized as a method which "cannot so conveniently be applied to these metaphysical matters," [2] is adopted by Spinoza and used consistently in his discussions of metaphysical matters throughout his chief philosophic work. Mere imitation of his predecessors cannot therefore explain his use of the geometrical method. Some other explanation will have to be found for it.

Many students of Spinoza regard his use of the geometrical method as a logical consequence of his mathematical way of looking at things. One of his early biographers declares that Spinoza had a "geometrical mind" (*l'esprit geometre*).[3] Erdmann says: "For no other reason than because it is a necessary consequence of the mathematical way of looking at things, the geometrical form of proof is of great significance, even where the proofs themselves are insipid and marred by inaccuracies." [4] Freudenthal maintains that "it was not

patristischen und scholastischen Zeit (10th ed., 1915), pp. 326–327. For other examples of attempts at the application of the geometrical method to philosophy, mostly of the type described by us here as partial geometrical method, see S. Hahn, *Thomas Bradwardinus* (Münster, 1905), pp. 13–14.

[1] Cf. Preface to *Opera Posthuma* quoted in *Spinoza Opera*, I, *Textgestaltung*, p. 623.

[2] *Secundae Responsiones* (*Oeuvres*, VII, p. 156, ll. 25–26).

[3] Pierre Bayle, *Dictionaire Historique et Critique* (1st ed., 1695–1697), under "Spinoza (Benoit de)"; A. Wolf, *The Oldest Biography of Spinoza*, p. 160.

[4] *Grundriss der Geschichte der Philosophie*, II, § 272.2 (English translation, II, p. 58).

therefore a capricious notion, which might as well have been dispensed with, that made Spinoza style his system *Ethica Ordine Geometrico Demonstrata*; on the contrary, the method called for in the title follows from the inner necessity of his thought." [1] And Joachim concludes that "the form of Spinoza's exposition is essential to its matter. He casts his system in a geometrical mould, because the subject-matter, as he conceives it, demands such treatment." [2]

But let us consider all the facts in the case and see whether there really is any ground for the assumption that the nature of Spinoza's philosophy demanded that it should be written in the geometrical form. The points which we shall try to establish are as follows: (1) Both Descartes and Lodewijk Meyer make a distinction between the geometrical method of demonstration, which may be either synthetic or analytic, and the geometrical form of literary exposition, which, whether synthetic or analytic, is to be modelled after the literary form of Euclid's *Elements*. (2) The geometrical method of demonstration of the synthetic type is nothing but valid syllogistic reasoning as practised throughout the history of philosophy. (3) The geometrical method of demonstration, whether synthetic or analytic, need not necessarily be written in the geometrical literary form, and, conversely, the use of the geometrical literary form is not determined by the subject-matter of which it treats. (4) Spinoza's mathematical way of looking at things means only the denial of design in nature and freedom in man, and this need not necessarily be written in the geometrical literary form.

The fullest discussion of the geometrical method is to be found in Descartes *Regulae ad Directionem Ingenii*. Though the phrase "geometrical method" in either two of its forms

---

[1] *Spinoza Leben und Lehre* (ed. Gebhardt, 1927), II, pp. 110–111.
[2] *A Study of the Ethics of Spinoza*, p. 13.

— *ordine geometrico* and *more geometrico* — does not occur
there, Descartes openly advocates that "in our search for
the direct road towards truth we should busy ourselves with
no object about which we cannot attain a certitude equal
to that of the demonstrations of arithmetic and geometry."[1]
This method, which by implication may be called the geometrical method, is contrasted by him with "that method
of philosophizing which others have already discovered and
those weapons of the schoolmen, probable syllogisms, which
are so well suited for dialectical combats."[2] The contrast
between the old syllogistic method of the schoolmen and the
new geometrical method which he proposes is described as
follows: The former deals with "probable knowledge"[3] or
"probable opinion";[4] its object is "dialectics"[5] and not the
attainment of truth; it had no utility save the solution of
empty problems.[6] The geometrical method, on the other
hand, he says, deals with "true and evident cognition,"[7] its
object is the discovery of truth, and it is to be employed to
solve useful problems. This new geometrical method, he
then continues, is based on intuition and deduction. It
starts with premises which must be self-evidently true, and
it arrives at conclusions by the method of inference, proceeding logically from the known to the unknown.[8]

In analyzing these statements of Descartes about the geometrical method, we find that it is nothing but what Aristotle
would call a scientific demonstration. Descartes' insistence
that truth can be attained only by premises which are self-
evidently true and by deduction is nothing but a repetition
of Aristotle's theory that demonstrative reasoning as ex-

[1] *Regulae ad Directionem Ingenii*, II (*Oeuvres*, X, p. 366, ll. 6–9).
[2] *Ibid.*, II (p. 363, ll. 21–24).   [3] *Ibid.*, II (p. 362, ll. 14–15).
[4] *Ibid.*, II (p. 363, ll. 14–15).   [5] *Ibid.*, II (p. 363, l. 23).
[6] *Ibid.*, IV (p. 373, ll. 26 ff.).   [7] *Ibid.*, II (p. 362, l. 5).
[8] *Ibid.*, IX and XI.

pressed in any syllogism must start with premises which are "true, primary, immediate, more known than, prior to, and the cause of, the conclusion." [1] Furthermore, if we study carefully Descartes' language we shall notice that he does not really contrast his own method with syllogisms in general but with what he calls "probable syllogisms" or what Aristotle would call a "dialectical (διαλεκτικός) syllogism" and a "contentious (ἐριστικός) syllogism," [2] for Descartes' "probable syllogisms" are syllogisms which consist of what Aristotle calls probabilities (τὰ ἔνδοξα), and "probabilities," according to Aristotle, yield a "dialectical syllogism" and a "contentious syllogism." [3] This is exactly what Descartes means when, speaking of "probable syllogisms," he says that they are so well suited for "contentions" (bellis) [4] or, as the French version translates it, "dialectical combats" (combats de la dialectique). [5] His geometrical method, as described by him so far, is thus not contrasted by him with the syllogistic method as such, but rather with the abuse of the syllogistic method.

But as Descartes goes on he adds a new point to his conception of the geometrical method. Ancient geometricians were acquainted with two methods of proof, one by analysis and the other by synthesis, though the proofs in Euclid's *Elements* are of the synthetic type. Descartes refers to the antiquity of the analytic method when he says: "Indeed I seem to recognize certain traces of this true mathematics in Pappus and Diophantus. . . . But my opinion is that these writers then with a sort of low cunning, deplorable in-

---

[1] *Analytica Posteriora*, I, 2, 71b, 21–22.

[2] *Topics*, I, 1, 100a, 29–30, and 100b, 23–24.

[3] *Ibid.*, 100a, 29–100b, 24.

[4] *Regulae ad Directionem Ingenii*, II (*Oeuvres*, X, p. 363, l. 23).

[5] *Régles pour la Direction de l'Esprit*, II (*Oeuvres de Descartes*, ed. Cousin, XI, p. 206).

deed, suppressed this knowledge." [1] These ancients, however, performed their analyses of geometrical problems by means of construction; Descartes performs them by means of algebraic calculations, the process of which is known as analytical geometry. By this change he extends the method of analysis to everything within the realm of mathematics, or, as he expresses himself, to any object in which "the question of measurement arises." [2] This he calls "universal mathematics." [3] But going still further, he applies the method of analysis to the other sciences, thus making the knowledge of all things mathematical. [4]

From this analysis of Descartes' own conception of the geometrical or mathematical method, it is quite clear that he means by it only the method of demonstration itself and not at all the literary form in which Euclid happens to couch the demonstration. Whichever kind of demonstration of the geometrical method is used, the synthetic or analytic, there is no indication in anything Descartes says that it has to be written in the form which Euclid employs in his *Elements*.

That the application of the geometrical method of demonstration to philosophic problems does not necessarily require the use of the external literary form of the Euclidian geometric propositions is still more evident from Descartes' *Secundae Responsiones*.

In a reply to one of his objectors who counselled him to propound the arguments of meditations in the geometrical method (*more geometrico*), [5] he distinguishes in the "geometrical mode of writing" (*modo scribendi geometrico*) two things, namely, the order of proof and the method of proof

[1] *Regulae ad Directionem Ingenii*, IV (*Oeuvres*, X, p. 376, ll. 21–26).
[2] *Ibid.*, IV (p. 378, ll. 3–4).
[3] *Ibid.*, IV (p. 378, ll. 8–9).
[4] *Ibid.*, IV (p. 379, ll. 5 ff.).
[5] *Secundae Objectiones* (*Oeuvres*, VII, p. 128, ll. 13–17).

(*ordinem scilicet, & rationem demonstrandi*).[1] As for the "order of proof," Descartes explains it, as he does in his *Regulae*, as consisting "merely in putting forward those things first that should be known without the aid of what comes subsequently, and arranging all other matters so that their proof depends solely on what precedes them." [2] This, as we have shown, is nothing but a repetition of what is generally considered to be true of any good syllogistic argument. The "method of proof" is described by Descartes, again as in his *Regulae*, as being twofold. One is analytic; the other is synthetic. The former reasons as it were *a priori*, from cause to effect; the latter reasons as it were *a posteriori*, from effect to cause,[3] the latter being, however, the only method employed by ancient geometers in their writings. Now, in his *Meditationes*, says Descartes, in so far as he tried to put forward those things first that should be known without the aid of what comes subsequently, he did certainly follow the geometrical order of proof. But he admits that, unlike the ancient geometers who had employed only the synthetic method of proof, he employed in his *Meditationes* the analytic method, and he did so for the very good reason that he did not believe that the synthetic method is applicable to the discussion of metaphysical matters. For the synthetic method of proof, he says, must start with certain presuppositions or "primary notions" (*primae notiones*) which are granted by all. Now, in geometry there are certain primary notions which "harmonize with the use of our senses, and are readily granted by all"; in metaphysics, however, "nothing causes more trouble than the making

---

[1] *Secundae Responsiones* (*Oeuvres*, VII, p. 155, ll. 8–10).

[2] *Ibid.* (p. 155, ll. 11–14).

[3] *Ibid.* (p. 155, ll. 23–24; p. 156, ll. 6–7). Cf. French version (*Oeuvres*, ed. Adam and Tannery, IX, pp. 121–122).

the perception of its primary notions clear and distinct . . . though in their own nature they are as intelligible as, or even more intelligible than, those the geometricians study." [1] "This is the reason," concludes Descartes, "why I used the form of Meditations rather than that of Disputations [and Questions], as do philosophers, or that of Theorems and Problems, as do geometers." [2] Still, despite his explanation of his preference for the analytic method over the synthetic method, he appends at the end of his reply to the second objections "something in the synthetic style," [3] as he describes it. This "something in the synthetic style" consists of his "arguments demonstrating the existence of God and the distinction between soul and body drawn up in geometrical fashion," [4] in which he begins like Euclid with a series of Definitions, Postulates, and Axioms or Common Notions, and then follows with Propositions each of which is proved by a demonstration. [5]

Here, then, as in his *Regulae ad Directionem Ingenii*, Descartes makes it quite clear that by the geometrical method in its primary and general sense he means nothing but what Aristotle would call a scientific demonstration consisting of premises which are self-evidently true and of a conclusion deduced from those premises by logical inference. Again as in his *Regulae*, the geometrical method is divided by him into two types, the analytic and the synthetic. Now, the analytic type of the geometrical method, we know, is as-

---

[1] *Ibid.* (p. 156, l. 2–p. 157, l. 10).

[2] *Ibid.* (p. 157, ll. 17–19). Cf. French version (*Oeuvres*, ed. Adam and Tannery, IX, p. 123).

[3] *Ibid.* (p. 159, ll. 13–14).

[4] *Ibid.* (p. 160, ll. 1 ff.).

[5] It is to be noted that, unlike Descartes, Spinoza includes no Postulates among the first principles which precede his propositions. Postulates are used by him, however, between Props. 13 and 14 of *Ethics*, II (repeated in *Ethics*, III) and at the beginning of Part III of *Principia Philosophiae Cartesianae*.

sociated historically with a certain external literary form, though Descartes makes no reference to it here. It is the form in which the few relics of the analytic demonstrations of the ancient geometricians and Descartes' own analytical geometry are written. But this external literary form was not essential, according to Descartes' own admission, to the geometrical method of the analytic type. In Descartes' application of this method to philosophical problems it took the form, as he himself says, of meditations. The external literary form of the synthetic type of the geometrical method is likewise associated historically with certain external literary forms which are alluded to by Descartes himself. In the past, he seems to say, it had taken two literary forms: first, that of "Disputations [and Questions]," by which he means the method used in the scholastic writings, and, second, that of "Theorems and Problems," by which he means the method used in Euclid's *Elements*. The inference to be drawn from this statement, again, is that the Euclidian literary form is not essential to the synthetic geometrical method when applied to philosophical problems, inasmuch as the scholastic "Disputations and Questions" is another type of literary form mentioned by Descartes as one which can be used in the synthetic geometrical method of demonstration, though he himself, as a concession to his correspondent, attempts to reduce a few of his philosophical arguments to the Euclidian literary form.

The same distinction within geometrical method between a method of demonstration and a method of literary exposition is to be found in Meyer's Preface to Spinoza's *Principia Philosophiae Cartesianae*. He speaks there of the "wretched plight of philosophy" (*miserimam Philosophiae fortem*)[1] which finds itself without a proper method. The method in

---

[1] *Opera*, I, p. 128, ll. 17–18.

vogue in the scholastic literature, which Descartes refers to
as "Disputations and Questions," is described by him as "a
method where the end is attained through definitions and
logical divisions which are indirectly connected with each
other and interspersed with numerous questions and explanations." [1] As against this he describes the new method
which was developed by those who were desirous to "leave
to posterity some studies besides mathematics established
with absolute certainty." He refers to this method as the
"mathematical method" (*methodo . . . mathematica*).[2] At first
it would seem that Meyer refers here to the Euclidian literary form. But as he proceeds and restates Descartes' words
in the *Secundae Responsiones* it becomes clear that he deals
here not with the geometrical literary form but rather with
the geometrical method of demonstration, which, following
Descartes, he divides into analytic and synthetic. Later,
speaking of the Euclidian literary form of demonstration, he
refers to it as "*more Geometris.*" [3] But in the entire discussion there is nothing to indicate that the application of the
geometrical literary form by Spinoza to Descartes' *Principia
Philosophiae* was the outgrowth of the mathematical method
of demonstration employed by Descartes. On the contrary,
the indications are that it was considered to be something
imposed upon it externally.

In Spinoza, beyond the mention of the fact that he has
reduced parts of Descartes' *Principia Philosophiae* to the
geometrical literary form [4] and references to its use in the
work which later came to be known as the *Ethics*,[5] there is no
discussion of its nature as a method of demonstration. He

[1] *Ibid.*, p. 127, ll. 24 ff.
[2] *Ibid.*, p. 128, l. 21.
[3] *Ibid.*, p. 129, l. 27.
[4] Epistola 13 (*Oeuvres*, IV, p. 63, l. 13).
[5] Epistola 2 (p. 8, l. 15); cf. Epistola 3 (p. 10, l. 7).

makes use, however, of certain mathematical analogies, such indeed as are also to be found in the works of Descartes. But in these mathematical analogies Spinoza goes much further than Descartes. In Descartes the mathematical analogies are used only as illustrations in his discussions of the method of demonstration. In no way do these analogies imply that Descartes conceived the universe as a whole to be governed by laws of necessity like those which prevail in mathematics. In his universe, according to his own statements, there was still room for final causes, for a divine will, and for human freedom. In Spinoza, on the other hand, the mathematical analogies are used as illustrations of the existence of inexorable laws of necessity throughout nature. Spinoza gives expression to this view when on several occasions he declares that all things follow from the infinite nature of God according to that same necessity by which it follows from the essence of a triangle that its three angles are equal to two right angles,[1] and when he declares that the human race would have been kept in darkness to all eternity with regard to final ends "if mathematics, which does not deal with ends, but with the essence and properties of forms, had not placed before us another rule of truth,"[2] or, finally, when in denying human freedom he declares, "I shall consider human actions and appetites just as if I were considering lines, planes, or bodies."[3]

It is these two principles — the denial of final causes in the universe and of freedom in human actions — that Spinoza wishes to illustrate by his use of mathematical analogies. It is only this, and nothing more, that his mathematical way of looking at things means. Beyond this, there

---

[1] *Ethics*, I, Prop. 17, Schol.; II, Prop. 49, Schol.; IV, Prop. 57, Schol.; *Cogitata Metaphysica*, II, 9.

[2] *Ethics*, I, Appendix (*Opera*, II, p. 79, ll. 32–34).

[3] *Ibid.*, III, Praef. (end).

is nowhere any indication that he in any way connected his use of the geometrical literary form with this his mathematical way of looking at things, nor can there be any such connection logically established on independent grounds. On the contrary, the fact that his *Short Treatise*, where his mathematical way of looking at things is already fully developed, is not written in the geometrical literary form would seem to indicate that the geometrical literary form was not a logical consequence of his mathematical way of looking at things. Furthermore, the fact that he had applied the geometrical literary form to the philosophy of Descartes, which does not look at things mathematically in Spinoza's sense, would also seem to indicate that there is no logical connection between the contents of a philosophy and the particular literary form in which it is written. Finally, the fact that Spinoza had intended to apply it to the grammar of the Hebrew language would similarly seem to indicate that there is no logical connection bteween the geometrical literary form and the subject-matter to which it is applied. The thought that may occur to one that the planned application of the geometrical form to the Hebrew grammar may somehow be connected with a metaphysical conception of language which students of Spinoza maintain to have detected in his theory of the priority of nouns to adjectives and verbs in the Hebrew language [1] may be dismissed as a passing fancy. Spinoza himself does not explicitly link his grammatical view as to the relation of adjectives and verbs to nouns with his metaphysical view as to the relation of modes to substance, and if he did ever link them at all in his mind,

---

[1] Cf. *Compendium Grammatices Linguae Hebraeae*, Chs. V and VIII; J. Bernays in "Anhang" to C. Schaarschmidt, *Des Cartes und Spinoza* (Bonn, 1850), p. 197; J. Freudenthal, *Spinoza Leben und Lehre* (ed. Gebhardt, 1927), I, p. 291; N. Porges, "Spinozas Compendium der hebräischen Grammatik," in *Chronicon Spinozanum*, IV (1924–1926), p. 146.

it must have been in the nature of a literary analogy. All those who have attached a metaphysical significance to this view of Spinoza have failed to notice the fact that an explicit analogy between the relation of adjectives and verbs to nouns and the relation of accidents to substance occurs also in the philosophical grammar of Profiat Duran,[1] and yet no implication of any metaphysical conception of language is to be discerned there.

If, as we have been trying to show, there is no logical connection between the substance of Spinoza's philosophy and the form in which it is written, his choice of the Euclidian geometrical form is to be explained on other grounds. Primarily, we may say, the reason for its choice was pedagogical, the clearness and distinctness with which the geometrical form was believed to delineate the main features of an argument and to bring them into high relief. It was used for the same reason that one uses outlines and diagrams. This pedagogical reason for the application of the geometrical form to philosophy is clearly stated by Descartes' objector, when he suggested to Descartes the use of this form. He says: "This is why it would be well worth the doing if, hard upon your solution of the difficulties, you advanced as premises certain definitions, postulates, and axioms, and thence drew conclusions, conducting the whole proof by the geometrical method, in the use of which you are so highly expert. Thus would you cause each reader to have everything in his mind, as it were, at a single glance, and to be penetrated throughout with a sense of the Divine being." [2] Equally pedagogical is the reason given by Meyer for the reduction of Descartes' philosophy to the Euclidian geometrical form by Spinoza. Conceiving the two types of geometrical method, the Euclid-

[1] *Ma'aseh Efod*, Ch. 9.
[2] *Secundae Objectiones* (*Oeuvres*, VII, p. 128, ll. 13–19).

ian synthetic and the Cartesian analytic, as mutually complementary, the former as the method by which mathematical truths are "written down" (*conscriptae*)[1] and the latter
as the method by which they are "discovered" (*inventae*),[2]
Meyer recommends the rewriting of Descartes' philosophy,
which was discovered by the analytic method, in the Euclidian synthetic method, for the benefit of those who, having
read Descartes' philosophy in the non-geometrical form in
which it is written, "are not able to follow it for themselves,
nor can they teach it to others,"[3] and also for the benefit of
the many who have made Descartes' opinions and dogmas
only a matter of memory and are unable to demonstrate
them and defend them against attacks.[4] It is thus always
for the benefit of the reader, and because of the clearness
with which it is supposed to state an argument, and not because the philosophic system itself demands it, that the geometrical form is made use of.

But there may have been another reason which had
prompted philosophers at the time of Descartes and Spinoza
to turn to the use of the geometrical form. It may have been
as a reaction against the new literary forms which since the
Renaissance, under the influence of the works of ancient
writers, had been imported into philosophic writings, where
it had taken the place of the syllogistic style. The Renaissance philosophers had an aversion toward the syllogistic
method of the mediaevals, not so much on intellectual
grounds as on purely aesthetic grounds; not so much because the method itself could not be properly used in the
discovery of truth or because of the ease with which the
method could be abused and be made to lend itself to give a
semblance of proof to things which were not true as because

[1] *Opera*, I, p. 129, l. 16.   [2] *Ibid.*
[3] *Ibid.*, p. 129, l. 8.   [4] *Ibid.*, p. 129, ll. 18 ff.

it was bare and bleak and skeleton-like. They were dissatisfied with syllogisms for the same reason that people are dissatisfied with food that is merely nourishment, with clothes that are merely warm, or with a house that is merely a shelter. The syllogistic method may have been practical and useful, but it lacked form and was not pleasing to the eye and the ear. They therefore began to experiment with new literary forms, more polished, more refined, and more resonant — dialogues after the manner of Plato, poetry after the manner of Lucretius, and rhetorical prose after the manner of Cicero. But all these new literary forms proved a disappointment. Instead of merely garbing the logical nakedness of the syllogism — that logical syllogism which must inevitably be implied in every sound argument — they sometimes served as a cloak to cover up the lack of any kind of logic and reasoning. Philosophy became metaphorical and effusive. What was thus gained in grace was lost in accuracy and precision. A new method in presenting philosophical arguments was needed. To return to the old syllogistic method openly and directly would have meant a return to scholasticism, for which the world was not yet ready. They therefore returned to it indirectly by adopting the geometrical form. To the philosophers of the seventeenth century the blessed word "mathematics" served as a veneer of respectability for the discredited syllogism.

In the case of Spinoza there may have been still another reason for his use of the geometrical form. It was in order to avoid the need of arguing against opponents. The *Ethics*, as we shall show, primarily consists of conclusions of an elaborate criticism of traditional philosophy. Had Spinoza followed the old traditional method, the method used by rabbis and schoolmen alike, the comparatively small volume of the *Ethics* would have run into many bulky tomes. That method required that the various views held by opponents on each problem should be stated, that the pros and cons for each view should be reproduced, that refutations and rebuttals should be marshalled, and that only then the author's own view should be given and its superiority to those of others pointed out. Spinoza, for reasons which can only be explained psychologically, did not want to go through all this elaborate formality. In a letter to Oldenburg he says, "It is not my custom to expose the errors of others," [1] and in another place he expresses a reluctance "to seem to be desirous of exposing the errors of others." [2] In still another place he declares himself not to be bound "to discuss what every one may dream." [3] By resorting to the use of the geometrical form he could avoid all this, at least openly. But Spinoza never meant to imply that by his use of the geometrical form his philosophy, like the geometry of Euclid, is the unfoldment of certain *a priori* self-evident truths. For his axioms, properly understood, are not necessarily self-evident truths, any more than his propositions are necessarily new truths discovered by demonstration. Most often they are merely restatements of generally accepted mediaeval brocards. It will be noticed that the "Axioms" mentioned in a letter from Oldenburg [4] and also in the geometric appendix to the *Short Treatise* are called "Propositions" in the *Ethics*, for the terms "definitions," "axioms," "propositions," and their like are used by Spinoza more or less indiscriminately as conventional labels to be pasted on here and there in order to give to his work the external appearance of a work of geometry. What the motives were that prompted Spinoza to depart from the old form of exposition

---

[1] Epistola 2 (*Oeuvres*, IV, p. 8, ll. 18–19).
[2] *Tractatus de Intellectus Emendatione*, § 95 (*Opera*, II, p. 34, ll. 31–32).
[3] *Ethics*, II, Prop. 49, Schol. (*Opera*, II, p. 133, l. 20).
[4] Epistola 3.

can be only conjectured, but among them there may have been the desire to produce a book which externally would be different from all other books on philosophy. He had something new to say, and he wished to say it in a new way. And perhaps, also, he chose the geometrical form in order to avoid the temptation of citing Scripture.

But still, the form in which the *Ethics* is written, we have reason to believe, is not the form in which it formulated itself in the mind of Spinoza. He must at first have thought out all its problems in their full detail after the manner of the rabbis and scholastics, and only afterwards, when he came to write them down, did he break them up into geometric propositions. There is thus behind our present *Ethics*, demonstrated in geometrical order, an *Ethics* demonstrated in rabbinical and scholastic order, just as behind Descartes' own fragmentary attempt to draw up his proofs of the existence of God and of the distinction between soul and body in geometrical fashion are the corresponding parts of the *Meditationes*, just as behind Spinoza's *Principia Philosophiae Cartesianae* is Descartes' *Principia Philosophiae*, and just as behind the geometric Appendix to Spinoza's own *Short Treatise* is Chapter II of Part I of that book. Now, Descartes himself admits that his geometric fragment does not give the full content of the arguments as they are unfolded in the *Meditationes*. "I should, however, like them kindly to notice," he says, "that I have not cared to include here so much as comes into my Meditations . . . nor shall I explain in such accurate detail that which I do include." [1] Spinoza similarly admits that the geometrical method might not convey easily to all the readers what he had in his mind, for in a Scholium, where he gives an outline of the topics dealt with in a subsequent group of propositions, he says:

[1] *Secundae Responsiones* (*Oeuvres*, VII, p. 159, ll. 15–19).

"Before, however, I begin to demonstrate these things by our full geometrical method, I should like briefly to set forth here these dictates of reason, in order that what I have in my mind about them may be easily comprehended by all." [1] Imagine now that Descartes' *Meditationes* and *Principia Philosophiae* and Chapter II of Spinoza's *Short Treatise*, I, were lost, and only Descartes' own geometric fragment, and Spinoza's *Principia Philosophiae Cartesianae*, and the geometric Appendix to the *Short Treatise* were left. In that case, to understand fully these extant geometrically written works we should have to reconstruct the lost works upon which they are based. Similarly, to understand our present *Ethics* we must construct that hypothetical *Ethics* which lies behind it.

But how are we to go about constructing that hypothetical *Ethics*? The answer to this question has already been given in the preceding chapter where we have discussed the method employed by us in the reconstruction of the reasoning that lies behind the *Ethics*. We may now proceed to the actual task of reconstruction.

[1] *Ethics*, IV, Prop. 18, Schol.

CHAPTER III

DEFINITION OF SUBSTANCE AND MODE

THERE are certain types of literature which are inseparably associated in our minds with some sort of formal, conventional beginning. We thus all expect a fairy tale to begin with "Once upon a time," and a Christmas ballad with "'Twas the night before Christmas." A Biblical narrative always suggests to our mind the phrase "And it came to pass," and epic poems, from the Iliad to the latest parody, begin with an invocation to the Muse. I suppose we should all be sorely disappointed if we woke up some fine morning to find that Caesar's *Commentaries on the Gallic Wars* did not begin with the familiar "Gallia est omnis divisa in partes tres." Now, like fairy tales, and Christmas ballads, and Caesar's *Commentaries*, metaphysical treatises in the Middle Ages as a rule set out on their philosophical investigation by a statement which might be reduced to the following formula: All Being is divided, etc.

The term "Being" which I have used here represents the Arabic *maujud*,[1] the Hebrew *nimẓa*,[2] and the Latin *ens*. All these three terms are meant to reproduce the Greek τò ὄv, which is used by Aristotle as the main subject of his tenfold division of categories. But at this point the mediaevals depart from Aristotle's method of procedure. They do not say outright at the very beginning that Being is divided into ten categories, and for the very good reason that they do not seem to take the Aristotelian tenfold classification of cate-

---

[1] ‏موجود‎.   [2] ‏נמצא‎.

gories — as does John Stuart Mill and others who have criticized or ridiculed it — to be a primary, logical, and accurate classification of Being. In their opinion, it would seem, when Aristotle wanted to be logical and accurate he simply divided Being into substance and accident; its subsequent subdivision into ten categories was meant to be merely tentative and was by no means fixed. It is with the logical division of Being into substance and accident, therefore, that the mediaevals mean to begin their metaphysical investigation. But here, again, they do not exactly say that outright. Instead of beginning directly with the statement that all Being is divided into substance and accident, they begin with a rather broader and more general statement, and by gradual paring, whittling, and edging finally narrow it down to the Aristotelian phraseology. Their opening statement usually reads that all Being is divided into that which dwells within a dwelling and that which does not dwell within a dwelling. The term "dwelling"[1] is then investigated, and a special kind of dwelling, named "subject,"[2] is differentiated from the others. At last the wished-for statement is arrived at, namely, that all Being is divided into that which is in itself and that which is in a subject, and the former is given the name of substance whereas the latter is given the name of accident. Thus the formula that everything which exists is either in itself or in another thing occurs in the writings of such philosophers as Joseph Ibn Zaddik,[3] Albo[4]

[1] משכן, مَحَلّ. Cf. my Crescas' Critique of Aristotle, p. 577.

[2] נושא, موضوع. ὑποκείμενον. Cf. ibid.

[3] 'Olam Katan, I, ii (p. 8): "Every existing thing of the things which exist inevitably falls under one of the following four classes: [a] It exists in itself, [b] it exists in another thing, [c] it exists neither in itself nor in another thing, or [d] it exists both in itself and in another thing."

[4] 'Ikkarim, II, 11: "Things which exist are divided first into two classes, those which exist in themselves and those which exist in other things."

and Burgersdijck,[1] and the formula that everything is either a substance or an accident occurs still more widely in the writings of such philosophers as Alfarabi,[2] Algazali,[3] Abraham Ibn Daud,[4] Jacob Anatolio,[5] and Burgersdijck.[6] A combination of these two formulae occurs in Eustachius a Sancto Paulo, who divides *ens* into *ens per se* and *ens per accidens*,[7] though he does not use the expressions *ens per se* and *ens per accidens* in the ordinary sense of substance and accident.[8] All these formulae may be traced to Aristotle's statement that "some things can exist apart and some cannot, and it is the former that are substances." [9]

This is how mediaeval thinkers begin their philosophy; and this is how Spinoza would have begun his *Ethics* had he chosen to write it *more scholastico rabbinicoque*. But as a matter of fact, even in its present artificial, geometrical form the *Ethics* begins with this statement, logically though not spatially. It is contained in Axiom I, which reads: "Everything which is, is either in itself or in another."

When we come, however, to Spinoza's formal definition of that thing which is in itself, labelled by the good old name

[1] *Institutiones Metaphysicae*, Lib. I, Cap. II, Thesis VIII: "Praeterea deprehendimus Entia quaedam per se subsistere, alia non per se, sed in iis subsistere, quae per se subsistunt."

[2] *Mehut ha-Nefesh*, in Edelmann's *Ḥemdah Genuzah*, I (p. 46): "Everything which exists must inevitably be either a substance or an accident."

[3] *Maḳaṣid al-Falasifah*, II, i (p. 79): "Existence is divided into substance and accident."

[4] *Emunah Ramah*, I, i (p. 4): "Things which exist are divided first into substance and accident."

[5] *Ruaḥ Ḥen*, Ch. 10: "All things which exist must inevitably be either substance or accident."

[6] *Institutiones Metaphysicae*, Lib. II, Cap. I, Thesis III: "Itaque partiemur Ens primo in substantiam et accidens."

[7] *Summa Philosophiae*, IV: *Metaphysica*, Pars I, Posterior Disputatio, Quaestio I: "Prima igitur divisio entis latissime sumti est in ens Rei, et ens Rationis: Secunda, entis rei, in ens Per se et ens Per accidens."

[8] Cf. *ibid.*, Quaestio IV.   [9] *Metaphysics*, XII, 5, 1070b, 36–1071a, 1.

"substance,"[1] and compare it with the mediaeval definition, we find that while in part they read alike, Spinoza's definition contains a new additional element. The mediaeval definition simply reads, as has been said, that substance is that which is in itself, i.e., not in a subject.[2] But Spinoza adds to "that which is not in itself" the statement "and is conceived through itself" (Def. III). Again, the mediaeval definition of accident is that which is in another thing.[3] Here, again, using the term "mode" (*modus*) which he identifies with the affections (*affectiones*)[4] of substance, Spinoza first defines it like the traditional accident as "that which is in another thing," but then adds the clause "through which also it is conceived" (Def. V). Furthermore, why did Spinoza reject the term "accident" (*accidens*) in his definitions at the beginning of the First Part of the *Ethics*, and replace it by the term "mode"? And why, too, did he not mention the term "subject" in his definitions of substance and mode? Shall we say that all these are matters of mere accident or carelessness or indifference? This might pass as an explanation if we considered the *Ethics* to be an accidentally, carelessly, and indifferently written book. But we are now working on the assumption that the *Ethics* is as careful a piece of

[1] In one of his letters he speaks, however, of "substantia sive ens." Epistola 9 (*Opera*, IV, p. 44, l. 17 and l. 35).

[2] *Maḳaṣid al-Falasifah*, II, i (p. 82): "Substance is a term applied to every existing thing not in a subject"; *Emunah Ramah*, I, 1 (p. 4): "Substance is that existing thing which is not in need of a subject"; Burgersdijck, *Institutiones Metaphysicae*, Lib. II, Cap. I, Thesis IV: "Substantia est Ens per se subsistens. *Per se subsistens* non excludit in hac definitione dependentiam ab omnibus causis (nam hoc sensu nullum Ens dici potest per se subsistere quam solus Deus) sed solummodo dependentiam a subjecto."

[3] *Emunah Ramah*, I, 1 (p. 4): "An accident is that which exists in [another] thing"; Thomas Aquinas, *Quaestiones Quodlibetales*, Quodlibetum IX, Quaest. 3, Art. 5, Ad Secundum: "Substantia est quod per se est; vel, accidens est quod est in alio."

[4] Cf. below, Vol. II, pp. 193–194.

writing even as the *Elements* of Euclid, where every term and phrase and statement has been carefully thought out and chosen, where every variation from what we may with right consider his literary sources must be accounted for; and it is to prove the accuracy of this assumption that is the main burden of our present study.

The solution that would naturally suggest itself to the reader, and one which is generally assumed by students of the *Ethics*, is that Spinoza is following here not the mediaeval authorities but rather Descartes. It is sometimes argued that all the elements of Spinoza's conception of substance are to be found in Descartes, for Descartes, too, considered substance not only as something existing by itself but also as something conceived by itself.[1] However, the formal definition of substance given by Descartes in *Principia Philosophiae*, I, 51, to which Spinoza makes reference in his *Cogitata Metaphysica*, I, 1, describes substance only in terms of existing by itself, without any mention of its being also conceived by itself, though Erdmann, in his exposition of Descartes' definition of mode and substance, introduces from other sources the distinction between "per aliud concipiuntur" and "per se concipiuntur." [2]

Then also with regard to his use of the term "mode" instead of "accident," it may again be traced to Descartes. In fact Spinoza himself ascribes his division of Being into substance and mode to Descartes.[3] Still, while it is true that the term "mode" does occur in the passage of Descartes[4] referred to by Spinoza, Descartes himself uses the term "accident" as synonymous with "mode" and the opposite of "substance." [5]

---

[1] Cf. A. Léon, *Les Éléments Cartésiens de la Doctrine Spinoziste*, p. 85.
[2] Cf. *Grundriss der Geschichte der Philosophie*, II, § 267.4.
[3] *Cogitata Metaphysica*, II, 5. Cf. also I, 1.
[4] *Principia Philosophiae*, I, 48 and 49. Cf. also I, 56.
[5] *Meditationes*, III (*Oeuvres*, VII, p. 40, l. 15): "modos, sive accidentia."

Why then did Spinoza restrict himself in the *Ethics* to the use of the term "mode" after having used the term "accident" as the equivalent of "mode" in some of his other writings? [1] That his subsequent rejection of the term "accident" is not unpremeditated may be gathered from the following statement in the *Cogitata Metaphysica*, I, 1: "In regard to this, however, and I say it deliberately, I wish it to be noted that Being is divided into substance and modes and not into substance and accident." [2]

The solution of these difficulties, therefore, seems to lie in an entirely different direction. Spinoza, I think, was forced to introduce this additional element in his definition of substance not so much because he differed from the mediaevals in the definition of that term as because he differed from them in the definition of mode. As far as substance itself is concerned, Spinoza's definition, as we shall presently see, does not essentially differ from the mediaeval; he only restricts its application by firmly insisting upon its rigid logical meaning. It is only in his conception of modes that Spinoza strikes out a line of his own; his modes are entirely different from Aristotelian accidents, and it is mainly for this reason that he discards the use of that term, and completely alters its definition by omitting the term "subject." The thesis which I am going to sustain, therefore, is that Spinoza's definition of substance contains nothing new, that the additional element it contains was not unknown to the mediaevals, and that Spinoza introduced this additional element in order to round up his definition of substance so as to make

---

[1] Epistola 4. In *Short Treatise*, Appendix I, Axiom 1, the reading is either "toevallen" (*accidentia*) or "wijzen" (*modificationes*). See *Opera*, I, p. 114 and p. 603. Cf. G. T. Richter, *Spinozas philosophische Terminologie* (Leipzig, 1913), p. 85, n. 507.

[2] Locke, too, substituted the term "mode" for "accident" (cf. *Essay concerning Human Understanding*, II, 12, § 3; 13, § 19). Leibniz, in his criticism of Locke, however, tries to reinstate the term "accident" (cf. *Nouveaux Essais*, II, 13, § 19).

it read as the diametrical opposite of his entirely new definition of mode.

In mediaeval philosophy the definition of substance is immediately followed by the classification of substances. As to
the method by which the different classes of substances are
deduced, something will be said in another connection. Suffice it for the present that the mediaevals speak invariably
of four or five substances, including matter, form, concrete
object, soul, and the separate Intelligences [1] — a classification
which the reader will recognize as a composite view made
up of several statements made by Aristotle.[2] All these substances belong to a class of being which is termed "the possible of existence," [3] with which is contrasted a single, unique
Being known as "the Necessary of Existence" [4] or God. The
relation between these two kinds of Being is that of cause
and effect. Now, generally speaking, it is the mediaeval
view that the Necessary of Existence or God cannot be called
substance, even though He is in himself, for God cannot be
subsumed with other things under a general term. Characteristic statements on this point are to be found in Algazali,[5] Asher Crescas,[6] and Moses ha-Lavi.[7] But while this view
is generally admitted, it is still maintained by Augustine,[8]

---

[1] Cf. *Maḳaṣid al-Falasifah*, II, i (p. 82); Shahrastani, ed. Cureton, p. 365; cf. my
Crescas' Critique of Aristotle, p. 575.

[2] Cf. *Metaphysics*, VII, 10, 1035a, 1, and *De Anima*, II, 1, 412a, 19.

[3] ‫ممكن الوجود‬, ‫אפשר המציאות‬.

[4] ‫واجب الوجود‬, ‫מחוייב המציאות‬. Cf. *Cogitata Metaphysica*, I, 1.

[5] *Maḳaṣid al-Falasifah*, II, ii (p. 144): "Eleventh, that of Him who is necessary
of existence, just as it cannot be said that He is an accident so it cannot be said that
He is a substance."

[6] Commentary on *Moreh Nebukim*, I, 57 (2): "But He is neither a substance nor
an accident."

[7] *Ma'amar Elohi*: "It has already been demonstrated that He who is necessary of existence does not come under the category of substance nor under any
of the other categories."

[8] *De Trinitate*, VI, 5 (Migne, *Patrologia Latina*, Vol. 42, Col. 928).

Gersonides,[1] and Descartes[2] that God can be called substance provided only that He is understood to be a substance
unlike any other substance. Burgersdijck says explicitly
that substance is divided into God and created being.[3]

In view of this application of the term "substance" to concrete objects, which must necessarily exist in some place, and
to form, which must necessarily exist in matter, and to soul,
which must reside in a body, a certain question naturally
arises in our mind. If at least three of the so-called substances in the Aristolelian classification always exist in something else, what, then, did the mediaevals mean when they
distinguished substance from accident as that which is in
itself and that which is in something else? Why should the
snub-nosedness of Socrates, for instance, be called accident,
on account of the existance of the snubness in Socrates' nose,
any more than Socrates' soul, which equally exists in his body?
Or, why should the "redness" of a "red table" be called an
accident, on account of its existence in a table, any more than
the table itself, which must exist in some definite place, that
is to say, in some other body? For this is the implication of
space according to Aristotle's definition of the term.[4]

The mediaevals were not unaware of the first-mentioned
difficulty, and they answered it as follows: An accident is
said to exist in something else as in a "subject," and to exist
in a subject means to exist in something without in any

---

[1] *Milḥamot Adonai*, III, 3 (p. 132): "You must know that there are certain attributes which must inevitably be attributed to God, as, for instance, the predication that God is substance, not that the term 'substance' is predicated of God and
other beings as a common genus but it is predicated of them *secundum prius et
posterius*." *Ibid.*, V, iii, 12 (p. 280): "It can also be shown that God is more truthfully to be called substance than is any other being."

[2] *Principia Philosophiae*, I, 51.

[3] *Institutiones Metaphysicae*, Lib. II, Cap. I, Thesis II: "Et substantiam deinde
subdividas in Deum et creaturam." Cf. quotation above p. 64, n. 2.

[4] *Physics*, IV, 4.

sense being the cause of the existence of that something. Incarnate soul, therefore, unlike snub-nosedness, is called substance because, while existing in the body, it is the cause of the body's life, and for this very same reason is form called substance, since it confers upon matter, in which it is, actual existence.[1]

I do not know whether the mediaevals have ever discussed directly the second difficulty we have raised, but we can easily answer it for them from their own point of view and out of their own statements. To say that a concrete object exists in something else, they would argue in the manner of Aristotle, may mean two things, either as a body exists in place or as a part exists in the whole.[2] Neither of these two kinds of existence in something else, however, makes a thing an accident, for in both these cases the thing might also exist without that something else. To exist in place, according to Aristotle's definition of place, means to exist in another body, from which the occupant might be removed, for one of the essential characteristics of place is that it must be external to the occupant.[3] Then, again, in the case of existing in the whole as a part, the part can be removed from the whole, if it is a discrete quantity; and the part will have to be a substance like the whole, if it is a continuous quantity. It is only when a thing exists in something else as in a subject, that is, when it cannot exist by itself without its subject, that it is called accident. The mediaevals could have found support for this distinction in the following passage of Aristotle: "I mean by a thing being in a subject (ὑποκείμενον) that which is in anything, not as a part, but so that it cannot exist separately from that in which it is."[4] The red

[1] Cf. my Crescas' Critique of Aristotle, p. 573, n. 9.
[2] Physics, IV, 3, 210a, 16 and 24; Metaphysics, V, 23, 1023a, 14-17.
[3] Physics, IV, 4, 211a, 1 ff.   [4] Categories, 2, 1a, 24-25.

table, therefore, is a substance, because it can exist without that particular place in which it happens to exist; the redness, however, is an accident, because, as that particular redness, it cannot exist without that particular table.

This is how, it appears to me, the mediaevals would have justified to their own satisfaction their formal distinction between substance and accident and their application of the term "substance" to concrete things. But I can see how Spinoza would have balked at such an explanation, and whoever has tried to approach the problems of philosophy by the same road as Spinoza, and to traverse the ground trod by that ex-pupil of the *Yeshibat 'Eẓ Ḥayyim* of Amsterdam, cannot help feeling that these were the problems that passed through his mind before he broke ground for the foundation of his new system. He would have argued against them somewhat as follows: It is true that concrete objects may be removed from the particular place in which they happen to be; still they cannot be removed from space in general. Everything in the universe must exist in space, which, as has been said before, means in another body. This is an Aristotelian principle which the mediaevals professed to follow. Aristotle says something to the effect that all things are in heaven (οὐρανῷ),[1] by which he does not mean the theological heaven to which martyrs and saints and others with proper introductions are admitted to enjoy a life of eternal bliss and beatitude. What he means is that the universe, which is finite, is all-surrounded by a sphere, which is the outermost of a series of concentric spheres, within which all things exist as in space. Consequently, if everything within the universe is thus within something else, namely, within the outermost sphere, and if a substance must be in itself, then nothing within the universe can be a substance. Or,

[1] Cf. *Physics*, IV, 2, 209a, 33; IV, 4, 211a, 24.

in other words, the red table can no more be a substance than the redness.

It is reasoning like this, if not exactly this very same reasoning, that must have led Spinoza to reject the mediaeval distinction between substance and accident, and the artificial distinction of existing in something else and existing in a subject. Everything that is in something else in any sense or manner, he seems to say, cannot be a substance. "That there is no such thing as a finite substance" is the starting point of his philosophy, and indeed it is the statement with which he begins his investigation of "What God Is," in his *Short Treatise*,[1] which is a kind of *Urethik*. It is a challenge hurled at all the mediaeval philosophers, ulemas, rabbis, and schoolmen alike, for they were all nursed by the same mother and fed from the same source. It denies the application of the term "substance" to finite things within the universe. Thus in one of his Dialogues, Reason, addressing Desire, says: "What you say, O Desire, that there are different substances, that, I tell you, is false; for I see clearly that there is but One, which exists through itself, and is a support to all other attributes. And if you will refer to the material and the mental as substances, in relation to the modes which are dependent upon them, why then, you must also call them modes in relation to the substance on which they depend."[2] Note that he does not reject the generally accepted definition of substance; on the contrary, he insists upon its rigid application. Only that which is really and absolutely in itself can be called substance, and so only that which is called the Necessary of Existence or God can be truly called substance. All the other things which belong to the so-called possible of existence are not substances; they are what the mediaevals would have called accidents, but which Spinoza prefers to call by a new

[1] I, 2.   [2] *Short Treatise*, I, First Dialogue, § 9.

name, modes, seeing that they are not exactly what is generally meant by accident. He confines the term "accident" to one of its more specific usages, and distinguishes it from mode as follows: "For accident is nothing but a mode of thought and exists only in regard to this [whereas mode is a real being]. For example, when I say that a triangle is moved, the motion is a mode not of the triangle but of the body moved. Therefore, in respect to the triangle, motion is only an accident, but in respect to the body, it is real being or mode; for motion cannot be conceived without a body, but it may without a triangle." [1]

If our account of the processes of Spinoza's mind thus far is right, we can readily see how at this point, with his rejection of finite substances and with his restricting the term "substance" to God alone, Spinoza was confronted with a perplexing problem. How should he define those discarded substances which he has renamed modes? As for his real substance, he could very well retain the old definition, being in itself, for God indeed is in himself. But could he just as well say of mode that it is that which is in something else? Spinoza could have used that definition if he had retained Aristotle's conception of a finite universe, bounded from without by an all-surrounding sphere, for then indeed all modes would have been within something else. But believing as Spinoza did in an infinite universe he could not naturally speak of modes as existing in something else, by this meaning Aristotle's space. Nor, again, could he say that they existed in a "subject," for the term "subject" to him has no meaning at all. And yet, if substance is to be defined as that which exists in itself, mode will, of course, have to be defined as that which exists in something else. But what might that something else be if it is not space nor subject?

[1] *Cogitata Metaphysica*, I, 1.

If we were justified in penetrating thus far behind the uttered statements of Spinoza in unfolding the hidden arguments that lie beneath them, we may be allowed to proceed a little further with the same method and to go through the slow paces of this imaginary tentative reasoning of his until we arrive at a happy conclusion. We can clearly see how Spinoza, in his groping for a new differentiation between substance and mode, would at first strike upon the other sense in which, according to Aristotle, a thing is said to be in something else, namely, as a part in the whole.[1] Substance is thus the whole which exists in itself, whereas mode is the part which exists in something else. Here at last we have arrived at a term with which we so often meet in works on Spinoza. But to Spinoza's mind, steeped in mediaeval philosophic lore as it undoubtedly was and trained as it also was in its rigorous logical discipline, the term "whole" would need further explanation. For there are several kinds of wholes,[2] and which of these, he would ask himself, should he say is substance? The kind of whole that would probably first suggest itself to him as the most applicable in the case in question would be that of a physical quantitative whole, for if substance is simply the whole of the modes it is nothing but the universe, and the universe to Spinoza as to the mediaevals is something physical and quantitative. But such a conception of substance as merely the aggregate sum of the modes is contrary to all the uttered statements of Spinoza. To Spinoza's mediaeval mode of thinking the difficulty of such a conception of substance would appear in the following manner. A quantitative whole must be either discrete, consisting of heterogeneous parts, or continuous, consisting of homogeneous parts. Substance, however, could be neither

[1] Cf. *Physics*, IV, 3, 210a, 16. See also *Short Treatise*, I, First Dialogue.
[2] *Metaphysics*, V, 25.

of these. It could not be a discrete quantitative whole, because the modes, if their nature is to be judged by the two
known modes, are each continuous. Even extension is continuous, for Spinoza was an Aristotelian, believing in the
continuity of matter. He was no atomist, and for this we
have ample evidence in his discussion of infinity.[1] As for
the second alternative, there is nothing contradictory in itself in saying that substance is a continuous quantitative
whole, for it is not impossible that Spinoza conceived a continuity between extension and thought. Still Spinoza would
reject this conception. For if substance were only the aggregate sum of modes, how could one insist upon the unity
and simplicity of substance without thereby declaring the
differences between modes a mere illusion? To such a view
Spinoza could by no means subscribe, for he was no mystic,
no idealist of the kind to whom everything that kicks and
knocks and resists is unreal. He was, many views to the
contrary notwithstanding, a hard-headed, clear-minded em-
piricist, like most of the mediaevals and like Aristotle.

Spinoza will thus take a final step and declare that substance is a whole which exists over and above and beyond
the sum of the modes, and saying this he will rest his case.
This may sound alarming and tantalizing, and it may also
appear as wholly inconsistent with what we have been accustomed to understand by Spinoza's repeated assertion
that God is an immanent cause and not a transeunt cause.
But we shall see in a subsequent chapter that the term "immanence" as used by Spinoza in its application to substance
is not contradictory to the term "transcendence" in its original meaning of being more general. Quite the contrary, the
immanence of Spinoza's substance is a transcendent immanence.[2] Spinoza's substance is thus a whole transcending

[1] See Epistola 12. Cf. below, Chapter VIII.   [2] Cf. below, pp. 323 ff.

the universe, the latter being the sum of the modes, and the relation of substance to the universe is conceived by him after the manner of the relation of the whole to the part, the whole in this particular case being a universal of a special kind, a real universal, as distinguished from the attributes which are only nominal universals.[1] By the same token, when Spinoza speaks of the modes as existing in another thing (*in alio*) he means that the modes, individually or in their aggregate totality, exist in substance in the same sense as when Aristotle says that "the finger is *in* the hand and generally the part *in* the whole,"[2] and that "man is *in* animal and generally species *in* genus."[3]

The term "universal," however, carries associations which would be only confusing in its use in connection with Spinoza. Aristotle himself would have simply spoken of genus and species. In Arabic and Hebrew literature philosophers also speak of genus and species rather than of universals, though the latter term is not altogether unknown.[4] It is also significant that the famous passage in Porphyry's *Isagoge* [5] to which legendary history assigns the origin of the problem of universals, just as grammar-school readers assign to the falling apple the origin of Newton's laws of motion — even that passage speaks of genera and species rather than of universals. Spinoza himself, though he makes use of the term "universal" quite frequently, says in one place: "Hence the fixed and eternal things . . . will be like universals to us, or, so to speak, the *genera* of the definitions of individual mutable things." [6] We shall therefore use here the term "genus," and describe Spinoza's conception of the relation between

---

[1] Cf. below, pp. 327–328.
[2] *Physics*, IV, 3, 210a, 15–16.
[3] *Ibid.*, 210a, 18.
[4] *Moreh Nebukim*, I, 51.   [5] Ch. I.
[6] *Tractatus de Intellectus Emendatione*, § 101 (*Opera*, I, p. 37, ll. 5–8).

mode and substance as that between the individual essence
and its genus.

We now come to the last step in our argument. In Aristotelian logic, universal terms like "genus" and "species"
perform certain functions in the formation of concepts. They
are the elements, or rather the causes, in the terms of which
the individual essence of a thing, the "what" of it, can be
conceived. They form its definition. Man is thus conceived
through his genus "animal" and his species "rational," and
he is thus also defined by the combination of these two terms.
And so everything that is in something else, as an individual
in its genus, may be thus said to be conceived by that something else. This is what Spinoza means by his definition of
mode as "that which is in another thing through which also
it is conceived"; that is to say, it is in another thing in the
sense that it is conceived through it, namely, as the individual
in its genus. Substance, on the contrary, "is in itself" absolutely, and "is conceived through itself," inasmuch as it is a
summum genus. But to be conceived through itself is really
a negation. It does not mean anything positively. All it
means is that it cannot be conceived through anything else.
This is the significance of Axiom II, which reads: "That
which cannot be conceived through another must be conceived through itself." The emphasis is that to be conceived
through itself merely means not to be conceived through
something else. The implication therefore is that Spinoza's
substance is inconceivable, and its essence undefinable and
hence unknowable.[1]

Thus the mediaeval definition of the term "substance"
has not undergone any change in Spinoza, though its application was restricted only to God. It is still defined as that
which is in itself. Even the additional fact of its being a

[1] Cf. below, p. 142.

summum genus, undefinable and unknowable, is not new; it is a mediaeval commonplace. That unique substance, God, was thus conceived throughout the Middle Ages among rational theologians. Says Maimonides, and he by no means stands alone in the views he is about to utter, for passages like these can be gathered at random from many a book: "There is no possibility of obtaining a knowledge of the essence of God." [1] Again he says: "The object is described by its definition, as, for example, man is described as a being that lives and has reason. . . . All agree that this kind of description cannot be given of God; for there are no previous causes to His existence, by which He could be defined: and on that account it is a well-known principle, accepted by all philosophers, who are precise in their statements, that no definition can be given of God." [2]

That the something else in which the modes are is substance and that mode is related to substance as the individual essence to its genus is clearly set forth by Spinoza in Proposition I. The proposition affirms the priority of substance to its affections, i.e. modes,[3] which is a truly Aristotelian principle, for the genus, according to him, is prior to, and better known than, the individual.[4] But of particular interest is the expression "prior in nature" (*prior est natura*) used by Spinoza. In Aristotle, the expression "prior in nature" (πρότερον τῇ φύσει) is used in two senses: first, in the sense of better and more excellent, and second, in the sense of being the cause of something.[5] In the latter sense it is very often used in Arabic and Hebrew as well as in Latin philosophic literature. But we find that the expression has acquired in the Middle Ages an additional meaning, namely, as the more universal

[1] *Moreh Nebukim*, I, 59.
[2] *Ibid.*, I, 52.
[3] Cf. below, Vol. II, pp. 193–194.
[4] *Topics*, VI, 4, 141a, 26 ff.
[5] *Categories*, 12, 14b, 4 ff.

to the less universal, as, for example, animality is prior in nature to humanity.[1] This seems to be nothing but a legitimate extension of its use in the sense of "cause," for the genus is considered by Aristotle as the cause of the individual essence.[2] Or it may also reflect Aristotle's statement that the whole is prior in nature to the parts.[3] Spinoza thus rightly says that "substance is prior in its nature to its affections" (Prop. I).

[1] *Maḳaṣid al-Falasifah*, II, i (p. 119): "With regard to [prior] in nature, as when we say, for instance, animality is prior to humanity."

Millot ha-Higgayon, Ch. 12: "Second, prior in nature, as, for instance, animal is prior to man."

Ruaḥ Ḥen, Ch. 8: "In the same way you say that animals are prior in nature to the human species."

Duns Scotus, *Quaestiones in Quatuor Libros Sententiarum*, Lib. II, Dist. I, Quaest. 2, No. 3: "Hic dicit Doctor quod *prius natura* potest dupliciter accipi. Primo positive ... sicut est de animali et rationali in homine, quia prius natura positive animal praecedit rationale."

[2] *Analytica Posteriora*, II, 2, 90a, 31.

[3] *Politics*, I, 2, 1253a, 19–20.

CHAPTER IV

UNITY OF SUBSTANCE

I

In his definition of substance we have seen how Spinoza, reasoning from the mediaeval definition of the term, has arrived at the conclusion that conditional being can in no sense whatever be called substance. The term is to be applied only to Necessary Being, or God. With this as a starting point, Spinoza now proceeds, in the First Part of the *Ethics*, to describe the properties of substance, beginning in Propositions II–VI with a discussion of its unity, which in manner of treatment, as we shall endeavor to show, runs along the line of the mediaeval discussions of the unity of God.

It is philosophic dualism of which Spinoza's discussion of the unity of substance is aimed to be a refutation, just as theological dualism was the target of mediaeval discussions of the unity of God. The philosophy against which Spinoza took the field, starting with the Aristotelian distinction of matter and form, passed through a hierarchy of beings until it ultimately arrived, again like Aristotle, at a being, unique and absolute, who is pure form. In this philosophy, it may be said, there is to be discerned a twofold dualism. Not only did it posit in the world itself a duality of matter and form, or, as it was better known in the fashionable philosophy of Spinoza's own time, of extension and thought, but it also maintained the duality of a material, multifarious, changeable world and an immaterial, simple, immutable God, who is pure form, whose essence is thought, and whose activity is thinking. Matter and form, in the traditional terminology, are two substances, which combined form all concrete beings, which are also called substances; and by the extension of the term "substance," for which he had several precedents,[1] Spinoza speaks of the mediaeval contrast between God and the world again as a contrast between two substances. It is upon this latter phase of dualism, the existence of an immaterial God over against a material world, that Spinoza is warring whenever we find him contending against the existence of two substances, in the *Ethics* as well as in the *Short Treatise*.

The object of Spinoza's criticism of this kind of dualism is not to abolish the materiality of the world, but rather to abolish the immateriality of God. He will endeavor to show that the assumption of an absolutely immaterial God is incompatible with the relation which the mediaevals assumed to obtain between God and the world, namely that of cause and effect. He will thus introduce into his discussion of the unity of substance the problem of creation — the first serious problem, it might be said, which the mediaeval religious thinkers encountered when they attempted to identify the Aristotelian pure form, a mere logical concept, with the personal God of tradition, and to use it as a working hypothesis to explain the origin of a created world as well as its governance. The difficulties of the theory of creation, of which the mediaevals were not unaware, were many and varied, all arising out of the conception of God as an immaterial, simple, and immutable being, combined with the Neoplatonic principle that "a simple element can produce only a simple thing." [2] Spinoza will hardly bring out new difficulties which have not already been thought of and fully discussed and answered by the mediaevals themselves, but he will insist that their answers are a kind of special pleading

[1] See above, pp. 67–68.   [2] *Moreh Nebukim*, II, 22.

which really does not solve the problem. Had the *Ethics* been written *more scholastico rabbinicoque*, Spinoza would have prefaced his argument in Propositions II–VI with words to the following effect: We shall now proceed to demonstrate that there is no God distinguished from the world after the manner of two substances, one spiritual and the other material. For to posit such a God would involve us in all the difficulties which you have yourselves noticed in the problem of creation, and from which, despite all your efforts, you have not been able to extricate yourselves completely. We shall see that, even in their present form, these five propositions contain a clear-cut, single, consecutive argument which in its external, logical outline is modelled after the mediaeval reasoning against the hypothesis of two deities and which substantially embodies the principal mediaeval arguments against creation.

To the mind of Spinoza, it would seem, the widely scattered mediaeval discussions of the problem of the unity of God [1] presented themselves in the form of a hypothetico-disjunctive syllogism. If there were two gods, either they would have to be absolutely unrelated to each other or there would have to be some kind of relation between them. He could clearly see why the mediaevals would have rejected both these alternatives as untenable. Two unrelated gods would imply the existence of two independent worlds, for in one world there could be no adequate division of labor between them; and two unrelated gods would contradict the very conception of God as something absolutely unrelated. To

---

[1] Spinoza discusses the problem of the unity of God directly in *Cogitata Metaphysica*, II, 2. He reproduces there two arguments which he characterizes as futile. Both these arguments are taken directly from Burgerdijck's *Institutiones Metaphysicae*, Lib. I, Cap. VI, but are also found in *Emunot we-Deʿot*, II, 1 and 2, and in *Ḥobot ha-Lebabot*, I, 7, First and Third Arguments. Cf. Freudenthal, "Spinoza und die Scholastik," in *Philosophische Aufsätze, Eduard Zeller . . . gewidmet*, p. 111.

assume such a formulation of the problem in the mind of Spinoza is nothing but to rearrange the mediaeval discussions and weld them into one composite argument.

God to the mediaevals meant the God of a world. Their conception of God, which was the hybrid product of the joining together of the Aristotelian logical principle of prime mover, or first cause, with the Biblical ethical teaching of a creator and supreme ruler, has derived from both these sources its main characteristic feature as that of cause and creator. A cause and creator, however these terms may have become attenuated, must of necessity be the cause and creator of something. God's thinking, which constitutes His sole activity, must either by necessity or by design objectify itself in a world at a certain stage in the process of emanation. An idle, quiescent, passive God, a God who has no world to operate upon, would be an impotent God and an object of commiseration and pity, as the hero of Chamisso's story who was without a shadow. It therefore follows that, granting two absolutely independent deities, there would have to be two absolutely independent worlds. But the existence of more than one world was generally agreed to be impossible. For this there was the overwhelming authority of Aristotle, who with an impressive array of arguments had shown in the latter part of the First Book of *De Caelo* (Chs. VIII–IX) that the existence of many worlds was impossible. It would thus be necessary first to establish the possibility of many worlds before it could be assumed that there was more than one God; and, in fact, Crescas, in his attempt to expose the flimsiness of the philosophic proofs for the unity of God, attacks the problem from that very angle, showing that the existence of more than one world is not impossible.[1]

[1] *Or Adonai*, I, ii, 15 and 19. Cf. my *Crescas' Critique of Aristotle*, p. 217 and pp. 472 ff., n. 127.

Since there must be only one world, within that only world, the argument would proceed, two absolutely independent and absolutely unrelated deities could not be conceived to exist and at the same time be active. "A duality could only be imagined in this way, either that at one time the one deity is active, the other at another time, or that both act simultaneously, nothing being done except by both together." [1] But either of these arrangements would be inconsistent with the absolute independence and omnipotence and self-sufficiency of the deities. To say that the two deities act each independently in their own spheres is likewise impossible, for "the whole existing world is one organic body, all parts of which are connected together. . . . Hence it is impossible to assume that one deity is engaged in forming one part, and another deity in forming another part, of that organic body of which all parts are closely connected together." [2] Here, again, Crescas tries to disprove the philosophic proof for unity by suggesting a possibility, with what success does not concern us here, of an adequate division of labor between two gods within this organic world.[3]

If two absolutely mutually independent deities are impossible, the mediaevals would then consider the case of two deities having something in common. Such deities, however, could not properly be called two unless in addition to their possessing something in common they also possessed something in which they differed. But what would that something be in which they differed? Usually in things which are said to have something in common and something in which they differ the identity implied is that of a common genus and the diversity is that of a specific difference, or the identity is that of a common species and the diversity is that of an individual difference, such as accidental qualities. It is for

[1] *Moreh Nebukim*, II, 1.   [2] *Ibid.*
[3] *Or Adonai*, I, ii, 19.

this reason that bodiless spiritual beings, between which there is no generic or specific or individual difference, cannot be counted. "Whatsoever is not a body does not admit of the idea of number except it be a force in a body, for then the individual forces may be numbered together with the matters or subjects in which they exist."[1] If two deities therefore existed, having something in common and something in which they differed, they would have to possess the metaphysical distinction of genus and species, or, still worse, they would have to possess physical qualities. Both these are contrary to the very nature of God, who must be absolutely simple and indivisible. The argument is stated as follows: "We say to him who believes that there is more than one God that the essence of the two gods must inevitably be one or more than one. If he says the essence is one, then the thing is one, and there is not more than one Creator; and if he says that the essence of the one deity is unlike that of the other, then it would be necessary to posit a certain difference between them."[2]

There is only one way, the mediaevals would conclude, in which purely immaterial beings can be counted, and that is when they are related to each other as cause and effect. Such is the case of the Intelligences which preside over the spheres. Though immaterial, still they are numbered, their number corresponding to that of the spheres.[3] The basis for their number, according to the view held by Avicenna, is that in the process of emanation they proceed in succession from one another, thus being the cause of one another. "It follows, therefore, that separate beings, which are neither bodies nor forces in bodies, do not admit of any idea of number except

[1] *Moreh Nebukim*, II, Introduction, Prop. 16.
[2] *Ḥobot ha-Lebabot*, I, 7 (4). Cf. *Emunot we-De'ot*, II, 2, and *Moreh Nebukim*, II, 1, and I, 75 (2).
[3] See *Moreh Nebukim*, II, 4.

when they are related to each other as cause and effect." [1]
Number in this sense, however, could not be applied to two
deities. If two deities were postulated to exist, they could
not bear to each other the relation of cause and effect, one
being produced by the other, for that would run counter to
the very conception of God as an uncaused being. "The
hypothesis that there exist two gods is inadmissible, because absolutely incorporeal beings cannot be counted, except as cause and effect." [2]

This then is the mediaeval argument against a duality of
gods as we assume it was formulated in Spinoza's mind.
It begins with the alternative that two deities either would
have to be absolutely different from each other or would have
to have something in common. Showing the impossibility of
the first alternative, it proceeds to reason against the second
alternative by pointing out that if two gods were not absolutely different from each other they would have to be absolutely the same, inasmuch as their natures could not be
divided by being partly different and partly the same. Nor,
having the same nature, could they be differentiated by
their relation to each other as cause and effect. Within this
framework Spinoza's five propositions arrange themselves
in logical order, forming the following consecutive argument:

There are no two substances, that is to say, an immaterial
God and a material world, for if there were, the following
two alternatives would be inevitable:

A. God would be absolutely different from the world, and
hence have nothing in common with it, for "two substances
having different attributes have nothing in common with
one another" (Prop. II). But then,

(1) There could be no causal relation between God and

---

[1] *Ibid.*, II, Introduction, Prop. 16.
[2] *Ibid.*, II, 1, First Proof.

the world, for "If two things have nothing in common with one another, one cannot be the cause of the other" (Prop. III).

B. Or, God and the world would not be absolutely different, but then, God and the world would have to be absolutely the same, for the following reasons:

(1) Things are said to be two only when they differ in essential or accidental qualities, for "two or more distinct things are distinguished from one another, either by the difference of the attributes of the substances, or by the difference of their affections" (Prop. IV).

(2) Consequently, if God and the world were of the same nature and differed neither in accidental nor in essential qualities, they could not be called two, for "in nature there cannot be two or more substances of the same nature or attribute" (Prop. V).

(3) To say that God and the world would differ in so far as one is the cause of the other is impossible, for "one substance cannot be produced by another substance" (Prop. VI).

The logical order of these propositions and their syllogistic form is thus quite apparent. But we must clothe this bare, skeleton-like outline with a body, in order to give to the propositions meaning and weight. Spinoza does not manipulate his terms according to certain rules of the game, as if they were pawns on the chess-board, for the mere pleasure of the play. There is always some concrete application in his reasoning. His propositions and their proofs, whenever they are not an interpretation of facts of nature, are to be taken as a criticism of the philosophy upon which he was nurtured.

Proposition II contains Spinoza's restatement of the mediaeval view concerning the distinction between God and the world. The essence of God, according to this view, is so different from the essence of the world that no attribute can be predicated of them in the same, or in any related, sense. All terms used in describing the divine nature are to be taken as homonymous terms, none of them having the meaning with which it is associated in our mind, and none of them conveying to our mind any direct knowledge of the divine nature, which must always remain unknowable and ineffable. When the mediaevals speak of a knowing God or a living God they do not mean to attribute to God a kind of knowledge or life which he shares in common with other beings, for knowledge and life in their application to God must have an absolutely different and unique meaning. "When they ascribe to God essential attributes, these so-called essential attributes should not have any similarity to the attributes of other things, and should according to their own opinion not be included in one and the same definition, just as there is no similarity between the essence of God and that of other beings." [1] Again, "this is a decisive proof that there is, in no way or sense, anything common to the attributes predicated of God, and those used in reference to ourselves; they have only the same names, and nothing else is common to them." [2] Referring to this view, Spinoza says: "Two substances having different attributes have nothing in common with one another" (Prop. II) — that is to say, when the same attributes, predicated of two substances, are homonymous terms, used in absolutely different and unrelated senses, the predication of these attributes does not imply any real relationship in the essence of the two substances. The term *attributa* in this proposition should be taken simply in the sense of predicates, which, as will be shown in another

---

[1] *Moreh Nebukim*, I, 56.   [2] *Ibid.*

chapter, is one of the senses in which the term is used by
Spinoza.[1]

The refutation of this view is given in Proposition III.
Spinoza seems to be challenging the mediaevals in the following words: If you say that the divine nature is absolutely
different from the nature of the world, how then can you interpret your traditional creation, as most of you do, in terms
of emanation and call your creative God an emanative cause?

The theory of emanation maintains that the entire universe with all its manifold finite beings is the unfolding of the
infinite divine nature, the product of its thinking. There is
nothing in the universe which is not involved in the nature
of God, and nothing happens in the universe which does not
emanate from Him. "Inasmuch as it has been demonstrated
that God is incorporeal and has also been established that
the universe is His work and that He is its efficient cause.
. . . We say that the universe has been created by divine
emanation and that God is the emanative cause of everything that comes into being within it." [2] It is for this reason
that God is said to know particulars by virtue of His knowledge of himself; [3] it is also for this reason that it is said that
by our contemplation upon the nature of the universe we may
arrive at the knowledge of the nature of God.[4] This kind of
relation which God is said to bear to the world is a causal
relation of a particular kind, unlike the causal relation of
corporeal agents to the objects upon which they operate. It
is called emanative causation. "Inasmuch as the actions of
the purely incorporeal Intelligence are clearly manifest in
the world, and they are especially manifest in every case of

[1] Cf. below, p. 228.
[2] *Moreh Nebukim*, II, 12.
[3] See *Milḥamot Adonai*, III, 4 (p. 138), and *Or Adonai*, II, i, 4 (p. 32b). Cf. below, Vol. II, p. 14.
[4] See *Ḥobot ha-Lebabot*, II, 1 ff.

change that does not originate in the mere combination of
elements, we cannot escape the conclusion that this agent,
not being corporeal, does not act by impact nor at a certain
definite distance. The action of the incorporeal Intelligence
is always termed emanation, on account of its similarity to a
water-spring." [1]

This principle of emanation, which was primarily introduced to obviate the difficulty of how an incorporeal agent
could act upon a corporeal object, was found to be insufficient
even in the eyes of the mediaevals, whose strictures upon
this point will be quoted later. Even after interposing a
series of immaterial intermediaries between God and the
world, they were still harassed by the question how could
matter ultimately arise if it were not to be found originally in
the nature of God. One of the solutions offered is that God as
the emanative cause of the universe does not act by necessity but by volition, and consequently all variety in nature,
due to the existence of matter, as well as matter itself, is to
be attributed to the design and determination of God. [2]

The principal points in this mediaeval view, so far as we
are here concerned, are three. God is the emanative cause
of the world, with all that it implies. But God is immaterial,
and how could a material world emanate from Him? The
answer is that God acts by volition and design.

In opposition to this, Spinoza denies the immateriality of
God as well as will and design in His action. He does not
hesitate to speak of God as the cause of the world, but he
insists that the causality must be mechanical and not inten-
tional. As against those "who think that God is a free cause,"
and that He creates "by a certain absolute will," he argues
that "I think that I have shown with sufficient clearness

[1] *Moreh Nebukim*, II, 12.
[2] *Ibid.*, II, 22.

(Prop. XVI) that from the supreme power of God, or from His infinite nature, infinite things in infinite ways, that is to say all things, have necessarily flowed, or continually follow by the same necessity, in the same way as it follows from the nature of a triangle, from eternity and to eternity, that its three angles are equal to two right angles." [1] This conception of God as a necessary cause is laid down by Spinoza in Axioms III, IV, and V, at the beginning of *Ethics*, I. The term "cause" which occurs in these axioms is to be taken as referring specifically to God, or substance, in its relation to the world. In Axiom III, he affirms that God acts by necessity: "From a given determinate cause an effect necessarily follows." Since God acts by necessity and not by volition, there is nothing in the nature of the world that is not in the nature of God; the two must be mutually implicative. "The knowledge of an effect depends upon and involves the knowledge of the cause" (Axiom IV), for "those things which have nothing mutually in common with one another cannot through one another be mutually understood, that is to say, the conception of the one does not involve the conception of the other" (Axiom V). Starting, therefore, with his own premise that God acts by necessity, he argues against the mediaevals that if God's nature be essentially different from the nature of the world, He could not be the cause of the world, for "if two things have nothing in common with one another, one cannot be the cause of the other" (Prop. III). In an earlier version of the same Proposition, the argument is stated more directly: "That which has not in itself something of another thing, can also not be a cause of the existence of such another thing" [2] — that is to say, if God is immaterial, He cannot be the cause of a material world.

----

[1] *Ethics*, I, Prop. 17, Schol.
[2] *Short Treatise*, Appendix I, Axiom 5.

Spinoza, however, knew that by this he had not yet fully succeeded in reducing his opponents to silence. To tell them that God could not be the cause of the material world, if He were assumed to be immaterial, would only evoke the reply that it was just to meet this difficulty that emanation was introduced to take the place of direct creation. God as the direct cause of matter would indeed be impossible. But emanation claims only that God is the cause of a single Intelligence, a purely spiritual being, as devoid of matter as God himself. It is this pure spirit of which God is the cause; and matter proceeds not directly from God but from the Intelligences. "In accordance with this axiom, Aristotle holds that the direct emanation from God must be one simple Intelligence, and nothing else."[1] Again, "from the Necessary Existent only one thing can proceed without an intermediary, but many things can proceed from Him by order of succession and through intermediaries."[2] Reduced to Spinoza's terminology, it may be said that there are two substances, namely, God and the first Intelligence, who are related to each other as cause and effect. Why should that be impossible?

The answer to this is to be found in Propositions IV, V, and VI, in which Spinoza will endeavor to show that the interposition of incorporeal intermediaries was merely a makeshift and did not really solve the problem how a purely spiritual God could produce a material world.

To begin with, Spinoza repeats the question raised with respect to the hypothesis of two deities, namely, by virtue of what could God and the first Intelligence be called two? In order to be susceptive of number, things must be distinguished either as separate substances or as separate modes;

[1] *Moreh Nebukim*, II, 22.
[2] *Maḳaṣid al-Falasifah*, II, ii, 10 (p. 143).

or, to put it in the words used by Spinoza elsewhere, the distinction between them must be either *realis* or *modalis*,[1] for extramental being, that is, real being (*ens reale*), as distinguished from fictitious being (*ens fictum*) and being of reason (*ens rationis*),[2] must be either substance or mode. Hence Proposition IV: "Two or more distinct things are distinguished from one another, either by the difference of the attributes of the substances, or by the difference of their affections."

Continuing this line of reasoning, he endeavors to prove that the first Intelligence, in the mediaeval theory, could not be distinguished from God and still have something in common with Him, but that the two would have to be either absolutely different or absolutely identical.

God and the first Intelligence, he argues, could not be said to be distinguished from each other *realiter* by differing only in part of their nature, that is to say, by their having something in common and something in which they differed. For since God is the highest genus, He could not share anything in common with any other being, as that would constitute His genus. If God is therefore to be distinguished from the first Intelligence *realiter*, He will have to differ from the latter in His entire nature, having no attribute in common with it. Spinoza thus says: "If they are distinguished only by difference of attributes, it will be granted that there is but one substance of the same attribute (Prop. V, Demonst.). God and the first Intelligence would therefore have to be absolutely different from each other.

Still less could it be said that God and the first Intelligence differed in accidental qualities. Spinoza does not attempt to refute this on the ground that the mediaeval immaterial God

---

[1] *Short Treatise*, Appendix I, Prop. 1, Demonst.
[2] Cf. *Cogitata Metaphysica*, I, 1. Cf. below, p. 161.

and pure Intelligences could not possess qualities which are accidental to matter. He knew quite well that for the mediaevals that would form no obstacle. They could interpret these qualities atrributed to God and the Intelligences in the same way as they interpreted the divine attributes, namely, either as external relations,[1] or as actions and negations.[2] He attacks it, however, from another angle. He seems to say to his imaginary opponents: However you would take these qualities, as relations, actions, or negations, you would have to admit that they are something external; that they are distinctions existing only in relation to our own mind, and in no way affecting the nature of God and the Intelligence. In their own nature and essence, therefore, God and the Intelligence would be identical and hence one. To quote him: "But if they are distinguished by difference of affections, since substance is prior by nature to its affections (Prop. I), the affections therefore being placed on one side, and the substance being considered in itself, or, in other words (Def. 3 and Ax. 6), truly considered, it cannot be conceived as distinguished from another substance" (Prop. V, Demonst.).

The upshot of this is that God and the first Intelligence would have to be either absolutely different or absolutely identical, inasmuch as "in nature there cannot be two or more substances of the same nature or attribute" (Prop. V).

Spinoza would have been quite satisfied, on mere logical grounds, in assuming that God and the first Intelligence are of absolutely the same nature and are to be distinguished only in so far as the former is related to the latter as cause to effect. But he would insist that this identity would mean that both God and the Intelligence must be material; that is to say, they must have extension as one of their attributes.

---

[1] Cf. *Cuzari*, II, 1, and *Emunah Ramah*, II, iii.
[2] Cf. *Moreh Nebukim*, I, 52 and 58. Cf. below, pp. 143-144.

His own view, as we shall see,[1] is only a modified form of such a doctrine. But the mediaeval thinkers were far from acknowledging such an identity. They were all agreed on the absolute immateriality of God, though there was some difference of opinion as to the immateriality of the Intelligences. Matter makes its first appearance in the Intelligences themselves, according to those who like Ibn Gabirol held the Intelligences to be material, or it arises from the particular nature of the Intelligences, according to those who believed that while the Intelligences are immaterial they possess in their nature a certain possibility which ultimately gives rise to matter. In either case, they all consider God to be different from the Intelligences; and still they all agree that God is the cause of the Intelligences. The difficulty raised by Spinoza in Proposition III thus occurs again, and is restated by him in Proposition VI: "One substance cannot be produced by another."

Proposition VI, as will have been noticed, is a repetition of Proposition III, and in fact its demonstration is based upon the latter proposition. Likewise the second demonstration of the Corollary of Proposition VI is a reproduction of the demonstration of Proposition III. Furthermore, in a letter from Oldenburg (Epistola III), as well as in Appendix I to the *Short Treatise*, the equivalents of Proposition III are given as axioms upon which the equivalents of Proposition VI are based as propositions. That both these should occur in the *Ethics* as propositions would seem to need some explanation. However, in the light of the logical outline in which we have shown these propositions to be connected, there is ample justification for this seemingly useless repetition.

Our discussion of these five propositions may be brought

[1] Cf. below, pp. 218 ff.

to a conclusion by the following remark on the Corollary in Proposition VI. The Corollary begins with the statement, "Hence it follows that there is nothing by which substance can be produced" ("Hinc sequitur substantiam ab alio produci non posse"), and ends with a similar statement, "Therefore absolutely there is nothing by which substance can be produced" ("Ergo substantia absolute ab alio produci non potest"). In *Short Treatise*, I, 2, the proof of the third proposition, "that one substance cannot produce another," which is the same as Proposition VI in *Ethics*, I, is given as follows: "Should any one again maintain the opposite, we ask whether the cause, which is supposed to produce this substance, has or has not the same attributes as the produced [substance]. The latter is impossible, because something cannot come from nothing." Similarly in the proof of the first proposition given in the foot-note in the same chapter of the *Short Treatise* it is said that, if there were a finite substance, "it would necessarily have something which it would have from nothing." Likewise in Epistola IV to Oldenburg Spinoza produces Proposition III, which he proves as follows: "Nam quum nihil sit in effectu commune cum causa, totum, quod haberet, haberet a nihilo." In the light of all these passages, the conclusion of the Corollary here may be interpreted to mean as follows: Therefore, if substance could be absolutely produced, it would have to be produced from nothing (Ergo, si substantia absolute produci posset, a nihilo deberet produci). The main point of the Corollary would thus be to show that if the material world were produced by an immaterial God, something would be produced from nothing. The force of this argument as well as its historical background will be dealt with in the second part of this chapter, in the discussion of the *Short Treatise*, to which we now turn.

II

The second chapter of the First Part of the *Short Treatise*, which bears the title "What God Is," is again, like Propositions II–VI of the *Ethics*, I, a criticism of mediaeval dualism. Our comments upon this chapter will therefore occasionally have to dwell upon matters which have already been dealt with in our discussion of the *Ethics*. Whenever such a repetition occurs, it is to be excused on the ground that it could not be avoided, unless we preferred to be economical at the expense of clearness and completeness.

Mediaeval dualism considers God as something essentially different from the world. God is pure form; the world is material. As a corollary of this, the world is conceived to have all the imperfections of which God as pure spirit is free. The world is furthermore the creation of God; the world is thus called conditional being whereas God is absolute being. Since creation is assumed to be in time, the world is still further contrasted with God as the created substance with the uncreated substance [1] or as the temporal with the eternal. The creation of the world was not by a single act but rather by a process of emanation. Matter did not come directly from God; it has made its appearance at a certain stage in the devolution of the issue of divine thought. God is pure thought, and His only activity is thinking. But as His thinking is a creative power, it becomes objectified in a thought, known as Intelligence, which, while immaterial like God himself, according to one of the prevailing views,[2] is of a less perfect order, inasmuch as by its nature it is only a possible being, having a cause for its existence. The thought of this Intelligence, which is said to possess a dual

[1] Cf. "de substantia increata, sive de Deo" in *Cogitata Metaphysica*, I, 2.
[2] Cf. above, p. 91, and below, p. 223.

nature, objectifies itself in another Intelligence and a sphere. So the process goes on until at a certain stage crass matter appears which is the basis of the sublunar world. The world thus possesses imperfections which are not found in the original thinking essence of God.

In the language of Spinoza these mediaeval contrasts between God and the world are expressed in the phrases "infinite substance" and "finite substance." It is Spinoza's purpose in his discussion of "What God Is" to abolish this dualism between the thinking essence of God and the material, or extended, essence of the world, to identify God with the wholeness of nature, and to conclude "that we posit extension as an attribute of God." [1] He begins in the first proposition by denying the old conception of a hierarchy of substances falling into a general division of spiritual and material substances, or infinite and finite, asserting "that there is no finite substance; but that every substance must be infinitely perfect in its kind." [2] If the mediaevals therefore are pleased to speak of the world as an emanation of the divine thinking essence, that divine thinking essence must contain the material element of which the world is made, "that is to say, that in the infinite understanding no substance can be more perfect than that which already exists in nature." [3]

Spinoza proves this proposition by the method employed by him elsewhere,[4] *ex absurdo contradictorio*, for "should any one want to maintain the opposite, we would ask the following question." Suppose, he says, God is a purely immaterial being and beside Him there is a material created substance. The question would then be raised: how did this material

---

[1] *Short Treatise*, I, 2, § 18 (*Opera*, I, p. 24, l. 11).
[2] *Ibid.*, § 2 (p. 19, ll. 9 ff.).   [3] *Ibid.* (p. 20, ll. 6–7).
[4] Cf. below, pp. 183, 378.

world come into being? You would have to resort to the
various theories of creation offered by the mediaevals. But
none of these is free from insurmountable difficulties. And
hereupon Spinoza proceeds to discuss some of the difficulties
of creation and their attempted solutions by the mediaevals.

In the classic writings of Jewish philosophers the discussion of the problem of creation opens with a consideration of
the Epicurean theory of a world having a beginning in time
but without necessarily having come into existence through
a God. Says Saadia: "After it had become perfectly clear
to me that all things are created, I began to inquire whether
they could have been produced by themselves or whether they
could not have been produced except by some agent not
themselves." [1] Says also Baḥya: "The propositions by which
may be proved that the world has a creator by whom it has
been created from nothing are three: First, a thing cannot
produce itself. . . . For anything coming into existence
after it has been without existence must inevitably satisfy
either one of these conditions — either it has come into existence through itself or it has come into existence through
a cause not itself." [2] Similar allusions to a theory of creation through itself, or what is better known as creation by
chance,[3] abound also in the writings of Maimonides,[4] Gersonides,[5] and Crescas.[6] Descartes, too, formulates the problem of creation in the form of a disjunctive proposition: "But
it seems to me to be self-evident that everything that exists
springs from a cause or from itself considered as a cause." [7]

Following his masters, Spinoza similarly begins his in-

[1] *Emunot we-De'ot*, I, 2.   [2] *Ḥobot ha-Lebabot*, I, 5.
[3] Cf. below, p. 318.
[4] *Moreh Nebukim*, II, 13 and 20.
[5] *Milḥamot Adonai*, VI, i, 6.
[6] *Or Adonai*, III, i, 3 (p. 63b).
[7] *Primae Responsiones* (*Oeuvres*, VII, p. 112, ll. 3–5).

quiry by asking "whether this substance is finite through itself . . . or whether it is thus finite through its cause." [1]

Spinoza's refutation of this first alternative is found in two versions, one given in the text and the other in the footnote. The latter is not much unlike the refutation given by Saadia. It reads as follows: "It could not have done so itself, because having been infinite it would have had to change its whole essence." [2] The following is Saadia's answer: "If we take any of the existent things and assume it to have made itself, we know that after its coming into existence it must possess a still greater power and ability to create something like itself. If it could therefore produce itself when it was weak and in a state of non-existence, it should be able to produce something like itself after it has become powerful and attained a state of existence. Seeing, however, that it cannot produce something like itself when it is powerful, certainly it could not have produced itself when it was weak." [3] The underlying assumption in both these refutations is that the substance, having made itself, could not so change its nature as to become less powerful or less infinite than before it has made itself. It is somewhat like the following argument quoted from Suarez by those who objected against Descartes: "If anything is self-derived and does not issue from a cause, it is necessarily unlimited and infinite." [4]

Thus disposing of creation through itself, Spinoza takes up the second alternative suggested by the mediaevals, namely, that "it is made finite by its cause, which is necessarily God." [5] Against this alternative Spinoza raises three objections, one of which is found both in the text and in the

---

[1] *Short Treatise*, I, 2, § 3 (*Opera*, I, p. 20, ll. 11–13).
[2] *Ibid.*, § 2, note 2 (p. 19, ll. 20–21).
[3] *Emunot we-De'ot*, I, 2.
[4] *Primae Objectiones* (*Oeuvres*, VII, p. 95, ll. 16–18).
[5] *Short Treatise*, I, 2, § 4 (*Opera*, I, p. 20, ll. 17–18).

foot-notes; the other two are given only in the foot-notes. It is my purpose to show that these arguments are directed against mediaeval attempts to remove two great difficulties with regard to the theory of creation, and furthermore to show that Spinoza's arguments themselves are taken from the mediaeval discussions.

One of the difficulties about creation in time which the mediaevals grappled with is its obvious inconsistency with the omnipotence and immutability of God, or, as Maimonides puts it, with the belief "that all wants, changes, and obstacles are absent from the essence of God." [1] An omnipotent and immutable God could not be conceived as being active at one time and inactive at another. And then, too, why did God choose one time rather than another for creation? To quote the argument from Maimonides: "An agent is active at one time and inactive at another, according as favorable or unfavorable circumstances arise. . . . As, however, God is not subject to accidents which could bring about a change in His will, and is not affected by obstacles and hindrances that might appear or disappear, it is impossible, they argue, to imagine that God is active at one time and inactive at another." [2]

In answer to this difficulty, Maimonides draws a distinction between the actions of God and the actions of created beings. Human action is an exercise of power, or free will, which is dependent upon external conditions; God's action is an exercise of pure or absolute will and is entirely self-sufficient. "Every being that is endowed with free will and performs certain acts in reference to another being, necessarily interrupts those acts at one time or another, in con-

[1] *Moreh Nebukim*, II, 18.
[2] *Ibid.*, II, 14, Sixth Method. Cf. *Milḥamot Adonai*, VI, i, 3 (p. 299), and *Or Adonai*, III, i, 1.

sequence of some obstacles or changes. . . . Thus changed circumstances change his will, and the will, when it meets with obstacles, is not carried into effect. This, however, is only the case when the causes of the actions are external; but when the action has no other purpose whatever but to fulfil the will, then the will does not depend on the existence of favorable circumstances. The being endowed with this will need not act continually even in the absence of all obstacles, because there does not exist anything for the sake of which it acts, and which, the absence of all obstacles, would necessitate the action: the act simply follows the will." [1]

A somewhat different turn to this same argument is given by Gersonides. Creation, he says, is an exercise not only of the divine absolute will but of the divine disinterested goodwill. "If God created the world for His own benefit, there would be some ground for this difficulty. But since it has been made clear that God derives no benefit from His creation and that creation is only an act of goodness and kindness, the time and manner of creation must be attributed to His will." [2]

The argument that any sort of finitude in the world, whether that of creation in time or that of magnitude, implies either a lack of power or a lack of good-will on the part of God is repeated by many other philosophers. Thus Leo Hebraeus asks: "Furthermore, the purpose of the Creator in creating the world was nothing but His will to do good. Since it is so, why should not the good have been made from eternity, seeing that no obstacle could have hindered the powerful God who is most perfect?" [3] Bruno similarly argues that if the world were finite God would have to be

---

[1] *Moreh Nebukim*, II, 18, Second Method.
[2] *Milḥamot Adonai*, VI, i, 18, Ninth Doubt.
[3] *Dialoghi d'Amore*, III, pp. 238–239 (Bari, 1929).

considered either as unable or as unwilling to make it infinite; in either case God would be evil, for "not to be
able is privatively evil, to be able and to be unwilling
would be positively and affirmatively evil." [1] Suarez, too,
is quoted by those who objected against Descartes as saying
that "all limitations proceed from a cause, and the reason
why anything is finite and limited is, either that its cause
could not, or that it would not, give it more being and perfection." [2] Finally, Abraham Herrera, in his tentative argument against the finite number of emanations, says that if
their number were finite, it would have to be "either because
God was unwilling to make them infinite . . . and thus His
goodness is not perfect, or because He was unable, and thus
He is lacking in power." [3]

Drawing upon these passages, without necessarily following them, Spinoza similarly argues that the creation of a
finite world by an infinite God would be incompatible with
divine power and with divine will or good-will. "Further,
if it is finite through its cause, this must be so either because
its cause *could* not give more, or because it *would* not give
more. That He should not have been able to give more would
contradict His omnipotence; that He should not have been
willing to give more, when He could well do so, savors of
ill-will, which is nowise in God, who is all *goodness* and
perfection." [4]

Both Maimonides and Gersonides, however, felt the weakness of their solution. To attribute creation in time to divine
will, or good-will, would indeed save divine omnipotence and
immutability, but it would still allow for change in divine

    [1] *De Immenso et Innumerabilibus*, I, 10 (*Opera Latina*, I, 1, Neapoli, 1879, p. 238).
Cf. J. L. McIntyre, *Giordano Bruno*, p. 191.
    [2] *Primae Objectiones* (*Oeuvres*, VII, p. 95, ll. 14–16).
    [3] *Sha'ar ha-Shamayim*, II, 4.
    [4] *Short Treatise*, I, 2, § 5 (*Opera*, I, p. 20, ll. 18 ff.).

will. "But, some might ask, even if we admit the correct-
ness of all this, is not change imputed in the fact that the
will of the being exists at one time and not at another?"[1]
While in one place Maimonides attempts to answer it by
drawing a rather arbitrary line of distinction between human
will and divine will, the latter of which he declares to be a
homonymous term,[2] in another place he answers it in the
following words: "The question remains, Why has this
thing been produced now and not long before, since the cause
has always been in existence? The answer is that a certain
relation between cause and product has been absent, if the
cause be corporeal; or, that the substance has not been
sufficiently prepared, if the cause be incorporeal."[3]

In a like manner Gersonides applies the same answer to
his own theory of creation. Unlike Maimonides he does not
believe in absolute *ex nihilo*. The world according to him
was created from a primordial, formless matter which co-
existed with God from eternity, the act of creation being
nothing but the investiture of the formless matter with form.
The choice of a particular time for creation was determined
not by a change in the will of God but by the nature of the
matter out of which the world was created. This, according
to him, would militate neither against the immutability of
the divine will nor against divine omnipotence: "One might
say that inasmuch as God exists always in the same manner,
His will must also remain always the same; by assuming
therefore that God wills to do a thing at one time and does
not will to do it at another, there must inevitably be a change
in the divine nature. To him we answer that the nature of
the material, primordial element is such that it requires that

---

[1] *Moreh Nebukim*, II, 18, Second Method, and cf. *Milḥamot Adonai*, VI, i, 18,
Ninth Doubt.　　[2] *Moreh Nebukim, loc. cit.*

[3] *Moreh Nebukim*, II, 12.

the existence of the good in it should have a beginning in time, inasmuch as that good must come to it from something without itself, as has been shown before, whence it has also been proved that the world must be created. This being the case, it is clear that the existence of the good in this material, primordial element is due to God, whereas the fact that that good did not exist in it from eternity is due to the imperfect nature of that primordial element, which imperfection has served us as a proof that the good in it must be created, for were it not for this, we have shown, the good in it would have come into being without an efficient cause, which would be absurd, as has already been pointed out. This being the case, the coming of the world into existence necessarily had to be at a certain time. There is no reason therefore for the question, why God did not create the world at an earlier time, because whatever time God created it before this time, the same question could still be asked. And just as God cannot be described as possessing the power to create in a thing two opposites at the same time, inasmuch as He is prevented from doing so by the nature of the object receiving the action, so also cannot God be described as having the power of making the good exist from eternity in the material element out of which the world was created, for the imperfection in the nature of that element requires that the good in it should be created in time." [1]

Against both these passages Crescas argues that absolute nothingness and formless matter cannot be said to possess any nature which would require that its creation should take place at a certain particular time. His argument against Maimonides reads as follows: "The question still remains, What has made God create at one time rather than at another? For it would seem that it could not be explained by

[1] *Milḥamot Adonai*, VI, i, 18, Ninth Doubt.

any other reason except that it was the will of God. For if it were for some other reason, that reason would inevitably have to be found either in the Agent who performed the action, or in the object upon which the action was performed, or in something outside both the Agent and the object, as, e.g., the organs through which the action was performed. It could not be in the Agent, for His relation to all times is the same; nor could it be in the object, for it is nothing but non-existence; nor *a fortiori* could it be in something external, for there is nothing external." [1] Against Gersonides he argues in this wise: "That the change would have taken place without a cause can be easily shown by what has already been said. For if the change of God's will had a cause, that cause would have to be found either in God or in the eternal, formless matter, inasmuch as there is nothing else besides these two. But the relation of God is the same to all times, and so also is the relation of that eternal, formless matter, and of all that arises from it, the same to all times. Thus there could be no cause for the change of will implied in choosing a particular time for creation." [2]

This tilt of Crescas against Maimonides and Gersonides is unquestionably the source of Spinoza's argument given in the foot-note: "To say to this that the nature of the thing required such [limitation] and that it could not therefore be otherwise, that is no reply: for the nature of a thing can require nothing while it does not exist." [3]

The second great difficulty of creation which the mediaevals grappled with is the explanation as to how this material, multifarious world could have arisen from the simple, immaterial divine thinking essence. "Ex nihilo nihil fit." This

---

[1] *Or Adonai*, III, i, 4 (p. 66b).
[2] *Ibid.* (p. 68b).
[3] *Short Treatise*, I, 2, § 5, note 3 (*Opera*, I, p. 20, ll. 23-25).

Aristotelian principle is repeated in Jewish philosophic literature from the earliest time.[1] Matter could not have originated in God, for it is excluded from His nature. Whence did it come then? The problem is stated by Jewish philosophers in the Neoplatonic formula that "a simple element can only produce a simple thing."[2] Crescas expresses the impossibility of matter arising directly from God in the following words: "Inasmuch as this matter [in Gersonides' theory] is extremely imperfect, it could not have come by necessity from God who is infinitely perfect."[3]

The theory of emanation which purported to be a solution of this difficulty was found to be unsatisfactory by both Maimonides and Gersonides. If everything must emanate from God and if in God there is nothing material, how could matter appear at all at any stage of emanation unless you say it sprang up out of nothing and is in no way traceable to God? It was this reasoning that forced Maimonides to make emanation a volitional process and Gersonides to accept the Platonic theory of the pre-existence of an eternal, formless matter. Their solutions, however, do not interest us now. We are interested only in their statement of the problem. Says Maimonides: "I ask the following question: Aristotle holds that the first Intelligence is the cause of the second, the second of the third, and so on, till the thousandth, if we assume a series of that number. Now the first Intelligence is undoubtedly simple. How then can the compound form of existing things come from such an Intelligence by fixed laws of nature, as Aristotle assumes? . . . By what law of nature did the spheres emanate from the Intelligences? What relation is there between material and immaterial beings?"[4] Says Gersonides: "This analogy, when closely examined,

---

[1] Cf. *Emunot we-De'ot*, I, 2, and *Ḥobot ha-Lebabot*, I, 5

[2] *Moreh Nebukim*, II, 22.   [3] *Or Adonai*, III, i, 4 (p. 68a).

[4] *Moreh Nebukim*, II, 22.

will be found to fall short of proving that matter can be created from absolute nothing. Only forms can arise in this manner, but not matter. In general, form can produce something of its own kind; hence it produces forms, for all forms are things of reason; but how could it produce materiality?"[1]

These discussions as to the rise of matter are reflected in the following argument of Spinoza, also given in a foot-note. "That there can be no finite substance is clear from this, namely, that, if so, it would necessarily have something which it would have from nothing, which is impossible. For whence can it derive that wherein it differs from God? Certainly not from God, for He has nothing imperfect or finite, etc. So, whence then but from nothing?"[2] We have already called attention to other passages where the same argument is advanced by Spinoza.

This first proposition of *Short Treatise*, I, 2, as will have been noticed, corresponds to Propositions II and III of *Ethics*, I. The second proposition, "that there are not two like substances,"[3] corresponds to Propositions IV and V of the *Ethics*. The argument that "if there were two alike they would necessarily limit one another"[4] is reminiscent of the argument after which it is modelled, namely, that if there were two deities they would limit each other by having a common genus and a specific difference.[5] The third proposition of the *Short Treatise*, I, 2, namely, "that one substance cannot produce another,"[6] corresponds to Proposition VI of the *Ethics*, and is proved by three arguments. The first[7] is the argument based upon the impossibility of something arising from nothing which we have already discussed. The

---

[1] *Milḥamot Adonai*, VI, i, 17 (p. 364). A parallel statement in *Ethics*, I, Prop. 15, Schol., is cited by Joël in *Lewi ben Gerson als Religionsphilosoph*, p. 78, n. 1.

[2] *Short Treatise*, I, 2, § 2, note 2 (*Opera*, I, p. 19, ll. 26-30).

[3] *Ibid.*, § 2 (p. 20, l. 4).   [4] *Short Treatise*, I, 2, § 6.

[5] Cf. above, p. 83.

[6] *Short Treatise*, I, 2, § 2 and § 7.   [7] *Ibid.*, § 8.

second,[1] however, is new and somewhat puzzling. It is my
purpose to show that it can be rendered clear and intelligible
by interpreting it as a criticism of Gersonides' theory that
the world was created from an eternal formless element.

In *Cogitata Metaphysica*, II, 10, in a passage which is
an undoubted allusion to Gersonides' theory of creation,[2]
Spinoza says as follows: "We will not pause to refute the
opinion of those who think that the world as chaos, or as
matter devoid of form, is co-eternal with God, and so far
independent of Him." Here, however, Spinoza does pause
to refute Gersonides, and with an argument raised by Gersonides himself. Gersonides begins to argue against his own
theory by saying that "it is inevitable that either some part
of this formless element remained after the world had been
created from it or no part of it remained." He then proceeds
to prove that neither of these alternatives is possible, adding
that "it is also past comprehension that the size of this primordial element should exactly agree with the size of which
the world must be, for it is evident that the size of the world
can be neither more nor less than what it is."[3] This is exactly
what Spinoza means by the following argument: "Further,
that which is created is by no means produced from nothing,
but must necessarily have been produced from that which is
existent (*die wezentlyk is*).[4] But that something should come
forth from that which is existent and that this latter should
not have that something less even after it had been produced
from it — that we cannot grasp with our understanding."[5]
If we take the last part of the passage to mean that the thing
"which is created," i.e., the world, after it was produced "from
that which is existent," i.e., the eternal formless matter,

---

[1] *Ibid.*, § 9.   [2] Cf. Joël, *Zur Genesis der Lehre Spinoza's*, p. 48.

[3] *Milḥamot Adonai*, VI, i, 18, First Doubt.

[4] On the meaning of *wezentlyk*, cf. below, p. 141, n. 4, and p. 382, n. 7.

[5] *Short Treatise*, I, 2, § 9 (*Opera*, I, p. 21, ll. 21–26).

could not be less than the latter had been before the world was produced from it, the meaning of the entire passage may be restated, in the light of Gersonides' argument, in the following manner: Further, since creation *ex nihilo* has been shown to be impossible, let us now consider creation from an eternal pre-existent formless element. This is, however, likewise inconceivable, for we cannot grasp with our understanding how the created world, the size of which must be determined by its own nature, should happen to agree exactly with the size of the eternal pre-existent element, and not be of a lesser size, so that no part of that element would remain unused after the world had been created from it. This unaccounted for agreement in size is characterized by Spinoza as something which "we cannot grasp with our understanding." Gersonides similarly characterizes it as something which is "past comprehension"[1] and as something which "I cannot comprehend" or "conceive of."[2]

If our interpretation of the last passage quoted from Spinoza is correct, then the argument contained therein as well as the argument contained in the parallel passage quoted from Gersonides is based upon an assumption which is found in Plato and repeated by Philo, namely, the assumption that the matter out of which the world was created was completely used up in the creation of the world so that nothing was left of it. Plato states it in the following passage: "Now the creation took up the whole of each of the four elements; for the Creator compounded the world out of all the fire and all the water and all the air and all the earth, leaving no part of any of them nor any power of them outside. He intended, in the first place, that the whole animal should be perfect, as far as possible, and that the parts of which he was formed should be perfect; and that he should be one,

רחוק ‎[1].   לא אשער ‎[2].

leaving no remnants out of which another such wor'l might be created."[1] Philo restates this view in the following passage: "It is unlikely that any material body has been left over and was moving about at random outside, seeing that God had wrought up and placed in orderly position all matter wherever found."[2] Eusebius quotes another passage from Philo's lost *De Providentia* as follows: "With a view to the creation of the world God estimated an exactly sufficient quantity of matter, so that there might be neither deficiency nor excess. . . . I shall therefore confidently assert that the world needed neither less nor more material substance for its furnishing."[3] This passage from Eusebius is reproduced in Hebrew by Azariah dei Rossi.[4]

The third argument reads as follows: "Lastly, if we would seek the cause of the substance which is the origin of the things which issue from its attributes, then it behoves us to seek also the cause of that cause, and then again the cause of that cause, *et sic in infinitum;* so that if we must necessarily stop and halt somewhere, as indeed we must, it is necessary to stop at this only substance."[5] In this passage Spinoza would seem to admit the impossibility of an infinite causal regression, and he would therefore contradict himself,[6] for elsewhere he denies this impossibility.[7] It seems to me, however, that the argument contained in this passage has an entirely different meaning.

It must be borne in mind that Spinoza advances it as a proof "that one substance cannot produce another," by

[1] *Timaeus*, 32C–33A. Translation by Jowett.
[2] *De Palantatione Noe*, II, 5. Translation by G. H. Whitaker.
[3] *Praeparatio Evangelica*, VII, 21. Translation by E. H. Gifford.
[4] *Me'or 'Enayim, Imre Binah*, Ch. 6 (ed. Cassel, p. 125).
[5] *Short Treatise*, I, 2, § 10 (*Opera*, I, p. 21, ll. 26–32).
[6] Cf. A. Wolf, *Spinoza's Short Treatise*, p. 174.
[7] *Epistola* 12. Cf. below, pp. 195 ff.

which he means to refute the theory that a material world was created by an immaterial God who in so far as He is immaterial is a transeunt cause. Like most of his other arguments it reasons against his opponents from their own premises. The passage therefore is to be divided into two parts, in the first of which he reproduces the premise of his opponents and in the latter of which he draws his own conclusions from the self-same premise. Spinoza seems to say to them as follows: Why do you assume the existence of two substances, God and the world, considering God as the prime cause and rejecting the existence of any other cause prior to Him? It is because you believe with Aristotle that things in change must have a cause and that the series of causes cannot be infinite, and so you argue that "if we would seek the cause of the substance [i.e., God] which is the origin of the things which issue from its attribute, then it behoves us to seek also the cause of that cause, and then again the cause of that cause, and so on *in infinitum*." Your postulating of a prime cause outside the world is therefore dictated by nothing but the alleged need of arbitrarily terminating the series of cause and effect. This being the case, why not stop the series with the world as a whole and postulate the prime cause as something immanent in the world, "so that if we must necessarily stop and halt somewhere, as indeed we must, it is necessary to stop at this only substance [i.e., the world]." The full force of this reasoning will be discussed in our comments on Proposition XVIII of *Ethics*, I.

The fourth and last proposition in this chapter of the *Short Treatise*, though containing in its proof many elements taken from the proofs of the preceding propositions, does not properly belong in our present discussion of the unity of substance. It will be treated subsequently in our discussion of the simplicity of substance.

CHAPTER V

SIMPLICITY OF SUBSTANCE

I. SIMPLICITY AND ATTRIBUTES

IN THE Appendix at the end of the First Part of the *Ethics*, Spinoza furnishes us with the unused titles for the unmarked chapters into which the book would have undoubtedly been divided had he chosen to write it after the manner of the scholastics and the rabbis. Using the terms "nature" and "properties" advisedly in their technical sense, he says: "In these chapters I have explained the nature of God and His properties." He then proceeds to enumerate these properties: (1) "That He necessarily exists; (2) that He is one; (3) that from the necessity alone of His own nature He is and acts; (4) that He is, and in what way He is, the free cause of all things; (5) that all things are in Him, and so depend upon Him that without Him they can neither be nor be conceived; and, finally, (6) that all things have been predetermined by Him, not indeed from freedom of will or from absolute good pleasure, but from His absolute nature or infinite power." The "nature of God," as we have already seen,[1] is treated in Proposition I, which supplements the definition of substance. Of the six "properties" enumerated by Spinoza the last four will be found to cover Propositions XIV–XXXVI, while the first may serve as a heading for Proposition XI. There remains therefore only the second property, "that He is one," which is to describe the contents of Propositions II–X and Propositions XII and XIII. We have already shown in the preceding chapter [2] that Proposi-

---

[1] Cf. above, pp. 61 ff.   [2] Cf. above, pp. 79 ff.

tions II–VI deal with the traditional problem of the unity
of God. We shall now endeavor to show that in Propositions VII–X and XII–XIII Spinoza similarly deals with
another traditional aspect of the same problem.

The expression "unity of God" was used by mediaeval philosophers in two senses. In the first place, it was used in the
sense of numerical unity, as an assertion of monotheism and
a denial of the existence of more than one God. In the second
place, it was used in the sense of essential unity, or simplicity,
as a denial of any kind of inner plurality in the divine nature.[1]
This distinction in the use of the term "unity" may be traced
to Aristotle's discussion of the various meanings of the term
"one,"[2] which is repeatedly reproduced with the usual
modifications and elaborations in mediaeval literature.[3]
Unity in the first sense is the subject of the mediaeval proofs
of the unity of God; unity in the second sense is the principle
underlying the mediaeval discussions of the nature of the
divine essence, or what is generally known as the problem of
divine attributes.[4] Spinoza follows the traditional method
of treatment. Having discussed the numerical unity of God
in Propositions II–VI, he now enters upon the discussion of
the essential unity, or simplicity, of God in Propositions
VII–X and XII–XIII.

The simplicity of God upon which the mediaevals so
strongly insisted was meant to emphasize the impropriety of
the assertion, or even of the implication, of any kind of inner
plurality in the divine essence. They especially mention
three of such inner pluralities which the idea of absolute
simplicity was meant to deny. First of all, it denies the ex-

[1] *Or Adonai*, I, iii, 4.

[2] *Metaphysics*, V, 6.

[3] *Makaṣid al-Falasifah*, II, i (p. 114); *Ḥobot ha-Lebabot*, I, 8; *Cuzari*, II, 2;
Emunah Ramah, II, ii, 1; *'Ikkarim*, II, 10.

[4] Cf. *'Ikkarim*, II, 7.

istence in God of accidental qualities. These had to be rejected on account of the belief in the absolute incorporeality of God which tradition, if not the actual asseverations of the Bible, had taken for granted — which belief was further intensified when the traditional God was identified with the Aristotelian pure form. "He is not a magnitude that any quality resulting from quantity as such could be possessed by Him; He is not affected by external influences, and therefore does not possess any quality resulting from emotion; He is not subject to physical conditions, and therefore does not possess strength or similar qualities; He is not an animate being, that He should have a certain disposition of the soul, or acquire certain properties, as meekness, modesty, etc., or be in a state to which animate beings as such are subject, as, e.g., in that of health or of illness. Hence it follows that no attribute coming under the category of quality can be predicated of God." [1]

But the simplicity of God denies more than that. It also denies the metaphysical or logical distinction of genus and species in the divine nature, or what are known as essential attributes as distinguished from accidental attributes. Arabic as well as Jewish philosophers are explicit in their denial of the distinction of genus and species in God. [2] It is this principle that underlies the following passage of Maimonides: "The object is described by its definition, as, e.g., man is described as a being that lives and has reason. . . . All agree that this kind of description cannot be given of God; for there is no previous cause to His essence, by which He could be defined. . . . An object is described by part of its definition, as when, e.g., man is described as a living being or as a rational being. . . . All agree that this kind of descrip-

---

[1] *Moreh Nebukim*, I, 52.
[2] *Makaṣid al-Falasifah*, II, ii, 11 (p. 145); *'Ikkarim*, II, 6 and 7.

tion is inappropriate in reference to God; for if we were to speak of a portion of His essence, we should consider His essence to be a compound."[1]

There is a third possible kind of distinction in the divine nature which is specifically rejected by the mediaevals in their discussion of the simplicity of God, namely, the distinction of essence and existence. There are certain historical reasons, to be dealt with subsequently, which induced the mediaevals to single out the predicate of existence for special discussion. Suffice it to say for the present that both Arabic and Jewish philosophers deal with this problem specifically in their general discussion of the nature of the divine essence. We may quote here the following typical passage from Maimonides, which occurs in the course of his discussion of attributes: "It is known that existence is an accident appertaining to all things, and therefore an element superadded to their essence. This must evidently be the case as regards everything the existence of which is due to some cause; its existence is an element superadded to its essence. But as regards a being whose existence is not due to any cause — God alone is that being, for His existence, as we have said, is absolute — existence and essence are perfectly identical. He is not a substance to which existence is joined as an accident, as an additional element."[2]

Simplicity in this sense, as a denial of any kind of internal plurality, physical as well as metaphysical and logical, is maintained by Spinoza with regard to substance. Of the three kinds of internal plurality especially rejected by the mediaevals, — the plurality of subject and accidental quality, of genus and species, and of essence and existence, — Spinoza mentions the last one specifically in Proposition VII. As for the second kind of internal plurality, he quotes

[1] *Moreh Nebukim*, I, 52.   [2] *Moreh Nebukim*, I, 57.

the mediaevals to the effect that "God is not a species of any genus," [1] which means the same as to say that in God there is no distinction of genus and species. This, as we have already seen,[2] is the implication of his definition of substance and of Proposition I, which is based upon it. It is this, too, which is meant when he says in one of his letters to Jellis that "of His [i.e., God's] essence we can form no general idea (*universalem . . . ideam*)."[3] Finally, as for the first kind of internal plurality, in Scholium 2 to Proposition VIII, which really belongs to Proposition VII, he dismisses, in unmistakable terms, the inherence in substance of accidental qualities, and almost in the words of Maimonides he says that those who attribute accidental qualities to substance do so because "they do not distinguish between the modifications of substances and substances themselves," and also because they "confound human nature with divine" and "readily attribute to God human affects." Substance is thus to Spinoza, like God to the mediaevals, absolutely simple, free from accidental as well as from essential attributes, and likewise impervious to the distinction of essence and existence.

The mediaeval insistence upon the absolute simplicity of God did not, however, mean to divest Him of all traits of personality. A God who has been conceived as creator and governor of the world, as lawgiver to man, and judge of human actions, could not possibly be conceived as impassive as a mathematical point and as indifferent as a metaphysical absolute. This belief in the personality of God is summed up by the mediaevals in the statement that "God, blessed be He, must be free of imperfections," [4] by which is meant that

---

[1] *Short Treatise*, I, 7, § 3.   [2] Cf. above, p. 77.
[3] Epistola 50 (*Opera*, IV, p. 240, ll. 2–3).
[4] *'Ikkarim*, I, 15; cf. II, 7.

"He must possess power and will and the other attributes without which He could not be thought of as perfect."[1] Spinoza restates this view in a letter addressed to Hudde in the following words: "That everything, which includes necessary existence, can have in itself no imperfection, but must express pure perfection."[2] Thus while on the one hand God must be absolutely simple and unqualifiable, on the other hand He must possess all those qualities which make for personality. How these two can be reconciled is the problem of attributes, which does not concern us for the present. The following brief statement from Albo will suffice as an indication of the mediaeval point of view: "All the attributes of perfection that are predicated of God or are conceived to exist in Him are predicated of Him and are conceived to exist in Him only in the sense in which they imply perfection but in none of the senses in which they would imply imperfection."[3] Of particular importance for us here is the use made by the mediaevals of the term "infinite" with regard to these attributes of perfection. In the first place, these attributes of God are to be infinite in number: "It must be understood that the perfections which exist in God are infinite in number."[4] In the second place, each of these attributes must be infinite in two senses: infinite in time, that is, eternal, and infinite in the degree of importance, that is, in its essential nature. "When we ascribe to God any of the attributes by which He may be described, whether negative or positive, that attribute must be taken to be infinite in two respects, infinite in time[5] and infinite in perfection or importance."[6] The term "infinite" applied to God thus means

---

[1] *Ibid.*, I, 15.   [2] Epistola 35.
[3] *'Ikkarim*, II, 21.   [4] *Ibid.*, II, 25.

[5] The term "time" has two meanings according to Albo, and infinite time in this passage is the equivalent of eternity. Cf. below, pp. 339, 363.

[6] *'Ikkarim*, II, 25.

to designate that He possesses an infinite number of attributes each of which is eternal and absolutely perfect. To quote: "It is with reference to this that the Cabalists designated God by the term Infinite (*En Sof*), to indicate that the perfections which are to be found in Him are infinite in the three senses which we have mentioned"[1] — that is to say, infinite in the number of attributes and each attribute infinite in time and in perfection.

Similarly to Spinoza, while God is absolutely simple and unqualifiable, He may still be described as possessing attributes, infinite in number, and each of them infinite in what the mediaevals called time and perfection. His definition of God at the beginning of the First Part of the *Ethics* is nothing but a restatement of the passages we have reproduced from Albo in the preceding paragraph. "By God, I understand Being absolutely infinite, that is to say, substance consisting of infinite attributes, each one of which expresses eternal and infinite essence."[2] Note the expression "eternal and infinite essence." By "eternal"[3] he means here what Albo calls "infinite in time," and by "infinite" he means again what Albo calls "infinite in perfection or importance." In his definition of God given in a letter to Oldenburg,[4] where incidentally the term "eternal" does not occur, Spinoza himself explains the term "infinite," by which each of the infinite attributes of God is described, as meaning "in the highest degree perfect of its kind." And what he has laid down of God in his definitions, he now tries to prove of substance in his propositions. First he shows that "every substance is necessarily infinite" (Prop. VIII), just as God is "absolutely infinite." Then, just as God is "substance con-

---

[1] *Ibid.*   [2] *Ethics*, I, Def. 6.

[3] For Spinoza's various uses of the term "eternal," see below, pp. 366 ff. and 375 ff.

[4] Epistola 2 (*Opera*, IV, p. 7, ll. 25–26).

sisting of infinite attributes," so substance possesses infinite attributes, for "the more reality or being a thing possesses, the more attributes belong to it" (Prop. IX), and inasmuch as substance has infinite reality or being, it must have infinite attributes. Finally, each attribute of substance must "express eternal and infinite essence," just as the attributes of God, for "each attribute of a substance must be conceived through itself" (Prop. X), and must therefore be identical with substance, and inasmuch as substance is infinite, each of its attributes must be infinite. In Jewish philosophy, too, the infinite nature of each attribute is deduced from the infinite nature of God. "For just as God, blessed be He, is infinite both in time and in importance, so is each of His attributes infinite both in time and in importance."[1]

The attempt of the mediaevals to preserve God's personality by endowing Him with infinite attributes while at the same time insisting upon His absolute simplicity has landed them, as we have already pointed out, in a self-contradiction. Attributes are either accidental or essential; they must be related to the subject either as color and size and weight and suchlike, or as genera and species, as, e.g., life and rationality are related to man. In either case they must imply a distinction of essence and attribute in the subject, though in the latter instance the distinction is only metaphysical or logical. Furthermore, attributes differ among themselves from each other, and therefore the assertion of an infinite number of attributes must imply a corresponding infinite number of differences in the nature of the subject. If the divine nature is to be free from any kind of plurality, how then can it have attributes? This difficulty constitutes the problem of divine attributes in mediaeval philosophy. The solutions offered will be touched upon in the sequel. In a

[1] 'Ikkarim, II, 25.

general way, it may be said that in the attempted solutions
two facts are sought to be established: first, all the attributes of God are in reality one attribute, and, whatever
differences there may appear to exist between them, they
do not affect the nature of God; second, whatever may be
the relation between essence and attribute, the assertion of
divine attributes does not contravene the simplicity of God's
essence.

Similarly Spinoza, after having stated in Propositions
VIII, IX, and X that substance has an infinite number of
attributes, proceeds to show that though assuming an infinite
number of attributes of which two "may be conceived as
really distinct, — that is to say, one without the assistance
of the other, — we cannot nevertheless thence conclude that
they constitute two beings or two different substances"
(Prop. X, Schol.), and that "no attribute of substance can
be truly conceived from which it follows that substance can
be divided" (Prop. XII), concluding that "substance absolutely infinite is indivisible" (Prop. XIII).

This then is the logical argument underlying Propositions
VII–X and XII–XIII. Had the *Ethics* been written *more
scholastico rabbinicoque* Spinoza would have prefaced these
propositions with the following words: We shall now proceed to show that just as substance is like God in its numerical unity (Props. II–VI), so it is also like God in its absolute
simplicity. That it has no distinction of genus and species
has already been stated (Def. III and Prop. I); that it
should have accidental qualities must be dismissed as something incomprehensible to a philosopher (Prop. VIII, Schol.
2). What is therefore left us to show is that like the philosophic God of the mediaevals substance has no distinction of
essence and existence (Prop. VII). Furthermore, though like
God "every substance is necessarily infinite" (Prop. VIII),

that is to say, consisting of infinite attributes (Prop. IX), each one of which expresses eternal and infinite essence (Prop. X), still this infinity of attributes does not imply that substance is in any sense divisible (Prop. X, Schol.; Props. XII–XIII).

With these general remarks we are now ready to discuss more fully the following three topics and the propositions in which they are treated: (1) the problem of essence and existence (Prop. VIII; Def. I); (2) the definition of the term "infinite" (Def. II; Def. VI; Props. VIII–X); (3) the relation of attribute to substance (Def. IV; Prop. X, Schol.; Props. XII–XIII).

II. ESSENCE AND EXISTENCE

The problem of essence and existence which is dwelt upon by Spinoza not only in his *Ethics* but also in his other writings, the terms in which the problem is couched, and the manner in which it is treated, are all part of the great philosophic heritage which had fallen to him from his predecessors. Two distinct traditions served him as sources of supply. One was the philosophic writings in Hebrew which have preserved the traditions of Arabic philosophy; the other was Descartes, who has preserved the traditions of the Latin scholastics. It can be shown that the two traditions had crossed at one time, and that the scholastic tradition of a later period was greatly indebted to the Arabico-Hebrew influence. But in Descartes, in whom the scholastic tradition reached its culminating point, owing to the influence of Anselm's ontological proof of the existence of God, the assertion of the identity of essence and existence in God assumed a meaning which was entirely different from that which it had in Jewish philosophy. In Jewish philosophy the assertion that in God essence and existence are identical, or however else it is phrased,[1] was merely another way of saying that God is necessary existence out of which arises the eternity, unity, simplicity, immutability, and unknowability of God, and in fact all those negations which tend to make God an absolute and infinite being. It does not however mean that thereby God becomes a "real" being (*ens reale*) as opposed to a being of reason and a fictitious being (*ens rationis, ens fictum*). Or, in other words, the fact that in the idea of God essence involved existence was not used to prove the actual existence of God, for in Jewish as well as in Arabic philosophy that mode of reasoning was not followed.[2] In Descartes the identity of essence and existence means all that, to be sure, but it also means something else in addition. It means also that this very idea of the identity of essence and existence in God proves that He is a "real" being. In Spinoza, as we shall endeavor to show, these two trends of thought meet, and upon the groundwork of philosophic lore inherited from the Hebrew books of his youth he raised the superstructure of Descartes' ontological proofs of the existence of God.

However complicated and important the problem of essence and existence may have become in the course of its development, and however great the significance it has assumed in its later history, the problem seems to me to have had a simple and humble origin. To my mind, it originated in the question as to the meaning of propositions in which the term "existent" forms the predicate, as, for instance, "A is existent." In order to appreciate the significance of this

[1] The other way of phrasing it is that God is existence without essence added thereto. See my "Crescas on the Problem of Divine Attributes," *Jewish Quarterly Review*, n.s., Vol. VII, p. 189, n. 85.

[2] Cf. my "Notes on the proofs of the Existence of God," *Hebrew Union College Annual*, I (1924), pp. 583 f.

question, we must bear in mind that Aristotle, and following him Arabic and Jewish logicians, held that every logical judgment must be synthetic, so that in every proposition the predicate must be a universal term belonging to one of the four or five predicables enumerated by Aristotle and Porphyry. It must be the genus of the subject, its species, a specific difference, a property or an accident. In mediaeval terminology the first three predicables are known as "essential attributes," the last two as "accidental attributes." The common characteristic of all these predicables is that they are all universal terms and are not identical with the essence of the subject. Essential attributes state the elements of which the essence of the subject is constituted or to which it belongs, and though not different from the essence of the subject they are either more extensive or less extensive than it, as, for instance, when the combination of animality and rationality, or either one of these, is predicated of man. Accidental attributes are something different from, and external to, the essence of the subject, adding some adventitious quality to it, as, for instance, when color and size and age are predicated of man. Nothing that is perfectly identical with the subject and co-extensive with it and is a mere verbal repetition of its essence can be affirmed in the predicate, for identity is not a logical relation. Aristotle laid it down as a rule when he stated that "individuals, and whatever is one in number, are predicated of no subject,"[1] and the mediaevals condemned as tautological any proposition like "A is A." In view of this the question may be justly raised as to what kind of predicate is the term "existent" in the proposition "A is existent." It cannot be identical with the essence of the subject, for then the proposition would be tantamount to saying that A is A. It is there-

[1] *Categories*, 2, 1b, 6–7.

fore concluded that existence is always an accident superadded to the essence of a thing.[1]

That existence is an element adventitious to the essence
of things would seem to be on the whole in accord with what
we know of Aristotle's views on the subject. According to
him the existence of things is not implied in the knowledge
of their essence which we may attain from their definition,
and thus while we may have an idea of man and knowledge
of his essence, and while we are even capable of defining him,
none of these can prove the actual existence of man. For all
definitions are answers to the question what a thing is but
not to the question whether a thing is. "But 'what man is'
and 'that man exists' are two different questions."[2] Again:
'Evidently those who define according to the present methods of definition do not demonstrate that a thing exists."[3]
To form conceptions of certain essences, to define them, to
describe them in formal propositions, does not imply that
they exist, for definitions and propositions may be purely
nominal in which words rather than things are the subject of
discourse. If a thing does actually exist, it only happens to
exist, just as it only happens to be white or black, large or
small. To assert therefore of such a thing that it is existent
is simply to attribute to it an accidental quality, just as to
say of a black or white thing that it is black or white. This
interpretation of Aristotle, to be sure, might be doubted.
It might be argued that while indeed there are nominal definitions in which existence is not implied, it may be still possible
that in real definitions existence is implied, and that to attribute existence to things that do actually exist is not to
attribute an accidental quality but rather to affirm some-

[1] This argument is reproduced by Crescas in the name of Avicenna in his *Or
Adonai*, I, iii, 1.
[2] *Analytica Posteriora*, II, 7, 92b, 10-11.
[3] *Ibid.*, 92b, 19-20.

thing that is involved in their essence. This indeed would seem to be Averroes' interpretation of Aristotle, for he maintains that existence is always involved in the essence of an actually existent subject.[1] Avicenna, however, and his Jewish followers, as Maimonides, for instance, by maintaining that existence is an accident superadded to the essence would seem to have understood Aristotle as explained above.

But even according to Avicenna and his school, God is an exception. In Him existence cannot be assumed to be added to His essence any more than any of the other attributes could be considered as accidental qualities. This is impossible by reason of the simplicity of the divine nature. It is because of this general principle that existence is accidental to the essence of created beings that the theologians of the Avicennian school have included in their discussion of the divine attributes the statement that God has no essence superadded to His existence, or that in God essence and existence are identical.[2]

It would seem that it was this traditional method of including the problem of essence and existence in the discussion of attributes or the simplicity of God that led Spinoza to lay down his seventh proposition. All of Spinoza's statements with regard to the nature of existence in relation to essence reflect the Avicennian and Maimonidean point of view. Repeating almost verbatim the words of Aristotle, he says that "the true definition of any one thing neither involves nor expresses anything except the nature of the thing involved."[3] Again, corresponding to the Avicennian formula that in created beings existence is an accident superadded to their essence, Spinoza says: "The essence of things produced

[1] Cf. quotation in Munk, *Guide des Égarés*, Vol. I, p. 231, n. 1.
[2] Cf. above, p. 122, n. 1.
[3] *Ethics*, I, Prop. 8, Schol. 2; cf. Epistola 34.

by God does not involve existence." [1] God is however different, for "I define God as a being to whose essence belongs existence." [2] And what is true of God is true also of substance: "It pertains to the nature of substance to exist." [3] The contrast between God and created beings is clearly brought out in the following passage: "Essence in God is not different from existence; indeed the one cannot be conceived without the other. In other things essence differs from existence, for the one may be conceived without the other." [4]

In his proof of Proposition VII, no less than in the proposition itself, Spinoza follows his predecessors. In Jewish philosophy, the negation of the distinction of essence and existence in God, as well as that of any other distinction, is based upon the view that any form of composition requires a cause to bring about that composition and that God can have no cause. "Everything that is composed of two elements has necessarily their composition as the cause of its existence as a composite being, and consequently in respect to its own essence it is not necessary of existence, for its existence depends upon the existence of its component parts and their combination." [5] Again: "Everything which is necessary of existence in respect to its own essence has no cause for its existence in any manner whatsoever or under any conditions whatsoever." [6] With this in mind Maimonides argues for the identity of essence and existence in God as follows: "It is known that existence is an accident appertaining to all things, and therefore an element superadded to their essence. This must evidently be the case as regards everything the existence of which is due to some cause; its

---

[1] *Ibid.*, I, Prop. 24.
[2] Epistola 83 (*Opera*, I, p. 335, l. 5).   [3] *Ethics*, I, Prop. 7.
[4] *Cogitata Metaphysica*, I, 2.   Cf. *Ethics*, I, Axiom 7.
[5] *Moreh Nebukim*, II, Introduction, Prop. 21.
[6] *Ibid.*, Prop. 20.

existence is an element superadded to its essence. But as regards a being whose existence is not due to any cause — God alone is that being, for His existence, as we have said, is absolute — existence and essence are perfectly identical; He is not a substance to which existence is joined as an accident, so as to constitute an additional element." [1]

The short proof of Proposition VII given by Spinoza follows the same line of reasoning. The essence of substance must involve existence, he argues, because substance has no cause, for "there is nothing by which substance can be produced." Were existence superadded to its essence, substance would require a cause to produce it. This state of being causeless, which the mediaevals as well as Spinoza himself usually designate by the expression "necessary existence," Spinoza also designates by the expression "cause of itself" (*causa sui*), a phrase which had already been in current use in philosophic literature.[2] *Causa sui*, like the mediaeval "necessary existence," is primarily nothing but a negation, meaning causelessness, and to Spinoza it is only a shorter way of saying that the essence of substance involves existence. He thus says in his first part of the definition of *causa sui*, "By cause of itself, I understand that, whose essence involves existence," [3] though the latter part of the definition, as we shall presently show, introduces a new idea into the phrase.

We thus have in Spinoza the following equation: necessary existence = *causa sui* = that whose essence involves existence. All of these expressions, as we have seen, mean primarily nothing but causelessness. An explicit statement to this effect is to be found in the following passage of Spinoza:

[1] *Ibid.*, I, 57.
[2] Cf. J. Freudenthal, "Spinoza und die Scholastik" in *Philosophische Aufsätze. Eduard Zeller . . . gewidmet*, p. 119; Martineau, *A Study of Spinoza*, p. 118, n. 1.
[3] *Ethics*, I, Def. 1.

"A thing must be conceived either through its essence alone
or through its proximate cause. Namely, if a thing be in
itself, or, as it is commonly termed, its own cause (*causa sui*),
then it must be understood through its essence alone; but
if a thing be not in itself, but requires a cause to exist, then it
must be understood through its proximate cause." [1] Now,
in Arabic and Jewish philosophy the concept of necessary
existence as applied to God is the main principle out of which
arise all the negations and affirmations about the divine
nature. It is from this that it is deduced that God is immaterial, that He is not an accident existing in a subject or a
form existing in matter, that His essence and existence are
identical, that He is not conditioned by any other cause nor
in any other way dependent upon another being, that He is
one, that He has no accidental qualities, that He is immutable, that He is the emanative cause of everything, that He
is indefinable, and that He is the source of the existence of
everything else. [2] By the same token Spinoza undertakes to
deduce from the concept of necessary existence, or its equivalents, a similar list of negations and affirmations about God.
Says he in one of his letters to Hudde: "I will briefly show
. . . what properties must be possessed by a Being that includes necessary existence. To wit: I. It must be eternal.
. . . II. It must be simple, not made up of parts. . . . III.
It cannot be conceived as determinate, but only as infinite.
. . . IV. It must be indivisible. . . . V. [It] can have in itself
no imperfection, but must express pure perfection. . . .
Lastly . . . there can only be a single Being, of which existence belongs to its nature." [3] Again: "From the fact alone,
that I define God as a Being to whose essence belongs exist-

---

[1] *Tractatus de Intellectus Emendatione*, § 92 (*Opera*, II, p. 34, ll. 9–13).
[2] *Maḳaṣid al-Falasifah*, II, ii (pp. 137 ff.).
[3] Epistola 35.

ence, I infer several of His properties; namely, that He necessarily exists, that He is one, unchangeable, infinite, etc." [1]

Not only from the mediaevals but also from Descartes has Spinoza derived the method of deducing the properties of God from the concept of necessary existence. "Indeed upon this truth alone, namely, that existence belongs to the nature of God, or that the concept of God involves a necessary existence as that of a triangle that the sum of its angles is equal to two right angles, or again that His existence and His essence are eternal truth, depends almost all our knowledge of God's attributes by which we are led to a love of God (or to the highest blessedness)." [2]

But from Descartes Spinoza has borrowed also the ontological proof. A being whose conception involves existence, according to this reasoning, must necessarily exist, and this sort of reasoning forms the basis of Spinoza's proofs of the existence of God in Proposition XI, to be discussed in a subsequent chapter. Now, according to Descartes, the term *a se*, which he applies to God in the same sense as *sui causa*,[3] has both a negative sense and a positive sense. In its negative sense it means that God has no cause; [4] in its positive sense it means that God stands to himself in the same way as an efficient cause does to its effect.[5] The term *causa sui* similarly in Spinoza is not a mere negation, meaning causelessness; it means also something positive: it is an assertion of self-sufficency and hence actual existence. He thus says in the second part of his definition of *causa sui*: "or that, whose nature cannot be conceived unless exist-

---

[1] Epistola 83.
[2] *Principia Philosophiae Cartesianae*, I, Prop. 5, Schol.
[3] *Primae Responsiones* (Oeuvres, VII, p. 109, ll. 16 and 21).
[4] *Ibid.* (p. 110, l. 24).
[5] *Ibid.* (p. 111, ll. 6–7).

ing." [1] Likewise Proposition VII of the First Part of the *Ethics*, while on the whole it is a reproduction of mediaeval Jewish discussions, contains also the additional Cartesian element, as is indicated in its phrasing. Spinoza does not say there as he says in *Cogitata Metaphysica*, I, 2, that essence in substance is not different from existence, but he says, "It pertains to the nature of substance to exist."

The identity of essence and existence is also the burden of the fourth proposition in the second chapter of the First Part of the *Short Treatise*. The wording of the proposition somewhat obscures its meaning. It reads as follows: "That in the infinite understanding of God there is no other substance than that which is formaliter in nature." [2] The purpose of this proposition, however, becomes clear when it is compared with its restatement at the end of the *Short Treatise*, Appendix I, Proposition IV: "To such an extent does existence pertain by nature to the essence of every substance, that it is impossible to posit in an infinite understanding the idea of the essence of a substance that does not exist in nature." It is clear that this fourth proposition, both in the main text and in the Appendix of the *Short Treatise*, is parallel to Proposition VII in *Ethics*, I, namely, that existence pertains to the nature of substance. In the *Short Treatise*, however, Spinoza utilizes the principle of the identity of essence and existence in substance as an argument for what is the main contention of Chapter 2 of the *Short Treatise*, I. The main contention of that chapter, as we have already shown, is to refute the mediaeval view that there are two substances, God and the world, the latter of which has no existence involved in its essence, inasmuch as it must acquire existence

---

[1] *Ethics*, I, Def. 1.
[2] *Short Treatise*, I, 2, § 2 (*Opera*, I, p. 20, ll. 6–7). But in § 11 (p. 21, ll. 33–34): "there is no substance or attribute" instead of "there is no other substance."

through an act of creation or emanation. Spinoza seems to say to his mediaeval opponents, in Proposition IV of the *Short Treatise*, I, 2, as follows: You maintain that the world [i.e., conditional substance] had existed prior to its creation only as an "idea" in the "infinite understanding [i.e., intellect] of God," and that only through an act of creation has it acquired existence. But any form of creation, however explained, I have already shown to you to be impossible.[1] Existence therefore must pertain to the essence of the world just as you say it pertains to the essence of God, and there is thus no such distinction between God and the world as that of creator and created, or absolute substance and conditional substance. He thus concludes, in the Corollary to Proposition IV in Appendix I at the end of the *Short Treatise*, that: "Nature is known through itself, and not through any other thing. It consists of infinite attributes, every one of them infinite and perfect in its kind; to its essence pertains existence, so that outside it there is no other essence or existence, and it thus coincides exactly with the essence of God, who alone is glorious and blessed." By "nature" here Spinoza means the universe; God is not outside of it, that is to say, pure form as opposed to matter, but the two are essentially the same, for, as he sums up his conclusions at the end of the four propositions in the same chapter of the *Short Treatise*, "we posit extension [i.e., matter] as an attribute of God."[2]

The proofs of the fourth proposition given in Chapter 2 of the *Short Treatise*, I, are not altogether new. They are only restatements of the arguments already used by Spinoza in his discussion of the first three propositions. We have already pointed out the literary origins of these arguments in our discussion of the unity of substance in the preceding chapter.

[1] Cf. above, Chapter IV.
[2] *Short Treatise*, I, 2, § 18 (*Opera*, I, p. 24, l. 11). But see below, pp. 299, 319 ff.

The sources quoted there will throw light upon Spinoza's reference here to an argument "from the infinite power of God, since in Him there can be no cause by which He might have been induced to create one sooner or more than another" [1] (First Argument). They will likewise help to elucidate his reference to an argument that God "cannot omit to do what is good" [2] (Third Argument), as well as his argument based upon the principle "that one substance cannot produce another" [3] (Fourth Argument). There is only left for us to account for his allusion to an argument "from the simplicity of His will" [4] (Second Argument). This I believe to reflect a passage in which Crescas attempts to refute Maimonides' solution of the problem of creation. It will be recalled that Maimonides endeavors to answer the question as to why God created the world at one time rather than at another, as well as to explain the other difficulties of creation, by the general statement that creation was an act of divine will. To this Crescas retorts somewhat as follows: If the world was created by divine will, then inasmuch as the world is composite, the will that has created it will have to be composite, for the creative will must be diffused throughout the parts of the object created. But this is impossible, since God's will, not being distinct from His essence, must be as simple as the essence itself. [5] Hence Spinoza's cryptic statement, "from the simplicity of His will." [6]

---

[1] *Short Treatise*, I, 2, § 11 (*Opera*, I, p. 21, l. 35–p. 22, l. 3).

[2] *Ibid*. (p. 22, ll. 3–4).   [3] *Ibid*. (p. 22, ll. 5–7).

[4] *Ibid*. (p. 22, l. 3).

[5] Cf. *Or Adonai*, III, i, 4 (p. 66b, ll. 42–45): "Granted that the proposition leads to the conclusion that there must be the will of an agent, this very same proposition would also have to make that will produce one simple object, for a will producing a composite object would itself have to be composite, inasmuch as the will must be diffused throughout the composite object which it produces."

[6] Cf. also Descartes' statement that "the will consists only of one single element, and is so to speak indivisible" (*Meditationes*, IV, *Oeuvres*, VII, p. 60, ll. 22–23).

III. DEFINITION OF THE TERM "INFINITE"

Coming now to Proposition VIII, that "every substance is necessarily infinite," we shall first endeavor to explain in what sense Spinoza uses the term "infinite." Here, too, it is to his predecessors that we must turn for help and information. Spinoza speaks of two kinds of infinite. There is, first, the "absolutely infinite" (*absolute infinitum*) (Def. VI). With this is contrasted, second, the "infinite in its own kind" (*in suo genere infinitum*) (Def. VI, Expl.). Corresponding to the "infinite in its own kind" there is the "finite in its own kind" (*in suo genere finitum*) (Def. II). These phrases are, to be sure, all defined by Spinoza, but his definitions, as will have been gathered, are in most cases brief restatements of generally accepted and well-known mediaeval concepts. What then is the origin and background of these phrases as well as of the ideas behind them?

In mediaeval discussions of infinity the term "infinite" is said to have two meanings. It may be an accident either of magnitude or of number, or it may be an essence, that is to say, a self-existent substance, immaterial like soul and intellect.[1] As an accident of magnitude it means an unlimited distance or length, something that has no end or boundary. As an accident of number, it means something that is endlessly addible or divisible. "Finite" as the antithesis of this kind of infinite means just the opposite, a distance that is bounded and a number that is limited, or, in other words, something comparable with others of its kind and exceeded by them.

But an essentially infinite substance means something

---

[1] See *Or Adonai*, I, i, 1 (p. 4a–b), based upon Averroes' Middle Commentaries on *Physics*, III, 4, 204a, 2–5, 204a, 32, and *Metaphysics*, XI, 10, 1066a, 35–1066b, 21. Cf. my *Crescas' Critique of Aristotle*, p. 137 and notes on pp. 329–335.

entirely different. It means a substance whose essence is unique and so incomparable that it cannot suffer any form of limitation and hence cannot have any form of positive description, for every description necessarily implies a limitation, or as Spinoza puts it: "determination is negation." [1] To call a substance infinite in this sense is like calling voice colorless. When voice is described as colorless it does not mean the negation of a property which we should expect it to have and which it may have, but rather the absolute exclusion of voice from the universe of color. By the same token, when substance is described as infinite in this sense, it means its absolute exclusion from any form of finitude, limitation, and description. The negation of finitude implied in this sense of the term "infinite" is what the mediaeval Jewish logicians would call "absolute negation" as contrasted with "particular negation" — a contrast which is expressed in the distinction between "A is not-B" and "A is not B." There is a suggestion of this distinction in Aristotle,[2] and Spinoza himself uses for these two kinds of negation the terms "negation" (*negatio*) and "privation" (*privatio*). "Thus privation is nothing else than denying of a thing something which we think belongs to its nature; negation is nothing else than denying of a thing something because it does not belong to its nature." [3] Of the parallel passages in Jewish philosophy the following may be quoted: "You already know from your reading in logic that negation is of two kinds. One is particular negation,[4] as, e.g., when we say 'Balaam does not see,' which is negation in the true sense of the term. The other is absolute negation,[5] that is to say, the denying of the subject that which does not natu-

---

[1] Epistola 50 (*Opera*, IV, p. 240, ll. 13–14): "determinatio negatio est." Cf. *Ethics*, I, Prop. 8, Schol. 1.   [2] *De Interpretatione*, Ch. 10; *Metaphysics*, V, 22.
[3] Epistola 21 (*Opera*, IV, p. 129, ll. 5–7).
[4] השלילה המיוחדת.   [5] השלילה המשולחת.   השלילה המשולחת.

rally belong to it, as, e.g., 'The wall does not see,' which is negation in a general sense." [1]

This mediaeval distinction between an essential and an accidental infinite is based upon the following passage in Aristotle: "The infinite is either that which is incapable of being traversed because it is not its nature to be traversed — this corresponds to the sense in which the voice is 'invisible' —, or that which admits only of incomplete traverse or scarcely admits of traverse, or that which, though it naturally admits of traverse, is not traversed or limited; further, a thing may be infinite in respect of addition or of subtraction or of both." [2]

The implication of the passage is this. The infinite is that which has no limit. The term is derived from magnitude and number, and must thus primarily apply to them or to any other thing which may be measured either quantitatively or qualitatively. We may therefore speak of infinite beauty as well as of infinite length and number. All such forms of measurement, however, imply a common standard and a comparison of the thing measured with other things of its kind. But the term "infinite" may be used also in a derivative sense as applied to things which are incapable of being measured on account of their uniqueness and incomprehensibility in a class in which they can be compared with others of their kind. "Infinite" in this sense is an absolute negation, the denial of a thing of any kind of determination and description, as something not belonging to its nature.

In view of this discussion, we may now explain the meaning of the different kinds of finite and infinite in Spinoza.

To be finite or limited means to be comparable, and since only like things can be compared, to be finite means to be included within a class of like things. "If between two things

[1] Narboni's commentary on *Moreh Nebukim*, I, 58.
[2] *Metaphysics*, XI, 10, 1066a, 35–1066b, 1; cf. *Physics*, III, 4, 204a, 2–7.

no relation can be found, there can be no similarity [and hence no comparison] between them, and there is no relation between two things that have no similarity to each other; as, e.g., we do not say that this heat is similar to that color, or this voice is similar to that sweetness. . . . You must know that two things of the same kind — i.e., whose essential properties are the same, distinguished from each other by greatness and smallness, strength and weakness, etc. — are necessarily similar." [1] Everything that suffers description may therefore be called finite in its own kind, for it cannot be described except in terms that properly belong to it and limit it. A thing finite is thus something that is similar in some respect to something else of its own kind with which it may be compared and be found greater or smaller, longer or shorter, more important or less important. Hence Spinoza's definition: "That thing is called finite in its own kind which can be limited by another thing of the same nature. For example, a body is called finite, because we always conceive another body which is greater. So a thought is limited by another thought; but a body is not limited by a thought, nor a thought by a body" (Def. II).

"Infinite in its own kind" means simply the superlative degree of comparison, its surpassing of all others of the same kind. It does not mean that the thing so described as infinite is unique and incomparable by possessing an infinite number of qualities, nor does it mean that any of its qualities is unique and incomparable. What it means is that certain ones of its qualities upon being compared with others of their kind will be found to surpass them all. Hence Spinoza's statement: "For of whatever is infinite only in its own kind, we can deny infinite attributes" (Def. VI, Expl.).

But "absolutely infinite" means an absolute exclusion

[1] *Moreh Nebukim*, I, 56.

from the universe of finitude, determination, and description. It implies uniqueness and incomparability; there is no kind to which it may be said to belong. It is *sui generis*. It is an individual essence of its own kind. The number of its attributes is infinite, and so is each of its attributes, and for this reason it suffers no description or determination. Spinoza thus says: "But to the essence of that which is absolutely infinite pertains whatever expresses essence and involves no negation" (Def. VI, Expl.).

It is as an "absolutely infinite" of this kind that God is described by the mediaevals, a description which denies the existence of any relation between the essence of God and that of other beings. "Since the existence of a relation between God and man, or between Him and other beings, has been denied, similarity must likewise be denied." [1] Even those who like Crescas contended for the existence of essential attributes likewise denied that there is any similarity between divine and human attributes, "for they widely differ . . . the one being finite and the other infinite," and "there can be no relation and comparison between the infinite and the finite." [2] In almost exactly the same words Spinoza says: "This I know, that between the finite and the infinite there is no comparison (*proportionem*); so that the difference between the greatest and most excellent creature and God is the same as the difference between God and the least creature." [3] The absolute infinity of God in this sense is described by Maimonides as follows: "Even these negative attributes must not be formed and applied to God, except in the way in which, as you know, sometimes an attribute is negatived in reference to a thing, although that attribute can naturally never be applied to it in the same sense, as, e.g., we say,

---

[1] *Ibid.*, I, 56.
[2] *Or Adonai*, I, iii, 3 (pp. 23b–24a).   [3] Epistola 54.

'This wall does not see.'" [1] Says also Judah ha-Levi: "As regards the negative attributes, such as Living, Only, First and Last, they are given to Him in order to negative their contrasts, but not to establish them in the sense we understand them. For we cannot understand life except accompanied by sensibility and movement. God, however, is above them. . . . One cannot, for instance, speak of time as being endowed with life, yet it does not follow that it is dead, since its nature has nothing to do with either life or death. In the same way one cannot call a stone ignorant, although we may say that it is not learned. Just as a stone is too low to be brought into connection with learning or ignorance, thus the essence of God is too exalted to have anything to do with life or death." [2] Exactly the same reasoning, though for a different purpose, is employed by Spinoza: "I say then, first, that privation is not the act of depriving, but simply and merely a state of want. . . . We say, for example, that a blind man is deprived of sight, because we readily imagine him as seeing. This imagination comes about either because we compare him with others who see, or because we compare his present condition with his past condition when he did see. . . . But when the decree of God and His nature are considered, we cannot say of that man any more than of a stone, that he is deprived of sight, for at that time sight pertains to that man no less inconsistently than to a stone." [3]

Hence the term "infinite" stands in Spinoza for such terms as "unique," "incomparable," "homonymous," "indeterminate," "incomprehensible," "ineffable," "indefinable," "unknowable," and many other similar terms. "Unknowable" and "indefinable," however, will be found its most

[1] *Moreh Nebukim*, I, 58.   [2] *Cuzari*, II, 2.
[3] Epistola 21.

convenient equivalents. It is in accordance with Aristotle's dictum that "the infinite so far as infinite is unknown," [1] which Spinoza himself repeats in connection with his argument that by an infinite number of methods "we can never arrive . . . at any knowledge whatever." [2]

In the three propositions from VIII to X Spinoza is trying to prove, as we have already indicated, that substance is everything that God has been laid down to be in his definition. Proposition VIII begins by showing that like God, who is "absolutely infinite," substance is also "necessarily infinite." Formally the proof of this proposition is based upon the identity of essence and existence in substance, as stated in Proposition VII, and upon the impossibility of two or more substances having the same nature or attributes, as stated in Proposition V. Materially, however, the proposition rests upon the very definition of substance. For Proposition VII, we may recall, is based upon the principle that substance has no prior cause, and Proposition V is likewise based upon the principle that substance can have no higher genus, both of which principles are implied in the definition of substance. So this proposition, too, is derived from the very nature and definition of substance as "something which is in itself and is conceived through itself." In fact, Propositions VII, VIII, IX, and X are all unfoldings of the implications of the definition of substance.

The next step in the analogy between substance and God is to show that by infinity in both cases is meant the possession of infinite attributes. This is the purpose of Proposition IX. The proposition as it stands is incomplete. Only the major premise is given. Its full significance, however, can be brought out by supplying the minor premise and conclusion.

[1] *Physics*, I, 4, 187b, 7.
[2] *Tractatus de Intellectus Emendatione*, § 13 (*Opera*, II, p. 13, ll. 17–23).

"The more reality or being a thing possesses, the more attributes belong to it." But substance possesses infinite
reality or being. Hence, to substance belong infinite attributes. In one of his letters to de Vries,[1] as well as in the
Scholium to Proposition X, in both of which places Proposition IX is reproduced, Spinoza actually adds the needed
conclusion.

There is one incidental comment which I should like to
make here with regard to the source of Proposition IX. It
seems to me that this proposition reflects Aristotle's discussion with regard to the character of a true *proprium* predicated of a subject. If it can be shown, says Aristotle, that A
is a *proprium* of B, it can also be shown that what is more A is
also a *proprium* of what is more B. To quote him in full:
"The confirmer however [must consider], whether what is
simply is the property of what is simply; for the more will be
the property of the more, the less also of the less, the least
of the least, and the most of the most; thus, since it is the
property of fire naturally to tend upwards, it would also be
the property of what is more fire naturally to tend more upwards, and in the same manner we must direct attention
from other things also, to all these."[2] That Aristotle speaks
of *proprium* (ἴδιον) whereas Spinoza here speaks of "attributes" is a matter of indifference. In mediaeval Hebrew literature the term *proprium* in a similar passage of Aristotle
is translated by the word which usually means "attribute."[3]

---

[1] Epistola 9 (*Opera*, IV, p. 45, ll. 2–4 and 20–22).

[2] *Topics*, V, 8, 137b, 33–138a, 3.

[3] Cf. *Emunah Ramah*, II, iv, 3 (p. 65): "These are some of the propositions
which are derived from the more (היותר) and less (והפחות). Aristotle mentions
them in the Book on *Dialectic* (נצוח = جدل), the title of which is translated by Alfarabi as the Book on *Topics* (המקומות = مواضع الجدل; cf. Steinschneider, *Al-
Farabi*, p. 53, n. 74). The proposition in question is as follows: If a certain thing
has a certain attribute (תואר), and if also the more that thing is the more it has
of that attribute, then the attribute belongs to the thing truly by necessity." This

Spinoza himself occasionally uses the term "attribute" in the sense of property.[1] Starting therefore with the definition of attribute as "that which the intellect perceives of substance, as if constituting the essence of substance" (Demonst. of Prop. IX) and assuming it to be thus a true *proprium* of substance, Spinoza concludes that "the more reality (*realitas*) or being (*esse*) a thing possesses the more attributes belong to it" (Prop. IX). Incidentally it may be remarked that since here as well as in his correspondence [2] Spinoza uses *realitas* as the equivalent of *esse* or of *entitas*,[3] the term *wezentheid* (or *wezeendhijd*), which in a corresponding passage in *Short Treatise*, I, 2, § 17,[4] is used in place of *realitas*, should be translated by *esse* (i.e., being, *Sein*) rather than *essentia* (i.e., essence, *Wesenheit*). Spinoza further uses *realitas* as the equivalent of *perfectio*,[5] for which use there is a parallel in Descartes.[6]

Proposition X concludes the analogy between substance and God by showing that each attribute of substance is infinite in all the various senses of infinity. "Each attribute of substance must be conceived through itself." To be conceived through itself, it has already been shown, means to be indefinable, and "indefinable" and "infinite," it has also been shown, are interchangeable terms.[7]

---

passage is based on *Topics*, V, 8, 137b, 14 ff., where the locus of more ($\mu\tilde{\alpha}\lambda\lambda o\nu$) and less ($\tilde{\eta}\tau\tau o\nu$) is discussed. The Greek term underlying the Hebrew term for "attribute" is *proprium* ($\tilde{\iota}\delta\iota o\nu$).

[1] Cf. below, p. 230.

[2] Epistola 9 (*Opera*, IV, p. 45, ll. 2–3 and 20).

[3] *Ethics*, IV, Praef. (*Opera*, II, p. 207, l. 27).

[4] *Opera*, I, p. 23, ll. 22–24; p. 534. Cf. above, p. 108, n. 4, and below, p. 382, n. 7.

[5] *Ethics*, II, Def. 6, *et passim*.

[6] *Meditationes*, III (*Oeuvres*, VII, p. 40, l. 28).

[7] See above, p. 76.

IV. Relation of Attribute to Substance

The God or substance of Spinoza, like the God of mediaeval rationalists, is unknowable in His essence. He may indeed, in Spinoza's view, be immediately perceived by intuition as a clear and distinct idea, but He is not subject to knowledge that defines its object in terms broader and more general. When Spinoza argues against the mediaeval conception of an unknowable God,[1] he simply argues for the view that God can be known, after a manner, even though He cannot be defined in terms of genus and species. "Of His [i.e., God's] essence," says Spinoza, "we can form no general idea."[2] Spinoza indeed will endeavor to prove the existence of God, but in this he will be merely carrying out the mediaeval tradition that while we can have no knowledge of God's essence we can prove His existence. "There is no possibility of obtaining a knowledge of the essence of God . . . the only thing that man can apprehend of Him is the fact that He exists."[3] Or again: "If knowledge is sought concerning a thing whose very existence is in doubt, the first question to be asked is whether it exists or not. When the question of its existence has been answered positively, the thing then to be asked about it is, What is it? How is it? Wherefore is it? Concerning God, however, man has no right to ask except the question as to whether He exists."[4]

But while the real nature of God must remain beyond comprehension, still God as a living and dynamic force in the world, conceived as creator, lawgiver, caretaker, guide, and guardian, makes himself known to mankind through His

---

[1] *Short Treatise*, I, 7, §§ 3 ff.
[2] Epistola 50 (*Opera*, IV, p. 240, ll. 2–3).
[3] *Moreh Nebukim*, I, 59.
[4] *Ḥobot ha-Lebabot*, I, 4.

actions and works, and assumes in their eyes a certain character and personality. This character and personality of
God was determined, in the Middle Ages, by a set of descriptive terms drawn from the literature of religious tradition.
In the philosophic terminology of the time, these descriptive terms were known by the name of divine attributes.
There were many kinds of attributes which, when taken in
their literal sense, would express the various relations that
may exist between attribute and subject. Some of these
divine attributes would constitute in their ordinary meaning
accidental qualities. Others would designate actions. Still
others would only express some external relations. It was,
however, generally agreed that attributes could not be taken
in a sense which would imply plurality in the divine essence
or a similarity between God and His creatures.[1] It was
therefore commonly recognized that attributes are not to be
taken in their literal sense. The Talmudic saying that "the
Torah speaks according to the language of men"[2] is quoted in
this connection by the mediaeval Jewish philosophers.[3]
Spinoza repeats it in his statement that "the Scripture . . .
continually speaks after the fashion of men."[4] How these
attributes could be interpreted so as not to contravene the absolute simplicity and uniqueness of God constituted the problem of divine attributes with which all the mediaeval Jewish
philosophers had to grapple. That attributes could not be
taken as accidental qualities was generally admitted.
Whether they should be interpreted as external relations
would seem to be a question upon which opinions differed,[5]

---

[1] See my "Crescas on the Problem of Divine Attributes," *Jewish Quarterly Review*, n.s., Vol. VII, p. 9, n. 11.

[2] *Berakot* 31b, and parallels.　　　　[3] *Moreh Nebukim*, I, 26.

[4] Epistola 19 (*Opera*, IV, p. 92, ll. 12–13); Epistola 21 (p. 132, ll. 34 f.).

[5] *Cuzari*, II, 2; *Emunah Ramah*, II, iii; *Hobot ha-Lebabot*, I, 10; *Moreh Nebukim*, I, 52 and 58.

though, I believe, it can be shown that the difference was merely in the use of terms. It was agreed by all, however, that attributes may be taken in the sense of actions. There was equally a general agreement that no attribute, in its literal and obvious sense, expresses the real essence of God, inasmuch as the essence of God must forever remain unknowable.

The mediaeval discussion about attributes is sometimes summed up in a distinction drawn between the name Jehovah and the other names of God. Says Judah ha-Levi: "All names of God, save the Tetragrammaton, are predicates and attributive descriptions, derived from the way His creatures are affected by His decrees and measures." [1] Says also Maimonides: "It is well known that all the names of God occurring in Scripture are derived from His actions, except one, namely, the Tetragrammaton, which consists of the letters *yod, he, waw, he*. This name is the *nomen proprium* [2] of God and is on that account called *Shem ha-Meforash*, that is to say, the name which indicates the essence of God in a manner which excludes the implication of its having anything in common with the essence of other beings. All the other glorious names are common appellatives,[3] inasmuch as they are derived from actions to which some of our own are similar." [4] In connection with these divine names Judah ha-Levi quotes Exodus 6, 3, where God says to Moses: "And I appeared unto Abraham, unto Isaac, and unto Jacob, by the name of God Almighty (*El Shaddai*), but by my name Jehovah was I not known to them." [5]

In Spinoza we find this view of the mediaevals restated in almost their own words. Quoting the same verse from

[1] *Cuzari*, II, 2.   [2] שם מיוחד.
[3] מורים בשתוף.
[5] *Cuzari*, II, 2.   [4] *Moreh Nebukim*, I, 61.

Exodus 6, 3,[1] he comments upon it as follows: "We must note that in Scripture no other name but Jehovah is ever found which indicates the absolute essence of God, without reference to created things. The Jews maintain, for this reason, that this is the only *nomen proprium* of God; that the other names are mere appellatives (*appellativa*); and, in truth, the other names of God, whether they be substantives or adjectives, are mere attributes, which belong to God in so far as He is conceived of in relation to created things or is manifested through them." He then concludes: "Now, as God tells Moses that He was not known to the patriarchs by the name of Jehovah, it follows that they were not cognizant of any attribute of God which expresses His absolute essence, but only of His deeds and promises — that is, of His power, as manifested in visible things."[2] Now, Spinoza has adopted the traditional term "attribute," and makes use of it as a description of the manner in which substance, unknowable in itself, manifests itself to the human mind. But how would Spinoza characterize his attributes if he were to classify them according to the mediaeval fashion? They are not accidents, nor relations, nor actions. They are, however, what, as we shall presently see, the mediaevals called essential attributes, that is to say, attributes which constitute the essence. He thus says: "By attribute, I under-

---

[1] In his comment on the divine name *El Shaddai* which occurs in this verse, Spinoza remarks that "*El Shaddai*, in Hebrew, signifies the God who suffices, in that He gives to every man that which suffices for him" (*Opera*, III, p. 169, ll. 3–5). Judah ha-Levi, in the corresponding passage quoted in the preceding paragraph, explains *El Shaddai* as meaning "power and dominion." Spinoza's explanation, however, is found in Rashi's commentary on the Bible (cf. Genesis 17, 1; 28, 3; 35, 11). Maimonides, though he like Rashi derives *El Shaddai* from a word meaning "sufficient," explains it to mean that "His existence is self-sufficient" (*Moreh Nebukim*, I, 63). These two etymologies of *El Shaddai* go back to still earlier sources.

[2] *Tractatus Theologico-Politicus*, Ch. 13 (*Opera*, III, p. 169, ll. 7–24).

stand that which the intellect perceives of substance, as if constituting its essence" (*Ethics*, I, Def. IV).

But here we are met with a difficulty, a natural difficulty, too, which has divided Spinoza scholars into two camps.

The definition may have two meanings, depending upon which of its elements is emphasized. If the expression "which the intellect perceives" is laid stress upon, it would seem that attributes are only *in intellectu*. Attributes would thus be only a subjective mode of thinking, expressing a relation to a perceiving subject and having no real existence in the essence. On the other hand, if only the latter part of the definition is taken notice of, namely, "constituting the essence of a substance," it would seem that the attributes are *extra intellectum*, real elements out of which the essence of the substance is composed. According to both interpretations, to be sure, it is the mind which perceives the attributes, but there is the following difference. According to the former interpretation, to be perceived by the mind means to be *invented* by the mind, for of themselves the attributes have no independent existence at all but are identical with the essence of the substance. According to the latter interpretation, to be perceived by the mind means only to be *discovered* by the mind, for even of themselves the attributes have independent existence in the essence of the substance.[1]

In the discussion of the subject two kinds of evidence have been adduced by scholars in support of their respective interpretations: literary and material. It is not my purpose here, however, to assemble and assess what has been said by either side in support of its own view and in objection to the other. On the whole, the abundance of both literary and material evidence is in favor of the subjective interpretation. This interpretation is in harmony both with the variety of

[1] Cf. Erdmann, *Grundriss der Geschichte der Philosophie*, II, § 272.6.

statements made by Spinoza about attributes and with the place which the attributes occupy in his system. Of the latter we shall have occasion to speak in other chapters. The main objection to this interpretation has been summed up in the statement that "no prae-Kantian reader would have put such a construction on Spinoza's language." [1] We shall therefore address ourselves to this particular objection and try to show that this very controversy between the upholders of the subjective and the objective interpretations of Spinoza's attributes is the question upon which mediaeval Jewish philosophers were divided in their theories of divine attributes, and also to point to certain facts which indicate that Spinoza has consciously and advisedly aligned himself with that group of Jewish philosophers who held a subjective theory of attributes.

The gravamen of the mediaeval discussion of divine attributes is what is known as the problem of essential attributes. By essential attributes are meant those elements which constitute the essence of a subject, or which are related to the essence of the subject as the genus and species are related to the essence of the object defined. It appears primarily as a problem in the exegesis of those adjectives which in the Bible or in the other traditional literature are ascribed to God. Admitting, as we have already pointed out, that attributes are not to be taken literally, that they cannot be interpreted as accidental qualities but may be interpreted as actions, the mediaevals raised the question as to whether any of these adjectives may be taken as being related to God in the same sense as the elements of a definition to the object defined, that is to say, as if constituting the divine essence. The problem, it must be remarked, was not whether the divine essence could be conceived as consisting of a genus and species. The

[1] Martineau, *A Study of Spinoza*, p. 184. Cf. Erdmann, *loc. cit.*

absolute simplicity of God is a principle established beyond any question, a simplicity which is to exclude metaphysical and logical plurality no less than physical composition. It is thus generally admitted that God is not a species and can have no genus.[1] The question was merely as to whether the assumption of essential attributes contravened that simplicity of essence. To put the question more bluntly: Assuming that the relation of God's attributes to His essence is analogous to that of the parts of a definition, genus and species, to the essence of the object defined, does that mean that the essence is simple or not? Those who reject essential attributes answer it in the negative; those who admit them answer it in the positive.

The basis of the problem, it seems to me, is to be found in the question as to the nature of the reality of genus and species, or, in other words, of universals. If universals have some kind of reality, then genus and species have some kind of real existence, and a subject to which are attributed terms related to it after the analogy of genus and species cannot be said to be absolutely simple. On the other hand, if universals have no reality at all, then genus and species are mere names, and definitions are purely nominal, and the essence of the subject defined is in reality simple. The problem of essential attributes is thus a problem of universals, the controversy between realism and nominalism. It is, however, not a conflict between Platonism and Aristotelianism. Platonic realism had no followers among the classical Jewish philosophers. It is as Aristotelians, and as interpreters of Aristotle's view, that Jewish philosophers latently formulated their respective theories of universals which are hid away in their discussions of divine attributes. For the real problem of universals, it may be said, began with the rejection of Pla-

[1] 'Ikkarim, II, 6 and 7. Cf. Short Treatise, I, 7, § 3.

tonic realism, when speculation became rife concerning those universals which were now said to exist only in the mind.

As spokesman of those who reject essential attributes we may take Maimonides.[1] While essential attributes, says Maimonides, denote the essence of the object and do not imply anything extraneous superadded to it, still they are to be rejected, for they imply that the essence itself is composed, as it were, of genus and species, which as universal terms are considered as previous causes to the existence of the individual essence.[2] It is here that the theory of universals comes into play. Like all Arabic and Jewish philosophers, Maimonides rejects Platonic realism, affirming that "species have no existence except in our own mind."[3] Still this assertion makes him neither a nominalist nor a conceptualist. Nominalism must be rejected as inconsistent with the entire trend of his argument, for if universals were mere words, definitions would be purely nominal, and Maimonides could not reject essential attributes on the ground that "there are no previous causes to His existence, by which He could be defined," and quote with approval those who maintain that "no definition can be given of God."[4] Conceptualism, or the theory that universals have ideal without real existence, is explicitly rejected by Maimonides in his repudiation of "the assertion of some thinkers, that ideas, i.e., the universals, are neither existent nor non-existent."[5] What Maimonides, as follower of Avicenna and in common with all his contemporaries, conceived of universals is that they have both ideal and real existence. Universals, to be sure, exist in the mind, but the human mind does not *invent* them

---

[1] The historical survey which follows is based upon my essay "Crescas on the Problem of Divine Attributes," *Jewish Quarterly Review*, n.s., Vol. VII (1916), pp. 1–44, 175–221.

[2] *Moreh Nebukim*, I, 51 and 52.

[3] *Ibid.*, III, 18. [4] *Ibid.*, I, 52. [5] *Ibid.*, I, 51.

out of nothing. What the mind does is only to *discover* them in the multifarious individuals. For prior to the rise of individual beings the universals exist in the mind of God as independent entities, and they remain as such even when they enter upon plurality in material form, though their presence in the individuals is not discernible except by mental activity. Consequently essential attributes, which are related to the subject as genus and species are related to the object defined, must necessarily imply some kind of plurality in the essence of the subject. This plurality, to be sure, would be only mentally discernible, but still it would be inconsistent with the conception of absolute simplicity.

As against this view there are those who maintain that essential attributes are admissible. They insist that universals have no reality at all; their existence in the mind means that they are invented by the mind. Genus and species are thus only generalizations, and definitions consisting of genus and species are only nominal. Averroes, whose view is quoted in Hebrew literature, is clearly outspoken on this point. "It is of the nature of essential attributes that they do not introduce any plurality into the subject which supports them actually. If they do import into them some kind of plurality, it is only in the same sense that the parts of a definition may be said to import some kind of plurality into the object defined, and that is what is called by philosophers an intellectual plurality in contradistinction to an actual plurality." [1] No less outspoken is Moses ha-Lavi in his admission of essential attributes. "Some attributes," he says, "are identical with the essence of the object described, as, for instance, when we describe man by the attribute 'animal.' . . . With reference to such attributes as are identical with

---

[1] Averroes, *Tahafut al-Tahafut*, V (ed. M. Bouyges, p. 300, ll. 12-15); paraphrased also by Narboni on *Moreh Nebukim*, I, 58.

the essence of the object described, it is evident that God can be described by them, inasmuch as they do not imply any addition to the essence at all." [1] The implication here again is that essential attributes, related to God after the analogy of the genus animal to man, are purely subjective terms, in reality being absolutely identical with the essence of God. Likewise Gersonides, in his argument against Maimonides' negative interpretation of attributes, justifies his own positive interpretation by pointing to their subjective character. He draws a distinction between two kinds of propositions, one in which the relation of subject and predicate is that of *discourse*, the other in which it is that of *existence* [2] — a distinction reminiscent of that made by Aristotle between *nominal* and *real* definitions. [3] Divine attributes are thus to him purely subjective and nominal predications of God, related to Him only in *discourse*, and implying no plurality in His essence, and may therefore be taken as positive terms. It can also be shown that Crescas' insistence upon the admissibility of positive essential attributes is based upon the view that attributes are purely subjective terms. The eclectic Albo, vacillating between the positive and negative interpretations of attributes, endeavors to justify the positive form of attributes by calling them "intellectual conceptions" [4] of divine perfection. "When I awaken from my reflections upon the plurality of attributes I begin to realize that all the attributes are nothing but intellectual conceptions of those perfections which must needs exist in Thy essence but which in reality are nothing but Thy essence." [5]

In view of this controversy over essential attributes in the

---

[1] *Ma'amar Elohi.*

[2] *Milḥamot Adonai*, III, 3: במאמר . . . במציאות.

[3] *Analytica Posteriora*, II, 10, 93b, 29 ff.

[4] בחינות שכליות.

[5] *'Iḳḳarim*, II, 25.

philosophic literature with which Spinoza had an intimate
acquaintance, and in view of this insistence upon the subjective nature of essential attributes on the part of many of
his Jewish predecessors, it is not unreasonable to assume that
it is not as a mere turn of speech that Spinoza always refers
to attribute in subjective terms, as when he describes
it, for instance, as that which the intellect perceives (*per-
cipit*)[1] concerning the substance, or as that which expresses
(*exprimit*)[2] or explains (*explicat*)[3] the essence of substance,
or as that under which God is considered (*consideratur*)[4] or
every entity is conceived (*concipi*),[5] or as that which is the
same as substance but is called attribute with respect to the
intellect (*respectu intellectus*).[6] There is, furthermore, evidence that Spinoza was acquainted with the moderately
realistic Avicennian and Maimonidean theory of universals
and that he disagreed with it and criticized it. "They have
set up general ideas," he says, . . . "These ideas, they state,
are in the understanding of God, as many of Plato's followers
have said, namely, that these general ideas (such as rational,
animal, and the like) have been created by God; and although those who follow Aristotle say, indeed, that these
things are not real things, only things of reason, they nevertheless regard them frequently as [real] things."[7] The
reference in this passage to the objective interpretation of
Aristotle's universals is clear. He finds it to differ only little
from Platonic realism. It would seem that Spinoza himself
considered universals, with the exception of only one uni-

---

[1] *Ethics*, I, Def. 4.

[2] *Ibid.*, I, Prop. 10, Schol.; Prop. 32, Demonst.

[3] *Tractatus Theologico-Politicus*, Ch. 13 (*Opera*, III, p. 169, l. 23).

[4] *Ethics*, II, Prop. 6; Prop. 7, Schol.; Epistola 64 (*Opera*, IV, p. 277, ll. 23–24 and 28–29).

[5] *Ethics*, I, Prop. 10, Schol.; cf. Epistola 9 (*Opera*, IV, p. 45, l. 2).

[6] Epistola 9 (*Opera*, IV, p. 46, l. 4).

[7] *Short Treatise*, I, 6, § 7.

versal, namely, substance,[1] as purely subjective concepts; and
what is true of universals is also true of attributes. It is thus
not in vain that in his formal definition of attribute Spinoza
says that he understands by it "that which the intellect [2]
perceives of substance, as if constituting its esssence," instead of merely saying, as does Descartes, that attributes
constitute the essence of substance.[3] Elsewhere, too, in
the *Ethics* as well as in his other writings attributes are
always spoken of in terms which suggest their subjective
character.[4] In one place he says explicitly that attributes
are distinguished only by reason.[5]

This subjective interpretation of attributes disposes of
the difficulty which is raised by those who follow the objective interpretation. "How that essence can be one and
self-identical, while its constituents are many, heterogeneous
and unrelated, is a question which is hopeless of solution." [6]

---

[1] Cf. below, pp. 327–328.

[2] By the term "intellect" in this definition Spinoza means the finite human intellect. When he says in *Ethics*, II, Prop. VII, Schol., that "we have already
demonstrated, that everything which can be perceived by the *infinite intellect* as
constituting the essence of substance pertains entirely to one substance, and consequently that substance thinking and substance extended are one and the same substance, which is now comprehended under this attribute and now under that," it
is not to be inferred that an attribute of substance is that which can be conceived
only by the "infinite intellect." What the passage means to say is that "*everything*
which can be conceived of by the *infinite intellect* as constituting the essence of substance" — and the infinite intellect can conceive of an infinite number of things as
constituting the essence of substance — is only an attribute of substance and not a
substance itself, and consequently extension and thought, which alone can be conceived by the finite human intellect as constituting the essence of substance, are
only attributes of substance and not substances themselves.

[3] *Principia Philosophiae*, I, 53: "Substantiae praecipua proprietas [= attri-
butum], quae ipsius naturam essetiamque constituit"; *Notae in Programma*
(*Œuvres*, VIII, 2, p. 349, ll. 1–2): "Attributum, quod ejus [substantiae] essentiam
naturamque constituit." See Erdmann, *Grundriss der Geschichte der Philosophie*,
II, § 272,6.

[4] See references above, p. 152. Cf. Busolt, *Die Grundzüge der Erkenntnisztheorie
und Metaphysik Spinozas*, pp. 107–111.   [5] *Cogitata Metaphysica*, I, 3.

[6] Martineau, *A Study of Spinoza*, p. 185.

The question had already been raised by Simon de Vries in a letter to Spinoza: "If I may say that each substance has only one attribute and if I had the idea of two attributes, then I could rightly conclude that where there are two different attributes there are also two different substances." [1] Spinoza's answer is like that given in Jewish literature by those who admitted essential attributes, namely, that attributes are merely different words expressing the same essence. "You desire, though there is no need, that I should illustrate by an example, how one and the same thing can be stamped with two names. In order not to seem miserly, I will give you two." [2] That essential attributes, as suggested in this quotation, are only names by which the essence is denoted is the view held by both those who admit the use of positive attributes and those who reject it. Even Maimonides speaks of essential attributes as being merely "the explanation of a name." [3] If he does reject their positive use, it is only because he endows essential attributes with some kind of objective reality. Were they all names only and nothing else, Maimonides would permit their positive use. Albo well restates Maimonides' view in the following passage: "You must know that God cannot be described by two things which would constitute His essence after the analogy of animality and rationality in Man. . . . He can, however, be described by any attribute which is only the explanation of the name by which He is called." [4]

In the mediaeval endeavor to reconcile the apparent contradiction between the plurality of attributes and the simplicity of essence an attempt is often made to reduce all the different attributes to one. It is shown that the variety of

[1] Epistola 8 (*Opera*, IV, p. 41, ll. 10–13).
[2] Epistola 9 (*Opera*, IV, p. 46, ll. 7–9).
[3] *Moreh Nebukim*, I, 51 and 52. Cf. below, pp. 229–230.
[4] '*Ikkarim*, II, 9.

attributes, however different they may appear to us, are in reality one, for they are all involved in our conception of God, they are conceived by us simultaneously, and they are always together in God. "These three attributes [life, power, wisdom] are conceived by our mind immediately and simultaneously without the aid of intermediate reasoning, for conceiving God as we do in the nature of a creator we at once think of Him as living, powerful, and wise. . . . But though these three attributes occur to our mind at once, it is impossible for our tongue to utter them at once, for we do not find in human speech a single word comprehending all the three attributes and we are compelled to resort to the use of three words." [1] Again: "We therefore say that the attributes ascribed to God, though different from each other when used with reference to us, are all one in Him. For with reference to ourselves, inasmuch as we conceive them or acquire them one after the other, we consider them as being different from each other; similarly, inasmuch as we acquire them after we have been without them, we naturally consider them as superadded to the essence. With reference to God, however, we must consider them as unified and unacquired in such a manner as not to imply any plurality in His essence." [2] It is the same reasoning that underlies the following passage of Spinoza: "From this it is apparent that although two attributes may be conceived as really distinct — that is to say, one without the assistance of the other — we cannot nevertheless thence conclude that they constitute two things or two different substances; for this is the nature of substance, that each of its attributes is conceived through itself, since all the attributes which substance possesses were always in it together, nor could one be produced by another;

[1] *Emunot we-De'ot*, II, 4.
[2] *'Ikkarim*, II, 21.

but each expresses the reality or being of substance" (Prop.
X, Schol.). The implications of this passage are these:
The two attributes appear to the mind as being distinct
from each other. In reality, however, they are one. For by
Proposition X, attributes, like substance, are *summa genera*
("conceived through itself"). The two attributes must
therefore be one and identical with substance. Furthermore,
the two attributes have not been acquired by substance
after it had been without them, nor are they conceived by
the mind one after the other or deduced one from the other.
They have always been in substance together, and are conceived by our mind simultaneously. Hence, the attributes
are only different words expressing the same reality and
being of substance.

Proposition XII is complementary to the definitions of
substance and attribute. While the definition of attribute
states affirmatively the subjective nature of attributes by
declaring that they are only perceived by the mind, the proposition denies any independent reality to attributes by
which the simplicity of the substance would be endangered.
"No attribute of substance can be truly conceived from
which it follows that substance can be divided." The conclusion is then reached in Proposition XIII, namely, that
"substance absolutely infinite is indivisible."

Spinoza's demonstrations for both these propositions are
practically the same. In both cases he begins with the same
hypothetico-disjunctive proposition and proceeds to show
in an identical manner that substance, because it is absolutely infinite, cannot be divided. It will be recalled that
Spinoza's "absolutely infinite" has been shown to correspond to what the mediaevals called "essentially infinite."
It is singularly worthy of notice that Spinoza's argument here
against the divisibility of an *absolutely infinite* substance is

the same as the mediaeval argument against the divisibility of an *essentially infinite* substance.

Spinoza's argument runs as follows:

I. If an absolutely infinite substance were divisible, the parts would either retain the nature of the whole or not.

II. If the parts retained the nature of the whole, there would then be many infinite substances, which is absurd.

III. If they did not retain the nature of the whole, then the whole would lose the nature of substance and cease to be.

The mediaeval argument against the divisibility of an essentially infinite substance, as given by Averroes, runs in a similar vein:

I. If an essentially infinite substance were divisible, the parts would either have the same nature as the whole or not.

II. If the parts had the same nature as the whole, then the parts of an infinite would be infinite, which is absurd.

III. If they did not have the same nature as the whole, then the whole would consist of heterogeneous parts and would thus lose its homogeneous and simple character.[1]

The discussion of attributes in this chapter has been confined to those phases of the problem which the exigencies of the interpretation of Propositions VII–X and XII–XIII required. Other phases of the problem will be discussed in the chapter on Extension and Thought.

[1] See Averroes' *Middle Commentaries* on *Physics*, III, 5, 204a, 20–32, and *Metaphysics*, XI, 10, 1066b, 11–21. Cf. my *Crescas' Critique of Aristotle*, p. 137, and note (d) on pp. 331–332.

CHAPT

PROOFS OF THE EX

I. THE ONTOL

THE first ten propositions of t
noza's proofs of the existenc
mediaeval philosophers. The
of God, placed by Spinoza ne
which, as we have already shown, is an exact reproduction
of a definition found in a standard work of a popular mediaeval Jewish philosopher.[1] Spinoza seems to address his imaginary opponents as follows:

All you mediaevals, to whatever school of thought you
may belong, have builded your philosophies on the conception of a God epitomized by you in a formal definition which
contains four characteristic expressions. You say that God
is (1) an *ens* in the highest sense of the term, by which you
mean that He is a being who exists necessarily. You also say
that He is (2) "absolutely infinite," by which you mean that
He is (3) "a substance consisting of infinite attributes,"
(4) "each of which expresses eternal and infinite essence"
(Def. VI). God so defined you call absolute substance; you
differentiate Him from the world which you call conditional
substance, and then you declare that the relation between
the absolute and the conditional substance is like that of
creator to created. In opposition to you, I deny at the very
outset the existence of a God outside the world and of His
relation to the world as creator. Still, unaccustomed as I am

[1] *'Ikkarim*, II, 25. Cf. above, p. 118.

to dispute about mere names,[1] I shall retain your own term substance as a philosophic surrogate to the pious name God, and in your own terms I am going to unfold a new conception of the nature of God and of His relation to the world.

To begin with, I shall abandon your distinction between absolute substance and conditional substance, but shall use the term substance in that restrictive sense in which you use the expression absolute substance. Then, what you call conditional substance, or the world, I shall call mode. Furthermore, unlike you, I shall not describe the relation of substance to mode as that of creator to created, but rather as that of whole to part, or, to be more exact, as that of universal to particular (Defs. II and V; Axioms I and II; Prop. I).[2] The reason for my disagreeing with you on the question of the causal relation between God and the world is that I find your doctrine of creation, however you may try to explain it, an untenable hypothesis (Props. II–VI).[3] Barring this difference between us, a difference which, I must confess, is fundamental and far-reaching in its effect, I am going to describe my substance in all those terms which you make use of in describing your God. Like your God, my substance is (1) the highest kind of *ens*, for existence appertains to its nature (Prop. VII). (2) It is also absolutely infinite (Prop. VIII). (3) Furthermore, it consists of infinite attributes (Prop. IX). (4) Finally, each of its attributes expresses eternal and infinite essence (Prop. X).[4] I have thus described my substance in all those terms which you use in your formal definition of God. Consequently, as I am now to reproduce your proofs of the existence of God to prove the existence of my substance, I shall bracket together the terms God and substance and

---

[1] Cf. *Cogitata Metaphysica*, I, 3, quoted below. Cf. below, p. 190, n. 3.
[2] Cf. above, Chapter III.   [3] Cf. above, Chapter IV.
[4] Cf. above, Chapter V.

say: "God, or substance consisting of infinite attributes, each of which expresses eternal and infinite essence, necessarily exists" (Prop. XI). Having made it clear by this time what I mean by the term God, I am no longer afraid of being misunderstood. Hereafter I shall drop the term substance and use in its stead the term God. And so he does.

The expression *necessario existit*, which Spinoza uses in the eleventh proposition, is to be understood to have two meanings. In the first place, it means that it can be shown apodictically, by necessary, logical reasoning, that God must exist. In the second place, it means that the existence which is proved of God belongs to that class known as necessary existence as opposed to possible existence. In a passage in the *Cogitata Metaphysica*, I, 1, Spinoza points out the distinction between these two classes of existence: "From the definition of Being, or, if you prefer, from its description,[1] it is now easily seen that Being should be divided into Being which because of its own nature necessarily exists, or Being whose essence involves existence, and Being whose essence involves only possible existence." In the course of our subsequent discussion of the proofs, especially of the second proof, it will become clear that the purpose of this proposition is to state not only that God exists but also that His existence is of the kind known as necessary existence. This double purpose of the proofs of the existence of God is clearly brought out by Spinoza in his *Principia Philosophiae Cartesianae*, I, Proposition V, Demonstration: "The concept of God includes necessary existence. Therefore it is true to say

[1] Definition (ὁρισμός, حد, גדר) is to be distinguished from description (ὑπογραφή, رسم, רשם). Cf. Maimonides, *Millot ha-Higgayon*, Ch. 10. Spinoza's hesitancy as to whether Being (*ens*) has a definition or only a description reflects the question raised by Hillel of Verona in his Commentary on Maimonides' Twenty-five Propositions (Prop. 25) as to whether substance has a definition in view of the fact that it is a *summum genus*. Cf. my *Crescas' Critique of Aristotle*, p. 575.

that He has a necessary existence in himself, or that He exists."
Similarly Crescas in conclusion of his summary of Maimonides' proofs of the existence of God seems to emphasize that
the proofs demonstrate not only that God exists but that He
exists with an existence which is necessary *per se*.[1]

It will be well for us to state in Spinoza's own terms what
he is driving at in his proofs of the existence of God and what
he is trying to establish thereby. Spinoza himself would
have said that he was trying to determine by these proofs
what kind of being (*ens*) God is. For being — or rather the
ideas we have of being — is, according to Spinoza, of four kinds
— a classification which seems to be derived from a Hebrew
source. Some ideas are real, and these are ideas which have
an extra-mental object as their source; others are unreal,
and of these some are fictitious, mere figments of the imagination, composite pictures of things perceived and experienced; others are rational, mere modes of thought, such as
the universals known as genera and species; and still others
are merely verbal, because they exist neither in the intellect
nor in the imagination, such as chimeras and ideas conveyed
by expressions like "a square circle."[2] None of these unreal
ideas are ideas of things, for they have no real object as their

---

[1] *Or Adonai*, I, i, 32.

[2] *Cogitata Metaphysica*, I, 1.

The source of this classification is to be found in the Hebrew philosophic manual
Ruaḥ Ḥen, Ch. 5. According to the *Ruaḥ Ḥen*, there is the following classification
of being:

1. Real beings, דברים אמתיים, which exist outside the mind and of which we
can form an idea either in the mind or in the imagination.

2. Unreal beings, דברים שאינם אמתיים, which exist neither in the mind nor outside the mind. They are fictitious beings, having existence only in the imagination,
אלא שיש לענין ההוא מציאות בדמיון המאמין. Previous to this in the same chapter
they are also called "verbal beings," שאין שם רק דבור לבד. This class is subdivided into two parts:

a. Factitious beings which have no existence in reality, ויצייר דברים שאינם
נמצאים כלל.

b. Factitious beings which not only have no existence in reality but whose nature

source, nor have they a counterpart outside the mind. Extra-mental existences only are real, and ideas in the mind are real only in so far as they represent those extra-mental existences. What Spinoza, therefore, is trying to establish by his proofs of the existence of God is that God is not a fictitious being, nor a verbal being, nor a being of reason, but a real being, who has existence outside our mind and who is the source and counterpart of the idea we have of Him. Substance, says Spinoza, is outside the intellect,[1] that is to say, it is not fabricated by the intellect. Only that conception of God, says he again, is a fiction which uses the name of God not in harmony with His real nature;[2] the true conception of God is that of "a body in nature whose idea is necessary in order to represent God immediately."[3]

In order to determine whether an idea is real or not one has to ascertain by means of the various approved sources of knowledge whether or not it has an extra-mental object

involves a contradiction, as the words "a square circle" או יצייר תכונת הדברים הנמצאים בהפך תכונתם, כמו שידמה הגלגל מרובע.

3. Beings of reason, which exist only in the mind but have no existence outside the mind, as genera and species, ויש דברים גם כן שנמצאים בשכל, ואין להם מציאות כלל בעצמן חוץ לשכל, והם המינים ושאר הכללים הגבוהים. The resemblance between this classification and that of Spinoza is striking. The only differences to be noted are as follows:

(1) The classification in *Ruaḥ Ḥen* applies the expression "verbal being" to both 2a and 2b. Spinoza applies it only to what in his classification corresponds to 2b.

(2) This classification considers the expression "a square circle" as something which is in the imagination. Spinoza says of a chimera, which to him is the equivalent of a "square circle," that it is neither in the intellect nor in the imagination (see *Cog. Met.*, I, 3).

Freudenthal is thus not quite right in saying that the distinction of *ens fictum*, *ens chimerae*, *ens rationis* and *ens reale* does not occur in Jewish philosophy. Cf. "Spinoza und die Scholastik" in *Philosophische Aufsätze, Eduard Zeller . . . gewidmet*, p. 103.

[1] Cf. *Ethics*, I, Prop. 4, Demonst.
[2] *Tractatus de Intellectus Emendatione*, § 54 (*Opera*, III, p. 20, note t).
[3] *Short Treatise*, Second Dialogue, § 12 (*Opera*, I, p. 34, ll. 15–17).

to correspond to it. Again and again Spinoza classifies the sources of knowledge. Not all of his classifications are of the same type; they are, however, all made up of various mediaeval classifications with some slight modifications of his own, as we hope to show in another chapter.[1] Roughly speaking, Spinoza maintains, clearly so in the *Short Treatise*, II, 1, that we may know things either directly or indirectly. Direct knowledge may be either sense perception in its many forms and derivations, or intuition, the latter of which is designated by Spinoza as "clear and distinct comprehension,"[2] "clear cognition,"[3] "intuitive science,"[4] or a perception "wherein a thing is perceived through its essence alone,"[5] that is to say, "intuitively, without any process of working."[6]   Indirect knowledge consists of the inference of the unknown from the known, which is described by Spinoza as "true belief,"[7] "art of reasoning,"[8] or that mode of perception "wherein the essence of one thing is concluded from the essence of another."[9]

Now, according to Spinoza, any one of these sources of knowledge is sufficiently valid to establish the reality of any idea we happen to have. Intuition and logical inference are as valid proofs for the reality of ideas as direct sense perception; to Spinoza, in fact, they are more valid, for sense perception and imagination alone may lead to falsity.[10]   Still, in

---

[1] Cf. below, Vol. II, Chapter XVI.

[2] *klaare en onderscheide bevatting*. *Short Treatise*, II, 1, § 2.

[3] *klaare Kennisse*. *Op. cit.*, II, 2, § 1.

[4] *scientia intuitiva*. *Ethics*, II, Prop. 40, Schol. 2.

[5] *ubi res percipitur per solam suam essentiam*. *Tractatus de Intellectus Emendatione*, § 19 (*Opera*, II, p. 10, l. 20).

[6] *sed intuitive, nullam operationem facientes*. *Ibid.*, § 24 (*Opera*, II, p. 12, ll. 13–14).

[7] *waar geloof*. *Short Treatise*, II, 1, § 2.

[8] *ratio*. *Ethics*, II, Prop. 40, Schol. 2.

[9] *ubi essentia rei ex alia re concluditur*. *Tractatus de Intellectus Emendatione*, § 19 (*Opera*, II, p. 10, l. 16).

[10] *Ethics*, II, Prop. 41.

the proof of the existence of God in the history of philosophy, not all of these sources of knowledge were of use. Direct sense perception had to be eliminated, for, in the words of Scripture, if a proof-text is necessary, "Man shall not see me and live" (Exodus 33, 20). In fact, Spinoza explicitly states that this verse should be taken in its literal sense as an answer to Moses' request that God should show himself to him in some perceptible form,[1] which, it may be remarked incidentally, is an oblique criticism of Maimonides' interpretation of the verse as meaning that God's essence cannot be comprehended by the human intellect in denial of Moses' request that God should become known to him in His true essence.[2] Historically, therefore, the proofs of the existence of God had to fall back upon the kind of knowledge which is either direct like Spinoza's intuition, or indirect, that is, by way of logical reasoning.

In the history of religious philosophy both these methods of proving the existence of God, the direct and the indirect, were made use of. When theologians, for instance, appeal to revelation as a proof of the existence of God, either to an act of historical revelation in the past or to the constantly repeated revelations in the religious experience of chosen or gifted individuals, they make the knowledge of God something direct and immediately perceived. Similarly when Cicero [3] and, following him, others maintain that the idea of God is innate in man, they also make it an object of immediate apprehension. Likewise the argument from *consensus gentium* rests, in its ultimate analysis, on the assumption that God is an object of immediate knowledge.[4] But,

---

[1] *Tractatus Theologico-Politicus*, Ch. 2 (*Opera*, III, p. 40, ll. 12 ff.).
[2] *Moreh Nebukim*, I, 64, and I, 4.
[3] *De Natura Deorum*, I, 17, §§ 44–45; II, 4, § 12.
[4] *Ibid.*

on the other hand, the cosmological argument and the argument from design proceed on the assumption that God cannot be immediately known; He can become known only indirectly by the art of reasoning. To Spinoza, however, be it noted, God is an object of direct knowledge, for God, according to him, is known to us as an intuition, as a clear and distinct idea, which is adequate and true. "That existence belongs to the essence of God," says Spinoza, "we can clearly and distinctly understand" (*Short Treatise*, I, 1, § 1); "The knowledge of the eternal and infinite essence of God which each idea involves is adequate and perfect" (*Ethics*, II, Prop. XLVI); and "By adequate idea, I understand an idea which, in so far as it is considered in itself, without reference to the object, has all the properties or internal signs of a true idea" (*Ethics*, II, Def. IV). To Spinoza, therefore, the reality of the idea of God, that is to say, the existence of God, is self-evident as an immediate fact of knowledge, for we can have a knowledge of God which is "as clear as that with which we also know our body." [1]

But here a difficulty arises. To say that God's existence is immediately perceived as an intuition and to declare intuition as a valid source of knowledge, which establishes the reality of the intuited idea, is to start out with a major premise which would seem to require no further demonstration, and to which no further demonstration could add anything, least of all a demonstration in the Aristotelian sense. For a demonstration, according to Aristotle, is "a syllogism which produces science" [2] — and the science it produces in the conclusion must be something not known directly from the major premise. It has indeed been asked whether even in the deductive syllogism of Aristotle the conclusion ever

---

[1] *Short Treatise*, II, 19, § 14 (*Opera*, I, p. 93, ll. 20–22).
[2] *Analytica Posteriora*, I, 2, 71b, 17–18.

really adds anything to the major premise.[1] Still, while there may be some justification for Aristotle in reasoning from the universal to the particular and in trying to prove syllogistically that Socrates is mortal from the immediately known and undemonstrable premise that all men are mortal, — for, after all, there may be a real inference in the syllogism in so far as there may be a real difference between the particular and the universal, — there does not seem to be even this saving grace in Spinoza's proof where the subject and the predicate in both the major premise and the conclusion are practically the same. For what Spinoza is practically trying to do is to prove syllogistically that God is existent from the immediately known and undemonstrable premise that God is existent. Logically it is analogous to an attempt to prove the mortality of Socrates by the syllogism:

The husband of Xanthippe is mortal,
Socrates is the husband of Xanthippe,
Therefore, Socrates is mortal,

in which there is no inference unless by Socrates' mortality here is meant that special kind of mortality which came to him as a result of the fact that he was the husband of Xanthippe. And yet Spinoza goes through all the motions of proving the existence of God. What need is there for proving that which at the very outset is assumed to be immediately known?

The answer that would naturally suggest itself is that we did not reproduce Spinoza's argument quite accurately, that the major premise in his syllogism does not in itself establish the existence of God; it only states the fact that we have an idea of God as an existent being, and the purpose of the syllogism therefore is to prove that our idea is real. We

[1] J. S. Mill, *System of Logic*, Bk. II, Chs. I and III.

should probably be referred to what is known as the ontological proof, to which class of reasoning most of Spinoza's proofs belong, and we should be reminded that in the ontological proof the major premise is always a statement of what our idea of God is and an assertion that our idea of God, whatever it be, whether of a greatest being, or of a most perfect being, or of a self-caused being, always involves existence, and that the purpose of the proof is to establish the reality of the idea. In refutation of this answer we may say that if the major premise is assumed not to establish the existence of God, then the conclusion does not establish it. Furthermore, we shall endeavor to show that in its classical formulation by the three authors with whom we shall chiefly concern ourselves here, Anselm, Descartes, and Spinoza, the reality of the idea of God was never sought to be proved by the syllogism, but it was already conceived to be established in the major premise by some other principle.

It is needless for us to repeat here in detail the stock objection to the ontological argument in its conventional formulation. The objection has become historically as famous as the proof itself. Generally speaking, it tries to point out that what the ontological proof establishes is that if God is conceived of as the greatest being, or the most perfect being, or a self-caused being, He must also be conceived of as existing outside the mind and cannot be conceived of as nonexistent. There is nothing in the proof, the objection continues, to show that the idea of God conceived of in any of those forms is not a fictitious and arbitrary idea fabricated by our mind. Now all these three protagonists of the ontological proof were aware of this objection, and they all tried to meet it squarely and directly. St. Anselm was challenged to answer it by Gaunilon, and he answered it. Descartes quotes the same objection from Thomas Aquinas and tries to rebut it.[1] Spinoza, too, was confronted with the stock objection by Oldenburg,[2] and he answered it.[3] Furthermore, he also quotes Thomas Aquinas as stating that "God cannot be proved *a priori*" and refutes that statement.[4] What is the force of all these answers, rebuttals, and refutations?

If we examine closely the answers given by St. Anselm, Descartes, and Spinoza to this most obvious objection, we shall find that they all try to show that the idea we have of God as an existing being does not depend for its proof upon the syllogism, but that its reality is immediately known, just as the reality of anything that is immediately perceived and experienced. God, they all seem to say, is an immediate object of knowledge, and the knowledge by which He becomes known to us is a valid source of knowledge. This is their proof for the existence of God. Nothing else is necessary to corroborate it. The kind of knowledge we have of God they hold to be as valid a proof for His existence as a miraculous revelation or a natural personal experience of His presence. There is no need to go further into this kind of immediate knowledge. As far as Spinoza is concerned, we shall discuss it fully in another chapter.[5]

That this is the meaning of the answer to the stock objection is clearly brought out in Descartes, and in his case the answer is generally so understood. The main point of his answer is that "whatever we clearly and distinctly perceive is true"[6] — true in the sense of its having objective reality,[7] of its not being an arbitrary and fictitious idea. The force of the ontological proof in Descartes, therefore, is its clearness and distinctness, its intuitive character, its immediacy

[1] *Primae Responsiones* (*Oeuvres*, VII, p. 115).
[2] Epistola 3.   [3] Epistola 4.
[4] *Short Treatise*, I, 1, § 10.   [5] Cf. below, Vol. II, pp. 155 ff.
[6] *Primae Responsiones* (*Oeuvres*, VII, p. 116).
[7] *Meditationes*, III (*Oeuvres*, VII, p. 46, ll. 8 f.).

after the manner of self-consciousness. It is this self-evident nature of the truth of the idea of God that distinguishes Descartes' ontological proof from his first proof in Meditation III, though both are alike in that they reason from the idea of God to His existence. In the first proof of Meditation III, the fact that we possess an idea of God is not in itself taken by Descartes to be a proof for His existence, for the idea might be arbitrary and fictitious. It is therefore necessary to establish the truth of the idea demonstratively, by reasoning from effect to cause, by showing that the idea we have of God could not have been produced except by a real object corresponding to it. In the ontological proof, on the other hand, the very nature of our idea of God is evidence of His existence, just as our thinking is evidence of our own existence and as our sense perception is evidence of the existence of the things perceived. It is not at all necessary to assume, as it is done, that Descartes' ontological proof is dependent upon his first and second proofs in Meditation III.[1] It is rather an independent proof, its basis being Descartes' theory of knowledge, according to which a clear and distinct idea like God is self-evidently true and contains objective reality.

Similarly Spinoza makes it unmistakably clear that his proof is primarily grounded upon the premise that God's existence is an immediate fact of our knowledge. In anticipation of the objection of Thomas Aquinas that "God cannot be proved *a priori*, because, indeed, He has no cause," he maintains that "God, however, the first cause of all things and even the cause of himself, manifests himself through himself."[2] The manifestation of God to us through

---

[1] Kuno Fischer, *Geschichte der neuern Philosophie*, I, 1 (3rd ed., Heidelberg, 1889), pp. 309 ff. Norman Smith, *Studies in the Cartesian Philosophy*, p. 58.

[2] *Short Treatise*, I, 1, § 10.

himself as evidenced by the clearness and distinctness and adequacy of the idea we have of Him directly and without any further reasoning proves His existence. Similar passages to the same effect are abundant in Spinoza's writings.[1]

If thus in both Descartes and Spinoza the ontological argument is really psychological, resting as it does upon the view that God is a direct object of our knowledge, can the same be asserted with equal certainty of St. Anselm's proof? On this point there exists a difference of opinion. On the one hand, attempts have been made to show that St. Anselm's argument is ultimately psychological like that of Descartes.[2] But, on the other hand, these attempts have been refuted on the ground that there is nothing in St. Anselm to warrant such a construction upon his argument.[3] In this entire controversy, however, one important passage in St. Anselm seems to have been lost sight of, namely, his answer to Gaunilon.

If we study the true meaning of Anselm's answer to Gaunilon's objection, we shall find that like Descartes and Spinoza he stresses the point that his ontological proof is based upon the premise that the existence of God is an immediate fact of consciousness. Gaunilon, as may be recalled, objected to the ontological proof by arguing that the idea of a being than whom a greater cannot be conceived no more proves the existence of God than the idea of an island than which a more excellent cannot be conceived proves the existence of that island. Anselm vehemently denies that there is

---

[1] See W. Apel, *Spinozas Verhältnis zum ontologischen Beweise* (Leipzig, 1911).

[2] Beda Adlhoch, "Der Gottesbeweis des hl. Anselm" in *Philosophisches Jahrbuch*, VIII–X (1895–1897), XV–XVI (1902–1903): "Verwegenheit also ist es nicht, wenn im Nachfolgenden zu beweisen versucht wird, das Argument sei ein psychologisches und geschichtsphilosophisches, kein ontologisches" (Vol. VIII, 1895, p. 56). See also G. Grunwald, *Geschichte der Gottesbeweise im Mittelalter*, pp. 31–33.

[3] Cf. C. Baeumker, *Vitelo*, p. 305.

any analogy between the idea of a being greater than all
other beings and the idea of an island more excellent than
all other islands, and exclaims: "But I call on your faith
and conscience to attest that this is most false." [1] We read
this answer and wonder. We say to ourselves: Simple Saint!
if the authority of faith and the dictates of a religious conscience are the ultimate arbiters in the controversy, why go
into all this trouble of proving the existence of God? Why
not quote Scripture and the church doctrine and be done
with it? There must therefore be some deeper meaning in
these simple words of Anselm. Is it not possible that in ap-
pealing to faith and to conscience Anselm is really invoking
the argument from revelation as attested by tradition by
which the existence of God is established as a fact of immediate personal experience? Such an argument from revelation
is common in Jewish philosophy,[2] and it may be considered
as partly psychological, in so far as the proof from revelation
derives its validity from the fact that it is an immediate experience, and partly historical and social, in so far as the
truth of the fact of revelation is attested by an unbroken
chain of tradition universally accredited within a certain
group.[3] It may thus be considered as the equivalent of the
argument from *consensus gentium*, which is also social and is
likewise ultimately based upon the immediacy of our knowledge of God, namely, the innateness of the idea of God.
Just as the general agreement of mankind is used by Cicero
as evidence that the idea of God is innate, so is the generally

---

[1] *Apologeticus*, Ch. I.

[2] Cf. *Moreh Nebukim*, II, 23.

[3] Such a historical proof based upon revelation is referred to by Spinoza in
Tractatus Theologico-Politicus, Ch. 4 (*Opera*, III, p. 61, ll. 28–31): "The truth of
a historical narrative, however assured, cannot give us the knowledge nor consequently the love of God, for love of God springs from knowledge of Him, and knowledge of Him should be derived from common notions (*comminubus notionibus*), in
themselves certain and known."

accredited religious tradition within the group taken by the Jewish philosophers to prove the veracity of the fact of revelation.[1] Anselm thus says to Gaunilon that the idea we have of God is unlike the idea we have of a most excellent island. The latter may be arbitrary and imaginary; the former is a true and necessary idea, being based upon the immediate experience of God's existence in the act of revelation as attested by religious tradition universally accepted.

That the ontological proof must ultimately rest upon a psychological basis may also be gathered from one kind of opposition to that argument among the scholastics. There were those who attacked the validity of the proof on the ground of their denial of the major premise, maintaining that the idea of God as a being whose essence involves existence was not immediately perceived by everybody. It was only well-trained philosophers, they argued, who perceived it as an immediate truth. But admitting that philosophers did perceive it as an immediate truth, these opponents of the ontological proof admitted the validity of the ontological proof for philosophers.[2] The particular theory of knowledge involved in this sort of reasoning is that indirect knowledge may in the course of time become direct knowledge which is immediately accepted without the need of demonstration. Spinoza himself intimates this particular view when he says that the desire to know things by the third kind of knowledge may arise from the second kind of knowledge.[3] The same view seems to be reflected also in Descartes' statement that "those propositions indeed which are immediately deduced from first principles are known now by intuition, now by deduction, i.e., in a way that differs according to our

---

[1] Cf. my "Notes on Proofs of the Existence of God in Jewish Philosophy" in *The Hebrew Union College Annual*, I (1924), p. 577.

[2] C. Baeumker, *Vitelo*, p. 301.   [3] *Ethics*, V, Prop. 28.

point of view." [1] And so, when the knowledge of God's existence becomes immediate and direct, whatever its origin, the existence of God is said to be proved ontologically instead of demonstratively, for to prove the existence of God ontologically means to perceive it directly as a given fact. The immediacy of the knowledge of God's existence is fully explained by Spinoza toward the end of the Second Dialogue in the *Short Treatise*, and there, too, he seems to intimate that it is not all men that do have at first such an immediate knowledge of God. "However, I tell you this, that so long as we have not such a clear idea of God . . . we cannot truly say that we are united with God."

We have thus shown, I believe, that Spinoza as well as Descartes and Anselm starts his ontological argument with a major premise that God's existence is a fact of immediate knowledge. It is not necessary, as is generally done, to set up a straw-man in the form of an untenable ontological argument as it is conventionally stated, to riddle it through and through, and then to take up the defence of one particular favorite, either Anselm, or Descartes, or Spinoza, and claim that his particular argument is immune from such criticism on the ground that it is not "ontological" but rather "psychological." [2] The point we have been trying to make is that all these three protagonists of the so-called ontological argument are alike in this respect. They are all making use of a "psychological" argument, and their syllogism is tantamount to saying that we know directly, as we can know anything at all, that God exists. There is nothing in the conclusion of the syllogism that is not contained in the major premise. But if this is so, the question may be raised, not

---

[1] *Regulae ad Directionem Ingenii*, III (*Oeuvres*, X, p. 370, ll. 10–13).

[2] Adlhoch does this with reference to Anselm; Apel with reference to Spinoza; Descartes is singled out by everybody as an exception.

only against Spinoza, but against Anselm and Descartes as well, What is the significance of the syllogism in the onto-logical proof?

The answer is that the syllogism adds nothing to the major premise. But still it is not altogether redundant. It may be said that the function of the ontological proof is like that of the proposition of an analytical judgment, in which the predi-cate adds nothing to the subject, and still its use is not alto-gether unjustifiable. Perhaps the comparison can be put in the following manner. Just as propositions are either ana-lytic or synthetic, so are syllogisms also either analytic or synthetic, and the relation of the analytical syllogism to the major premise is like that of the analytical proposition to the subject. To be more specific: The ontological proof for the existence of God is an analytical syllogism just as the proposition "God is existent" is an analytical judgment, and the relation of the syllogism in the ontological proof to the major premise is like the relation of the proposition "God is existent" to the subject "God." Neither of them adds anything to the contents of its respective subject or major premise with which it starts, but both of them analyze the contents of their respective subject and major premise.

It was not Kant who was the first to draw the distinction between analytical and synthetical judgments. It has been shown that the scholastics before him had recognized it and expressed it by the distinction between *per se nota* and *per aliud nota* or by similar other distinctions, such as *per se* and *per accidens* or *in materia necessaria* and *in materia contigenti.*[1] It can also be shown that it was not unknown to Arabic and Jewish philosophers, and having known that distinction, they asked themselves what kind of relation was expressed in an analytical proposition. That the relation

[1] Cf. P. Coffey, *The Science of Logic*, I, p. 70.

could not be real and hence the judgment could not be real they all seem to agree. They only seem to question whether there could be a justifiable logical relation which was not real. Thus in the proposition "God is existent," argues Avicenna, followed by a chorus of Jewish philosophers, since essence and existence are identical, the proposition is tautological, and is tantamount to saying "God is God." [1] And similarly Maimonides argues that in a proposition where the predicate is identical with the subject there is no real logical relation but only the explanation of a name.[2] Likewise Gersonides maintains that in the proposition "God is existent" the term "God" is a subject only "in discourse," not "in existence." [3]

All this may be considered as a sort of anticipation of John Stuart Mill's conclusion that an analytical judgment is only verbal, or that it is explicative, as others call it. And so may we also say of the analytical or ontological proof that it is only verbal and explicative. It is indeed true to say of an ontological proof what John Stuart Mill says of every form of Aristotle's deductive syllogism. It contains no real inference. It adds nothing to what is already known from the major premise. But still its use is justifiable. For it translates a conviction into an argument. It elicits a truth which is only implicitly contained in the major premise. It puts an immediate fact of consciousness in the form of a syllogistic reasoning. It resolves an idea into its component parts. Thus when Spinoza proves the existence of God ontologically, he does not pretend to arrive at a newly discovered fact, but rather to restate in formal language a fact already known.

[1] *Or Adonai*, I, iii, 1. Cf. above, p. 123.
[2] *Moreh Nebukim*, I, 51; cf. 52. Cf. above, p. 154.
[3] *Milḥamot Adonai*, III, 3. Cf. above, p. 151.

Truly speaking, if the ontological proof were to be put into a syllogistic formula in such a way as to bring out its entire force, it would have to be as follows:

Everything which is immediately perceived to exist exists.

God is immediately perceived to exist.

Therefore, God exists.

Now, none of the ontological proofs in their various forms as given by its three main exponents, Anselm, Decartes, and Spinoza, prove directly that God exists. What they prove is that the existence of God is known to us by a certain kind of immediate knowledge. Their various proofs can be reduced to the following syllogism:

If we have an idea of God as the greatest, or as the most perfect, or as a self-caused being, then God is immediately perceived by us to exist.

But we have an idea of God as the greatest, or as the most perfect, or as a self-caused being.

Therefore, God is immediately perceived by us to exist.

Their direct proof of the existence of God is their respective views that our immediate knowledge of God's existence which is implied in the idea we have of God as the greatest, or as the most perfect, or as a self-caused being is valid knowledge.

II. Spinoza's Four Proofs

The foregoing discussion of the nature of the ontological proof may serve as a general approach to the understanding of all of Spinoza's proofs of the existence of God. Whatever may be said in criticism of this mode of ontological reasoning hardly concerns those of us who are now mainly interested in the objective understanding of Spinoza's thought, rather than in passing criticism on it. It may perhaps be that the alleged immediacy of the idea of God is nothing but an after-thought of a departed traditional belief, just as the catless grin which Alice saw in Wonderland was nothing but an after-image of a departed grinning cat; or it may be that Spinoza is claiming "an arbitrary right to accept anything he pleases as self-evident"; [1] and it may perhaps also be, as we have been trying to show, that the reasoning by which it is sought to dissolve this idea into a syllogism, despite the cogency of its logical form, is nothing but the breaking up of a complex term into its component parts. But however slight this proof may appear to us, it certainly carried conviction to the mind of Spinoza and of others like him to whom an immediately and intuitively conceived idea by its very clearness and distinctness connoted as much reality as, aye even greater reality than, the undimmed perceptions of unimpaired senses. And perhaps we should be inclined to give more weight to this reasoning if we could only bear in mind that Spinoza's God is not the God of traditional theology, that his "God" is merely an appeasive term for the most comprehensive principle of the universe, which he supposed to be conceived apriorily as the ideal triangle, but unlike the ideal triangle, being the working principle of the universe and not its mere ideal pattern, its *a priori* conception involved an extra-mental reality which the *a priori* conception of a triangle did not. With these considerations looming before our mind, there remains for us only to deal with the external structure of the proofs, their origin, their individual history, their growth, and the final form in which they appear before us.

It may be recalled that Descartes has three proofs of the

[1] F. Pollock, *Spinoza*, p. 129.

existence of God, two of them in Meditation III[1] and a third
in Meditation V, corresponding respectively to the three
proofs in the *Discours de la Méthode*, IV,[2] in the *Principia
Philosophiae*, I, 18–19, 20–21, and 14, and in the geometrical
formulation of the arguments demonstrating the existence of
God at the end of *Secundae Responsiones*, Propositions II,
III, and I. The first two of these three proofs we shall designate respectively as the first and second proof of Meditation III, and the third as the ontological proof. All the proofs
for the existence of God adduced by Spinoza in his various
works may be traced to these three Cartesian proofs, and
may be divided accordingly into three groups:

First, Descartes' first proof of Meditation III to be found
in *Principia Philosophiae Cartesianae*, I, Proposition VI, and
in the proof designated as *a posteriori* in *Short Treatise*, I, I,
and referred to also in a letter to Jelles (Epistola XL) and
in a note to the *Tractatus de Intellectus Emendatione*, § 76
(*Opera*, II, p. 29, note a).

Second, Descartes' second proof of Meditation III to be
found in *Principia Philosophiae Cartesianae*, I, Proposition
VII, and in the third proof of *Ethics*, I, Proposition XI.

Third, Descartes' ontological proof to be found in *Principia Philosophiae Cartesianae*, I, Proposition V; in the
a priori proof of *Short Treatise*, I, I; in the first proof of
Ethics, I, Proposition XI; and in letters to Blyenbergh
(Epistola XXI) and Hudde (Epistola XXXIV).

The fourth proof in the *Ethics* is a modification of Descartes' second proof of Meditation III, and the second proof
in the *Ethics*, we shall try to show, has been suggested by
Descartes' ontological proof, but it contains many elements
borrowed from mediaeval Jewish and Arabic philosophy.

[1] (1) *Oeuvres*, VII, p. 45, ll. 9 ff., (2) *ibid.*, p. 47, ll. 24 ff.
[2] (1) *Oeuvres*, VI, p. 33, ll. 25 ff., (2) *ibid.*, p. 34, ll. 24 ff., (3) *ibid.*, p. 36, ll. 4 ff.

We shall here deal with the four proofs of the *Ethics*, correlating with them the parallel proofs found in the other writings of Spinoza.

FIRST PROOF

What is mainly of interest to us in Spinoza's first proof in the *Ethics* and its parallels elsewhere is the various forms in which he reproduces Descartes' ontological argument. Spinoza does not summarize Descartes, he does not epitomize him, nor does he merely paraphrase him. He rather selects what he considers to be the salient features of Descartes' argument and moulds them into a form of his own. If we compare the various versions of Descartes' ontological proof as given by Spinoza, we shall find that the Demonstration of Proposition V in *Principia Philosophiae Cartesianae*, I, and the first part of the *a priori* proof in *Short Treatise*, I, 1, represent one type; that the proofs in Epistolae XXI and XXXIV and the second part of the *a priori* proof in *Short Treatise*, I, 1, introduced by the remark "otherwise also thus," represent another type; and that the first proof of Proposition XI in *Ethics*, I, represents a third type. How these three types of Descartes' ontological proof were chiselled out from the unhewn and rugged block of Descartes' rather discursive and informal discussion of the ontological proof can be best shown by trying to outline the salient features of Descartes' argument as they must have formulated themselves in Spinoza's mind.

The starting point of Descartes' argument is the presence of the idea of God in our mind. This idea of God, he contends, could not have reached our mind through the medium of our senses, nor is it a factitious idea, depending solely on our thought. We rather derive this idea of God, so to speak, from "the storehouse of our mind."¹ It is the first and fore-most of the clear and distinct and true ideas born within us.

But how do we know that the idea of God is not factitious? To this Descartes answers that we know it by the fact that the idea is unique and absolutely unlike any other idea, "for really I discern in many ways that this idea is not something factitious, and depending solely on my thought, but that it is the image of a true and immutable nature . . . because I cannot conceive anything but God himself to whose essence existence [necessarily] pertains."²

That existence pertains to the essence of God is known by us, according to Descartes, in two ways. In Meditation V, in *Principia Philosophiae*, I, 14, and in the geometrical formulation of the arguments demonstrating the existence of God at the end of *Secundae Responsiones*, Proposition I, he says that it is implied in our immediate idea of God as "a Being supremely perfect,"³ for since existence is perfection it must be included in that idea as something pertaining to the essence of God. In his *Primae Responsiones*, however, he declares that the pertinence of existence to essence in God is also implied in our idea of God as a self-caused being, or, as he expresses himself, in a being who possesses necessary existence,⁴ for necessary existence is the equivalent of existence *per se*,⁵ which, according to Descartes, means self-caused as well as causeless.⁶ It is therefore natural for Descartes sometimes to leave out this intermediary step of

---

¹ *Meditationes*, V (*Oeuvres*, VII, p. 67, ll. 22 f.). Cf. *Meditationes*, III (*Oeuvres*, VII, p. 51, ll. 18 ff.).

² *Meditationes*, V (*Oeuvres*, VII, p. 68, ll. 10 ff.).

³ *Meditationes*, V (*Oeuvres*, VII, p. 67, l. 9).

⁴ *Primae Responsiones* (*Oeuvres*, VII, p. 117, ll. 5 ff.).

⁵ See Gerhardt, *Die Philosophischen Schriften von Gottfried Wilhelm Leibnitz*, IV, p. 406: "Car l'Estre necessaire et l'estre par son Essence ne sont qu'une même chose."

⁶ *Primae Responsiones* (*Oeuvres*, VII, pp. 109 ff.).

perfection or self-causation, by which we know that God's essence involves existence, and to speak of our immediate conception of God as that of a being whose essence involves existence.

Upon this assumption of the pertinence of existence to the essence of God Descartes builds his ontological proof. We find it in two forms.

In the first form, the major premise states that "all which I know clearly and distinctly as pertaining to this subject [i.e., of the innate idea] does really belong to it," [1] or as he puts it in *Primae Responsiones*, "That which we clearly and distinctly understand to belong to the true and immutable nature of anything, its essence, or form, can be affirmed of that thing." [2] The minor premise states that we clearly and distinctly understand that to exist belongs to the nature of God, and hence the conclusion that we can affirm of God that He exists. This is also the form used in the geometrical formulation of the arguments demonstrating the existence of God at the end of *Secundae Responsiones*, Proposition I. It is this form of the argument that is reproduced by Spinoza in Proposition V of *Principia Philosophiae Cartesianae*, I, and in the first part of the *a priori* proof of *Short Treatise*, I, 1, the phraseology of the *Primae Responsiones* being especially noticeable in the latter.

In the second form, Descartes draws a comparison between the idea of God and that of a triangle. Both have "a determinate nature, form, or essence, which is immutable and eternal." [3] That determinate nature, form, or essence in the case of the triangle is implied in its definition; but in the case of God it is implied in our idea of Him as all-perfection

---

[1] *Meditationes*, V (*Oeuvres*, VII, p. 65, ll. 17 ff.).
[2] *Primae Responsiones* (*Oeuvres*, VII, p. 118, ll. 22 ff.).
[3] *Meditationes*, V (*Oeuvres*, VII, p. 64, ll. 15 ff.).

or as self-causality. Thus from the definition of a triangle diverse properties follow, viz., "that its three angles are equal to two right angles, that the greatest side is subtended by the greatest angle, and the like." [1] Similarly from our idea of God as an all-perfect or self-caused being it follows "that an [actual] and eternal existence pertains to His nature." [2] The nerve of the argument, or, as Spinoza would say, the force of the argument (*vis argumenti*),[3] is the conclusion "that existence can no more be separated from the essence of God than can its having its three angles equal to two right angles be separated from the essence of a [rectilinear] triangle." [4] It is this form of the argument that is briefly restated by Spinoza in Epistola XXI, when he says: "If the nature of God is known to us, then the assertion that God exists follows as necessarily from our own nature as it follows necessarily from the nature of a triangle that its three angles are equal to two right angles." [5] In the second part of the *a priori* proof of *Short Treatise*, I, 1, it is reproduced rather incompletely: "The essences of things are from all eternity, and unto all eternity shall remain immutable. The existence of God is essence. Therefore, etc." The conclusion, in the light of our quotations from Descartes, should read as follows: Therefore, the essence and existence of God are together from all eternity, and unto all eternity shall remain unchanged, that is to say, existence can never be separated from the essence of God.

In the *Ethics*, Spinoza uses the first form of Descartes'

---

[1] *Meditationes*, V (*Oeuvres*, VII, p. 64, ll. 18 ff.).

The use of the triangle having its three angles equal to two right angles as an illustration for the idea of necessity is to be found in Aristotle, *Physics*, II, 9, 200a, 17 ff.

[2] *Meditationes*, V (*Oeuvres*, VII, p. 65, l. 24).

[3] Epistola 12 (*Opera*, IV, p. 62, l. 5).

[4] *Meditationes*, V (*Oeuvres*, VII, p. 66, ll. 8 ff.).   Cf. French version (*Opera*, IX, p. 52).   [5] Epistola 21 (*Opera*, IV, p. 130, ll. 4-7).

ontological proof with some modification. Reduced to a syllogism, the major premise therein is the statement that everything whose essence involves existence exists. The minor premise is the statement that God's essence involves existence. But the conclusion, that God exists, is arrived at indirectly by proving the contrary to be absurd. This is like the reasoning employed in St. Anselm's proof. In a letter to Schuller, Spinoza expresses a preference for this kind of proof, namely, the *reductio ad absurdum*, when the proposition is negative.[1] It is also to be noted that in this proof Spinoza finds that existence must pertain to the essence of God not in the idea of perfection, as does Descartes in Meditation V, but rather in the idea of self-causality, for Spinoza refers here to Proposition VII, the demonstration of which is based upon the premise that subtance, or, as he now calls it, God, cannot be produced by an external cause and must therefore be self-caused. But we have already seen that Descartes himself, in *Primae Responsiones*, makes self-causality the basis of the identification of essence and existence in God. There is therefore no foundation for the oft-repeated statement that Descartes bases his ontological proof on the idea of God as a most perfect being, whereas Spinoza bases his ontological proof on the idea of God as a self-caused being.[2] The two, as we have seen, are identified by Descartes himself.

In the light, however, of what we have said, namely, that the basis of the ontological proof is the assertion that we

---

[1] Epistola 64 (*Opera*, IV, p. 278, ll. 8 ff.): "deducendo rem ad absurdum." Cf. Epistola 63 from Schuller. See above, p. 97, and below, p. 378.

[2] It may be said that Leibniz advocated the substitution of "existence *per se*" for "perfection" as a criticism of Descartes, whereas Spinoza evidently did so as an interpretation of Descartes. Cf. A. Hannequin, "La preuve ontologique cartésienne défendue contre Leibnitz" in *Revue de Métaphysique et de Morale*, IV (1896), pp. 435, 436.

have a valid immediate perception of God's existence and that the so-called ontological proofs merely show how our valid immediate perception of God's existence is implied in our idea of God as the greatest or the most perfect being, or, in this particular proof, as a being whose essence involves existence, Spinoza's first proof in the *Ethics* is really to be reduced to the following syllogism:

> If we have a clear and distinct idea of God as a being whose essence involves existence, then God is immediately perceived by us to exist.
>
> But we have a clear and distinct idea of God as a being whose essence involves existence.
>
> Therefore, God is immediately perceived by us to exist.

SECOND PROOF

Against his own ontological proof based upon the inseparableness of existence from the essence of God Descartes himself raises a difficulty which he considers of no little moment. "We are so much accustomed to distinguish existence from essence in the case of other things," he says, "that we do not with sufficient readiness notice how existence belongs to the essence of God in a greater degree than in the case of other things." [1] In order to remove this difficulty, Descartes draws a distinction, or rather recalls an old distinction, between possible and necessary existence, declaring that "in the concept or idea of everything that is clearly and distinctly conceived, possible existence is contained, but necessary existence never, except in the idea of God alone." [2] It may be here remarked that by necessary existence, as already pointed out, is meant existence *per se*, which, according to Descartes

---

[1] *Primae Responsiones* (*Oeuvres*, VII, p. 116, ll. 9 f.).
[2] *Ibid.* (ll. 20 ff.).

himself, has a negative aspect in the sense of uncaused as
well as a positive aspect in the sense of self-caused.[1] With
this distinction drawn, Descartes substitutes the expression
"necessary existence" for the mere word "existence" in his
ontological proof, arriving at his conclusion that God exists
not from the premise that existence is involved in the essence
of God, but rather from the premise that necessary existence
is involved in it. It will have been noticed that in his restatement of Descartes in *Principia Philosophiae Cartesianae*, I,
Proposition V, Spinoza has already made use of this substitution, declaring that "the concept of God includes necessary
existence," that is to say, necessary existence and not merely
existence. In the *Short Treatise*, I, 1, however, and in the
first proof in *Ethics*, I, Proposition XI, the term "existence"
without the adjective "necessary" is used.

Now in the second proof in the *Ethics* Spinoza takes up
again this new phrase "necessary existence" and builds
around it a new proof. But why did Spinoza make a new
proof out of it? Why did he not embody it in his first proof
as did Descartes and as he himself did in his restatement of
Descartes in his *Principia*? The answer would seem to be
found in the fact that the phrase "necessary existence" had
brought to Spinoza's mind the recollection of the mediaeval
discussions about possible and necessary existence and of
a mediaeval cosmological proof based upon that distinction,
and all this appeared to him to warrant the framing of an
entirely new and distinct proof. Thus Spinoza's second
proof is of a composite nature. It is ontological and Cartesian in form, but its substance is enriched by borrowings
from mediaeval sources. We shall attempt to disentangle
this complicated and involved proof and reduce it to its
simple constituent elements.

[1] See above, p. 180, n. 6.

In mediaeval Jewish philosophy, under the influence of Aristotle, a distinction is made between an internal cause, which resides in the nature of the thing itself, and an external cause, which resides outside of the thing. If the cause resides in the thing itself, an effect must follow from that cause unless there is an external impediment to prevent it. That external impediment may also be considered as a sort of cause, and thus we have a further distinction between a cause which produces existence and a cause which prevents or negates existence. Similar distinctions are familiar also to students of scholastic philosophy.[1]   In Maimonides these distinctions are implied in the following statement: "Everything that passes from potentiality to actuality has something different from itself as the cause of its transition, and that cause is necessarily outside itself, for if the cause of the transition existed in the thing itself and there was no obstacle to prevent the transition, the thing would never have been in a state of potentiality but would have always been in a state of actuality."[2]   In the commentaries upon this passage, distinct technical terms for the contrast between effective causes and impedimental causes are introduced.[3]

Then, again, in mediaeval Jewish philosophy, in the attempt to prove that God is everlasting and can never be

[1] For the distinction between external and internal cause (*causa extrinseca, causa intrinseca*), see *Metaphysics*, XII, 4, 1070b, 22–23; *Summa Theologica*, Prima Secundae, Quaest. 1, Art. 3, Obj. 1. See also *Principia Philosophiae Cartesianae*, I, Axiom 11. Cf. below, pp. 319 ff.

For the impedimental cause, see *Summa Theologica*, Pars I, Quaest. 115, Art. 6, Obj. 3: *Si effectus coelestis corporis non ex necessitate proveniat, hoc est propter aliquam causam impedientem.*

[2] *Moreh Nebukim*, II, Introduction, Prop. 18.

[3] See commentary of Shem-Ṭob on *Moreh Nebukim*, ad. loc.: מוציא, effective cause; מעיק, מונע (Arabic: عائق. Cf. *Cuzari*, V, 20, p. 338, l. 19: עאיק = מונע), impedimental cause. The impedimental cause is also mentioned by Avicenna in his *Al-Shifa'*. Cf. M. Horten, *Die Metaphysik Avicennas*, p. 267.

deprived of His existence, it is argued that God's existence could not be negated or taken away except by some cause, but that cause would have to be either like God himself or unlike himself; and as neither of these is possible, it is concluded that God's existence can never be negated. To quote: "God is everlasting, and will never cease to exist. For a being proved to have no beginning cannot pass away. Just as the coming of the non-existent into existence must have a cause, so also the disappearance of a thing from existence requires a cause. Nothing vanishes from existence on its own account, but on account of its opposite. God, however, has nothing opposite Him, nor, for that matter, anything like Him. For if anything were like Him in every respect, it would be identical with God himself and they could not therefore be described as two. As for assuming something opposite God to be the cause of His ceasing to exist, it is likewise impossible for the following reason. That opposite thing could not be without beginning, for it has already been proved that God's existence alone is without beginning, nor could it have been created, for everything created must be an effect produced by the eternal God; but, if so, how can the effect make its cause disappear?" [1]

Then, also, in mediaeval Jewish philosophy, in consequence of an Avicennian view, the origin of which I have discussed in another place,[2] a distinction is made between "necessary existence *per se*" and "possible existence *per se*." Necessary existence *per se* is that which Spinoza would call *causa sui*, something whose existence is independent of any cause.[3] "Everything that is necessary of existence in respect to its own essence has no cause for its existence in any man-

---

[1] *Cuzari*, V, 18, 5.
[2] Cf. my *Crescas' Critique of Aristotle*, pp. 109–112, 680 ff.
[3] Cf. above, p. 127; below, p. 252.

ner whatsoever." [1] Possible existence *per se* is that which owes its existence to some cause. "Everything that has a cause for its existence is in respect to its own essence only possible of existence, for if its causes exist, the thing likewise will exist." [2] Furthermore, the possible *per se* is said to become impossible in the absence of the cause upon which its existence depends, for "if its causes have never existed, or if they have ceased to exist, or if their causal relation to the thing has changed, then the thing itself will not exist." [3] But, still, when the cause from which it follows by necessity does exist, then the thing, though only possible by its own nature, is said to be necessary with reference to its cause. It may thus be said that within everything possible there is the distinction of being possible in itself but necessary with reference to its cause. According to this view, therefore, there is a fourfold classification of being, divided first into two main groups, into that which is causeless and hence necessary by itself and that which requires a cause for its existence, the latter of which being then subdivided into its three aspects, namely, possible in itself, necessary by its cause, and impossible in the absence of any cause. [4]

This fourfold classification of being is reproduced by Spinoza in *Cogitata Metaphysica*, I, 3, when he divides all things into necessary, impossible, possible, and contingent. Necessary existence, in Spinoza as in mediaeval philosophy, is exemplified by God. As an illustration for the impossible Spinoza mentions the "chimera," [5] which like the words "a

---

[1] *Moreh Nebukim*, II, Introduction, Prop. 20.
[2] *Ibid.*, Prop. 19.   [3] *Ibid.*
[4] See commentary of Shem-Ṭob on *Moreh Nebukim*, II, Introduction, Prop. 19.
[5] So also in Descartes, as, for instance, in the French version of Meditation III (*Oeuvres*, IX, p. 34). Aristotle's illustration of a non-existent being is a goat-stag (τραγέλαφος) and sphinx. Cf. *De Interpretatione*, I, 16a, 16–17; *Physics*, IV, 1, 208a, 30.

square circle" exists neither in the intellect nor in the imagination and is rightly called a verbal being. The term "possible" is used by Spinoza in the general sense of being brought about or being made necessary by a cause, and the term "contingent" is used by him to designate that aspect of the possible wherein it was said by the mediaevals to be possible in consideration of its own essence. "A thing is said to be possible when we understand its efficient cause, but do not know whether it is determined. Therefore, we may consider that to be possible which is neither necessary [i.e., by itself] nor impossible [i.e., by itself]. If now we attend merely to the essence of a thing and not to its cause, we say it is contingent; that is, when we consider anything between the extremes God and chimeras." That these two terms "possible" and "contingent" were meant by Spinoza for the two aspects of the possible as used by the mediaevals may be gathered from the context of the passage quoted and from parallel passages in the other works of Spinoza.[1] He then makes the following statement: "If any one wishes to call that contingent which I call possible and possible what I call contingent I shall not contradict him. For I am not accustomed to dispute about mere names. It will be sufficient if it is only admitted that these arise not because of something real, but only because of a deficiency in our perception (*defectus nostrae perceptionis*)."[2] The last statement is a repetition of what is said earlier in the same chapter: "For some, these two terms are considered defects of things, although, in truth, they are nothing more than a deficiency in our intellect (*defectus nostri intellectus*)."[3] The reference is no doubt to

---

[1] Cf. *Principia Philosophiae Cartesianae*, I, Prop. 7, Lemma 1, Nota 1; *Tractatus de Intellectus Emendatione*, § 53 (*Opera*, II, p. 19, ll. 30 ff.); *Ethics*, I, Prop. 33, Schol. 1; IV, Defs. 3 and 4. Cf. below, pp. 310, 399, 410.

[2] *Cogitata Metaphysica*, I, 3. Cf. *Metaphysics*, V, 30, 1025a, 24; below, p. 399, and Vol. II, pp. 13, 109, 160.   [3] Cf. *Ethics*, I, Prop. 33, Schol. 1.

the controversy between Avicenna and Averroes as to whether possibility is merely a conceptual aspect or a real property of being.[1] It is also to be noted that Spinoza's lofty declaration here in *Cogitata Metaphysica*, I, 3, that "I am not accustomed to dispute about mere names," as well as Blyenbergh's statement in one of his letters to Spinoza that "you have taught me that one must not quarrel over words,"[2] is reminiscent of a similar expression used in Hebrew, Arabic, Latin, and Greek philosophic writings.[3]

Coming now to Spinoza's second proof in the *Ethics*, we find that it is replete with all those distinctions and lines of reasoning which we have abstracted from mediaeval sources. Spinoza refers to the distinction between an internal and an external cause when he speaks of a reason or cause which "must either be contained in the nature of the thing or lie outside it."[4] He also distinguishes between a positive cause and an impedimental cause when he says that if a thing

---

[1] See commentary of Shem-Ṭob on *Moreh Nebukim*, II, Introduction, Prop. 19.

[2] Epistola 20 (*Opera*, IV, p. 101, ll. 4–5 and 24).

[3] Cf. Abraham Ibn Daud, *Emunah Ramah*, I, 6 (p. 20): . . . וקראנוהו אנחנו נפש ואתה אם לא ישר בעיניך זה השם, תשים לו איזה שם שתרצה, כי אין קפידא אצלנו בשמות. "We call soul *nefesh*. . . . If this name does not please you, call it by whatever other name you like, for we are not sticklers for names." Similarly Algazali in his *Tahafot al-Falasifat*, III (ed. Maurice Bouyges, p. 109, l. 9), says: فان لم تسموا هذا فعلا فلا مضايقة فى التسميات, which in the published Latin translation from the Hebrew version of Averroes' *Tahafot al-Tahafot* (*Happalat ha-Happalah, Destructio Destructionis*) is rendered as follows: "si autem non appellabilis hoc actionem non est disputatio de nominibus." (ואם לא תקראו זה פעל, הנה אין לחץ בשמות.) This translation was accessible to Spinoza. Descartes makes use of the same expression in a letter to Henry More. Cf. *Correspondance*, DXXXVII (*Oeuvres*, V, p. 269, ll. 25–26): "Ego vero non soleo quidem de nominibus disputare."

Similar expressions occurring in Greek and in other Arabic sources are quoted by S. Horovitz in his *Die Psychologie bei den jüdischen Religions-Philosophen des Mittelalters*, p. 216, n. 13. As Greek examples he quotes from Alexander Aphrodisiensis, *Scripta Minora* (ed. Bruns), II, p. 183, l. 17: ὀνομάτων μὲν οὖν οὐδεὶς φθόνος, and from Galen, *Opera* (ed. Kühn), I, p. 155: ἡμεῖς δὲ οὐδὲν διαφερόμεθα πρὸς τοὺς, τὰ ὀνόματα ἐξαλλάττοντας.

[4] "Haec vera ratio seu causa vel in natura rei contineri debet, vel extra ipsam."

exists, "there must be a reason or cause why it exists; and if it does not exist, there must be a reason or cause which hinders its existence or which negates it." [1] Furthermore, he follows the main outline of the mediaeval argument for the everlastingness of God when he argues that if a reason or cause be granted "which hinders God from existing, or which negates His existence . . . it must be either in the nature itself of God or must lie outside it, that is to say, in another substance of another nature. . . . But substance possessing another nature could have nothing in common with God, and therefore could not give Him existence nor negate it." [2] Finally, he reproduces the mediaeval and his own classification of being into necessary, possible, and impossible when he states that "the nature of the thing itself shows the reason why a square circle does not exist . . . and the reason, on the other hand, why substance exists follows from its nature alone," [3] and when he further says that it is not from its own nature "but from the order of corporeal nature generally," i.e., its cause, that "it must follow, either that a triangle necessarily exists, or that it is impossible for it to exist." [4]

But more than this. There is a mediaeval proof for the existence of God based upon the distinction between necessary existence and possible existence which, as we shall now

[1] "Ratio, seu causa dari debet, cur existit; si autem non existit, ratio etiam, seu causa dari debet, quae impedit, quominus existat, sive quae ejus existentiam tollat."

[2] "Si . . . ratio . . . causa dari possit . . . quae impedit, quominus Deus existat, vel quae ejus existentiam tollat . . . ea, vel in ipsa Dei natura, vel extra ipsam dari deberet, hoc est, in alia substantia alterius naturae. . . . At substantia, quae alterius esset naturae, nihil cum Deo commune habere, adeoque, neque ejus existentiam ponere, neque tollere posset."

[3] "Ex. gr. rationem, cur circulus quadratus non existat, ipsa ejus natura indicat; . . . Cur autem contra substantia existat, ex sola etiam ejus natura sequitur."

[4] "At ratio, cur circulus vel triangulus existit, vel cur non existit, ex eorum natura non sequitur, sed ex ordine universae naturae corporeae; ex eo enim sequi debet, vel jam triangulum necessario existere, vel impossibile esse, ut jam existat."

proceed to show, served Spinoza as a pattern for his second proof. This mediaeval proof is one of the several forms of what is known as the cosmological proof. Spinoza, as we shall see, has changed it into an ontological proof.

In order to recreate the complete setting of this second proof of Spinoza, it is necessary for us to trace the development of the cosmological proof out of which it has arisen.[1] The cosmological proof is based upon the principle of causality, reasoning from effect to cause, which, when expressed in its most general terms, asserts that every form of coming into being or change requires a cause. The principle of causality alone, however, was not considered sufficient to be used as a proof for the existence of God. It had to be supplemented by some other principle. In Plato[2] that supplementary principle was the creation of the world. The cosmological proof as used by him may therefore be reduced to the following syllogism:

Everything that comes into existence must have a cause.

The world came into existence.

Therefore, the world must have a cause.

This form of the cosmological proof was also used by the Moslem Mutakallimun and their Jewish followers, among whom it was known as the proof from creation, though its identity with the Platonic proof from efficient causation was not always recognized.[3] With the denial of a created universe by Aristotle the cosmological proof assumed a new form. The principle of causality was still retained, but the theory of creation was replaced by the theory of the impos-

---

[1] Cf. my "Notes on Proofs of the Existence of God in Jewish Philosophy" in *The Hebrew Union College Annual*, I (1924), pp. 584 ff.

[2] *Timaeus* 28 A.

[3] See my "Notes on the Proofs of the Existence of God in Jewish Philosophy," *op. cit.*, p. 584, n. 44.

sibility of an infinite regress. In Aristotle two versions of this
type of the cosmological proof occur, one couched in terms
of motion and the other in terms of potentiality and actuality.
Assuming the world to be a process of motion or a process of
the actualization of the potential, and assuming also that
both these processes require a cause and that there can be
no infinite series of causes of any kind, the two forms of the
proof run as follows:

A

Every series of things moved and moving must have
an unmoved mover.
The world is a series of things moved and moving.
Therefore, the world must have an unmoved mover.

B

Every series of transitions from potentiality into actuality must have a cause which is pure actuality.
The world is a series of transitions from potentiality
into actuality.
Therefore, the world must have a cause which is pure
actuality.

The first of these versions is given by Aristotle in the
Eighth Book of the *Physics*, the second in the *Metaphysics*.[1]

To these two Aristotelian versions of the cosmological proof
Avicenna, and before him Alfarabi, added a third version
couched in terms of possibility and necessity. This new version was introduced by them because they considered it to
be more general and more universally applicable than the
others. It will be noticed that this new version does not
essentially differ from the other two, for motion, potentiality,
and possibility are only different ways in which the principle
of causality is expressed and are in a sense interchangeable

[1] *Metaphysics*, IX, 8, 1049b, 24 f., and XII, 7, 1072b, 3 f.

terms. In Greek the same term, δύναμις, means both potentiality and possibility, and Aristotle defines motion as the
actuality of that which is potential so far as it is potential [1]
and also as the actuality of that which is movable so far as
it is movable.[2] Maimonides, who besides the two Aristotelian
versions of the proof uses also the Avicennian version, introduces the latter by the following remark: "This is taken
from the words of Aristotle, though he gives it in a different
form." [3]   From Maimonides it was taken over by Thomas
Aquinas, who makes use of it as the third of his five proofs
of the existence of God.[4]   From him it was passed on into
modern philosophy, so that Kant uses the Avicennian version as his model cosmological proof. We shall endeavor to
show that this is also the basis of Spinoza's second proof.

The Avicennian version as reproduced by Maimonides —
for it was Maimonides from whom Spinoza most likely drew
his knowledge of it — is divided into two parts. In the first
part, it tries to establish the fact that in the universe among
all the things that actually exist there must be one which has
eternal existence, inasmuch as it is impossible either that all
things should be eternal or that all things should be transient.
In the second part, drawing upon the distinction between
necessary and possible (and also impossible) existence, it
tries to prove that the eternal being must have necessary
existence, that is to say, it must be independent of any cause,
or, as Spinoza would say, it must be *causa sui*. The proof
for this is based, again, as in Aristotle's versions, upon the
impossibility of an infinite regress. Reduced to its syllogistic
form, Avicenna's version of the proof runs as follows:

[1] *Physics*, III, 1, 201a, 10–11.
[2] *Physics*, III, 2, 202a, 7–8.
[3] *Moreh Nebukim*, II, 1.
[4] *Summa Theologica*, Pars I, Quaest. 2, Art. 3. Cf. *Contra Gentiles*, Lib. I, Cap. 13.

> Every series of transitions from possible existence
> into necessary existence must have a cause which
> has necessary existence.
>
> The world is a series of transitions from possible exist-
> ence into necessary existence.
>
> Therefore, the world must have a cause which has
> necessary existence.

A modification of the Avicennian proof was introduced
by Crescas.[1] Crescas denies the impossibility of an infinite
series of causes and effects and thereby removes one of the
premises of the Aristotelian proofs of the existence of God
in all of its forms. But still he retains the principle of
causality, maintaining that everything possible, i.e., everything which by its own nature may or may not exist, must
have a cause to give preference to existence over non-existence. That cause must itself be uncaused, that is, it must
have necessary existence. Once such a cause is given, argues
Crescas, it may have an infinite number of effects arranged
in a causal series, for infinity is not impossible.[2] How Crescas
conceived of this possibility does not concern us here.[3] Suffice
it to say that on the mere principle of causation, namely,
that any series of causes and effects, whether infinite or
finite, must have a first uncaused cause, Crescas establishes
a new cosmological proof for the existence of God. The
characteristic feature of this proof, in contradistinction to
the Aristotelian and the Avicennian, as will have been
noticed, is the elimination of the principle of the impossibility of an infinite series of causes and effects. But still like
the older Aristotelian proofs it retains the principle of causality, which principle is couched, as in Avicenna's proof, in
terms of possibility and necessity. Truly considered, Crescas'

---

[1] Or Adonai, I, iii, 2.   [2] Or Adonai, I, ii, 3.
[3] Cf. my Crescas' Critique of Aristotle, pp. 67–69, 490–497.

new proof is simply a restoration of the Platonic proof from
efficient causation or of the proof from creation as used by
Moslem and Jewish theologians, the only difference between
them being that whereas the older proof starts with the conception of a universe created in time Crescas' proof starts
with the conception of a universe which is only possible by
its own nature. Reduced to its syllogistic formula, Crescas'
proof runs as follows:

> Every series of possible beings must have a cause
> which is necessary being.
> The world is a series of possible beings.
> Therefore, the world must have a cause which is
> necessary being.

It is this proof of Crescas that Spinoza quotes, or rather
paraphrases, in a letter to Meyer (Epistola XII) at the end of
his lengthy refutation of the ancient arguments against
infinity: "But here I should like it to be noted in passing
that the more recent Peripatetics, as I at least think, misunderstood the argument of the Ancients by which they
strove to prove the existence of God. For, as I find it in the
works of a certain Jew, named Rab Ghasdai,[1] it reads as follows. If there is an infinite regression of causes, then all
things which exist will be things that have been caused.
But it cannot pertain to anything that has been caused that
it should necessarily exist in virtue of its own nature. Therefore there is in nature nothing to whose essence it pertains
that it should exist necessarily. But this is absurd: and there
therefore also that.[2] Therefore the force of the argument lies
not in the idea that it is impossible for the infinite actually to

---

[1] On this form of transliteration of Crescas' first name, see below, p. 295, n. 1.

[2] The original passage in the *Or Adonai*, I, iii, 2, reads as follows: "Whether
causes and effects are finite or infinite, there is no escape from the conclusion that
there must be something which is the cause of all of them as a whole, for if there
were nothing but effects, those effects would have only possible existence *per se* and

exist, or that a regression of causes to infinity is impossible, but only in the impossibility of supposing that things which do not exist necessarily in virtue of their own nature, are not determined to existence by something which does exist necessarily in virtue of its own nature, and which is a cause, not an effect."

It is evident that Spinoza understood well the portent and significance of Crescas' proof. He only seems to be mistaken in its historical background when he describes it as a restoration of the original argument of the "ancients" (presumably Aristotle and his followers) which was corrupted by the misunderstanding of the "more recent Peripatetics" (presumably the scholastics). Quite the contrary, Crescas' argument is in direct opposition to the argument of those "ancients," though it may be considered, as we have pointed out, as a restoration of an argument still more ancient, namely, that of Plato.

We are now going to show how this cosmological proof of Avicenna couched in terms of possibility and necessity and as modified by Crescas by the elimination of the principle of the impossibility of an infinite series of causes and effects was taken up by Spinoza and remodelled into an ontological proof.

Just as Avicenna begins his proof with a classification of being, so Spinoza begins his proof with a classification of our ideas of being. Real beings, says Avicenna, fall, in the main, into two classes. There is one being, and one only, whose existence is necessary by his very nature; all others owe their existence to some external cause; in themselves they are only possible; but if the cause of their existence is present they

would thus need something to cause the preponderance of their existence over their non-existence. But that which would bring about this preponderance of their existence would be the cause of those effects, and that is what is meant by God."

are called necessary with reference to their cause, and if that cause is removed they become thereby impossible. Similarly Spinoza classifies our ideas of being with reference to their reality or existence as that which is necessary by its own nature and those which by their own nature are only possible, but become necessary by virtue of some cause from which they follow by necessity, or become impossible when that cause is absent. To this class belong our ideas of all beings which require a cause. Only one new class is introduced here by Spinoza, that which is impossible by its own nature, which is contrasted both with that which is necessary by its own nature and with that which is possible by its own nature. But this class, too, was not unknown to mediaeval Jewish philosophers, though Spinoza's immediate source may have been Descartes.[1] As an illustration of an idea whose existence is necessary by its own nature Spinoza cites substance or God. A square circle is his example of an idea whose existence is impossible by its own nature [2] — it is only a "verbal being," as he says elsewhere. The existence of a circle or a triangle is taken by him as a typical illustration of an idea which in itself has only possible existence and becomes either necessary or impossible according as the cause is present or absent.

Thus far Spinoza has been closely following Avicenna. But when on the basis of this classification of our ideas of

[1] Anything whose nature involves a self-contradiction is called impossible by its own nature and according to Jewish philosophers cannot be made possible even by God in the ordinary course of nature. Cf. Maimonides, *Moreh Nebukim*, I, 75, First and Fifth Arguments, and Descartes, *Meditationes*, VI (*Oeuvres*, VII, p. 71, ll. 18–20).

[2] Spinoza does not mention here the illustration of a chimera. Were it not for his note in *Cogitata Metaphysica*, I, 1, that "by chimera is understood a being which by nature involves a contradiction," one would be tempted to say that its impossibility is due only to the lack of proper causation and not to a self-contradiction in its nature.

being he attempts to construct a proof for the existence of God he leaves Avicenna behind. To begin with, like Crescas, he eliminates the impossibility of an infinite series of causes. But then he leaves Crescas, too. For Crescas still reasons cosmologically and *a posteriori*, from effect to cause, from the existence of things possible to the existence of a thing necessary. But Spinoza starts with an immediately perceived idea of a being whose existence is necessary by its own nature, the clearness and distinctness of which idea is in itself proof for its reality, and tries to resolve this immediately perceived truth into an analytical syllogism, which, as we have seen, is the main function of the ontological proof. The passage from the major premise to the conclusion is achieved, as in his first proof and as in Anselm's proof, by showing the absurdity of the contrary. Thus the Avicennian cosmological proof as modified by Crescas is transformed by Spinoza into an ontological proof after the manner of Descartes. Reduced to its syllogistic formula, Spinoza's second proof runs as follows:

> If we have a clear and distinct idea of God as a being whose existence is necessary by His own nature, then God is immediately perceived by us to exist.
>
> But we have a clear and distinct idea of God as a being whose existence is necessary by His own nature.
>
> Therefore, God is immediately perceived by us to exist.

The basis of the ontological proof, as we have seen, is our valid immediate perception of God's existence. This form of the proof merely shows how our valid immediate perception of God's existence is implied in our clear and distinct idea of God as a being whose existence is necessary by His own nature.

THIRD AND FOURTH PROOFS

It is almost an anti-climax to pass from that involved and complicated second proof of Spinoza to his third and fourth proofs which are based upon a single source, namely, Descartes' second proof in Meditation III. There is one phase, however, which is of interest, namely, Spinoza's endeavor to convert Descartes' proof from a cosmological argument, as it is reproduced by him in his third proof, to an ontological argument, as he gives it in his fourth proof. We have already seen how Spinoza has done it with another cosmological argument in his second proof. Generally speaking, it may be said that whatever any one may attempt to prove of God demonstratively, *a posteriori*, can also be proved of him ontologically, *a priori*, if it is assumed that the thing to be proved forms our immediate and self-evidently true idea of God. Now, in his second proof in Meditation III, Descartes takes the attributes of creation, conservation, or power, just as in his ontological proof he takes the attribute of perfection and self-causality, and argues that creation, conservation, or power must imply existence no less than perfection and self-causality. But there is the following difference, as it is at first assumed by Descartes, between creation, conservation, or power, on the one hand, and perfection and self-causality, on the other. The latter two are immediately perceived as our very idea of God and hence they yield an ontological proof, but the former are not immediately perceived as our very idea of God; they are derived demonstratively, *a posteriori*, from His actions, and hence they yield a cosmological proof. But here Spinoza seems to argue that power, too, is immediately perceived as our idea of God, just as perfection and self-causality in the view of Descartes, and as greatness in the view of Anselm. Why not then construct an ontological proof on the attribute of power? This reasoning marks the relation between the third and the fourth proofs of Spinoza. In his third proof Spinoza reproduces Descartes' second proof of Meditation III in its original cosmological form. In his fourth proof he converts it into an ontological proof. The relation between the third and fourth proofs is clearly brought out in Spinoza's own introductory words to the fourth proof: "In this last demonstration I wished to prove the existence of God *a posteriori*, in order that the demonstration might be the more easily understood, and not because the existence of God does not follow *a priori* from the same grounds."

But to come to the proofs themselves. Perhaps by way of general introduction I may say what I intend to do in the next few paragraphs. I intend to show, in the first place, that Descartes' second proof in Meditation III is only a modification of the traditional proof from creation. In the second place, I intend to explain why Descartes describes this proof either (*a*) as a proof from man's existence or (*b*) as a proof from man's conservation. In the third place, I intend to explain how it happens that this proof is restated by Spinoza in his third proof as a proof from power.

Descartes' second proof in Meditation III is described by himself as a proof from the individual's consciousness of his own existence to the existence of God.[1] It is thus a cosmological proof, reasoning from effect to cause, and, truly speaking, it is only verbally different from the proof of creation which, as has already been mentioned, was made use of by Plato and by Moslem and Jewish theologians as well as by Christian theologians.[2] The only difference between the old proof from creation and Descartes' second proof is

---

[1] *Meditationes*, III (*Oeuvres*, VII, p. 48, ll. 1 f.).
[2] John of Damascus, *De Fide Orthodoxa*, I, 3, First Proof.

that the older proof argues from the existence of the world whereas Descartes argues from man's own existence or life.[1] But this change in the vocabulary of the proof, or rather this new additional vocabulary, is already to be found in the writings of early authors. St. Augustine, for instance, in reproducing the argument from creation, says: "And therefore, whether we consider the whole body of the world . . . or whether we consider all life . . . all can only be through Him who absolutely is."[2] Similarly, Maimonides, in arguing for the existence of an eternal being in the universe, says: "Consequently nothing whatever would exist [if all things were transient]; but as we see things existing and find ourselves in existence, we conclude . . . there must be an eternal being that is not subject to destruction."[3] An analogy between St. Augustine's contention that we have a consciousness of our own existence and a similar contention by Descartes in his discussion of the nature of the human mind has been pointed out by one of his objectors.[4]

These quotations are sufficient to show that the vocabulary used by Descartes in his second proof in Meditation III has grown out of the older proof from creation. But it can be further shown that there is a structural similarity between the old argument from creation and Descartes' argument from man's consciousness of his own existence. We have already shown in a previous chapter [5] how the argument for the creation of the world started with the tentative question

---

[1] Kuno Fischer designates Descartes' second proof as "anthropological." *Geschichte der neuern Philosophie*, I, 1 (3rd ed., Heidelberg, 1889), p. 308.

[2] *De Civitate Dei*, VIII, 6: "Ac per hoc sive universi mundi corpus . . . sive omnem vitam . . . nisi ab illo esse non posse, qui simpliciter est." This change in the vocabulary of the argument is sometimes described as a change from a cosmological form to a psychological. See C. Baeumker, *Vitelo*, pp. 320 ff.

[3] *Moreh Nebukim*, II, 1, Third Argument.

[4] *Objectiones Quartae* (*Oeuvres*, VII, p. 197, ll. 24 ff.).

[5] Cf. above, pp. 98 ff.

whether the world came into being by itself or by some external cause. Similarly, Descartes' proof from man's consciousness of his own existence begins with the question, "From whom do I then derive my existence? Perhaps from myself or from my parents, or from some other source less perfect than God?" [1] He concludes naturally that it must be derived from God.

Allied with the argument from creation is the argument from the divine government or conservation of the world.[2] This argument, instead of reasoning from the single and completed act of creation, reasons from divine providence, that is to say, from God's guidance and governance and conservation of the world. "Conservation" is a mediaeval term for the continuation of existence after the world was created,[3] and it is considered as direct an effect of God's causality as the act of creation itself.[4] This argument from divine government or conservation of the world is another form of cosmological reasoning, and it was considered as somewhat superior to the argument from creation, for it can be used even if the world is supposed to be eternal, inasmuch as God can be conceived as the governor of the world and the cause of its conservation without the world necessarily hav-

---

[1] *Meditationes*, III (*Oeuvres*, VII, p. 167, ll. 3 ff.).

[2] John of Damascus, *De Fide Orthodoxa*, I, 3, Second Proof: "Secunda ex earum conservatione et gubernatione. — Porro ipsa quoque rerum creatarum compages, conservatio, atque gubernatio, nos docent Deum esse, qui universum hoc coagmentarit, sustentet, et conservet, eique provideat." In John of Damascus this proof from conservation and government is distinguished from the proof of design as well as from the proof of creation. Cf. *Contra Gentiles*, Lib. I, Cap. 13, end.

[3] *Contra Gentiles*, Lib. III, Cap. 65: "Conservatio rei non est nisi continuatio esse ipsius."

[4] See *Moreh Nebukim*, I, 69: "Here I wish to show that God is the cause of every event that takes place in the world, just as He is the creator of the whole universe as it now exists." Again: "God, however, is himself the form of the universe, as we have already shown, and it is He who causes its continuance and permanency." Cf. *Ethics*, I, Prop. 24, Corol.; Epistola 18 (*Opera*, IV, p. 82, ll. 24 ff. and 4 ff.); Epistola 20 (p. 98, ll. 15 ff. and 33 ff.); *Meditationes*, III (*Oeuvres*, VII, p. 49, ll. 5 f.).

ing come into existence in time.[1] Thus we find that Descartes proposes a change in the form of his proof from man's existence or creation by transforming it into a proof from conservation, declaring that, even if we assume that we have always existed and need no author of our existence, we still need an author of our conservation.[2] It might therefore be said that Descartes' argument from man's existence corresponds to the argument from creation and his argument from man's conservation corresponds to the argument from divine government. Spinoza, in his *Principia Philosophiae Cartesianae*, I, Proposition VII, explicitly rejects the argument from existence and retains only the argument from conservation. Here in *Ethics*, I, Proposition XI, Third Proof, however, in summarizing Descartes' second proof in Meditation III, he continues to use the term "existence," which would seem to be a return to the "existence" form of Descartes' proof. But "existence" may mean both to "come into existence" and to "continue to exist." In this proof in the *Ethics* it may therefore be taken in the latter sense.

From the act of creation it is deduced, in mediaeval philosophy, that God possesses the attribute of power, or that He is omnipotent.[3] Though wisdom and will may enter into the act of creation, still it is said that it is through "power" that God creates.[4] It is for this reason that Descartes speaks of the "power" to create or to conserve, and Spinoza still

[1] The compatibility of the belief in the existence of God with the belief in the eternity of the universe is assumed by Maimonides. See *Moreh Nebukim*, I, 76, Sixth Argument: "But he seems to forget that we are at issue with those who, whilst they believe in the existence of God, admit at the same time the eternity of the universe."

[2] *Meditationes*, III (*Oeuvres*, VII, p. 49, ll. 12 ff.).

[3] *Emunot we-De'ot*, II, 4; *Cuzari*, V, 18, 7–9.

[4] *Ibid.* Cf. Thomas Aquinas, *Summa Theologica*, Pars I, Quaest. 9, Art. 2: "Omnes enim creaturae, antequam essent, non erant possibiles esse . . . sed per solam potentiam divinam, in quantum Deus poterat eas in esse producere."

more explicitly says: "*posse existere potentia est*" (*Ethics*, I, Proposition XI, Third Proof), and he also speaks of "*potentia conservandi*" (*Prin. Phil. Cart.*, I, Prop. VII, Lemma II). Descartes' second argument may therefore be referred to, as indeed Spinoza does seem to refer to it, as the argument from power, and it may be considered as one of the variations of the mediaeval arguments from creation or divine government.

Reduced to its syllogistic formula, Descartes' second argument in Meditation III as restated by Spinoza in his third proof may be given as follows:

> Everything that continues in its existence must have a cause.
>
> We and the world continue in our existence.
>
> Therefore, we and the world must have a cause.

This syllogistic form is clearly brought out in Spinoza's *Principia*. In the *Ethics* it is somewhat obscured, owing to Spinoza's predilection for indirect proof of the *reductio ad absurdum* type of argument. But it can be easily brought into accord with the argument employed in the *Principia*. It is an *a posteriori*, cosmological argument, pure and simple, only verbally different from the arguments from creation or government.

The proof in the form in which it is given in the *Ethics* may be fully unfolded as follows:

We have the idea of the existence of ourselves as finite beings and we also have the idea of the existence of God as an infinite being.

There are three possibilities as to the truth of these ideas. First, they are both false, and therefore "nothing exists." [1] Second, only the idea of our own existence is true, and

---

[1] "Ergo vel nihil existit."

therefore, "there is nothing which necessarily exists excepting things finite." [1]

Third, both ideas are true, and therefore a "being absolutely infinite also necessarily exists." [2]

The first of these possibilities is to be rejected, for "we ourselves exist." [3]

The second possibility is to be rejected, for "if, therefore, there is nothing which necessarily exists excepting things finite, it follows that things finite are more powerful than the absolutely infinite being, and this (as is self-evident) is absurd." [4] The force of this argument is to be understood in the light of Descartes' argument against our being ourselves the authors of our existence. Descartes' argument originally is that if we were ourselves the authors of our existence we should have endowed ourselves with every perfection of which we possessed any idea and which we include in our idea of God. Spinoza presents here the same argument in the form of a *reductio ad absurdum*. He proceeds as follows: If we exist and God does not exist, then we must exist "in ourselves," [5] that is to say, we must be the authors of our own existence. Therefore, the idea we have of our own existence is more powerful than the idea we have of God's existence, inasmuch as "inability to exist is impotence, and, on the other hand, ability to exist is power." [6] But we have set out with the assumption that we have an idea of God as as infinite being and of ourselves as finite beings. Hence, a self-contradiction.

[1] "Si itaque id, quod jam necessario existit, non nisi entia finita sunt."
[2] "Vel Ens absolute infinitum necessario etiam existit."
[3] "Atqui nos . . . existimus."
[4] "Si itaque id, quod jam necessario existit, non nisi entia finita sunt, sunt ergo entia finita potentiora Ente absolute infinito: atque hoc (*ut per se notum*) absurdum est."
[5] "Atqui nos, vel in nobis, vel in alio, quod necessario existit, existimus."
[6] "Posse non existere impotentia est, et contra posse existere potentia est."

Consequently, the third possibility must be true, and "therefore the being absolutely infinite, that is to say, God, necessarily exists." [1]

So much for Spinoza's third proof. We shall turn now to his fourth proof.

Suppose we say that our clear and distinct idea of God is that of a being of the highest power, i.e., of the highest power to create or to conserve, just as Anselm said that it is the idea of the greatest being and as Descartes himself said that it is the idea of the most perfect being or of a self-caused being. We should then be able to frame an ontological proof from the idea of God as the cause of existence or conservation. Descartes himself has already performed this conversion of his second proof into an ontological proof from "power" in the following passage in his *Primae Responsiones:* [2] "Further, because we cannot think of God's existence as being possible, without at the same time, and by taking heed of His immeasurable power, acknowledging that He can exist by His own might, we hence conclude that He really exists and has existed from all eternity; for the light of nature makes it most plain that what can exist by its own power always exists. And thus we shall understand that necessary existence is comprised in the idea of a being of the highest power, not by any intellectual fiction, but because it belongs to the true and immutable nature of that being to exist." Descartes thus has three forms of the ontological proof:

1. From the idea of a most perfect being.
2. From the idea of a self-caused being.
3. From the idea of a most powerful being.

What Spinoza is really trying to do in his fourth proof is

---

[1] "Ergo ens absolute infinitum, hoc est (*per Defin. 6.*) Deum, necessario existit."
[2] *Oeuvres*, VII, p. 119, ll. 11 ff.

simply to reproduce the third form of Descartes' ontological proof.

Reduced to a syllogism, Spinoza's fourth proof runs as follows:

> If we have a clear and distinct idea of God as a being of the highest power, then God is immediately perceived by us to exist.
>
> But we have a clear and distinct idea of God as a being of the highest power.
>
> Therefore, God is immediately perceived by us to exist.

Here, again, the proof merely shows how our valid immediate perception of God's existence is implied in our clear and distinct idea of God as a being of the highest power. The basis of the ontological proof, as we have said, is this valid immediate perception of God's existence.

There remains now only the last part of the Scholium of Proposition XI to be explained, the part which contains a provisional objection quoted in the name of "many persons" against "this demonstration." In order to simplify the discussion of this part of the Scholium, we shall preface it by a few general remarks.

First, the demonstration of which Spinoza says here that its force may not be easily grasped by many persons refers to the third proof and not to the fourth proof given at the beginning of the Scholium. It will have been noticed that the fourth proof is not given by Spinoza as an independent proof but as a Scholium to the third proof. And so when he says in that Scholium that "many persons, nevertheless, will perhaps not be able easily to see the force of this demonstration," the reference is to the third proof.

Second, the provisional objection raised in the Scholium is to be read in the light of Spinoza's discussion in his Scholium to Proposition VII in *Principia Philosophiae Cartesianae*, I.

Third, the answer to this provisional objection is to be read in the light of Spinoza's Demonstration of Lemma I of the same Proposition in his *Principia*.

In the Scholium to Proposition VII in the *Principia*, Spinoza discusses Descartes' distinction between "difficult" (*difficile*) and "easy" (*facile*) creation or conservation. He interprets these terms as referring to the production of "more perfect" (*perfectius*) and "less perfect" (*imperfectius*) things respectively. In this Scholium to Proposition XI here in the *Ethics* Spinoza reproduces the same distinction, explaining the expression "more difficult to produce" (*factu difficiliores*) as referring to that "to which they conceive more attributes pertain." By the same token we may say that "easy" production is the production of that to which they perceive less attributes pertain. We may thus further conclude that by his distinction between "more difficult" and "easy" production here Spinoza again means, as in the *Principia*, the distinction between the production of the "more perfect" and the production of the "less perfect."

With this distinction in view, says Spinoza, "many persons" will try to refute the third proof. The third proof, it will be recalled, starts with the hypothesis that we have two ideas, one of God as an infinite being and another of man as a finite being, and proceeds to argue that if man exists and God does not exist it will be contrary to the hypothesis. But these "many persons" will say, contends Spinoza, that the distinction between God and man as infinite and finite means a distinction between infinite perfection and finite perfection or between having an infinite number and a finite number of properties. But it has just been said that the difference between the "more perfect" and the "less perfect" corresponds respectively to the difference between "difficult" existence or production and "easy" existence or production. Accordingly, the existence denied of God and the existence affirmed of man are of two different kinds entirely, one being infinitely "difficult" existence and the other being "easy" existence. To deny therefore infinitely difficult existence of God while affirming easy existence of man does not imply a contradiction of our idea of God as an infinite or most perfect being. Quite the contrary, it is because we conceive of God as an infinite and most perfect being that His existence becomes infinitely difficult, and hence He does not exist, whereas man, being conceived as finite and imperfect, thereby has existence which is easy, and hence he does exist. Spinoza could have put into the mouth of these "many persons" the following illustration. Suppose we have two ideas, one of our possessing a million dollars and the other of our possessing one dollar. The first idea is more perfect than the second, inasmuch as more attributes or properties pertain to it. But because the idea of having a million dollars is more perfect their existence is more difficult and consequently they do not exist in our pocket, whereas the idea of having one dollar is less perfect; therefore its existence is easy and it does exist in our pocket.

To this provisional objection tentatively raised in the name of "many persons" Spinoza answers by recalling his old distinction between things "which are produced by external causes" [1] and things "which can be produced by no external cause." Of the former, he argues, it is indeed true to say that the greater the perfection the more difficult its existence and the smaller the perfection the easier the existence. Hence the idea of a million dollars has less possibility of existence than that of one dollar, for the perfection

---

[1] *Ethics*, I, Prop. 11, Schol. Cf. *Principia Philosophiae Cartesianae*, I, Prop. 7, Lemma I, Nota I.

as well as the existence of a million dollars is not intrinsic. The perfections of beings dependent upon external causes are themselves external perfections, and the more of them there are the more dependent the existence of the beings becomes upon external causes. "For whatever perfection or reality those things may have which are produced by external causes, whether they consist of many parts or of few, they owe it all to the virtue of an external cause, and therefore their existence springs from the perfection of an external cause alone and not from their own." [1] But if you have an idea of anything with a set of internal perfections, growing out of its own nature, then the possibility of its existence increases in proportion to the number of perfections, so that if we get an idea of an infinitely perfect being its existence becomes absolutely necessary. "In an idea or concept of everything, existence either as possible or as necessary is contained." [2] "For, as we cannot affirm existence of nothing, as we detract from the perfection of a concept and conceive its content to approach zero as its limit, so much do we detract from its possible existence. If we conceive this degree of perfection to be infinitely diminished, even to zero, it will contain no existence, or but an absolutely impossible one. On the other hand, if we increase this degree of perfection to infinity we conceive that it has the highest possible existence and so to be absolutely necessary." [3] This kind of internal perfection which grows out of the nature of things, as distinguished from external "marks of perfection which men from ignorance and tradition are accustomed to esteem as such," [4] is to be understood only as "so much reality or being." [5] God, therefore, who is conceived as having an infinite number of perfections growing out of His own nature,

---

[1] *Ethics*, I, Prop. 11, Schol.
[2] *Principia Philosophiae Cartesianae*, I, Axiom 6. Cf. Prop. 7, Lemma I, Demonst.
[3] *Ibid.*, Prop. 7, Lemma I, Demonst.
[4] *Ibid.*, Prop. 7, Lemma I, Nota 2.   [5] *Ibid.*

has the most reality and being.[1] You cannot argue, as would those "many persons," that because God is infinitely perfect His existence is infinitely difficult, and hence He does not exist. Only external perfections may be said to increase the difficulty of existence; internal perfections, on the contrary, increase the possibility of existence. Such internal "perfection consequently does not prevent the existence of a thing, but establishes it; imperfection, on the other hand, prevents existence, and so of no existence can we be more sure than of the existence of the Being absolutely infinite or perfect, that is to say, God." [2]

To sum up our main conclusions: Historically there were two kinds of proofs for the existence of God, based upon two kinds of knowledge, indirect and direct. The indirect kind of knowledge gave us the various cosmological and teleological proofs. The direct kind of knowledge gave us the proofs based upon revelation, the innateness of the idea of God, and universal assent. The ontological proof as stated by Anselm, Descartes, and Spinoza is not an independent proof. It is only a different way of formulating the old proofs based upon direct knowledge. In Anselm, it is a modified form of the argument from universal assent. In Descartes and Spinoza it is a modified form of the argument from the innateness of the idea of God.

Of the four proofs for the existence of God given by Spinoza in the *Ethics*, the *first* and *third* correspond respectively to Descartes' ontological proof in Meditation V and his cosmological proof in the second proof of Meditation III. Descartes' first proof in Meditation III is not reproduced by Spinoza in the *Ethics*, but is reproduced by him in the *Short Treatise* and in his *Principia Philosophiae Cartesianae*, and is referred to in his correspondence and in *De Intellectus*

[1] Cf. *Ethics*, I, Prop. 9.   [2] *Ethics*, I, Prop. 11, Schol.

Emendatione Tractatus. Spinoza's *second* proof in the *Ethics* is a modification of Descartes' ontological proof in Meditation V, enriched by elements borrowed from a cosmological proof in Hebrew philosophic sources. Spinoza's *fourth* proof in the *Ethics* is the conversion of his *third* proof, which is cosmological, into ontological form, which conversion was also made by Descartes himself.

The idea of God which is assumed in the ontological proof to imply existence is differently phrased in the different forms of the proof. In Anselm, it is the idea of the greatest being. In Descartes, it is the idea of the most perfect being, or of a self-caused being, or of the most powerful being. Spinoza's three ontological proofs — the *first*, *second*, and *fourth* proofs in the *Ethics* — make use of three descriptions which may be reduced to two. In the *first* proof, the idea of God is that of a being whose essence involves existence. In the *second* proof, it is that of a being whose existence is necessary *per se*. These two can be reduced to what Descartes described as a self-caused being. In the *fourth* proof, it is the idea of a being who is most powerful. This difference in terminology, however, is only verbal. Any other term, such, for instance, as the most real being (*ens realissimum*), can be used, if it is assumed to be that which is immediately perceived of God, without introducing anything new in the ontological proof. The recurrent claims for the discovery of new ontological proofs for the existence of God which we meet in philosophic literature generally prove, upon analysis, to be nothing but the substitution of some new terms for such older terms as the greatest, the most perfect, the self-caused, and the most powerful. Oftentimes, these so-called newly discovered ontological proofs are not even ontological, but rather disguised cosmological proofs.

CHAPTER VII

EXTENSION AND THOUGHT

I. The Framework of Spinoza's Universe

In our analysis of the *Ethics* so far we have found that of the first thirteen propositions twelve deal with the traditional problem of the nature of God, which we have discussed in the chapters on the definition, unity, and simplicity of substance, and one proposition deals with the proofs of the existence of God. The remaining propositions of the First Part of the *Ethics* similarly deal with a problem which in traditional philosophy would go under the title of the relation of God to the world. Spinoza starts out in Proposition XIV with a recapitulation of his denial, both in *Short Treatise*, I, 2, and in Propositions II–VI in the First Part of the *Ethics*, of the fundamental belief of all mediaeval philosophers that between God and the world there is a distinction of pure form and matter, the two constituting, as it were, two substances. "Besides God," he therefore maintains, "no substance can be nor can be conceived" (Prop. XIV). His demonstration of this proposition is again a summary of what he has already said in the *Short Treatise*, I, 2, and in Propositions II–VI, namely, if the world were of a nature absolutely distinct from that of God, all the difficulties which the mediaevals themselves had pointed out against the assumption of the existence of two deities [1] or against the assumption of the emanation of a material world out of an immaterial cause by the ordinary process of necessary causality [2] would recur and would be unanswerable (Dem-

[1] Cf. above, p. 83.   [2] Cf. above, p. 88.

onst.). He thus concludes that there cannot be anything in the nature of the universe, including matter, which is not in God himself, who according to all traditional opinions is the sole cause of the universe. "Hence it follows with the greatest clearness, firstly, that God is one, that is to say (Def. VI), in nature there is but one substance" (Corol. I). But this one substance or God, again according to all traditional opinions,[1] "is absolutely infinite" (*ibid.*), and therefore cannot be fully known by the finite intellect.[2] It is only the infinite intellect (*infinitus intellectus*),[3] i.e., the infinite intellect of God (*infinitus Dei intellectus*),[4] that can perceive everything which pertains to this one substance, that is to say, its infinite attributes. The finite "human mind can only get to know those things which the idea of an actually existing body involves, or what can be inferred from this idea."[5] But inasmuch as "this idea of the body neither involves nor expresses any other attributes of God than extension and thought,"[6] it follows that the human mind knows God "in so far only as He is considered under the attribute of extension"[7] and "under the attribute of thought, and not in so far as He is considered under any other attribute."[8] And so, just as his discussion of the impossibility of two substances in the *Short Treatise* culminates in the statement "that we posit extension as an attribute of God,"[9] so also here Spinoza concludes with the statement that "it follows, secondly, that the thing extended and the thing thinking are either attributes of God or affections of the attributes of God" (Corol. II).

---

[1] Cf. above, p. 117.　　　　　　　　[2] Cf. above, p. 142.
[3] *Ethics*, II, Prop. 7, Schol. (*Opera*, II, p. 90, l. 4).
[4] Epistola 66 (*Opera*, IV, p. 280, ll. 8–9).
[5] Epistola 64 (*Opera*, IV, p. 277, ll. 10–13).
[6] *Ibid.* (ll. 18–19).　　　　　　　　[7] *Ibid.* (ll. 23–24).
[8] *Ibid.* (ll. 28–29).　　　　　　　　[9] *Short Treatise*, I, 2, § 18.

The last expression, "or affections of the attributes of God," is a reference to the modal system of extension and thought, which Spinoza describes most fully and clearly in the *Short Treatise* [1] and his correspondence with Schuller.[2] The full scheme of Spinoza's system of extension and thought may be pieced together from these two main sources. In its bare outline it is as follows: There is, to begin with, substance or God with infinite attributes. Of these only two attributes are known to us, extension and thought. From these attributes there follows a series of modes, to wit, (1) immediate infinite modes, (2) a mediate infinite mode, and (3) finite modes. Of extension, the immediate infinite mode is motion-and-rest; of thought, the immediate infinite mode is the absolutely infinite intellect (*intellectus absolute infinitus*). Only one mediate infinite mode is specifically named by Spinoza, and that is the face of the whole universe (*facies totius universi*). He does not make it clear, however, whether it is a mode of extension or of thought or of both. The finite modes are the particular things (*res particulares*). Substance and its attributes are called by Spinoza *natura naturans*, the entire modal system of extension and thought is called by him *natura naturata*, and within the latter he distinguishes between the two classes of infinite modes, which he calls "general," and the single class of finite modes, which he calls "particular."

As a skeleton framework to hold together and to unify the fragmentary pieces of the visible universe, this scheme of Spinoza is to be regarded as one of the stages, an advanced stage, to be sure, in the long development of similar schemes since man began to distinguish between the visible and the invisible and to discern behind phenomenal sporadic changes

[1] *Ibid.*, I, 8–9.
[2] Epistolae 63–64.

a certain unity and a certain causal connection. Any attempt to interpret this scheme of Spinoza as an adumbration of any specific theories of modern science is justifiable in the same sense as the Stoics were justified in transforming the gods and goddesses of Olympia into the natural forces and moral principles of their own philosophy, or as Philo and the mediaeval Jewish, Christian, and Moslem theologians were justified in investing the God and angels of the Bible with significances of their own philosophic principles. There is indeed a justification in all such attempts at allegorical methods of interpretation, whether applied to Homer, the Bible, or the works of Spinoza, but only in so far as they are confined to an effort to show that all these systems of myths, religion, and philosophy were inspired by a common striving to see the universe as a whole and to interpret it as a unit, and how in reaching out for the truth they almost attained it. But the allegorical method of interpretation becomes a perversion of truth when confused with the method of historical research. The first step in understanding any author is to find out what he means by what he says and how he came to say it in a certain particular manner. In Spinoza's skeleton framework of the universe, the terms used are those of traditional philosophy, and the concepts represented by these terms, as well as the connection between them, are likewise reminiscent of skeleton frameworks of the universe invented by his predecessors. We happen to know also that philosophers throughout the ages have come to whatever new views they have happened to arrive at as a result of criticism of older views and a modification of the views criticized by them. We have already seen how Spinoza's propositions in the *Ethics* so far can be best explained as a criticism and modification of his mediaeval philosophic background. We shall therefore try to show how the entire scheme of Spinoza's theory of extension and thought has grown out of a typical scheme held by mediaeval philosophers.

The mediaeval skeleton framework of the universe in its bare outline and without any discussion of its finer subtle points starts out, like that of Spinoza, with God who is infinite in His perfections; but unlike Spinoza's, it assumes God to be pure form, whose sole activity is thinking. The product of God's thinking is an Intelligence, which is likewise pure form and the activity of which is likewise thinking. But this Intelligence, owing to the dual aspect of its existence, being, on the one hand, necessary of existence, for it is the inevitable product of divine thinking, and, on the other hand, only possible of existence, for by its own nature and without a cause it could not have come into being, contains also a duality in its nature, the duality of necessity and possibility. Out of the necessary element in its nature there emanates another Intelligence, which is again pure form and the activity of which is again thinking; but out of its possible element there proceeds a sphere which is material and the activity of which is motion. As the astronomy of the Middle Ages posited a plurality of such concentric celestial spheres, the number of which varied according to different views but is generally spoken of as nine,[1] the process is repeated until we come to the last in the series of the concentric spheres, the so-called lunar sphere, and to the last in the series of the Intelligences, generally spoken of as the Tenth or Active Intelligence. This so-called Tenth Intelligence, like all the others, has in its nature the duality of possibility and necessity. Out of its possibility there arises the underlying general matter which is common to all the sublunar things and the nature of which is pure possibility and potentiality. Then by the motion of the spheres — their common circular

[1] Cf. *Moreh Nebukim*, II, 4.

motion as well as the particular variations in their common circular motion — this common underlying matter is predisposed for the assumption of the general as well as the particular forms by which the simple elements and the compound things are differentiated among themselves from each other. The forms themselves — from the primary forms of the four elements to souls and minds, which are also called forms — flow from the activity of the Tenth Intelligence,[1] which means that they ultimately flow from God.

Thus, according to this scheme, the entire universe is divided into matter and form. These two exist together in the physical part of the universe, but form exists apart from matter in the world of the Intelligences [2] and in God. While on the whole matter owes its existence to God as its ultimate cause, it does not come directly from God, inasmuch as God is pure form, and by a mediaeval principle, which may be formulated as *omne materiale e materiali*,[3] matter cannot arise from form. Matter arises somewhere in the process of emanation at a stage removed from God, and its origin is accounted for by what I have described elsewhere as "emergent emanation." [4]

In order to simplify the process of showing how Spinoza derived his own scheme from the mediaeval scheme, it is necessary for us to separate in the latter its essential from its non-essential elements. The essential element in the scheme is the main philosophic thesis that God is pure form and

---

[1] The most obvious sources from which Spinoza could have derived his knowledge of this mediaeval scheme are *Moreh Nebukim*, I, 72; II, 4; and Shem-Ṭob's commentary on *Moreh Nebukim*, II, 13.

[2] For a difference of opinion, however, with regard to the immateriality of the Intelligences, see below, p. 223.

[3] Cf. my paper, "The Problem of the Origin of Matter in Mediaeval Jewish Philosophy and Its Analogy to the Modern Problem of the Origin of Life," in *Proceedings of the Sixth International Congress of Philosophy*, p. 602.

[4] Cf. *ibid.*, pp. 603–604.

hence the material universe did not proceed from Him directly. The non-essential elements are the assumptions which happened to be part of the mediaeval scientific conception of the universe, namely, the theory of celestial spheres, the theory of the plurality of Intelligences, and the theory that the universe was finite in extent, being enclosed within an all-surrounding sphere. They were, however, not essential to the scheme itself. The non-essential character of these scientific assumptions in the mediaeval scheme is attested by the fact that in the history of philosophy, even before Spinoza, they had been eliminated or modified one by one without affecting the main philosophic thesis of the immateriality of God. The theory of the finite extent of the universe, which was an Aristotelian heritage in the history of philosophy, was attacked by Crescas [1] at the beginning of the fifteenth century, as it was again attacked by Bruno [2] about two centuries later, so that by the time of Spinoza the infinity of the universe was already treated as a philosophic commonplace. The theory of celestial spheres was eliminated from consideration in respectable scientific circles with the fall of the Ptolemaic astronomy in the sixteenth century, and even before that time two important features of that theory, namely, the difference between the matter and the motion of the celestial bodies and those of terrestrial bodies, had been disposed of by Crescas.[3] With the elimination of the celestial spheres there would necessarily have to follow the elimination of the plurality of the Intelligences, for the number of the Intelligences, according to the mediaeval view itself, was determined by the number of the spheres.[4] But still one Intelligence of pure form would have to remain

[1] Cf. my *Crescas' Critique of Aristotle*, pp. 115–117.
[2] Cf. *ibid.*, pp. 115, 118.   [3] Cf. *ibid.*, pp. 118–120.
[4] Cf. *Moreh Nebukim*, II, 4.

for as long as the main thesis of God as pure form remained and for as long as the origin of the material world was explained not as an act of special creation out of nothing but as a process of emanation out of the substance of God. Thus the mediaeval scheme, stripped of its non-essential accessories and modified to fit the new scientific conceptions of the universe, must have presented itself to the mind of Spinoza as follows: There is God, a pure form, whose sole activity is thinking. The product of God's thought is an Intelligence, which is also pure form, but in the nature of which there is a duality of necessity and possibility. Out of this Intelligence emanates the physical universe, its matter out of the possibility of the Intelligence's nature, and its form, motion, and thought out of the necessity of the Intelligence's nature.

It is this main thesis, which on the whole had survived all the changing conceptions of the universe up to the time of Spinoza and from which the intermediary Intelligence was eliminated only whenever emanation gave place, as, for instance, in the case of Descartes, to a special act of creation out of nothing, that Spinoza constantly and repeatedly makes the subject of a frontal attack.[1] He does not dwell on the absurdity of the mediaeval theories of celestial spheres or on the plurality of Intelligences, for these were already dead issues in his own time and were not essential, as we have seen, to the main thesis. He does indeed discuss the problem of infinity, but not especially with reference to the infinite extent of the universe, but with reference to certain general aspects of the problem which were still vital issues in his own time, and he does it only in a letter in which he answers a question addressed to him and in a scholium to a proposition in which he refutes some unnamed opponents.[2] The

[1] Cf. above, Chapter IV.   [2] Cf. below, Chapter VIII.

main thesis, however, is attacked by him directly. He shows
that if God is pure form, then the interposition of another
form between God and the universe will not remove the difficulty of how matter could arise from form by the ordinary
process of necessary causality.[1] As an escape from this difficulty he takes the bold step of making the material universe
proceed by necessity directly from God, with the inevitable
consequence that God himself becomes material, or, to use
his own terms, extension becomes an attribute of God. In
a letter to Oldenburg Spinoza seems to allude to this method
of reasoning leading to his conclusion with regard to extension when he says: "And, on the other hand, things which
they [the theologians], on account of their prejudices, regard
as created, I contend to be attributes of God, and as misunderstood by them."[2]

The conclusion arrived at by Spinoza that God was material is not new in the history of philosophy. The most
notable exponents of this view in European philosophy are
the Stoics, who may have perhaps arrived at their materialism, like Spinoza, as a result of a criticism of the Platonic
and Aristotelian dualism.[3] Though the Stoic view was not
unknown to mediaeval Jewish philosophers, for in a work
written in Arabic by an unknown Jewish or Moslem author
and preserved in a Hebrew translation it is quoted in the
name of Zeno, i.e., Zeno of Citium,[4] still none of them had
ever attempted to bridge the gulf between God and the
world by endowing God with materiality. Ibn Gabirol's
Fons Vitae, to be sure, is said to have given rise to such a

---

[1] Cf. above, p. 91.   [2] Epistola 6 (*Opera*, IV, p. 36, ll. 21–23).

[3] This explanation for the Stoic materialism has been suggested by Zeller, but
is rejected by him. Cf. Zeller, *Philosophie der Griechen*, III, 1 (4th edition),
pp. 125 ff. English translation: *Stoics, Epicureans and Sceptics*, pp. 127 ff.

[4] See David Kaufmann, *Die Spuren Al-Batlajûsi's in der jüdischen Religions-
Philosophie* (Budapest, 1880). Hebrew Text, p. 36, ll. 10 ff.

view in David of Dinant,[1] but this is far from being a true
representation of the real view of Ibn Gabirol. Ibn Gabirol
goes only so far as to assert, as do also Baḥya Ibn Pakuda [2]
and Judah ha-Levi,[3] that the distinction of matter and form
is also to be found in the Intelligences or angels, a view
which was taken over from him by Duns Scotus and his
followers and maintained by them against Thomas Aquinas. Leo Hebraeus refers to this view and ascribes it to
Plato.[4] God himself, even according to Ibn Gabirol, was
free of matter. Crescas, to be sure, comes near attributing
extension to God when, after defining space as extension
and assuming it to be infinite and the world to be in it, he
quotes in support of his view the old rabbinic dictum that
God is the place of the world.[5] Logically, if God is the place
of the world and the place of the world is extension, God
must have extension as one of His attributes. But Crescas
stops short of drawing this daring conclusion. God still continues to be to him pure form, and in the problem of creation, in order to bridge the gulf between the immaterial God
and the material world, he has to resort to the solution of
endowing God with will and purpose and design. It is said
that in Bruno there is an intimation that extension is one
of God's attributes,[6] but if this really represents Bruno's
reasoned-out view, then to say of Bruno, as does Pollock,

[1] Cf. Erdmann, *Grundriss der Geschichte der Philosophie*, §§ 192 and 188. But
according to Albertus Magnus, David of Dinant's view that God is "principium materiale omnium" was due to the influence of Alexander of Aphrodisias: "Alexander
etiam in quodam libello quem fecit de *Principio incorporeae et corporeae substantiae*,
quem secutus est quidam David de Dinanto in libro quem scripsit de *Tomis*, hoc
est, de divisionibus, dicit Deum esse principium materiale omnium" (*Summa Theo-
logiae*, Pars I, Tract. IV, Quaest. 20, Membrum 2, Quaestio Incidens).

[2] *Ḥobot ha-Lebabot*, I, 6.

[3] *Cuzari*, IV, 3. Cf. commentaries *Ḳol Yehudah* and *Oẓar Neḥmad* on V, 18, 6.

[4] *Dialoghi d'Amore*, III, p. 244 (Bari, 1929). Cf. p. 246, where Avicebron is
referred to.   [5] Cf. my *Crescas' Critique of Aristotle*, p. 123.

[6] Pollock, *Spinoza*, p. 104. Cf. *De la Causa*, III, p. 261, ll. 14–18 (ed. Lagarde).

that "he rejects the notion of formless matter" [1] is to put the
wrong emphasis on his view. What should have been said
is that he rejects the notion of matterless form. Clearer
than all these intimations as to an extended God is the statement made by Henry More in a letter to Descartes, which
reads: "God seems to be an extended thing." [2]

Spinoza, however, did not come to his view by merely
adopting the statements of the Stoics or of Bruno or of More,
or by merely carrying out to its logical conclusion the hint
thrown out by Crescas. He had been forced to it, as we have
shown in a previous chapter,[3] by the logic of the situation
and as a result of his thorough and critical examination of
the various mediaeval solutions of the problem of the rise
of matter out of an immaterial God. Finding all the solutions
of this difficulty under the theory of emanation unsatisfactory, and refusing to resort to the theory of creation *ex nihilo*
or to the theory of the co-existence of an eternal matter
alongside God, he was forced to the conclusion that God
was not immaterial.

II. Properties, Attributes, and Modes

We have thus seen how the main outline of Spinoza's
skeleton framework has developed out of the mediaeval
framework. We shall now try to show in a similar manner
the development of the individual parts within that framework — the infinity of God's attributes, the two known
attributes of extension and thought, and the modal system
under the two known attributes.

[1] *Ibid.*

[2] Descartes, *Correspondance*, DXXXI (*Oeuvres*, V, p. 238, l. 21): "Res enim
extensa Deus videtur esse." Cf. Dunin-Borkowski, *Der junge De Spinoza*, pp.
359 ff.

[3] Cf. above, Chapter IV.

The infinity of God's attributes is implied throughout the mediaeval discussions of the nature of God, especially in the oft-repeated statement that God is indescribable.[1] A close and almost verbal resemblance to Spinoza's statement as to the infinity of attributes is to be found in Crescas, who, in discussing a certain Talmudic passage in which the excessive enumeration of divine attributes is discouraged, explains it on the ground that such an enumeration "would appear as an attempt to limit that which is infinite in number."[2] His pupil Joseph Albo puts it still more directly when he says: "It must be understood that the perfections which exist in God are unlimited in number, that is to say, they are infinite with reference to their plurality."[3] The term "perfection" is used here by Albo as synonymous with "attribute." With these mediaeval thinkers, to whom God was immaterial and separate from the world and to whom the attributes were expressions of divine perfections, it was only logical that they should insist not only upon the infinite degree of perfection of each attribute but also upon the infinite number of attributes. For them to say that God possessed an infinite number of attributes meant nothing more than to say that God's powers and perfections were inexhaustible. But with the gradual disappearance of the separation of God and the world, if not their complete identification, in the Renaissance philosophy, as for instance in the philosophy of Bruno, and with the general acceptance in opposition to Aristotle of the belief in an infinite number of worlds, the ascription of infinite attributes to God naturally assumed a new meaning. To the minds of some people it must have conveyed the idea of the existence of an infinite number of independent worlds.

---

[1] Cf. *Moreh Nebukim*, I, 59.
[2] *Or Adonai*, I, iii, 3 (p. 24a).
[3] *'Ikkarim*, II, 25. Cf. above, p. 117.

Thus Schuller asks of Spinoza whether or not "there must be constituted as many worlds as there are attributes of God."[1] Spinoza tries to set him aright on this point. In his answer to Schuller,[2] where reference is made to the Scholium to Proposition VII, Part II, and in other places where the infinite attributes are discussed,[3] Spinoza makes it quite clear that by infinite attributes he does not mean an infinite number of independent worlds, but rather an infinite number of aspects of one single infinite universe, analogous to the mediaeval conception of the infinite attributes of God.

The infinite attributes of God, however, are not known to us. Only some of them we are able to affirm of God, and even these, according to the mediaevals, do not tell us anything about the true essence of God. They are only inadequate terms by which we express the various ways in which God manifests himself through nature. The selection of attributes which are admissible of God constitutes one phase of the problem of attributes in mediaeval Jewish philosophy, and various lists have been drawn up by various philosophers. Saadia [4] enumerates life, power, and knowledge. Baḥya Ibn Pakuda [5] mentions existence, unity, and eternity. Ibn Zaddik's [6] list contains existence, power, knowledge, abundance, justice, goodness, mercifulness, life, truth. Judah ha-Levi,[7] dividing attributes into actional, relational, and negational, mentions under them respectively the following groups: (a) making poor and rich, casting

---

[1] Epistola 63.   [2] Epistola 64.

[3] Cf. *Short Treatise*, I, 1, § 8, note 3 (*Opera*, I, p. 17, ll. 33 ff.).

[4] *Emunot we-De'ot*, II, 4: חי, יכול, חכם.

[5] *Ḥobot ha-Lebabot*, I, 10: נמצא, אחד, קדמון.

[6] *'Olam Ḳaṭan*, III (pp. 57 ff.): מציאות, גבור, חכם, עשיר, צדיק, מטיב, רחמן, חי, אמת.

[7] *Cuzari*, II, 1: (a) מוריש ומעשיר, משפיל אף מרומם, רחום וחנון, קנא ונוקם, נבור, שדי; (b) ברוך ומבורך, מהולל, קדוש, רם ונשא; (c) חי, אחד, ראשון ואחרון

down and exalting, merciful and gracious, jealous and re-
vengeful, strong, almighty; (*b*) blessed and praised, glorified,
holy, exalted and extolled; (*c*) living, one, first and last.
Abraham Ibn Daud [1] mentions eight: unity, truth, existence,
eternity, life, knowledge, will, and power, but concludes:
"We do not contend that there are no other attributes which
may be similarly affirmed of God, provided only that it be
made clear that they are to be understood in such a way as
to imply no plurality in His essence." [2] Descartes likewise
enumerates a similar list of attributes "in so far as they may
be known by the light of nature alone." [3] His list mentions
eternal, omniscient, omnipotent, the source of all goodness
and truth, creator of all things, and infinite perfection.

Spinoza does not altogether disregard these traditional
attributes of God. But they are not to him what he would
call "the proper attributes of God" [4] in the specific sense in
which he uses the term "attribute," namely, "that which
the intellect perceives of substance, as if constituting its essence." [5] They are called by him *propria*, "that is to say,
without them God would indeed be no God, but still it is
not they that constitute God: for they reveal nothing of the
character of substance, through which alone God exists." [6]
The contrast between attributes and properties is also implied in his opening statement in the Appendix to the First
Part of the *Ethics*, where he divides the contents of the First
Part into two problems, namely, (1) "the nature of God and
(2) its properties." [7] By "the nature of God" he means
there the attributes. Similarly in the *Tractatus de Intellectus*

---

[1] *Emunah Ramah*, II, iii (p. 52): האחד, האמתי, הנמצא, הנצחי, החי, היודע,
הרוצה, היכול. [2] *Ibid.* (p. 56).

[3] *Principia Philosophiae*, I, 22.

[4] *Short Treatise*, I, 2, § 28. [5] *Ethics*, I, Def. 4.

[6] *Short Treatise*, I, 3, § 1, and note 1.

[7] Cf. above, p. 112.

Emendatione he says of "one" and "infinite" that "these
are not attributes of God which set forth His essence." [1]
These properties are further described by Spinoza either as
being "an extraneous denomination, such as that He exists
through himself, is eternal, one, immutable, etc.," or as
having "reference to His activity." [2] What he means here
by an "extraneous denomination" is not quite clear. But
a passage in the *Cogitata Metaphysica* may throw light upon
it. In that passage, using the traditional term "attribute"
rather loosely in the sense of his own term "property," he
enumerates the following eleven properties: eternity, unity,
greatness, immutability, simplicity, life, understanding, will,
power, creation, concurrence. These, he says, are divided
by some into incommunicable (*incommunicabilia*) and com-
municable (*communicabilia*) [3] — a division which he characterizes as "more nominal than real," for all of them are
to be incommunicable or homonymous, inasmuch as there
can be no similarity in their meaning when applied to God
and when applied to other beings. Spinoza himself divides
them into those which explain God's "active essence"
(*actuosam ejus essentiam*), such as "understanding, will, life,
omnipotence, etc.," and those which only explain "His mode
of existence" (*ejus modi existendi*), such as "unity, eternity,
necessity, etc." [4] Now, in his correspondence, Spinoza speaks
of the properties as being explanations of the expression
necessary existence [5] or of the identity of essence and existence,[6] the latter of which, as we have shown, is itself derived
from the nature of necessary existence.[7] Taking, therefore,

---

[1] § 76, note z (*Opera*, II, p. 29).   [2] *Short Treatise*, I, 2, § 29.
[3] This distinction has been traced by Freudenthal to Thomas Aquinas and Heereboord. Cf. "Spinoza und die Scholastik," in *Philosophische Aufsätze, Eduard
Zeller . . . gewidmet*, p. 116.
[4] *Cogitata Metaphysica*, II, 11.
[5] Epistola 35.   [6] Epistola 83.   [7] Cf. above, pp. 126 ff.

all these passages together, we may conclude that the "extraneous denomination" is an explanation of God's "mode of existence" or of the expression "necessary existence." And thus Spinoza's properties correspond to what Maimonides described as (1) explanation of a name,[1] and (2) actions,[2] both of which are distinguished by him from essential attributes. In a letter to Oldenburg, evidently referring to these lists of attributes, Spinoza writes: "I say that many attributes which they [the theologians of his time] and all others at least who are known to me attribute to God, I regard as things created."[3] By "things created" (*creaturas*) he undoubtedly means what Maimonides calls "actions."

According to Joël the distinction between attributes and properties referred to by Spinoza is analogous to the distinction made by Crescas between essential attributes and attributes merely as intellectual conceptions.[4] The analogy is wrong on several grounds. First, the intellectually conceived attributes of Crescas may have a closer relation to Spinoza's definition of attributes [5] than to his definition of properties. Second, Crescas' intellectually conceived attributes imply a certain conceptual theory of universals which Spinoza's properties do not. Third, Crescas' intellectually conceived attributes, as I have shown, are one of several forms of anti-realistic conceptions of attributes in Jewish philosophy,[6] of which Maimonides' "explanation of a name" is an extreme type, and which, incidentally, may be traced to

[1] *Moreh Nebukim*, I, 51.

[2] *Ibid.*, I, 52.

[3] Epistola 6 (*Opera*, IV, p. 36, ll. 19–21).

[4] Joël, *Zur Genesis der Lehre Spinoza's*, pp. 19 ff.; Joachim, *A Study of the Ethics of Spinoza*, p. 42, n.

[5] Cf. above, p. 152.

[6] Cf. my "Crescas on the Problem of Divine Attributes" in *Jewish Quarterly Review*, n.s., VII (1916), pp. 1–44, 175–221. Cf. above, pp. 150 ff.

the nominal definition mentioned by Aristotle and described by him also as the explanation of a name.[1] The fact that Spinoza divides properties into those which are explanations of the expression necessary existence and those which describe actions shows quite clearly that they are traceable to what Maimonides describes as explanations of a name and actions.

But even as *propria*, not all the attributes that have been used by the mediaevals with reference to God are of interest to Spinoza. Many of them are only adjectives which happen to have been applied to God in the traditional literature of religion. Spinoza passes them by and confines himself only to those which are of a philosophic character. "We shall not trouble ourselves very much about the ideas that people have of God, but we shall only inquire briefly into what the philosophers can tell us about it."[2] Of these so-called philosophic *propria*, or, as he calls them here, "attributes which do not pertain to God," he reproduces a list which concludes with the phrase "and so forth": "A being existing through or of itself, cause of all things, omniscient, almighty, eternal, simple, infinite, the highest good, of infinite compassion."[3] In a foot-note to this passage, he describes these attributes which do not pertain to God as "certain modes which may be attributed to God" either in consideration of both his known attributes, such as eternal, self-subsisting, infinite, cause of all things, immutable, or in consideration of the attribute of thought only, such as omniscient, wise, etc., or in consideration of extension only, such as omnipresent, fills all, etc. A list of *propria* under the loose name of attributes is given in the *Cogitata Metaphysica*, namely, eternity, unity, greatness, immutability, simplicity, life, understand-

[1] *Analytica Posteriora*, II, 10, 93b, 29–37.
[2] *Short Treatise*, I, 7, § 2.   [3] *Ibid.*

ing, will, power, creation, concurrence.[1]   In a letter to Hudde
he enumerates four *propria*, eternal, simple, infinite, indivisible, all of which are reduced by him to the single property of
perfection.[2]   In a later letter to Hudde he refers not only
to these four properties but also to "the remaining similar
properties" and to their reduction by him to one property.[3]
In a letter to Tschirnhaus he mentions as properties the assertions "that He exists necessarily, that He is unique, immutable, infinite, etc." [4] In the Appendix to the First Part
of the *Ethics* there is an indirect reference to properties, of
which he mentions necessary existence, one, acting by the
necessity of His own nature, cause of all things, all things
being in Him, predestination.[5] A list of three *propria* is
given by him in the *Short Treatise*, namely, that God is
the cause of all things, divine providence, and divine predestination.[6]

These *propria*, which in traditional philosophy had passed
for divine attributes, do not according to Spinoza reveal
anything of the nature of God. Even in mediaeval philosophy they were taken, as a rule, as homonymous terms to be
understood in a sense entirely unrelated to their ordinary
meaning. It was well, indeed, for the mediaevals to give
up their inquiry about the nature of God at this point, for
to them God was absolutely distinct from the universe, as
pure form must be distinct from matter, and consequently
what they called attributes could not tell us anything of the
nature or essence of God or what God is. They told us only
what He is not or what He does in the world — the so-called

---

[1] *Cogitata Metaphysica*, II, 1–11. The origin of this list in various Latin sources
is given by Freudenthal, "Spinoza und die Scholastik," in *Philosophische Aufsätze
Eduard Zeller . . . gewidmet*, p. 110.

[2] Epistola 35.   [3] Epistola 36.   [4] Epistola 83.

[5] Appendix to *Ethics*, I.

[6] *Short Treatise*, I, 3, 5, and 6.

negative and actional interpretations of divine attributes.[1]
But according to Spinoza God is as material as the world,
and His essence, therefore, apart from His actions, does reveal itself in the nature of the physical universe. God or substance, to be sure, is unknown to us in His infinite fullness,
and even that part of Him which is known to us is known to
us only through attributes which are not substance itself but
only "that which intellect perceives of substance."[2] Still,
the intellect perceives them "as if constituting its essence,"[3]
that is to say, as if constituting the essence of substance.
While the mediaevals considered the essence of God unknown, because the knowledge gained of God's essence is
not so positive as the knowledge that one may gain, according to their theory of knowledge, of the essence of other
beings, Spinoza considered the essence of God in so far as
it could be known through nature as positive as, and even
more positive than, the knowledge one may gain, according
to his own theory of knowledge, of the essence of any particular being. One must therefore go, according to Spinoza,
to the physical universe, to consider its ways, and to be wise
as to the nature of God.

If we are to attempt to reconstruct hypothetically the
process of Spinoza's study of nature and of his reasoning
which ultimately led him to the discovery of the two known
attributes of God, we must assume that he started with the
Aristotelian method of classifying being. Three classifications of being are to be found in Aristotle, namely, the ten
categories, substance and accident, and matter and form.
Of these three classifications, the first must have been dismissed by Spinoza outright as something unuseful for his
purpose. Not only did it seem to him, as to others after

---

[1] *Moreh Nebukim*, I, 52.
[2] *Ethics*, I, Def. 4.   [3] *Ibid.*

him, to be logically faulty, but it is also reducible to lower
forms, for it is based upon the distinction of substance and
accident, the nine categories outside of substance being
nothing but an enumeration of various accidents casually
selected.[1] The classification of substance and accident, or
rather of substance and mode, to be sure, is used by Spinoza
as the ultimate classification of being in his own system,[2]
and rightly so, since in his own system only one substance is
assumed. In the system of Aristotle, however, where three
kinds of substances are assumed, the classification of substance and accident could not be ultimate, since substance
presupposes already the distinction of matter and form, for
the three substances in Aristotle are matter, form, and concrete things composed of matter and form.[3] Spinoza must
have therefore started his revision of the mediaeval scheme
with the last of the Aristotelian classifications of being,
namely, matter and form.

Then as a next step, we may assume, Spinoza must have
modified Aristotle's classification of matter and form to suit
his own particular theory of the materiality of God. In
Aristotle, as we have seen, matter and form are substances,
each of them existing "in itself." Though in concrete composite things form does not exist "in itself," [4] for it is inseparable from matter and cannot exist apart from matter,
still form can also be pure and exist "in itself" apart from
matter, as in the case of his own God. To Spinoza, however,
form could never be pure and exist apart from matter, for
even God, he has already shown, must be material. Matter
and form, therefore, could not be substances; they could be
only attributes of substance, and there could be only one
such substance, and that is God. Particular things are not

---

[1] Cf. above, p. 62.　　　　　　[2] Cf. above, pp. 63 f.
[3] Cf. above, p. 67.　　　　　　[4] Cf. above, p. 68.

substances. That they cannot be substances he has already shown from the very same terms used in the mediaeval definition of substance.[1]

Then Spinoza must have taken one further step and changed the terms "matter" and "form" into "extension" and "thought." The reason for his doing so will become clear to us when we consider the ambiguity of the old terms matter and form. In Aristotle and throughout the Middle Ages matter and form were correlative terms. They were applied simultaneously to everything within the hierarchy of beings that lie between the lowest matter and the highest form. They could not therefore be used by Spinoza in his own specific and restricted sense with reference to the two known attributes of God without leading to some confusion. It was in fact this multifariousness of meaning of the terms matter and form that led mediaeval philosophers to classify them according to their different applications and to label them by certain distinguishing adjectives, so that in Thomas Aquinas there are no less than fifty-one varieties of matter and no less than one hundred and twenty-one varieties of form.[2] In order therefore to avoid confusion, Spinoza had to find certain equivalents for matter and form which would have the traditional sanction of expressing the same contrast and which would also stand respectively for one traditional specific matter and for one traditional specific form.

Such two terms he found in extension and thought. The common matter underlying the four elements, according to Aristotle and his commentators, is something extended; in fact, it is the first kind of matter that is extended, and hence could be called extension. There is indeed a difference of opinion among his mediaeval commentators as to whether

[1] Cf. above, Chapter III.
[2] Cf. L. Schütz, *Thomas-Lexikon* (1895): "Materia" under c and "Forma" under b.

extension was the underlying common matter of the four elements itself or whether it was a sort of form of a still further inextended matter, in which case the underlying common matter of the four elements would be itself composed of matter and form, respectively known as prime matter (*materia prima*) and corporeal form (*forma corporeitatis*). The latter was the opinion of the leading Arabic and Jewish philosophers, such as Alfarabi, Avicenna, Algazali, Averroes, Joseph Ibn Ẓaddiḳ, Abraham Ibn Daud, and Joseph Ibn Aknin, though there was a difference of opinion among them as to the nature of the *forma corporeitatis*. The origin and history of this controversy about the *forma corporeitatis* have been discussed by me elsewhere.[1] Crescas, however, argues for the elimination of the inextended prime matter and makes the *forma corporeitatis* or extension itself at once the prime matter and the underlying common matter of the four elements.[2] The same view was also held, according to the testimony of Isaac Abrabanel, by his son Judah Abrabanel,[3] better known as Leo Hebraeus, author of the *Dialoghi d'Amore*. However it is, the common matter underlying the four elements was conceived to have extension as something inseparable from it, on which account it could be spoken of as extension. A further justification for the substitution of extension for matter by Spinoza was the fact that Descartes defined matter as extension,[4] though, perhaps, not in the same sense in which Crescas identified the two. The reason for Spinoza's substitution of thought for form is quite obvious, for the highest form or God is spoken of by Aristotle and throughout the Middle Ages as pure thought.

[1] Cf. my *Crescas' Critique of Aristotle* in the notes on pp. 579–590, of which a summary is given on pp. 99–101.

[2] *Ibid.*, pp. 102–104, 261–263; notes 26–32 on pp. 598–602.

[3] *Ibid.*, p. 600.

[4] *Principia Philosophiae*, II, 4, and cf. Spinoza, Epistola 83.

But "extension" and "thought" are abstract terms which "the intellect perceives of substance, as if constituting its essence."[1] It is only through their respective activities that they become manifest to our senses. Now, in Aristotle and throughout the Middle Ages God as pure thought was conceived as an active principle. Thought meant thinking, and that process of thinking is always active and is never in a state of quiescence. This is the trend of Aristotle's statements when he says of God's thought that it "thinks itself because it shares the nature of the object of thought. . . . For that which is capable of receiving the object of thought, i.e. the essence, is thought. And it is *active* when it *possesses* this object. Therefore the latter ⟨possession⟩ rather than the former ⟨receptivity⟩ is the divine element which thought seems to contain."[2] Maimonides re-echoes these statements when he declares that "God is the *intellectus*, the *intelligens*, and the *intelligibile*," and that "God is an intellect which always is in action."[3] Extension or matter, however, is different, according to Aristotle and the mediaevals and also Descartes;[4] it is never active, it is always passive. It is set into motion by an external agent, which ultimately terminates in God, who is the cause of motion in matter, but who is himself not matter and is not in motion. The view is most clearly set forth by Maimonides: "The principles of any individual compound substance are matter and form, and there must needs be an agent, that is to say, a mover which sets the substratum in motion, and thereby renders it predisposed to receive a certain form. The agent which thus predisposes the matter of a certain individual being is called

[1] *Ethics*, I, Def. 4.
[2] *Metaphysics*, XII, 7, 1072b, 19–23.
[3] *Moreh Nebukim*, I, 68.
[4] *Principia Philosophiae Cartesianae*, II, Prop. 12, and cf. Descartes, *Principia Philosophiae*, II, 36.

the immediate mover. Here the necessity arises of inquiring
into the nature of motion, the moving agent and the thing
moved. But this has already been explained sufficiently;
and the opinion of Aristotle may be formulated in the words
that matter is not the cause of its own motion.[1] This is the
important proposition which leads to the investigation of
the existence of the prime mover." [2]

Spinoza accepts the old philosophic view with regard to
God's thought that it is the act of thinking and that God is
therefore an intellect which is always in action. But he dis-
agrees with the old philosophic conception of matter as
something inert. In one of his letters he directly criticizes
Descartes for maintaining that the variety of things can be
deduced "from extension in no other way than by supposing
that this was the effect produced in extension by motion
which was started by God," [3] and gives as his own view that
it must be "explained through an attribute, which expresses
eternal and infinite essence." [4] Since according to his own
view extension is an attribute of God just as thought is, extension must be active no less than thought, and just as
thought is thinking so extension is motion, not motion im-
parted to it by an external agent, but something which expresses the activity of its own nature. These actional aspects
of the attributes of extension and thought are what Spinoza
calls immediate infinite modes.

[1] Cf. *Metaphysics*, I, 3, 984a, 21–25; XII, 6, 1071b, 28–30.
[2] *Moreh Nebukim*, II, Introduction, Prop. 25; *Crescas' Critique of Aristotle*,
p. 315.   [3] Letter from Tschirnhaus (Epistola 82).
[4] Letter to Tschirnhaus (Epistola 83). Spinoza's statement that "matter is
badly defined by Descartes as extension" is not to be taken literally as an objection to Descartes' identification of matter with extension. It is to be taken in connection with the entire letter of Tschirnhaus and as referring especially to the latter's restatement of the opinion of Descartes that the variety of things can be
deduced "from extension in no other way than by supposing that this was the effect
produced in extension by motion which was started by God." Cf. also the definition of matter in *Cogitata Metaphysica*, II, 10 (*Opera*, I, p. 269, ll. 31–33).

The immediate infinite mode of thought is designated by Spinoza in four ways: (1) Intellect (*Intellectus, Verstaan*).[1] (2) Absolutely infinite intellect (*intellectus absolute infinitus*).[2] (3) An infinite power of thought (*potentia infinita cogitandi*).[3] (4) The idea of God (*idea Dei*).[4] The term *intellectus* in the first two designations is to be understood here not only in the sense of the thinking subject but also in the sense of the act of thinking, that is to say, not only in the sense of the intellect, νοῦς, but also in the sense of intellection, νόησις, on the principle reproduced by Maimonides as the common opinion of the philosophers that "God is the *intellectus*, the *intelligens*, and the *intelligibile*" and that "all intellect is identical with its action; the intellect in action is not a thing different from its action, for the true nature and essence of the intellect is comprehension." [5] This principle is also reproduced by Spinoza.[6] When it is recalled that according to Spinoza there is no potential intellect but that every intellect is actual,[7] it will become clear how the term *intellectus*, which literally means the understanding subject, is used by him in the sense of the act of understanding. When, therefore, in the third designation he describes the infinite mode of thought as *potentia infinita cogitandi*, the term *potentia* is not to be taken in the sense of potentiality or faculty or the power to do something but in the sense of the power displayed in doing something, for ordinarily, as says Maimonides, "when we assume the intellect to be potential, we necessarily distinguish two things, the potential intellect and the potential intelligible object." [8]

---

[1] Letter from Schuller (Epistola 63), and *Short Treatise*, I, 9.
[2] Letter to Schuller (Epistola 64).   [3] Epistola 32 (*Opera*, IV, p. 173, l. 18).
[4] *Ethics*, II, Props. 3, 4, and 8. Cf. I, Prop. 21, Demonst.
[5] *Moreh Nebukim*, I, 68. Cf. below, Vol. II, pp. 24, 45.
[6] *Ethics*, II, Prop. 7, Schol. Cf. below, Vol. II, pp. 24, 45.
[7] *Ethics*, II, Prop. 48, Schol., and *Ethics*, I, Prop. 31, Schol.
[8] *Moreh Nebukim*, I, 68.

The active sense of the term *intellectus* is made clear by Spinoza himself in his description of the immediate infinite mode of thought in the *Short Treatise*. He says that "it has been from all eternity, and to all eternity will remain immutable. . . . It has one function, namely, to understand clearly and distinctly all things at all times." [1] The emphasis in these statements is on the terms "eternity," "immutable," and "at all times," and they reflect the following statements of Maimonides: "Now it has been proved that God is an intellect which *always* is in action, and that . . . there is in Him at no time a mere potentiality, that He does not comprehend at one time, and is without comprehension at another time, but He is an intellect in action *always*." [2] Spinoza continues to describe there the function of the infinite mode of thought as that "which produces invariably an infinite and most perfect satisfaction, which cannot omit to do what it does." [3] This seems to reflect Aristotle's description of the constant activity of the First Principle or God: "And its life is such as the best which we enjoy, and enjoy for but a short time. For it is ever in this state (which we cannot be), since its actuality is also pleasure . . . and the act of contemplation is what is most pleasant and best." [4]

The expression *idea Dei* we take to be the equivalent of the expression *intellectus absolute infinitus* as a description of the immediate infinite mode of thought. These two expressions, however, indicate two different aspects of that immediate infinite mode. The term *intellectus*, as we have seen, literally refers to the thinking subject, the νοῦς in Aristotle's enumeration of the threefold aspect of God's thinking, namely, the νοῦς, the νόησις, and the νοητόν or

---

[1] *Short Treatise*, I, 9, § 3.   [2] *Moreh Nebukim*, I, 68.
[3] *Short Treatise*, I, 9, § 3.
[4] *Metaphysics*, XII, 7, 1072b, 14–24.

νοούμενον. The term *idea* in *idea Dei* is a transliteration of εἶδος in the specific sense of εἶδος νοητόν (*forma intelligibilis*),[1] and hence it reflects the object of thought, the νοητόν or νοούμενον in Aristotle's threefold enumeration. But inasmuch as in God, according to Aristotle, Maimonides, and Spinoza himself, the thinking subject, the act of thinking, and the object of thought are identical, the expressions *intellectus absolute infinitus* and *idea Dei* are identical in meaning, both designating the immediate infinite mode of thought.

That the relation between the "idea of God" and the "absolutely infinite intellect" was conceived by Spinoza to be like that of object of thought to the thinking subject, which, of course, in God are identical, may be shown from the following passage. In Proposition IV of *Ethics*, II, Spinoza says that "the idea of God . . . can be one only." In the Demonstration of this proposition he proves it by the contention that "the infinite intellect comprehends nothing but the attributes of God and His affections," which are all united in God as one. This passage makes it quite clear that the "idea of God" was considered by Spinoza to be related to the "infinite intellect" as the object of thought to the thinking subject with which it is identical. Another prooftext may perhaps be found also in the following passage: "We must remember, besides, that our mind, in so far as it truly perceives things, is a part of the infinite intellect of God (Corol. Prop. XI, Part II), and therefore it must be that the clear and distinct ideas of the mind are as true as the ideas of God (*Dei ideae*)."[2] If in this passage the plural "*Dei ideae*" means the ideas of God in the "infinite intellect of God" rather than the ideas of God in "our mind," then it is quite evident that the relation between the "idea of

---

[1] *Metaphysics*, XII, 9, 1075a, 3–5. Cf. below, Vol. II, pp. 46–48, 93.
[2] *Ethics*, II, Prop. 43, Schol., end.

God" and the "infinite intellect of God," i.e., the absolutely
infinite intellect, is like that between the clear and distinct
ideas of our mind and our mind, that is to say, like the relation between the object of thought and the thinking subject, which two are identical in God.

Some students of Spinoza take the *idea Dei* as the mediate
infinite mode of thought corresponding to the *facies totius
universi* which they take as the mediate infinite mode of
extension.[1] This view, however, is dictated only by the
necessity of finding a special mediate infinite mode of thought
in order to round out the symmetry of the modal system.
No statement in Spinoza could be found which would definitely corroborate it. On the contrary, the following passage in the *Short Treatise* would seem to contradict it. Says
Spinoza: "And since, as a matter of fact, nature or God is
one being of which infinite attributes are predicated, and
which contains in itself all the essences of created things, it
necessarily follows that of all this there is produced in thought
an infinite idea (*oneyndige Idea*), which comprehends *objective* the whole of nature just as it is *realiter*." [2] The "infinite idea" in this passage undoubtedly refers to the *idea
Dei*, and from the context of the passage it is quite clear
that it cannot be a mediate mode of thought, for right after
this statement Spinoza says definitely: "Wherefore also, in
the ninth chapter of the First Part, I called this idea a creation created immediately by God." [3] Furthermore, the use
of the *idea Dei* in the Demonstration of Proposition XXI of
Ethics, I, leaves no doubt that it is an immediate rather than
a mediate mode of thought.[4]

---

[1] Pollock, *Spinoza*, pp. 187–188, referring also to Ed. Böhmer, "Spinozana," in
Zeitschrift für Philosophie und philosophische Kritik, 42 (1863), pp. 107–116;
Joachim, *A Study of the Ethics of Spinoza*, p. 94.

[2] *Short Treatise*, Appendix II, § 4 (*Opera*, I, p. 117, ll. 24–29).

[3] *Ibid.* (p. 117, ll. 29–31; p. 607, § 10).   [4] Cf. below, p. 378.

The immediate infinite mode of extension is designated by
Spinoza in two ways: (1) Motion.[1] (2) Motion and rest.[2]
The addition of rest to motion must have been suggested to
him by Descartes, who speaks of motion and rest as "two
diverse modes of a body in motion."[3] Whether Descartes
himself meant by this addition that rest was a real entity,
or whether he used it only as a rhetorical flourish, is a question which has been raised in connection with another passage in Descartes.[4] But it would seem that Spinoza had
taken it to mean something positive, in opposition to Aristotle and the mediaevals, to whom rest was only the privation
of motion.[5] The positive character of rest is affirmed by
Spinoza when he says that "as is self-evident, the same force
is required to give a body at rest a certain velocity as is required to bring the same body with that given velocity to
rest,"[6] or when he says that "by force we understand the
quantity of motion. . . . In bodies at rest by force of re-
sistance we understand the quantity of rest."[7] It is interesting to note that Crescas in his criticism of Aristotle similarly
maintains, though in a different sense, that there is a quantity of rest as there is a quantity of motion.[8] It has been
suggested that by motion and rest Spinoza means energy in
motion and energy in position, or kinetic and potential
energy.[9]

[1] Letter from Schuller (Epistola 63), and Short Treatise, I, 9.

[2] Short Treatise, I, 2, § 19, note 7 (Opera, I, p. 25, ll. 26–27); II, notes to Preface;
II, 19, § 6 (Opera, I, p. 90, ll. 26–27); II, 20, § 4, note 4 (Opera, I, p. 98, l. 35);
Appendix II, § 15 (Opera, I, p. 120, l. 24); Ethics, I, Prop. 32, Corol. 2; Epistola 64;
Meyer's Preface to Principia Philosophiae Cartesianae (Opera, I, p. 132, l. 13).

[3] Principia Philosophiae, II, 27.

[4] Pollock, Spinoza, p. 110.   [5] Physics, IV, 12, 221b, 12–13.

[6] Principia Philosophiae Cartesianae, II, Def. 8 (2).

[7] Ibid., Prop. 22, Demonst., and Prop. 37, Corol. Cf. E. Schmitt, Die unendliche
Modi bei Spinoza (Leipzig, 1910), p. 47, n. 2.

[8] Cf. my Crescas' Critique of Aristotle, pp. 287–288.

[9] Pollock, Spinoza, p. 113.

In the history of philosophy an immediate creation of God has been sometimes called a son of God. Thus Philo describes the intelligible world, which was an immediate creation of God and created by Him from eternity, as a son of God, whereas time, which is not an immediate creation of God but is the offspring of the cosmos, is described by him as a grandson of God.[1] This designation has gone over to Christian theology, and Spinoza refers to the Christian side of it elsewhere in his works.[2] But Philo's statement is also reproduced by Azariah dei Rossi,[3] and it is also reflected in Leo Hebraeus' *Dialoghi d'Amore*.[4] Following tradition, therefore, Spinoza characterizes the immediacy of these two infinite modes by saying of motion that it is "a son, product, or effect created immediately by God," and of understanding that it "is also a son, product, or immediate creation of God, created by Him from all eternity."[5]

Spinoza's God, though He can no longer be contrasted with the universe as the immaterial with the material, can still be contrasted with it as the simple whole with the aggregate whole. His God, as we shall show in the next chapter, is not identical with the physical universe. He transcends it in a certain special sense of the term transcendence.[6] And so, the aggregate totality of the physical universe, in so far as it is the necessary result of the activity of God's attributes of extension and thought, is called by Spinoza also an infinite mode of God, but in order to differentiate it from the other infinite modes he calls it a mediate infinite mode. This distinction between immediate and mediate infinite modes,

[1] *Quod Deus Sit Immutabilis*, VI, 31.
[2] *Cogitata Metaphysica*, I, 10; Epistola 73; *Ethics*, IV, Prop. 68, Schol.
[3] *Me 'or 'Enayim, Imre Binah*, Ch. 4, p. 100 (ed. Cassel).
[4] *Dialoghi d'Amore*, III, p. 244 (Bari, 1929).
[5] *Short Treatise*, I, 9, §§ 2-3.
[6] Cf. below, p. 322.

however, does not occur in all the writings of Spinoza. In
the *Short Treatise* he does not mention it. On the contrary,
the distinction drawn there is not between two kinds of infinite modes but rather between infinite modes, as motion
in extension and understanding in thought, and particular
things, the former of which are immediately created by God
whereas the latter are said to be created by God by a sub-
sidiary instrumental cause. God is therefore called by him
the proximate cause of the infinite modes but the remote
cause, in a certain sense, of the particular things.[1] But the
distinction between immediate and mediate infinite modes
is referred to several times in the *Ethics*,[2] and a mediate
infinite mode is specifically named by Spinoza in a letter to
Schuller.[3]

The name given by Spinoza to that mediate infinite mode
is "the face of the whole universe" (*facies totius universi*).[4]
The phraseology of this expression is reminiscent of the
Biblical manner of describing the totality or wholeness of
a certain extent of territory. Thus when the Bible wants to
say "over the entire earth," it says "upon the face of all the
earth," which in the Vulgate is translated by *super faciem
totius terrae* (Dan. 8, 5), or by *super faciem universae terrae*
(Gen. 7, 3, I Sam. 30, 16), or by *super faciem omnis terrae*
(II Sam. 18, 8, Zech. 5, 3). The term *facies* may also reflect
the Greek πρόσωπον in the sense of "person," for the Latin
facies as well as the Hebrew word for "face" [5] has acquired the
meaning of "person" under the influence of the Greek term.
Accordingly the *facies totius universi* may mean the whole
universe taken as an individual, in conformity with Spinoza's statement that "we may easily conceive the whole of

[1] *Short Treatise*, I, 3, § 2 (8). But cf. *Ethics*, I, Prop. 28, Schol.
[2] *Ethics*, I, Prop. 23, Demonst.; Prop. 28, Schol.; Appendix (*Opera*, II, p. 80,
l. 17). [3] Epistola 64.
[4] *Ibid.* [5] פנים.

nature to be one individual." [1] In coining or adopting this expression for the mediate modes, Spinoza may have also been influenced by the Cabalistic term "faces" (*parzufim*, from πρόσωπον), which stands for the mediate emanations from the Infinite (*En Sof*), following from Him through the mediacy of the Sefirot. Abraham Herrera in his *Puerta del Cielo* refers to these mediate emanations as the "faces of the universe of the infinite." In the Spanish original, the phrase reads: "parzupim del mundo del ynfinito." [2] In the Hebrew version, the same term "parzupim," or rather "parzufim," is used. [3] In the abridged Latin version made from the Hebrew, the phrase reads: "Personæ Systematis(,) Infiniti." [4] Whether Spinoza had before him the Spanish original in manuscript or the Hebrew version printed in Amsterdam in 1655, twenty years prior to the writing of his letter to Schuller, dated "29 Julii, 1675," where the phrase "facies totius universi" occurs, it can be easily seen how Herrera's description of his mediate emanations by the phrase "*parzupim* of the universe of the infinite" suggested to him the phrase "facies totius universi" as a description of his own mediate infinite mode.

The expression "the face of the whole universe" is explained by Spinoza himself as meaning "the whole universe which, although it varies in infinite ways, yet remains always the same." [5] This explanation, it seems to me, may refer to two principles in Spinoza's philosophy.

In the first place, it may refer to the Cartesian and

[1] Scholium to Lemma 7, after Prop. 13 of *Ethics*, II.

[2] Cf. *Livro Quarto de La Puerta del Cielo De Abraham Cohen de Herrera*, Cap. 3, fol. 38b. MS. in the Library of the "Portugeesch Israëlietisch Seminarium Ets Haïm" in Amsterdam. A copy of this passage was made for me through the courtesy of the Librarian, Dr. J. S. da Silva Rosa.

[3] *Sha'ar ha-Shamayim*, II, 3: ‏ופרצופי עולם האין סוף‎.

[4] *Porta Cælorum*, II, 3, p. 45.

[5] Epistola 64.

Spinozistic principle of the preservation of the proportion of motion and rest.[1] According to this principle, the preservation of the proportion of motion and rest in the parts composing the body of an individual results in the preservation of the form (*forma*)[2] or shape (*figura*)[3] of that individual as a whole. Consequently the preservation of the proportion of motion and rest in the particular parts which compose the physical universe and constitute it as an individual whole will preserve the face (*facies*), i.e., the form (*forma*) and shape (*figura*), of the universe as a whole. As Spinoza says elsewhere: "Thus, if we advance *ad infinitum*, we may easily conceive the whole of nature to be one individual, whose parts, that is to say, all bodies, differ in infinite ways without any change of the whole individual."[4]

In the second place, it may refer to the principle of "the order and interdependence of nature as a whole" (*totius naturae ordo et cohaerentia*),[5] *facies* thus meaning *ordo et cohaerentia*. This principle is also spoken of by Spinoza as "the order of the whole of nature or the connection of causes" (*ordo totius naturae, sive causarum connexio*),[6] or as "the fixed and unchangeable order of nature or the chain of natural events" (*fixux et immutabilis naturae ordo sive rerum naturae concatenatio*),[7] or as "the concatenation of causes" (*concatenatio causarum*).[8] With reference to this principle, too, nature as a whole may be considered as an individual consisting of parts, "inasmuch as the power of nature is simply the aggregate of the powers of all her individual

---

[1] See Lemma 7, after Prop. 13 of *Ethics*, II. Cf. below, Vol. II, p. 69, n. 4.
[2] *Ethics*, IV, Prop. 39, Demonst.
[3] See Axiom 3 preceding Lemma 4, after Prop. 13 of *Ethics*, II.
[4] Scholium to Lemma 7, after Prop. 13 of *Ethics*, II.
[5] *Tractatus Theologico-Politicus*, Ch. 16 (*Opera*, III, p. 191, ll. 5-6).
[6] *Ethics*, II, Prop. 7, Schol.
[7] *Tractatus Theologico-Politicus*, Ch. 3 (*Opera*, III, p. 45, ll. 34-35).
[8] *Ibid.*, Ch. 4 (*Opera*, III, p. 58, l. 21).

components."¹ Now, this order of nature, according to Spinoza, may be explained either by the attribute of thought or by the attribute of extension, according as the component parts of the universe are considered either as modes of thought or as modes of extension.² By the same token, we may infer that according to Spinoza the order or the face of the whole universe may be also explained by the joint activity of both attributes, if the component parts of the universe are considered as modes of both thought and extension.

Consequently, the mediate infinite mode designated by Spinoza as "the face of the whole universe," if taken with reference to the principle of the preservation of the proportion of motion and rest, will be a mode of extension only, but if taken with reference to the principle of the order of the whole of nature, will be a mode of both extension and thought. As Spinoza does not say that "the face of the whole universe" is a mode of extension only and as he nowhere specifically mentions a mediate infinite mode of thought, we may conclude that "the face of the whole universe" is a mediate infinite mode of both extension and thought.

In our presentation of the system of infinite modes we have in some respects parted from the interpretations which one may find in the Spinoza literature, and in some other respects we have placed ourselves on the side of one class of interpreters as against that of another class.³ Among the interpreters of Spinoza there are some who take the "face of the whole universe" to be only a mode of exten-

¹ *Ibid.*, Ch. 16 (*Opera*, III, p. 189, ll. 21–23).
² *Ethics*, II, Prop. 7, Schol.
³ For a classification of the various interpretations of infinite modes, see E. Schmitt, *Die unendliche Modi bei Spinoza* (Leipzig, 1910), pp. 5 ff.

sion,[1] but in order to preserve the symmetry of extension
and thought, they supply by conjecture the missing mediate
infinite mode of thought out of other parts of Spinoza's
writings. Two Spinozistic expressions have been borrowed to fill up that lacuna in Spinoza's list of infinite
modes: (1) God's idea (*idea Dei*).[2] (2) "The constant form
of reasoned thought or Necessary Logical laws."[3] Support for the first conjecture is adduced from the fact that
certain descriptions of the *idea Dei* would seem to make it
the ideal counterpart of the *facies totius universi*.[4] Martineau,
who is the author of the second conjecture, does not adduce
any textual support for his view. I am inclined to reject
both these conjectures, for the following reasons. As we
have already seen, the expression *facies totius universi* may
include both the modes of extension and the modes of
thought. Then, as we have also shown,[5] the *idea Dei* is an
immediate mode of thought and the equivalent of the *intellectus absolute infinitus*. Finally, Martineau's "Necessary Logical laws" cannot be a mediate infinite mode parallel to the *facies totius universi*, for from a statement in
Meyer's Preface to Spinoza's *Principia Philosophiae Cartesianae* it may be indirectly inferred that the "Necessary
Logical laws" are parallel to "motion and rest" and consequently must be identical with the "absolutely infinite
intellect" and are therefore an immediate infinite mode. The
passage reads as follows: "And as the human body is not
absolute, but its extension is determined according to natural
laws of motion and rest, so also mind or human spirit is not

---

[1] See *ibid.*, p. 116, n. 4, where a list of authors holding different interpretations
of the *facies totius universi* is given. Cf. Pollock, *Spinoza*, p. 188.

[2] Pollock, *Spinoza*, p. 187; Joachim, *A Study of the Ethics of Spinoza*, p. 94.

[3] Martineau, *A Study of Spinoza*, p. 200.

[4] Joachim, *op. cit.*, p. 95.

[5] Cf. above, pp. 239 ff.

absolute but is determined through ideas by natural laws of thought." [1]

In the philosophy of Aristotle and in the Aristotelian philosophy reproduced by the mediaevals sometimes for the purpose of refutation, a distinction is drawn between the universe as a whole and the particular things within it. The universe as a whole is said to be eternal and immutable, to have neither beginning nor end, never to have been different nor ever to change, but always to remain the same.[2] The particular things in the sublunary part of the universe, however, are different. They are called transient and are said to be subject to constant change [3] and to the process of generation and corruption.[4] Following tradition, Spinoza similarly distinguishes between the "general," which are the infinite modes, and the "particular," which are the particular things.[5] The infinite modes are described by him as eternal and immutable [6] and as remaining always the same,[7] whereas the particular things are described by him as "transient . . . which did not exist from all time, or have had a beginning" [8] and as "individual mutable things." [9]

But these transient things, according to the mediaeval Aristotelians, do not act sporadically and haphazardly. They are all subject to the necessary and immutable laws which govern the universe as a whole and the influence of which reaches every part of it. This view has been summed up in the following statement of Maimonides: "This whole order [of the universe], both above and here below, is never dis-

---

[1] Preface to the *Principia Philosophiae Cartesianae* (*Opera*, I, p. 132, ll. 12 ff.).
[2] *Moreh Nebukim*, II, 13, Third Theory.
[3] *Ibid.*, II, 10.   [4] *Ibid.*, II, 11.
[5] *Short Treatise*, I, 8.
[6] *Ibid.*, I, 9.   [7] Epistola 64.
[8] *Short Treatise*, II, 5, § 5 (*Opera*, I, p. 62, ll. 32 ff.). Cf. § 2 (p. 563).
[9] *Tractatus de Intellectus Emendatione*, § 100 (*Opera*, II, p. 36, l. 22).

turbed or interrupted, and nothing new is produced in it which is not in its nature and nothing happens in it which is contrary to law." [1] Furthermore, even according to Maimonides himself, to whom the world does not follow from God by mere necessity but by knowledge, God's eternal knowledge is of such a nature that in determining the changes in particular things it determines them in such a way that they follow "according to an imperishable and immutable order." [2] So also Spinoza maintains that the "individual mutable things" (*haec singularia mutabilia*) "are produced and are ordered" according to "fixed and eternal things" (*res fixae aeternaeque*), that is to say, the infinite modes, which are of an eternal and immutable nature. The sequence of individual mutable things is, therefore, "to be sought from fixed and eternal things only, and also from the laws inscribed in them, as it were in true codes." [3]

These fixed and eternal things, though they are themselves only modes which by definition can neither be nor be conceived without substance,[4] may still be considered with reference to the individual mutable things which are dependent upon them as substance is considered by Spinoza with reference to modes, that is to say, the individual mutable things can neither be nor be conceived without the infinite modes. The relation between them, therefore, is like that between substance and mode, namely, the relation between the whole and the part or between the universal and the particular.[5] This is the significance of the following passage: "It may indeed be said that these individual mutable things so intimately and essentially, if I may so speak, depend upon those that are fixed that the former without the latter can neither

[1] *Moreh Nebukim*, II, 13.   [2] *Ibid.*, III, 21.
[3] *Tractatus de Intellectus Emendatione*, § 101 (*Opera*, II, p. 36, ll. 35 ff.).
[4] *Ethics*, I, Def. 5.   [5] See above, pp. 74 ff.

be nor be conceived. Hence these fixed and eternal things, although they may be individual (*singularia*), nevertheless, on account of their presence everywhere and their extensive power, will be like universals to us, or so to speak, the *genera* of the definitions of individual mutable things, and proximate causes of all things." [1]

If this interpretation of the passage just quoted is correct, then the "fixed and eternal things" do not refer directly to substance or to attribute but only to the infinite modes, both the immediate and the mediate, though, of course, indirectly they may include also substance and attribute, inasmuch as they, too, are fixed and eternal and are the cause of the existence of the infinite modes. According to some interpreters of Spinoza, however, the fixed and eternal things refer directly to substance, attribute, and even finite modes. [2] The application of the expression "fixed and eternal things" to the infinite modes, that is to say, to the absolutely infinite intellect, motion and rest, and the face of the whole universe, reflects the expression "eternal things" which was applied by the mediaevals to the Intelligences, motion, and the universe as a whole, when these were assumed with Aristotle to be eternal. [3] The expression goes back to Aristotle himself. [4] Again, the characterization of the infinite modes as *singularia* in the passage quoted is in conformity with what we have said above, namely, that Spinoza's substance or God is in some respect transcending the universe and is a simple whole as contrasted with the universe, or, as he

---

[1] *Tractatus de Intellectus Emendatione*, § 101 (*Opera*, II, p. 37, ll. 3 ff.).

[2] For different interpretations of the meaning of the *res fixae et aeternae*, see E. Schmitt, *Die unendliche Modi bei Spinoza* (Leipzig, 1910), pp. 68–69.

[3] See my *Crescas' Critique of Aristotle*, pp. 287, 291, and note 18 on p. 645, note 31 on p. 662, note 32 on p. 663. The Hebrew expression underlying "eternal things" is: הדברים הנצחיים.

[4] τὰ ἀεὶ ὄντα, *Physics*, IV, 12, 221b, 3–4.

calls it, *natura naturata*, which is an aggregate whole. Consequently, substance is the only true whole or universal, and the infinite modes are in their relation to it only *singularia*.

In mediaeval philosophy a distinction is made between the possible *per se*, the possible *per se* but necessary in consideration of its cause, and the necessary *per se*. This distinction is based upon an Avicennian proposition which is reproduced by Maimonides as follows: "Everything that has a cause for its existence is in respect to its own essence only possible of existence, for if the causes exist, the thing likewise will exist, but if the causes have never existed, or if they have ceased to exist, or if their causal relation to the thing has changed, then the thing itself will not exist." [1] The origin, history, and implications of this proposition I have discussed elsewhere.[2] According to this threefold division of possibility and necessity, the particular things are called possible *per se*, the celestial spheres are called possible *per se* but necessary in consideration of their cause, and God is called necessary *per se* — a division based upon the Aristotelian division of the universe into the transiently movable, the eternally movable, and the eternally immovable.[3] Spinoza reproduces this mediaeval threefold division of possibility and necessity in different connections in several places in his works.[4] But here he applies it to his theory of infinite modes. He changes, however, the terms "possible" and "necessary" to "transient" and "eternal," with which, as we have seen, they are connected.[5] The particular things,

---

[1] *Moreh Nebukim*, II, Introd., Prop. 19; cf. my *Crescas' Critique of Aristotle*, p. 303.

[2] *Crescas' Critique of Aristotle*, pp. 109–111, 681–685.

[3] *Metaphysics*, V, 5, 1015a, 33–34. See *Crescas' Critique of Aristotle*, p. 109 and pp. 680 ff.

[4] See above, pp. 187 ff.

[5] Cf. my *Crescas' Critique of Aristotle*, pp. 109 ff. and 680 ff.

he says, are transient, i.e., possible *per se*. The infinite modes, while transient or possible *per se*, are not to be considered as transient or possible in consideration of their cause. God is eternal, i.e., necessary *per se*. "Now some objects are in themselves transient; others, indeed, are not transient by virtue of their cause. There is yet a third that is eternal and imperishable through its own power and might. The transient are all the particular things which did not exist from all time, or have had a beginning. The others are all those modes [marginal note adds: the general modes] which we have stated to be the cause of the particular modes. But the third is God." [1]

But while Spinoza operates on the whole with mediaeval conceptions and uses mediaeval terms, he always tries to emphasize the two points upon which he fundamentally differs from the mediaevals, namely, the necessity of God's causality and the denial of God's immateriality. This emphasis upon his two points of difference from the mediaevals may be discerned in the explanations he offers for the meaning of the old expression *natura naturans* as applied to God in contrast to *natura naturata* as applied to the world.

The distinction between God and the world, according to the mediaevals, is twofold. In the first place, God is the cause and the world His effect, and by cause they mean an intelligent cause, a creator, acting by design and with a purpose. In the second place, God is immaterial and the world material, so that God, if He is to be called substance at all,[2] is a substance beyond all substances, a superior or immaterial substance as against the world which consists of material substances. These two distinctions between God and the world are sometimes illustrated by the contrast be-

---

[1] *Short Treatise*, II, 5, § 5 (*Opera*, I, p. 62, ll. 28 ff.). Cf. § 2 (p. 563).
[2] Cf. above, p. 67.

tween the expressions *natura naturans* and *natura naturata*.
Whatever the origin of these two expressions and whatever
their variety of meanings,[1] it is sufficient for our present
purpose to know that they were used by Thomas Aquinas in
a sense which implied the two fundamental distinctions between God and the world as we have stated them. God,
says he, is called *natura naturans* because He is "the universal cause of all things that happen naturally,"[2] by which
he means, of course, that God is an intelligent and purposive
cause. This universal cause, he says again in another place,
belongs "to some superior substance, in which sense God is
said by some to be *natura naturans.*"[3] Spinoza seems to
refer to this last passage when he says of the *natura naturans*
that "the Thomists likewise understand God by it, but
their *natura naturans* was a being (so they called it) beyond
all substances."[4]

Now, Spinoza wanted to make use of these two expressions
as respective designations of what in his philosophy corresponded to God and the world in mediaeval philosophy,
namely, God and the modes. But still he did not want to use
them in their old meaning by which they connoted a distinction between an intelligent cause and a premeditated effect
or between an immaterial substance and a material substance. What did he do? He simply revised their meaning.
Defining *natura naturans* as including substance and its attributes and *natura naturata* as including all the modes, the
infinite as well as the finite,[5] he describes the differences between them in such terms that when we study them closely

---

[1] Cf. H. Siebeck, "Ueber die Entstehung der Termini *natura naturans* und *natura naturata*," in *Archiv für Geschichte der Philosophie*, 3 (1889–1890), pp. 370 ff.

[2] *Commentaria in Librum Beati Dionysii De Divinis Nominibus*, Caput 4, Lectio 21.

[3] *Summa Theologica*, Prima Secundae, Quaest. 85, Art. 6.

[4] *Short Treatise*, I, 8.   [5] *Ibid.*, I, 8; Epistola 9.

we discover that they are aimed directly against the Thomistic conception of the meaning of these expressions. In the first place, wishing to make it clear that, while he retains the original meaning of *natura naturans* as that of a universal cause, he does not mean by it an intelligent and purposive cause, Spinoza says that "by *natura naturans* we are to understand . . . God in so far as He is considered as a free cause," [1] by which he means to say, in so far as He acts by the necessity of His own nature,[2] whereas "by *natura naturata* I understand everything which follows from the necessity of the nature of God, or of any one of God's attributes." [3] In the second place, in opposition to the Thomists, who used the two expressions to designate a distinction between God as an immaterial substance and the world as a material substance, Spinoza, who denies finite substances and considers the distinction between God and the world as that between substance and mode, explains *natura naturans* by his own definition of substance and *natura naturata* by his own definition of mode. He thus says again: "By *natura naturans* we are to understand that which is in itself and is conceived through itself," whereas "by *natura naturata* I understand . . . all the modes of God's attributes in so far as they are considered as things which are in God, and which without God can neither be nor can be conceived." [4]

Another difference between Spinoza and the mediaevals, again growing out of his attribution of materiality to God, is his contention that the "two attributes may be conceived as really distinct — that is to say, one without the assistance of the other." [5] This passage, like so many other utterances

[1] *Ethics*, I, Prop. 29, Schol.
[2] *Ibid.*, I, Def. 7.
[3] *Ibid.*, I, Prop. 29, Schol.
[4] *Ibid.*, I, Prop. 29, Schol., and cf. Defs. 4 and 5.
[5] *Ibid.*, I, Prop. 10, Schol.

of Spinoza, is to be understood as a veiled criticism of the
mediaevals — in this case, of their conception of the inter-
relation of matter and form. According to Aristotle and the
mediaevals, though there exists a pure form, such as God
and the Intelligences, still in the physical universe matter
and form are only relative terms. Not only does not either
one of them exist without the other, but neither one of them
can be conceived without the other. Matter is matter only
with reference to some form, and form is form only with
reference to some matter. Furthermore, since God is pure
form, then matter, under the theory of emanation, must
ultimately have been produced by pure form, and it is form
which continues to be the active, producing principle in
matter. Matter itself is non-being; it is inert. It is form
which constitutes the existence of bodies,[1] and it is form
which sets matter in motion.[2] Form is said to exist in matter,
and matter is said to exist through form.[3] As against this,
Spinoza maintains that extension and thought, which in his
philosophy are the successors of matter and form,[4] are two
attributes of substance, existing in it together from eternity,
each having the same sort of existence as the other, and each
having its own independent form of activity, extension that
of motion and rest, and thought that of thinking. Unlike
form which produces motion in matter, thought does not
produce motion in extension. Motion is an activity of extension itself. Extension and thought, again, are not correlative terms, which cannot be conceived but through each
other; they can be conceived independently of each other
with reference to substance only. Nor does thought exist in
extension any more than extension exists through thought.

[1] Cf. my *Crescas' Critique of Aristotle*, pp. 257 ff.
[2] *Ibid.*, pp. 89, 299, 672–673.   [3] *Ibid.*, pp. 99, 257 ff., 577, n. 15.
[4] Cf. above, p. 234.

"For this is the nature of substance, that each of its attributes is conceived through itself, since all the attributes which substance possesses were always together, nor could one be produced by another; but each expresses the reality or being of substance." [1]

But still, though distinct from each other, extension and thought, again unlike matter and form, do not imply a plurality in the nature of substance. The reason why the mediaevals considered matter and form to constitute a plurality [2] wherever they existed together is not that they could be physically separated but that they were considered by them two distinct substances, each of which was supposed to exist in itself [3] and each of which was also supposed to be in contrast to the other, matter being potential, form actual, matter being the cause of corruption, form the cause of generation. [4] But according to Spinoza, extension and thought are not two substances but attributes of one substance, and they are only that "which intellect perceives of substance, as if constituting its essence." [5] There is no contrast between them of potentiality and actuality, or of imperfection and perfection. They are both expressing two different phases of the activity of substance, which in substance itself are one. Consequently, from the fact that the two attributes are conceived as distinct from each other it is not to be concluded that "they constitute two beings or two different substances" [6] after the manner of the Aristotelian and mediaeval matter and form. The independence of each attribute which Spinoza insists upon is merely to emphasize his denial of the interdependence of matter and form

---

[1] *Ethics*, I, Prop. 10, Schol.
[2] Cf. above, p. 113.
[3] Cf. above, p. 67.
[4] Cf. above, p. 236.
[5] *Ethics*, I, Def. 4.
[6] *Ibid.*, I, Prop. 10, Schol.

in mediaeval philosophy; it is not an independence which implies the reality of the attributes in their relation to substance or a reality in the difference between themselves, with the result that the unity of substance can no longer be logically maintained. The relation of the attributes to each other is of the same order as their relation to substance. Just as the difference between attribute and substance is only a conception of the human mind, so the difference between the attributes themselves is only a form of conception in the human mind, "for this is the nature of substance, that each of its attributes is *conceived* through itself." [1] It is in this sense only that the "two attributes may be *conceived* as really distinct — that is to say, one without the assistance of the other." [2]

Still, while extension is an attribute of God, it must not be confused with corporeality in the popular anthropomorphic conception of God. Spinoza dismisses this popular form of anthropomorphism which imagines "God to be like a man, composed of body and soul and subject to passion," without much ado, "for all men who have in any way looked into the divine nature deny that God is corporeal." [3] Behind this last statement there are the long discussions of the rabbis and of all the religious philosophers since Philo, who sought to spiritualize or to explain away the anthropomorphic expressions in certain portions of the Bible. Maimonides speaks for all of them when he emphasizes the importance of "God's incorporeality and His exemption from all passions," as doctrines "which must be explained to every one according to his capacity, and they must be taught by way of

---

[1] *Ibid.*   [2] *Ibid.*
[3] *Ibid.*, I, Prop. 15, Schol. This Scholium belongs to Prop. 14; cf. Freudenthal, "Spinozastudien," in *Zeitschrift für Philosophie*, 108 (1896), p. 251, n. 2. The rest of this chapter is a discussion of the first part of this Scholium.

tradition to children and women, to the stupid and igno-rant." [1]

The argument, however, which Spinoza reproduces in the name of philosophers for the incorporeality of God does not represent any of the standard philosophical arguments re-produced by Maimonides,[2] but it does represent the argu-ment quoted with approval by Maimonides in the name of the Kalam. The argument in Spinoza reads as follows: "That He cannot be so they conclusively prove by showing that by body we understand a certain quantity possessing length, breadth, and depth, limited by some fixed shape; and that to attribute this to God, a being absolutely infinite, is the greatest absurdity." The Kalam argument in Mai-monides reads as follows: "If God were corporeal, He would be finite, which is true; and if He were finite, He would have a certain dimension and a certain fixed shape, which is equally a correct conclusion." [3] Spinoza's passage is clearly a para-phrase of Maimonides' passage with the additional inclusion of the current definition of "body."

But the mediaevals, proceeds Spinoza, deny of God not only body but also matter and extension in general, and thus by removing from divine nature "substance itself, corporeal or extended," they affirm "that it was created by God." This leads Spinoza to a recapitulation of his arguments against creation, namely: if God is pure form, how could matter have arisen from Him? Of course, the mediaevals have their different solutions of the problem of the origin of matter; none of them sufficiently explains, however, "by what di-vine power it could have been created." This is quite a good summary of his main points against creation.[4] He concludes,

---

[1] *Moreh Nebukim*, I, 35.   [2] *Ibid.*, and II, 1.
[3] *Ibid.*, I, 76, Third Argument.
[4] Cf. above, Chapter IV.

as he always does after an argument against creation, "that extended substance is one of the infinite attributes of God."

Spinoza then reproduces two arguments by which the philosophers have endeavored to prove the incorporeality of God:

"First, that corporeal substance, in so far as it is substance, consists, as they suppose, of parts, and therefore they deny that it can be infinite, and consequently that it can pertain to God." So far I have been unable to find the source of this argument in the form in which it is given here by Spinoza. My impression is that it is a composite argument made up of the following parts: (1) The standard argument for the incorporeality of God on the ground that God is one and indivisible, whereas corporeality implies composition and divisibility. Maimonides puts this argument as follows: "There is no unity unless one discards corporeality, for a corporeal thing is not one, but composed of matter and form, which are two distinct things by definition; and furthermore it is divisible." [1] Exactly the same argument is given by Descartes [2] and also by Spinoza in the *Short Treatise*.[3] (2) The Aristotelian denial of the existence of an infinite corporeal magnitude,[4] which is reproduced by Maimonides [5] and elaborately discussed by Crescas.[6] That this argument is of a composite nature may be inferred from the following statement with which Spinoza introduces it: "But for the sake of a fuller explanation, I will refute my adversaries' *arguments*, which, *taken altogether* (*omnia*), come to this."

---

[1] *Moreh Nebukim*, I, 35.

[2] *Principia Philosophiae*, I, 23; *Principia Philosophiae Cartesianae*, I, Prop. 16. Cf. below, p. 268.

[3] *Short Treatise*, I, 2, § 18 (*Opera*, I, p. 24, ll. 12–15). Cf. below, p. 269.

[4] *Physics*, III, 5, 204a, 8 ff.; *Metaphysics*, XI, 10, 1066b, 1 ff.

[5] *Moreh Nebukim*, II, Introduction, Prop. I.

[6] *Or Adonai*, I, i, 1; I, ii, 1; cf. my *Crescas' Critique of Aristotle*, pp. 135 ff.

"Taken altogether" is undoubtedly a reference to the composite nature of the argument. A further proof that the argument as reproduced here in the *Ethics* is of a composite nature is the fact that in the *Short Treatise* [1] it is reproduced in its simple form, without any mention of infinity.

"A second argument is assumed from the absolute perfection of God. For God, they say, since He is a being absolutely perfect, cannot be passive; but corporeal substance, since it is divisible, can be passive." This argument, too, is found in Descartes [2] and in the *Short Treatise*,[3] and is implied in Maimonides' fourth proof for the existence, unity, and incorporeality of God from the concept of actuality and potentiality.[4]

The remaining parts of the Scholium to Proposition XV, which is taken up with a refutation of the alleged arguments against the possibility of an infinite corporeal substance, will be discussed in the next chapter.

---

[1] *Short Treatise*, I, 2, § 18 (*Opera*, I, p. 24, ll. 11–15).
[2] *Principia Philosophiae*, I, 23.
[3] *Short Treatise*, I, 2, § 18 (*Opera* I, p. 24, ll. 15–18).
[4] *Moreh Nebukim*, II, 1, Fourth Argument.

CHAPTER VIII

INFINITY OF EXTENSION

THE arguments of his "opponents" against the possibility of an infinite corporeal substance are introduced by Spinoza incidentally in connection with his discussion in the *Ethics* of the traditional rejection of extension as an attribute of God. The cause of this rejection, declares Spinoza, is to be found in the alleged incompatibility of extension with the infinity of the divine nature, for extension, assumed to be divisible and consisting of parts, cannot be infinite.[1] And thereupon Spinoza proceeds to adduce, as he says, "one or two," but actually three, of the "many examples" by which his opponents have tried to show, on the assumption of the divisibility of corporeal substance, that it could not be infinite. In the *Short Treatise*, however, this traditional argument for the rejection of extension as a divine attribute is reproduced without any reference to the problem of infinity. According to this earlier version of the argument, extension is said to be rejected as an attribute of God because, being divisible and consisting of parts, it is incompatible with the simplicity of the divine nature.[2] In both these places Spinoza's refutation of the argument is the same — an attempt to show that extension need not necessarily be divisible and composed of parts. This he does by drawing a distinction between extension as an attribute and extension as a mode and by showing that while the latter is divisible the

---

[1] *Ethics*, I, Prop. 15, Schol.: "First, that corporeal substance, in so far as it is substance, consists, as they suppose, of parts, and therefore they deny that it can be infinite, and consequently that it can pertain to God."

[2] *Short Treatise*, I, 2, § 18 (*Opera*, I, p. 24, ll. 11–15): "For since extension is divisible, the perfect being would have to consist of parts, and this is altogether inapplicable to God, because He is a simple being."

former is simple. In the *Short Treatise* [1] this distinction is
clearly drawn; in the *Ethics* [2] there is only an emphasis on
the indivisibility and simplicity of substance, with the implied
inference that modes only are composed of parts and divisible. But here, again, in the *Short Treatise* the refutation aims
to establish merely the simplicity of extension, whereas in
the *Ethics* it aims to establish its infinity as well as its simplicity. In the *Ethics*, furthermore, Spinoza reinforces his
refutation of his opponents by introducing a new distinction, namely, a distinction between quantity regarded "as
it exists in the imagination" and quantity regarded "as it
exists in the intellect," the former being "finite, divisible,
and composed of parts" and the latter being "infinite, one,
and indivisible" — a distinction, he says, which will be
"plain enough to all who know how to distinguish between
the imagination and the intellect." [3] Both these distinctions
mentioned in the *Ethics* occur also in two different places in
the *Tractatus de Intellectus Emendatione*. In one place there,
Spinoza says that the idea of quantity, if the understanding
(*intellectus*) forms it absolutely, is infinite, whereas the idea
of quantity, if the understanding perceives it by means of
a cause, is finite. [4] This distinction is undoubtedly identical
with his distinction between extension as an attribute and
extension as a mode, the former of which is infinite and the
latter finite. In another place he speaks of the errors into
which those "who do not accurately distinguish between intellect and imagination" easily fall, and he mentions as one of
the errors their belief that extension must be finite. [5] Finally,
these distinctions between substance and mode and between

[1] *Short Treatise*, I, 2, §§ 21–22 (*Opera*, I, p. 26, ll. 6–7).
[2] *Ethics*, I, Prop. 15, Schol. (*Opera*, II, p. 58, l. 16–p. 59, l. 1).
[3] *Ibid.* (*Opera*, II, p. 59, ll. 20–32).
[4] *Tractatus de Intellectus Emendatione*, § 108 (*Opera*, II, p. 39, ll. 4–14).
[5] *Ibid.*, § 87 (p. 32, l. 35–p. 33, l. 3).

intellect and imagination, with the addition of a third distinction, namely, that between the infinite and the indefinite,
occur again in one of Spinoza's letters to Meyer.[1]

It is the purpose of this chapter to isolate the problem of
the infinity of extension from the problem of the applicability of extension as an attribute of God, and to place this
aspect of Spinoza's discussion of the problem of infinity, both
the arguments of his unnamed opponents and also his
criticism thereof, in the light of its historical setting. We
shall deal here with certain texts of Crescas some of which
have already impressed Joël and other students of Jewish
philosophy with their obvious resemblance to certain passages in Spinoza's discussion of infinity.[2] As mere parallel
passages they are interesting enough, if only to increase the
number of such parallels that may be culled from the wide
philosophic literature of the Middle Ages. It may perhaps
be of somewhat greater significance if it is shown that even
Spinoza's refutations are found among those offered by
Crescas, but here, too, as we shall see, they may be found
also in the works of other writers. But the matter grows in
importance when we notice that the three "distinctions"
mentioned by Spinoza in his letter remind one of three refutations by Crescas of three arguments which correspond
respectively to the three "examples" of Spinoza. The matter becomes of still greater importance when, as we hope
to show, Spinoza's entire discussion of the indivisibility of
infinite extension is found to involve many difficulties which
can be cleared up by the aid of a thorough understanding
of Crescas' position on the same subject.

[1] Epistola 12.

[2] Cf. M. Joël, *Don Chasdai Creskas' religionsphilosophische Lehren*, p. 22, n. 1.
Cross-references to Spinoza are also to be found in: M. Schreiner, *Der Kalâm in
der jüdischer Literatur*, p. 27, n. 5; I. I. Efros, *The Problem of Space in Jewish
Mediaeval Philosophy*, pp. 93, 97, 107; M. Waxman, *The Philosophy of Don Hasdai
Crescas*, p. 40, n. 36.

It is safe to say that whomsoever in particular and directly Spinoza may have had in mind when assailing his opponents for denying the infinity of corporeal substance, it is ultimately the views and arguments advanced by Aristotle that he is contending with. Aristotle it was who boldly came out against the conception of an infinite which had been held by some of his predecessors, and it is in his writings that we find the most elaborate discussion of the subject. With a long array of arguments, in which all his characteristic theories of physics and metaphysics come into play, Aristotle exploded the theory of the existence of any possible phase of the infinite. This negation of the infinite, with the avalanche of arguments found in Aristotle's *Physics*, *Metaphysics*, and *De Caelo*,[1] had passed into the stock-in-trade of philosophic lore of mediaeval thought, where it played an important part, for it enters as an element into one of the chief proofs for the existence of God, namely, the cosmological proof based upon the assumption of the impossibility of an infinite regress. A few new arguments against infinity may have been added later, the old arguments of Aristotle may have been changed, garbled, misinterpreted, split up, and reclassified, but it is always to Aristotle that any mediaeval discussion of the impossibility of an infinite can be traced. It is, therefore, of the utmost importance for us to know to what extent the reasons attributed by Spinoza to his unnamed opponents for denying the infinity of corporeal substance do actually agree with what we know to be the views of Aristotle.

If we were to believe Spinoza, the main reason why Aristotle and his followers rejected infinity was their belief that corporeal substance is composed of parts. "Wherefore the whole heap of arguments," he says, "by which philosophers

[1] *Physics*, III, 4–8; *Metaphysics*, XI, 10; *De Caelo*, I, 5–7.

commonly endeavor to show that extended substance is finite, falls to the ground by its own weight, for all these arguments suppose that corporeal substance is made up of parts." [1] It would also seem that it is not the mere divisibility of extended substance that Spinoza understood to be the assumption underlying the arguments against infinity, but rather its divisibility into heterogeneous parts and its composition of those parts, so that extended substance, according to Spinoza, was not considered by his opponents as a continuous quantity. Thus he says: "Wherefore those who think that extended substance is made up of parts or of bodies really distinct from one another are talking foolishly, not to say madly. It is as though one should attempt by the mere addition and aggregation of many circles to make up a square, or a triangle, or something else different in its whole essence." [2] He furthermore compares the relation of the parts of which corporeal substance is supposed to be composed to that of points to a line. "In the same way, others, who have persuaded themselves that a line is made up of points, could also find many arguments by which they would prove that a line is not divisible to infinity." [3] Finally, Spinoza seems to imply that the assumption of the divisibility of corporeal substance, which is supposed to underlie the rejection of its infinity, is analogous to the belief in the discontinuity of nature as held by those who admit the existence of a vacuum, and thus he concludes the argument that "since, therefore, it is supposed that there is no vacuum in nature (about which I will speak at another time), but that all the parts must be united, so that no vacuum can exist, it follows that they cannot be really separated; that is to say,

---

[1] Epistola 12 (*Opera*, IV, p. 55, l. 16–p. 56, l. 1).
[2] *Ibid.* (p. 55, ll. 11–16).
[3] *Ibid.* (p. 56, ll. 2–4).

that corporeal substance, in so far as it is substance, cannot be divided." [1]

And yet how strangely un-Aristotelian are these views attributed by Spinoza to Aristotle. Aristotle, as we know him from his own writings, no more considered corporeal substance to consist of heterogeneous parts than a line to consist of points, for both body and line are to him continuous quantities and infinitely divisible. "It is impossible," he says, "that anything continuous should be composed of indivisibles; as, for instance, a line of points, since a line is a continued quantity, but a point is indivisible." [2] And what is true of a line is also true, according to Aristotle, of the other magnitudes, for "there is the same reasoning with respect to magnitude, time, and motion; for either each or no one of these consists of indivisibles and is divided into indivisibles." [3] Following out this line of reasoning, he concludes that "it is also evident that everything which is continuous is divisible into things always divisible." [4] And it is because of his belief in the continuity of corporeal substance that Aristotle rejects the existence of a vacuum and maintains "that there is not an interval different from bodies, either separable or actual — an interval which divides the whole body, so that it is not continuous, as Democritus and Leucippus say, and many other physicists — or even perhaps as something which is outside the whole body, which remains continuous." [5] Thus for every view ascribed by Spinoza to his opponents we may find in Aristotle a statement to the contrary.

Then there is another difficulty. Spinoza argues that his opponents denied the existence of an infinite because they

[1] *Ethics*, I, Prop. 15, Schol. (*Opera*, II, p. 59, ll. 16–19).
[2] *Physics*, VI, 1, 231a, 24–26.
[3] *Ibid.*, 231b, 18–20.   [4] *Ibid.*, 231b, 15–16.
[5] *Ibid.*, IV, 6, 213a, 31–213b, 2.

erroneously believed that infinite substance must be divisible, whereas he maintains that infinite substance is indivisible. Now, Aristotle himself discusses the possibility of an indivisible infinite substance, but, while admitting that there is an indivisible substance and that that substance can be called infinite, he argues that the term "infinite" when applied to that indivisible substance will not mean infinite except in the sense in which a voice is called "invisible," but that, he concludes, is not what he means by the term "infinite" when he investigates whether an infinite exists.[1] How then can Spinoza argue against those who deny the existence of an infinite and at the same time use the term "infinite" in a sense which is explicitly rejected by his opponents? Is he not committing here the fallacy of equivocation?

It has been suggested that in attacking his opponents for conceiving corporeal substance as an aggregate of distinct bodies it was Descartes whom Spinoza was aiming at.[2] In proof of this a passage is cited in which Descartes rejects extension as a divine attribute on account of its divisibility. A closer examination of this passage, however, will reveal that while it contains one of those arguments which Spinoza says are found "in authors, by which they endeavor to show that corporeal substance is unworthy of divine nature, and cannot pertain to it," [3] that argument is not used by Descartes to prove that corporeal substance cannot be infinite. Descartes simply endeavors to show that inasmuch as extension is divisible, and inasmuch as divisibility indicates imperfection, extension cannot be an attribute of God.[4] This

---

[1] *Ibid.*, III, 5, 204a, 8–14; *Metaphysics*, XI, 10, 1066b, 1–7.

[2] Cf. H. H. Joachim, *A Study of the Ethics of Spinoza*, p. 30, n. 1.

[3] *Ethics*, I, Prop. 15, Schol. (*Opera*, II, p. 58, ll. 13–16).

[4] *Principia Philosophiae*, I, 23: "Thus since in corporeal nature divisibility is included in local extension, and divisibility indicates imperfection, it is certain that God is not body." Compare Spinoza's *Principia Philosophiae Cartesianae*, I, Prop. 16.

exactly corresponds to the second of the two arguments
which Spinoza ascribes, both in the *Ethics* and in the *Short
Treatise*, to those who denied extension as an attribute of
God.[1] It is in this sense only that Tschirnhaus said to Leibniz, evidently in the name of Spinoza, that Descartes erroneously attributed divisibility to extension.[2] But it does
not mean that Descartes believed in the heterogeneity of
matter and its divisibility into irreducible parts on account
of which he had to deny its infinity. Quite the contrary,
Descartes believed that matter, whose essence is extension,[3]
is infinite in extent.[4] Furthermore, Descartes was far from
considering corporeal substance to consist of parts really
distinct from one another, for, by denying the existence of
atoms [5] and of a vacuum,[6] he held extension to be continuous
and infinite in divisibility.[7] Though he admits "that certain sensible bodies are composed of insensible particles," [8]

---

[1] *Ethics*, I, Prop. 15, Schol. (*Opera*, II, p. 58, ll. 9–13): "A second argument is
assumed from the absolute perfection of God. For God, they say, since He is a being absolutely perfect, cannot suffer; but corporeal substance, since it is divisible,
can suffer: it follows, therefore, that it does not pertain to God's essence." *Short
Treatise*, I, 2, § 18 (*Opera*, I, p. 24, ll. 13–15): "Moreover, when extension is divided
it is passive, and with God (who is never passive, and cannot be affected by any
other being, because He is the first efficient cause of all) this can by no means be
the cause." See Wolf's note on p. 178. Cf. above, p. 260.

[2] "Extensionem non inferre divisibilitatem, inque eo lapsum esse Cartesium."
Cf. K. I. Gerhardt, "Leibniz und Spinoza," in *Sitzungsberichte der königlich
preussischen Akademie der Wissenschaften zu Berlin*, 1889, p. 1077, reprinted also
in L. Stein, *Leibniz und Spinoza*, p. 283.

[3] Cf. *Principia Philosophiae*, II, 4, and *Principia Philosophiae Cartesianae*, II,
Prop. 2.

[4] Cf. *Principia Philosophiae*, II, 21, and *Principia Philosophiae Cartesianae*,
II, Prop. 6.

[5] Cf. *Principia Philosophiae*, II, 20, and *Principia Philosophiae Cartesianae*, II,
Prop. 5.

[6] Cf. *Principia Philosophiae*, II, 16–19, and *Principia Philosophiae Cartesianae*,
II, Prop. 3.

[7] Cf. *Principia Philosophiae*, II, 34, and *Principia Philosophiae Cartesianae*,
II, Prop. 5, Demonst.

[8] *Principia Philosophiae*, IV, 201.

he himself takes great pains to point out that these parts are not indivisible and insists that his view has more in common with that of Aristotle than with that of Democritus.[1] All that we may gather, therefore, from Descartes' own statements is that, while extension is divisible and hence cannot be applied to God, it is not divisible into indivisible parts in the same way as, according to Spinoza's arguments here against his opponents, a line would have to be divisible if it were conceived to consist of points.

It was thus not Aristotle and his followers whom Spinoza could have meant when he ascribed to his opponents the discreteness of corporeal substance as the reason for their denying its infinity. Still less could he have meant Descartes, for Descartes not only like Aristotle believed in the continuity of extension, but also like Spinoza held it to be infinite. Unless, therefore, we are inclined to say that Spinoza willfully imposed upon his opponents views which they would disclaim or that he unwarily misunderstood their position, we are bound to look for some new meaning that may lie concealed behind his uttered words. We must particularly try to find out whether it is not possible that Spinoza uses here the terms "indivisible" and "divisible" in some special and generally unknown sense, for it is in the discovery of such a special, uncommon use of these two terms, it would seem, that we may find an answer to the questions raised by us. We must therefore acquaint ourselves thoroughly with the sources from which we have reason to believe Spinoza had drawn his knowledge of the ancient controversy about infinity in order to learn the exact meaning of the terms he uses, to fill out the gaps in his fragmentary statements, and to restate the full implications of his argument of which his words are sometimes mere suggestions.

[1] *Ibid.*, IV, 202.

Allowing ourselves to be guided by the gentle hand of Averroes through the uncharted texts of Aristotle's writings, for it was Averroes by whom Spinoza's predecessors had been so wisely guided in their pursuit of the same subject, we may restate for our purpose certain pertinent facts with regard to Aristotle's conception of infinity. (1) An infinite, by definition, must be divisible, for "if it is indivisible, it will not be infinite, unless in the same manner as voice is invisible. Those, however, who say that there is the infinite do not assert that it thus subsists, nor do we investigate it as a thing of this kind, but as that which cannot be passed through." [1] (2) A divisible infinite must be one of the following three: (*a*) A quantity existing as an accident in a corporeal subject. (*b*) An incorporeal quantity. (*c*) An incorporeal substance.[2] An accidental quantity existing in a corporeal subject is dismissed as something irrelevant to the conception of infinity under discussion. Then an incorporeal infinite quantity is dismissed on the ground that there is no incorporeal quantity. To quote Averroes: "It cannot be an incorporeal quantity, for since number and magnitude are inseparable from sensible objects, it follows that whatever is an accident of number and magnitude must likewise be inseparable, and infinity is such an accident, for finitude and infinity are two accidents existing in number and magnitude, inasmuch as the essence of number and magnitude is not identical with the essence of the infinite." [3] Finally, an infinite incorporeal substance is rejected on the ground of the

---

[1] *Physics*, III, 5, 204a, 12–14. Cf. *Metaphysics*, XI, 10, 1066b, 5–7.

[2] Cf. Averroes' Middle Commentary on the Physics, Book III, Summa iii, Chapter 4: "If the infinite is divisible, it must inevitably be an incorporeal quantity or a quantity existing in a subject or one of the incorporeal substances." Paraphrased also by Crescas, *Or Adonai*, I, i, 1 (p. 4a). Cf. my *Crescas' Critique of Aristotle*, pp. 137 and 330.

[3] Averroes, *loc. cit.* Paraphrased also by Crescas, *loc. cit.* (p. 4a–b). Cf. *Crescas' Critique of Aristotle*, pp. 137 and 330.

absurdities that would ensue if it were supposed to be divisible. We shall quote the argument on this last point in three versions:

In Aristotle the argument is given as follows: "It is also evident that it is not possible for the infinite to be, as subsisting in energy and as essence and a principle: for whatever part of it is assumed will be infinite, if it is partible: for the essence of infinite and the infinite are the same, since the infinite is essence or substance, and is not predicated of a subject. Hence it is either indivisible, or divisible into infinites. But it is impossible that there can be many infinites in the same thing. As air, however, is part of air, so likewise infinite is a part of infinite, if it is essence and a principle. It is, therefore, impartible and indivisible. But this is impossible, since it is infinite in energy; for it is necessary that it should be a certain quantum." [1]

Averroes' version of the same argument runs as follows: "After we have shown that the infinite cannot be an incorporeal nor a corporeal quantity, there is nothing left but that it should be an incorporeal substance, of the kind we affirm of soul and intellect, so that the thing assumed to be infinite, that is, described as infinite, and infinite being itself are one in definition and essence and not different in reason. However, if we assume the infinite to be of this kind, its essence thus being at one with its definition, then, as a result of its being infinite, we shall be confronted with the question whether it is divisible or indivisible. [In the first case,] if it be divisible, then the definition of a part and the whole of it will be the same in this respect, as must necessarily be the case in simple, homoeomerous things. But if this be so, then the part of the infinite will be infinite. For the parts must inevitably either be different from the infinite whole or not

[1] *Physics*, III, 5, 204a, 20–29. Cf. *Metaphysics*, XI, 10, 1066b, 11–19.

be different therefrom. If they be different, then the infinite will be composite and not simple; if they be not different, then the definition of the part will be the same as that of the whole, for this reasoning must necessarily follow in the case of all things that are homoeomerous. Just as part of air is air, and part of flesh is flesh, so part of infinite is infinite, forasmuch as the part and the whole in each of these are one in definition and essence. If a difference is found in the parts of homoeomerous bodies, it is due only to the subject which is the receptacle of the parts and not to the form, for if we imagine the form of a homoeomerous body without a subject, the parts and the whole thereof will be the same in all respects and without any difference. [In the second case,] if we say that the infinite incorporeal substance is indivisible, which must be the case of an incorporeal *qua* incorporeal, then it cannot be said to be infinite except in the sense in which a point is said to be infinite. In general, the treatment of the existence of an incorporeal infinite is irrelevant to the subject under discussion." [1]

This Averroian version of Aristotle's argument is briefly restated by Crescas in the following terms: "Again, we cannot help asking ourselves whether this incorporeal substance is divisible or indivisible. If it is divisible, since it is also incorporeal, simple, and homoeomerous, the definition of any of its parts will be identical with that of the whole, and since the whole is now assumed to be infinite, any part thereof will likewise have to be infinite. But it is of the utmost absurdity that the whole and a part thereof should be alike [in infinity]. And if it is indivisible, which, indeed, as an incorporeal, it must be, we can no longer call it infinite, except as a point is said to be infinite." [2]

---

[1] Averroes, *loc. cit.*, quoted in my *Crescas' Critique of Aristotle*, pp. 331–332.
[2] *Or Adonai, loc. cit.* (p. 4a). Cf. *Crescas' Critique of Aristotle*, p. 137.

The gravamen of this Aristotelian argument against an infinite incorporeal substance, as will have been gathered, is that if it were divisible its parts would each have to be either infinite or finite, neither of which is possible. It is this argument that is reproduced by Spinoza in his first "example": "If corporeal substance, they say, be infinite, let us conceive it to be divided into two parts; each part, therefore, will be either finite or infinite. If each part be finite, then the infinite is composed of two finite parts, which is absurd. If each part be infinite, there is then an infinite twice as great as another infinite, which is also absurd." [1] It will be recalled that it is by this very same reasoning that Spinoza has proved in Propositions XII and XIII that an infinite must be indivisible. [2]

It is simply a matter of ordinary good reasoning that any attempt at a refutation of Aristotle's arguments against infinity will have to proceed from his own premises and will have to use terms in his own sense. The infinite will have to be a quantitative term, "for it is necessary that it should be a certain quantum," [3] as Aristotle plainly puts it. It will have to be divisible. This at once renders it futile to seek to establish an infinite incorporeal substance which is not quantitative and not divisible and of which the use of the term infinite merely means its exclusion from the universe of finitude in the same sense as a point is said to be infinite. The infinite, the existence of which any criticism of Aristotle will seek to establish, will thus have to be an incorporeal quantity, inasmuch as an infinite quantity existing as an accident in a corporeal subject has been disposed of by Aristotle himself as something inconsistent with the conception of infinity. But an infinite quantity has been rejected

---

[1] *Ethics*, I, Prop. 15, Schol. (*Opera*, II, p. 57, ll. 28-33).
[2] Cf. above, pp. 156-157.   [3] Cf. quotation above, p. 272, n. 1.

by Aristotle on the ground that no incorporeal quantity exists. The first step, therefore, in proving the existence of an infinite will be to establish the existence of an incorporeal quantity. Furthermore, this incorporeal quantity, while it will be divisible in conformity with the definition of the term infinite, will at the same time also have to be homoeomerous, as everything incorporeal perforce must be, and consequently, as a second step, a way will have to be found by which the parts into which it is divisible will not each be infinite like the whole nor finite unlike the whole.

It is exactly this process of reasoning that is employed by Crescas in his criticism of Aristotle. Endeavoring to show that an infinite is possible, he first seeks to establish the existence of an incorporeal quantity. He does so by proving, by arguments which do not concern us here, that a vacuum does exist, not indeed within the universe, dispersed throughout the pores of bodies and thus breaking up their continuity, as was held by Democritus, but rather outside the universe, the view held by the Pythagoreans.[1] The vacuum is nothing but tridimensional extension, or, as Crescas calls it, "incorporeal dimensions" as contrasted with a plenum which is "corporeal dimensions."[2] The significance of this distinction may be fully appreciated when compared with the view of Aristotle. Tridimensionality, according to Aristotle, is either the essence of matter or a form of matter, for there is a difference of opinion among his commentators on that point.[3] In either case, tridimensionality is always corporeal, for even if it is a form of matter, as a form it cannot exist without matter. But to Crescas the vacuum outside the universe is tridimensionality which has an independent,

---

[1] Cf. my *Crescas' Critique of Aristotle*, pp. 53–60.

[2] *Or Adonai*, I, ii, I (p. 14b). Cf. *Crescas' Critique of Aristotle*, p. 187.

[3] Cf. *Crescas' Critique of Aristotle*, p. 101 and n. 18 on pp. 579–590. Cf. above, pp. 234–235.

incorporeal existence. Furthermore, this incorporeal tridimensionality, argues Crescas, is a continuous quantity, i.e., a
magnitude, inasmuch as it is described in terms of a continuous quantity rather than in those of a discrete quantity, for it
is said to be "great and small" rather than "much and few." [1]
As such it is infinite in divisibility. But Crescas argues also
that it must likewise be infinite in extent, "for if it had a
limit it would have to terminate either at a body or at another vacuum. That it should terminate at a body, however,
is impossible. It will, therefore, have to terminate at another
vacuum, and that will go on to infinity." [2]

But here Crescas seems to become conscious of the difficulty raised by Aristotle, in Averroes' version of the argument, against an infinite incorporeal substance. The infinite
vacuum is divisible, but it is also homoeomerous. This
being the case, the parts of the infinite vacuum will either
be identical with the whole in definition or not. If they are,
then the parts will each be infinite like the whole; if they are
not, then the whole will be composed of heterogeneous parts.
The passage in which Crescas refutes Aristotle's argument
and in which he also seems to touch upon this difficulty may
be given here in full: "We say that the argument is fallacious
and a begging of the question. For he who assumes the existence of an incorporeal infinite magnitude likewise affirms
the existence of an incorporeal quantity. By the same token,
it does not follow that the definition of the infinite would have
to apply to its parts, just as such reasoning does not follow
in the case of a mathematical line. Nor would there have to
be any composition in it except of parts of itself." [3]

This passage of Crescas is evidently meant to be a refuta-

---

[1] *Or Adonai,* I, ii, 1 (p. 15a). Cf. my *Crescas' Critique of Aristotle,* p. 189.
[2] *Ibid.*
[3] *Or Adonai, loc. cit.* (p. 14a). Cf. *Crescas' Critique of Aristotle,* p. 179.

tion of the argument contained in the passage quoted above
from Averroes and of which Crescas himself has given a paraphrase. It will be recalled that Averroes argues against two
possible alternatives in the case where the infinite is assumed
to be both homoeomerous and divisible. First, if the parts
are each infinite like the whole, then the parts of an infinite
will be infinite, which is absurd. Second, if the parts are
each finite, then the infinite whole is composed of dissimilar
parts and is therefore no longer homoeomerous, which is
contrary to the assumption. Now, in this passage Crescas
evidently tries to answer both these alternatives. As against
the first, he seems to say that though the parts are assumed
to be of the same kind as the whole, they are not each infinite like the whole, for "it does not follow that the definition of the infinite would have to apply to all its parts, just
as such reasoning does not follow in the case of a mathematical line." As against the second, he seems to say that
though the parts are finite, the infinite whole would not be
composed of dissimilar parts, for "nor would there have to
be any composition in it except of parts of itself."

When we examine, however, this passage closely, we find
that its reasoning is not quite fully explained. In the first
place, Crescas does not fully explain why in an infinite
which is assumed to be homoeomerous and infinite in essence
the parts should not each be infinite like the whole. He
merely asserts that it would not have to be so in the case of
an infinite, just as something similar would not have to follow in the case of a mathematical line. But we may ask
ourselves: The infinite under discussion is infinite in its
essence just as a mathematical line is linear in its essence,
and since the parts of the line are linear like the whole, why
should not also the parts of the infinite be infinite like the
whole? In the second place, when Crescas, arguing appar-

ently against the second alternative, tries to show that the infinite would not be composed of dissimilar parts even if its parts were each finite, he simply says "nor would there have to be any composition in it except of parts of itself." What is the meaning of this statement?

Joël, probably starting with the *a priori* belief that Crescas must have used the analogy of the mathematical line in the same way as it is used by Spinoza in his letter to Meyer, paraphrases this passage as follows: "So wenig die Linie aus Punkten bestehe, so wenig habe man sich die unendliche Ausdehnung aus Theilen zusammengesetzt zu denken." [1] This paraphrase seems to take the passage as a refutation of an argument which assumes that the infinite is composed of heterogeneous parts. But as we have seen, quite the contrary, the analogy of the mathematical line is meant to be a refutation of that part of the argument, paraphrased by Crescas himself from Averroes, in which it is urged that if the infinite does not consist of heterogeneous parts, then the parts of the infinite will each have to be infinite.

In order to get at the meaning of this difficult passage we must call to our aid everything that was possibly known to Crescas about a mathematical line and its definition and out of this try to reconstruct imaginatively what he could have meant by his allusion to a mathematical line as a solution of the difficulty raised against the existence of an infinite. Two main facts about a mathematical line must have been known to Crescas. In the first place, he was acquainted with Euclid's definitions of a line, of which there are two. But it must have been the second of these definitions [2] with which Crescas operated, for it is this second definition which is most frequently quoted in the texts with which Crescas was ac-

---

[1] M. Joël, *Don Chasdai Creskas' religionsphilosophische Lehren*, p. 22.
[2] *Elements*, Book I, Def. 3.

quainted.[1] This definition reads: "The extremities of a line are points." In the second place, Crescas was well acquainted with Aristotle's statements that a line is a continuous quantity [2] and that "everything which is continuous is divisible into things always divisible." [3] According to these statements, then, a line is divisible into parts which are lines, and presumably a line can also be said to be composed of those lines into which it is divisible. Now the following question may be raised against these statements of Aristotle. Since the parts into which a line is divisible and of which they are also composed are according to Aristotle lines, they must also be defined as lines. But by Euclid's second definition of a line, the extremities of a line are said to be points. Consequently, if a line is divided into as well as composed of lines, a line must be also divided into and composed of points. But this is contrary to Aristotle's statement that a line is a continuous quantity and does not consist of points.[4]

This question must have undoubtedly been in the mind of Crescas when he made his allusion to the definition of a mathematical line. In his brief statement that the definition of the parts, of both the infinite and the line, is not identical with that of the whole and that both would not be composed except of parts of themselves, he gives us some clue as to what his answer to this question would be. He would answer it by saying that incorporeal quantities, which are continuous and homoeomerous like a mathematical line and the infinite vacuum, have no parts. Parts are to be found only in discrete quantities, such as number, which is made up of different units, or in corporeal continuous quantities where the parts differ from the whole in accidental qualities, as,

---

[1] Averroes' *Epitome of the Physics*, III (Hebrew version), p. 10b. Cf. Isaac Israeli, *Sefer Yesodot*, II, p. 45 (ed. Fried).

[2] *Physics*, VI, 1, 231a, 24.   [3] *Ibid.*, VI, 1, 231b, 15–16.

[4] *Ibid.*, VI, 1, 231a, 24–26.

for instance, the parts of an actual line which differ from the whole in length. If Aristotle does speak of a mathematical line as being infinitely divisible, the divisibility is merely in thought and in capacity; in reality infinite divisibility means nothing but a denial that the line consists of parts different from the whole. Or, to put the matter in other words, in the case of a discrete quantity, or of a corporeal continuous quantity, the whole is both divisible into parts and composed of those parts into which it is divisible; but in the case of an incorporeal continuous quantity, while the whole is infinitely divisible into parts, it is not composed of those parts into which it is infinitely divisible. In the case of the former, the parts are actual and co-exist with the whole; in the case of the latter, the parts are only potential and do not co-exist with the whole. This is what is behind Crescas' statement that the definition of the whole need not necessarily apply to the parts, for the parts are never actual and do never co-exist with the whole, and this is also what he means by saying that the whole is not composed "except of parts of itself," i.e., of parts which do not exist outside the whole or beside the whole. If Crescas had carried out his argument in full he would have drawn upon Aristotle's discussion as to "whether the formula [i.e., definition] of the parts must be present in the formula of the whole or not," [1] in the course of which discussion Aristotle says: "For even if the line when divided passes away into its halves, or the man into bones and muscles and flesh, it does not follow that they are composed of these as parts of their essence, but rather as matter; and these are parts of the concrete thing, but not of the form, i.e., of that to which the formula refers." [2]

[1] *Metaphysics*, VII, 10, 1034b, 23–24.
[2] *Metaphysics*, VII, 10, 1035a, 17–21. This interpretation of Crescas' passage is fully worked out in my *Crescas' Critique of Aristotle*, pp. 391–394.

In other words, to be divisible does not always mean to be composed.

The essential point in Crescas' answer to Aristotle's argument rests, as we have seen, upon the distinction between the vacuum outside the world and the plenum within it, or between incorporeal extension and corporeal extension. The answer given by Spinoza to the same argument, reproduced by him in his first "example," is based upon a similar distinction. What Crescas calls incorporeal extension or vacuum or space logically corresponds to what Spinoza calls extended substance or the attribute of extension, and what Crescas calls corporeal extension corresponds to what Spinoza calls the particular modes of extension.[1] To both of them, the former is infinite, whereas the latter is finite. Spinoza thus says in his letter to Meyer, and it is in answer to the first "example" mentioned in the *Ethics*, that the argument is based upon a failure to distinguish "between that which must be infinite from its very nature, or in virtue of its definition, and that which has no limits, not indeed in virtue of its essence, but in virtue of its cause."[2] From a comparison of his subsequent elaboration of this distinction in the letter with his corresponding discussion of the same distinction in the *Ethics*,[3] in the *Short Treatise*,[4] and in the *Tractatus de Intellectus Emendatione*[5] it is clear that the distinction is that between extension as an attribute and as a mode. That the latter is described by the expression "in virtue of its cause" may be explained by the fact that Spinoza regards the relation of substance to mode as that of cause to effect.[6]

[1] Cf. *Crescas' Critique of Aristotle*, pp. 116–118.
[2] Epistola 12 (*Opera*, IV, p. 53, ll. 2–5).
[3] *Ethics*, I, Prop. 15, Schol. (*Opera*, II, p. 58, l. 16–p. 59, l. 19).
[4] *Short Treatise*, I, 2, §§ 21–22 (*Opera*, I, p. 26, ll. 6–17).
[5] *Tractatus de Intellectus Emendatione*, §108 (*Opera*, II, p. 39, ll. 4–14).
[6] Cf. above, p. 76, and below, p. 324.

With his adoption of the old distinction between the two kinds of extension, Spinoza also follows his predecessors in his description thereof. But before we take up this point, we have to explain Spinoza's use of the terms "indivisible" and "divisible" in these descriptions. We have seen how the term "divisible" may apply to three different kinds of divisibility. First, it may apply to what the mediaevals would call an incorporeal continuous quantity, such as Crescas' vacuum or a mathematical line, which is free of any accidents. This is said to be divisible to infinity into parts which are homogeneous with the whole, that is to say, a vacuum into vacuums and a line into lines. Second, it may apply to what the mediaevals would call a corporeal continuous quantity which is subject to qualitative or quantitative accidents. This is said to be divisible into parts which while not generically different from the whole differ from it and from one another by certain qualitative or quantitative accidents. Thus, to use the illustration given by Averroes in the passage quoted above, while parts of air are air and parts of flesh are flesh, the parts differ from the whole and from one another in size or quality or in some other accident. Third, it may apply to a discrete quantity which is said to be divisible into parts which are heterogeneous with the whole and of which the whole is composed. Now, the first of these three kinds of divisibility is divisibility only in potentiality but not in actuality, for no actual division into infinity is possible. To say therefore of a thing that it is potentially infinitely divisible is tantamount to saying that actually it is indivisible. In fact, Aristotle himself, who defines a continuous quantity as that which is infinitely divisible, describes such a quantity also as indivisible, on account of its not being infinitely divisible in actuality. "Since, however, the term indivisible (ἀδιαίρετον) has two meanings, according as a whole is not potentially divisible or is actually undivided, there is nothing to hinder us from thinking an indivisible whole, when we think of length (that being actually undivided)." [1] Drawing upon this passage of Aristotle, Thomas Aquinas similarly says: "Now the indivisible is threefold, as is said in *De Anima*, III. First, the continuous is indivisible, since actually it is undivided, although potentially divisible. . . . The third kind of indivisible is what is altogether indivisible, as a point and unity, which cannot be divided either actually or potentially." [2]

Now, in order to remove the difficulties we have pointed out at the beginning of the chapter with regard to Spinoza's reproduction of the views of his opponents and also in order to make the infinite extension which Spinoza affirms to be of the same kind with reference to divisibility as that which Aristotle denies, we must assume that when Spinoza in his arguments against Aristotle's denial of an infinite extension insists that extension is indivisible he does not mean that it is indivisible like a point, that is to say, indivisible even potentially, but rather that it is indivisible like a continuous quantity in Aristotle's own use of the term, which means that it is indivisible in actuality. He is thus not arguing against Aristotle from a new assumption which Aristotle would not admit, but he is rather arguing against him from Aristotle's own assumption. And, similarly, when he argues that his Aristotelian opponents believe that extension is divisible and is composed of parts, he does not mean to say that they believe that extension is divisible into, and com-

---

[1] *De Anima*, III, 6, 430b, 6–8.

[2] *Summa Theologica*, Pars I, Quaest. 85, Art. 8: "Dicitur autem indivisibile tripliciter, ut dicitur in 3 de Anima (text. 23 et deinceps): uno modo sicut continuum est indivisibile, quia est indivisum in actu, licet sit divisibile in potentia. . . . Tertio modo dicitur indivisibile quod est omnino indivisibile, ut punctus et unitas, quae nec actu nec potentia dividuntur" (quoted also by Schütz in *Thomas-Lexikon* (1895), under "indivisibilis").

posed of, heterogeneous parts as if it were a discrete quantity;
what he means to say is that, thinking as they do of extension only as that which is subject to accidental differences,
they believe it to be divisible into parts which are quantitatively different from one another, and from such an assumption they argue against the existence of an infinite extension
in the same way as one would argue against the infinite
divisibility of a line or of matter if one started out with the
assumption that a line is composed of points and that matter is composed of heterogeneous atoms dispersed in a
vacuum. The point which I have been trying to make is
this: When Spinoza charges his opponents with a belief that
extension is divisible, he does not mean to say that extension
is held by them to be divisible into indivisible parts. What
he means to say is that in their use of the divisibility of extension as an argument against its infinity they failed to
distinguish between extension as an attribute, or what the
mediaevals would call an incorporeal extension, and extension
as a mode, or what the mediaevals would call a corporeal extension. The former, because it is divisible into homogeneous
parts, can be called indivisible, and can therefore be infinite.
The latter, however, because it is divisible into parts which
are quantitatively different, cannot be infinite.

The attribute of extension is described by Spinoza in the
same terms in which the infinite incorporeal substance is
described in the passage quoted above from Averroes. It is
"infinite from its very nature, or in virtue of its definition"
or "in virtue of its essence." [1] Like Crescas' incorporeal extension it is continuous and has no parts, for "part and whole
are not true or real entities, but only things of reason, and
consequently there are in nature [i.e., substantial extension]

[1] Epistola 12 (*Opera*, IV, p. 53, ll. 2-5).

neither whole nor parts." [1] It, therefore, "cannot be divided
into parts, or can have no parts"; [2] but, as we have already
pointed out, by this Spinoza simply means what Aristotle
would have sometimes described as being continuous and
infinitely divisible and what Crescas would have characterized as not being composed except of parts of itself. The
mode of extension, on the other hand, is "composed of finite
parts . . . and divisible" [3] just as any corporeal object, in
the view of his predecessors, is divisible either into heterogeneous parts or into parts which are qualitatively or quantitatively different from each other. "Further," says Spinoza,
"as regards the parts in nature, we maintain that division,
as has also been said already before, never takes place in
substance, but always and only in the modes of substance.
Thus, if I want to divide water, I only divide the mode of
substance, and not substance itself." [4] Similarly, in the passage quoted above from Averroes, we read: "Just as part
of air is air, and part of flesh is flesh, so part of infinite is
infinite, forasmuch as the part and the whole in each of these
are one in definition and essence. If a difference is found in
the parts of homoeomerous bodies [like air and flesh], it is
due only to the subject which is the receptacle of the parts
and not to the form, for if we imagine the form of a homoeomerous body without a subject, the parts and the whole
thereof will be the same in all respects and without any
difference." To be sure, Bruno, too, in his criticism of
Aristotle's rejection of infinity dwells upon the absence
of parts in the infinite,[5] but there is more in Spinoza's state-

---

[1] *Short Treatise*, I, 2, § 19 (*Opera*, I, p. 24, ll. 19–21).

[2] Epistola 12 (*Opera*, IV, p. 53, ll. 12–13).

[3] *Ethics*, I, Prop. 15, Schol. (*Opera*, II, p. 59, ll. 2–3).

[4] *Short Treatise*, I, 2, § 21 (*Opera*, IV, p. 26, ll. 6–11). The same illustration from
water occurs also in *Ethics*, I, Prop. 15, Schol. (*Opera*, II, p. 59, l. 35–p. 60, l. 3).

[5] Cf. *De l'infinito universo et Mondi*, Dial. II, p. 337 (ed. Lagarde).

ment than in Bruno's, and the excess is strongly reminiscent of Crescas.

Thus when Spinoza maintains against Aristotle the existence of an infinite, indivisible extension, he does not reject Aristotle's conception of the infinite as something divisible. The indivisibility of his extension is not like the indivisibility of a point, but rather like the indivisibility which Aristotle sometimes applies to a continuous quantity which is otherwise described by him as infinitely divisible. Again, when he charges his opponents with considering extension as divisible and composed of distinct points, he does not mean that they held extension to be a discrete quantity, similar to the discreteness of a line if it were supposed to consist of points; he only means to say that, denying the existence of pure extension, they considered extension divisible and composed of parts on account of the qualitative or quantitative differences in the parts of the material subject in which it existed, and thus they argued against the infinity of extension in the same way as one could argue against the infinite divisibility of a line or of matter if one started with the assumption that a line was composed of points and that matter was made up of heterogeneous parts dispersed in a vacuum.

Against the existence of an infinite extension there is another argument the purpose of which is to show that the assumption of an infinite would give rise to the absurdity of one infinite being greater than another. This argument appears under various forms in many works of Hebrew and Arabic philosophic literature, and it also occurs in the writings of Bruno. We shall restate here two versions of this argument.

One version is found in Saadia,[1] in Gersonides, followed by Crescas, and in Bruno. In Gersonides, the argument is

---

[1] *Emunot we-De'ot*, I, 3, Eighth Theory (4).

illustrated by the movements of the heavenly spheres and is aimed against the eternity and hence the infinity of time in the past. Several propositions are assumed in this argument. First, some of the heavenly spheres move faster than others. Second, in the same given time, the fast-moving spheres perform a greater number of rotations than the slow-moving. Third, one infinite cannot be greater than another. Out of these propositions the argument may be formulated as follows: If time be infinite in the past, then the fast-moving and slow-moving spheres will have performed an infinite number of rotations. But since the number of rotations of the fast-moving sphere must be greater than that of the slow-moving, one infinite will be greater than another.[1] In Bruno's argument the same difficulty is raised, but the illustration is taken from the division of infinite distance into an infinite number of paces (or feet) and an infinite number of miles.[2] Spinoza's second "example" follows closely these two arguments, resembling in form more that of Bruno than that of Gersonides. "Again, if infinite quantity is measured by equal parts of a foot each, it must contain an infinite number of such parts, and similarly if it be measured by equal parts

---

[1] *Milḥamot Adonai*, VI, i, 11 (pp. 341–342): "Having laid down these premises, I contend that, if past time were infinite in quantity, it would follow that there could be no swift motion and slow motion among the spheres. The argument runs as follows: The number of rotations performed by the swift-moving sphere in the past time, which is assumed to be infinite, must of necessity be infinite, and the same must be true of the number of rotations performed by the slow-moving sphere. But inasmuch as one infinite number cannot be greater nor smaller than another infinite number, it will follow that no one sphere is of swifter motion than another, for if one sphere moved more swiftly than another, the number of rotations of the swift sphere would of necessity be greater."

This argument is reproduced in *Or Adonai*, III, i, 3 (p. 64a).

[2] *De l'infinito universo et Mondi*, Dial. II (p. 338): "El. Particolarmente di quello che fa al proposito nostro de gl' infiniti passi, et infinite migla che uerrebono á fare un infinito minore, et un' altro infinito maggiore nell' immensitudine de l'uniuerso." Cf. on the same page: "la dimensione infinita non é meno de infiniti piedi, che de infinite migla."

of an inch each; and therefore one infinite number will be twelve times greater than another infinite number." [1]

In his answer Bruno endeavors to show that in the infinite there can be no distinction of number and measure. "It is an absurdity to say that in the infinite one part is greater and another is smaller, and one part has a greater proportion to the whole and another a smaller." [2] Again: "In the innumerable and the immeasurable there is no place for more or less, few or many, nor for any distinction of number or measure." [3] A similar statement is also made by Galileo: "These are some of those difficulties which arise from discourses which our finite understanding makes about infinites, by ascribing to them attributes which we give to things finite and terminate, which I think most improper, because those attributes of majority, minority, and equality agree not with infinites, of which we cannot say that one is greater than, less than, or equal to another." [4] Exactly the same sort of answer is given by Crescas to Gersonides' argument, and, strangely enough, it contains some of the same expressions: "The fast spheres will, indeed, in a certain time perform the same number of rotations that slow spheres will perform in a greater time, when the number of their rota-

---

[1] *Ethics*, I, Prop. 15, Schol. (*Opera*, II, p. 57, ll. 33–37).

[2] *Op. cit.*, pp. 337–338: "Essendo che implica contradittione che ne l'infinito sia parte maggiore, et parte minore, et parte che habbia maggiore et minore proportione á quello."

[3] *De Immenso et Innumerabilibus*, II, 8 (*Opera Latina*, I, 1, p. 284):

"Innumero nempe atque immenso non locus ullus
Esse potest pluris, modici, pauci, atque minoris,
Quae numeri et mensi discrimina cernimus esse."

(English translation quoted from J. Lewis McIntyre's *Giordano Bruno*, p. 188.)

[4] *Discorsi e Dimostrazioni matematiche intorno a due Nuove Scienze*, I, in *Le Opere di Galileo Galilei* (Firenze, 1890–1909), Vol. 8, p. 77, ll. 35 ff., quoted by Bertrand Russell in his *Scientific Method in Philosophy*, p. 192, from Tho. Weston's translation, p. 47.

tions is of such a kind as can be described by the terms much and few, great and small, within a certain time limit, that is to say, when both the number and the time are finite, and this indeed is due to the fact that the fast sphere and the slow sphere cannot perform the same number of rotations in equal time. But when the time or the number of rotations is infinite, neither of these can be described by the terms much and few, great and small, equal and unequal, for all these terms are determinations of measure, and measurability does not apply to an infinite. Hence, no absurdity will ensue if both the fast and the slow spheres have performed an infinite number of rotations in the past, inasmuch as the number of their rotations cannot be properly described as great and small and unequal." [1]

A similar distinction is to be discovered in Descartes' differentiation between the infinite and the indefinite. From the illustrations he gives it is clear that by the indefinite he means that whose parts cannot be expressed by any number. He furthermore describes the indefinite as that which has no limits only "in a certain sense," from which it may be inferred that the real infinite is that which has no limits. The difference between the indefinite and the infinite, according to Descartes, is therefore a difference between that whose parts cannot be expressed by any number and that which has no limits. By this distinction Descartes, like Crescas and Bruno, disposes of such questions against the existence of an infinite as, e.g., "whether the half of an infinite line is infinite." [2]

The other version of the argument is found in Avicenna, [3]

---

[1] Or Adonai, III, i, 4 (p. 67b).

[2] Principia Philosophiae, I, 26, and Principia Philosophiae Cartesianae, II, Prop. 5, Schol.

[3] Al-Najat, II: Physics (Rome, 1593), p. 33, reproduced in Carra de Vaux's Avicenne, p. 201.

Algazali,[1] Saadia and Baḥya,[2] Abraham ibn Daud,[3] and Altabrizi.[4] Crescas cites it in the name of Altabrizi in an abridged and modified form. We quote it here from Crescas: "Suppose we have a line infinite only in one direction. To this line we apply an infinite line [which is likewise infinite only in one direction], having the finite end of the second line fall on some point near the finite end of the first line. It would then follow that one infinite [i.e. the first line] would be greater than another infinite [i.e., the second line]. But this is impossible, for it is well known that one infinite cannot be greater than another." [5]

The refutation given by Crescas of this argument is again based upon the distinction between the infinite in the sense of the indefinite or of its being incapable of measurement and the infinite in the sense of its having no limits. To quote: "The impossibility of one infinite being greater than another is true only with respect to measurability, that is to say, when we use the term 'greater' in the sense of being greater by a certain measure, and that indeed is impossible because an infinite is immeasurable. In this sense, to be sure, the first one-side infinite line [in Altabrizi's argument] will not be greater than the second one-side infinite line, inasmuch as neither of them is measurable in its totality. Thus indeed the first line is not greater than the second, though it extends beyond the second on the side which is finite." [6] What Crescas is trying to do is to point out the possibility of an extension

---

[1] *Maḳaṣid al-Falasifah*, II, i (p. 126), quoted by me in *Crescas' Critique of Aristotle*, p. 347.

[2] *Emunot we-De'ot*, I, 3, Eighth Theory (3); *Ḥobot ha-Lebabot*, I, 5.

[3] *Emunah Ramah*, I, 4.

[4] Commentary on Maimonides' Twenty-five Propositions, Prop. I, quoted in my *Crescas' Critique of Aristotle*, pp. 145–146.

[5] *Or Adonai*, I, i, 1 (p. 5a–b). Cf. *Crescas' Critique of Aristotle*, p. 149.

[6] *Or Adonai*, I, ii, 1 (p. 15a). Cf. *Crescas' Critique of Aristotle*, pp. 190–191.

which is infinite in the sense that its parts cannot be equated
with or explained by any number and still is not infinite in
the sense that it has no limits. Such, for instance, are the
lines in Altabrizi's argument, which are infinite on one side
but finite on the other. When two such immeasurable but limited infinites are given, then while indeed one of them cannot
be conceived as greater than the other in the sense that the
total number of its parts can be expressed by a number which
is greater, still it can be conceived as greater than the other
in the sense that it can extend beyond the other on the
limited side. The reason why one immeasurable infinite cannot be said to be greater than another, says Crescas, is that
their parts cannot be expressed by any number and therefore the terms great and small are inapplicable to them.

It is, therefore, as a refutation of his second "example"
in the *Ethics* that Spinoza in his letter to Meyer charges his
opponents with the failure to make a distinction "between
that which is called infinite because it has no limits, and that
whose parts we cannot equate with or explain by any number,
although we know its maximum and minimum," [1] concluding
that, had they made such a distinction, "they would also have
understood which kind of infinite can be conceived as greater
than another infinite, without any complication, and which
cannot be so conceived." [2] The wording of Spinoza's answer
is strikingly reminiscent of both Crescas and Descartes.

Back again to Aristotle, by way of Averroes, Altabrizi, and
Crescas, we must go for the source of Spinoza's third "example." In the *De Caelo*, Aristotle advances a series of arguments to prove from the circular movements of the heavenly
spheres that the heavens cannot be infinite, for if they were
infinite they could not revolve in a circle. One of these

---

[1] Epistola 12 (*Opera*, IV, p. 53, ll. 5–8).   [2] *Ibid.* (p. 53, ll. 14–15).

arguments, reproduced by Crescas from Averroes, runs as follows:[1]

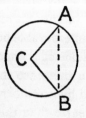

Let *ACB* be an infinite circle.
Let *CA* and *CB* be infinite radii.
Let *CA* revolve on its centre *C*.
Let *CB* be fixed.

If an infinite sphere could rotate upon itself, then *CA* would sometimes have to fall on *CB*.

But the distance *AB* is infinite, and an infinite distance cannot be traversed.

Consequently, *CA* could never fall on *CB*.

Hence, no infinite body could have circular motion.

An argument advanced by Altabrizi seems to be a modification of this Aristotelian argument. It is more general than the Aristotelian argument in that it is detached from the illustration of the movements of the spheres. Crescas reproduces it in the name of "one of the moderns" as a reinforcement of Aristotle's argument. In Crescas' restatement it read as follows: "The same difficulty [according to this version of the argument] would arise in the case of any two lines emerging from a common point if they were supposed to be infinite. The distance between any two such lines at the point where they are intersected by a common chord would undoubtedly increase in proportion to the extension of the lines, and as the lines are assumed to be infinite, the distance between them would likewise have to be infinite.

[1] *Or Adonai*, I, i, 1 (p. 7a). Cf. *De Caelo*, I, 5, 271b, 27–272a, 7; *Crescas' Critique of Aristotle*, pp. 169 and 379–380.

But this is self-evidently impossible." [1] In almost exactly
the same terms Spinoza states his third "example." "Lastly,
if from one point of any infinite quantity it be imagined that
two lines, *AB*, *AC*, which at first are at a certain and determinate distance from one another, be infinitely extended, it
is plain that the distance between *B* and *C* will be continually increased, and at length from being determinate will be
indeterminable." [2]

In his answer Crescas again brings into play the distinction between the infinite and the indefinite. He endeavors
to show that while any given distance between any two points
in the infinitely extending lines must be finite, the distance
between them may be said to be infinite in the sense that
whatever distance we take there is always a greater distance
beyond it. It is analogous to what Aristotle says of magnitude and number that, while they are both finite in actuality
they are infinite in capacity, in so far as magnitude is infinitely divisible and number is infinitely addible. They are
in this sense infinite, "for the infinite is not that beyond
which there is nothing, but it is that of which there is always
something beyond." [3] To quote him in part: "To this the
opponent of Aristotle may answer that distance increases
[infinitely] in the same manner as number is said to increase
[infinitely], but it always remains limited. That the possibility of infinite increase is not incompatible with its being
actually limited may be seen from the case of infinite decrease, for the examination into contraries is by one and the
same science. [4] It has been demonstrated in the book on *Conic
Sections* that it is possible for a distance infinitely to decrease

[1] *Or Adonai, loc. cit.* Cf. *Crescas' Critique of Aristotle*, pp. 171 and 381–382.
[2] *Ethics*, I, Prop. 15 (*Opera*, II, p. 57, ll. 37 ff.).
[3] *Physics*, III, 6, 207a, 1–2.
[4] Cf. *Metaphysics*, XI, 3, 1061a, 19.

and still never completely to disappear.[1] It is possible to assume, for instance, two lines which, by how much farther they are extended, are brought by so much nearer to each other, and still will never meet, even if they are produced to infinity. If, in the case of decrease, there is a certain distance which always remains and does not disappear, *a fortiori* in the case of increase it should be possible for a distance, though infinitely increased, always to remain limited.[2] . . . This, to be sure, is remote from the imagination, but reason compels us to assume it." [3]

Now, Spinoza does not furnish us with any direct answer to the third "example," though his distinction between the infinite and the indefinite may apply to it. But when he says in his letter to Meyer that his opponents failed to distinguish, thirdly, "between that which we can only understand but cannot imagine, and that which we can also imagine," [4] may we not assume that it is a reminiscence of the last statement by which Crescas concludes his lengthy refutation of the argument which is the exact prototype of the third "example"? Had Spinoza taken the trouble to give a full expression to what he had in mind when he quoted reminiscently this third distinction, he would undoubtedly have given us a paraphrase of this last quoted of Crescas' refutations, as he did, in part, at least, of his two other distinctions; or, perhaps, he would have gone still further and said

---

[1] Apollonius, *Conic Sections*, II, Theorem 13. See Munk, *Guide des Égarés*, I, p. 410, n. 2.

[2] *Or Adonai*, I, ii, 1 (p. 16a). Cf. *Crescas' Critique of Aristotle*, p. 207.

[3] *Or Adonai*, *loc. cit.* (p. 16b). Cf. *Crescas' Critique of Aristotle*, p. 211. That the last statement of Crescas about imagination and reason refers to the entire argument and not merely to the passage immediately preceding it may be gathered from Maimonides, who, speaking of the problem cited from the *Conic Sections*, similarly remarks: "This is a fact which cannot easily be conceived, and which does not come within the scope of the imagination" (*Moreh Nebukim*, I, 73, Prop. 10).

[4] *Epistola* 12 (*Opera*, IV, p. 53, ll. 8–10).

with a generous but rather patronizing gesture: *Nam, ut ipsam apud Judæum quendam Rab Ghasdaj*[1] *vocatum, reperio, sic sonat.*[2]

[1] The transliteration of Ḥasdai (חסדאי) by "Ghasdai" follows Spinoza's own method of transliterating the Hebrew *Ḥet* (ח) by *gh*. Cf. his *Compendium Grammatices Linguae Hebrææ*, Cap. II (*Opera*, I, p. 288, l. 18). The form "Jaçdai" (*Opera*, IV, p. 61, l. 35) which occurs in Leibniz's copy of the letter evidently represents the Spanish-Portuguese transliteration of the name. In old Spanish documents published by Fritz Baer in his *Die Juden im Christlichen Spanien*, I (1929), the name is usually written "Azday." But the following forms also occur: "Adzay" (p. 712), "Atzay" (pp. 499, 676), "Azay" (pp. 616, 723), "Azdray" (p. 1000), "nAzday" (p. 676), "Nazday" (p. 699). In these documents the personal name is generally followed by the surname "Cresques," but it occurs also without it (pp. 741, 1000), as here in Spinoza's letter. In Giovanni Francesco Pico della Mirandola's *Examen Doctrinae Vanitatis Gentium*, VI, 2, the name is transliterated "Hasdai" and is not followed by the surname. Nor is the surname given in the references to Crescas in the works of Isaac ben Shem-Ṭob and Shem-Ṭob ben Joseph ben Shem-Ṭob. Cf. my *Crescas' Critique of Aristotle*, pp. 32–33.

[2] Epistola 12 (*Opera*, IV, p. 61, ll. 17–18).

CHAPTER IX

THE CAUSALITY OF GOD

I. MATERIALITY AND CAUSALITY OF GOD

AFTER recapitulating his position as to the materiality of God in Proposition XIV, Spinoza proceeds in logical order to state his conclusion that there is nothing in the material world which is not in God, or, to put it in the words of his own Proposition XV, "whatever is, is in God, and nothing can either be or be conceived without God." Taken by itself, this proposition would seem to be nothing but a repetition of the ordinary assertions of the omnipresence of God which are current in the literature of every religion. In fact, Spinoza himself acknowledges as much when he says that "like Paul, and perhaps also like all ancient philosophers . . . I assert that all things live and move in God; and I would dare to say that I agree also with all the ancient Hebrews as far as it is possible to surmise from their traditions." [1] By "all ancient philosophers" he undoubtedly refers not only to the Stoic poets Aratus and Cleanthes, to whom Paul himself refers in his statement "as certain also of your own poets have said," [2] and not only to the Stoics in general, whose God was material like the God of Spinoza, but also to those who like Aristotle conceived of God as immaterial, for, though immaterial and hence separated from the universe, that God was still He in whom the universe could be said to have its being, inasmuch as He was its formal, efficient, and final cause. [3] Similarly by the "ancient Hebrews" Spinoza does not refer only to the teachings

[1] Epistola 73.   [2] Acts 17, 28. Cf. Commentaries *ad loc*.   [3] Cf. below, p. 302.

of the Hebrew Bible but also, and perhaps more particularly, to the teachings of Judaism at the time of Paul, in its Palestinian and Hellenistic branches, for the omnipresence of God is emphasized by both of these branches of Judaism. The classic expression on this point, used by both the rabbis and Philo, is the statement which is quoted constantly in the Middle Ages by Jewish as well as Christian philosophers, namely, that God is the place of the world.[1] The belief in the omnipresence of God has continued to be a religious commonplace in Judaism as well as Christianity and Mohammedanism, and has been maintained by every shade of religious opinion, though, perhaps, not always without some slight shade of logical inconsistency. The most pertinent passage for our present purpose, both on account of its source and on account of its phrasing, is the following quotation from the Hymn of Unity, which is included in the Jewish liturgy: "Thou encompassest all and fillest all; and since Thou art all, Thou art in all. . . . Thou art not separated or detached from anything, nor is any place empty or devoid of Thee. . . . Thou art and existeth in all; all is Thine, and all is from Thee."[2]

But while the proposition taken by itself contains nothing new, it is used by Spinoza in a different sense. He himself alludes to that difference in its use when he says in his reference to Paul and all ancient philosophers that he agrees with their assertion, "though in another way." What the difference between them is becomes clear in Proposition XV, for this proposition is to be understood as a criticism of the mediaeval inconsistency in first affirming that all things are in God and then denying that matter is in God. For when

---

[1] *Genesis Rabbah* 68, 9 *et al.*, Philo, *De Somniis*, I, 11; Crescas, *Or Adonai*, I, ii, 1; Leibniz, *Nouveaux Essais*, II, 13, § 17. Cf. my *Crescas' Critique of Aristotle*, pp. 123, 201.   [2] *Shir ha-Yiḥud*, III.

the mediaevals reiterated their statements that God is all
and all is from God and in God, they had to make a mental
reservation with regard to matter. God was not matter, and
matter was not from God nor in God. Matter existed by the
side of God, according to Aristotle; it was created by God *ex
nihilo*, according to the generally accepted view of all the
three religions; it appeared somewhere in the process of
emanation, according to the emanationists. The statement
that God is all and all is from God and in God could not be
taken in its full and literal sense that "whatever is, is in God"
except by one who like Spinoza asserted that God was material.

But is it only this that Proposition XV means to assert,
namely, that matter as well as form is in God, or does it
mean more than this? Does it not mean a complete denial
of the separation of God from the world, with the inevitable
consequence of the disappearance of God as a distinct being
either in thought or in reality?

In the history of philosophy Spinoza's conception of God
has been characterized by different names. In his own day,
it was called deism of the type that flourished then in France,[1]
and it was also stigmatized as a disguised kind of atheism.[2]
When this imputation of atheism was renewed by Jacobi,[3]
Hegel quibbled about its being akosmism rather than atheism.[4] Novalis met the charge of atheism by declaring Spinoza
a God-intoxicated man [5] — a declaration which explains
Spinoza's profuse use of the term God rather than its meaning. The term pantheism is the one which has been most

---

[1] *Epistola* 42.   [2] *Epistola* 43.

[3] *Ueber die Lehre des Spinoza in briefen au den Herrn Moses Mendelssohn*, 1785.
Cf. Jacobi's *Werke* (1819), Vol. IV, 1, p. 216.

[4] *Encyclopädie der philosophischen Wissenschaften*, I, § 50 (ed. Bolland), p. 74;
Vorlesungen über die Geschichte der Philosophie (ed. Bolland), p. 891.

[5] *Schriften* (ed. Paul Kluckhohn, Leipzig [1892]), Vol. III, p. 318, § 253.

often applied to it. Avenarius, who has stratified the writings of Spinoza on the basis of the use of the terms Nature, God, and Substance, just as the higher critics stratify the Pentateuch on the basis of the use of the terms Jehovah and Elohim, has discovered three phases in the development of Spinoza's pantheism, which he designates by the following terms: Naturalist All-in-one, Theistic All-in-one, and Substantive All-in-one [1] — a distinction in which one will find it hard to discover any difference. Windelband brushes all these subtleties aside and declares outright that Spinoza's conception of God is "complete and unreserved pantheism." [2]

The problem before us, however, is not to devise a fitting term by which Spinoza's conception of God can be adequately described, but rather to find out whether his God is absolutely identical with the aggregate totality of particular things or whether He does in some way transcend it. When we leave what others have said about Spinoza's God and turn to what he himself has said about Him, we find that the matter does not become any clearer. Though he makes reference to the characterization of his religion as one which "does not rise above the religion of the Deists," [3] he does not definitely disclaim it. Perhaps he saw no need of disclaiming it, since the author of that statement had done it himself when he said that "unless I am mistaken in my conjecture, this man does not include himself in the ranks of the Deists, and does not allow men to return to the least bit of religious worship." [4] Nor does he disclaim the charge of atheism except in so far as

---

[1] *Naturalistische All-Einheit, Theisitische All-Einheit, Substanzialistische All-Einheit.* Cf. R. Avenarius, *Ueber die beiden ersten Phasen des Spinozischen Pantheismus* (Leipzig, 1868).

[2] *Geschichte der Philosophie* (3rd edition), p. 336; English translation, *A History of Philosophy*, p. 409.   [3] Epistolae 42 and 43.

[4] Epistola 42.

the term meant in his time a man who is "wont to desire inordinately honors and riches." [1] No more conclusive than this evidence from silence are his positive statements. While in one place he asserts that "those who think that the *Tractatus Theologico-Politicus* rests on this, namely, that God and nature (by which they mean a certain mass, or corporeal matter) are one and the same, are mistaken," [2] in another place he asserts that "I could not separate God from nature as all of whom I have any knowledge have done," [3] and in still another place he identifies the terms God and nature. [4] All that one can with certainty gather from these passages is that while Spinoza did not identify God with nature conceived as an inert mass of matter, he did identify Him with it when conceived in all its infinite attributes. Nor, finally, can we get more light on the question from his statement that "the universe is God," [5] for here, too, the statement may merely mean, as may be judged from the context, "that all things [that is to say, including matter] emanate necessarily from the nature of God." [6] But does it also mean that God is nothing but the aggregate of particular things which constitute the universe?

Since the uttered statements of Spinoza do not throw any light on the question, we shall try the use of the historical critical method in order to solve our problem. We shall give an analysis of the salient features of the traditional conception of God which Spinoza constantly uses as the target for his criticism. We shall also try to find out what elements of it he criticized and ultimately rejected. Finally we shall try to reconstitute Spinoza's conception of God out of those

---

[1] Epistola 43.   [2] Epistola 73.
[3] Epistola 6.
[4] *Short Treatise*, I, 2, § 12 (*Opera*, I, p. 22, ll. 9–13).
[5] Epistola 43.
[6] *Ibid.*

elements of the traditional God which were left by him uncriticized.

The God of tradition whom Spinoza tries to dethrone is sometimes depicted by him disdainfully in all his anthropomorphic crudity as He was pictured in the minds of the vulgar.[1] But this may be considered only as an occasional departure from what is really his general practice. As a rule, the conception of God which he criticizes is that of the philosophers, of the "men who have in any way looked into the divine nature."[2] This conception of God is marked by two main characteristics, immateriality and causality. All the problems raised about the nature of God by philosophers throughout the Middle Ages can be grouped together under these two terms. The immateriality of God it is which gives rise to His unity, simplicity, immutability, and incomparability, out of which springs the complexity of problems which go under the general name of attributes. But such a conception of God's immateriality takes God completely out of the universe, which is not what the mediaeval philosophers wanted to do. And so, immediately after they establish the absolute immateriality of God, they turn around and try to introduce God back into the universe by establishing a certain causal relation between them. It is through the causality of God that the world comes into being and is ruled and guided by Him. God's omnipresence, omniscience, omnipotence, and benevolence of which they all speak are nothing but different ways of expressing the fact of divine causality. These, then, are the two main characteristics of the God of traditional philosophy. Now Spinoza's criticism of this conception of God in *Ethics*, I, falls into two parts, corresponding to these its two main characteristics, immate-

[1] E.g., *Ethics*, I, Prop. 15, Schol.
[2] *Ibid.*

riality and causality. The first fifteen propositions are all a
criticism of the immateriality of God, culminating in Proposition XV in the statement that "whatever is, is in God,"
which, as we have shown, means that everything, including
matter, is in God. Beginning now with Proposition XVI to
the end of the First Part, he criticizes the old conceptions of
the causality of God. In this chapter, however, we shall deal
only with Propositions XVI–XVIII.

In order to be able to follow Spinoza's criticism, we must
first give a formal statement of what the mediaevals meant
by divine causality. Causes have been divided by Aristotle
into four: the material, the formal, the efficient, and the
final. Beginning with this commonplace of philosophy, the
mediaevals asked themselves which of these causes God is.
He cannot be the material cause, they said, for God is immaterial. He must therefore be the three other causes. Maimonides is worth quoting on this point. "It has been shown
in the science of physics that everything, except the First
Cause, owes its origin to the following four causes — the
material, the formal, the efficient, and the final. These are
sometimes proximate, sometimes remote, but each by itself
is called a cause. They also believe — and I do not differ
from their belief — that God, blessed be He, is the efficient,
formal, and final cause." [1]

Now, in opposition to the mediaevals, as we have already
seen, Spinoza makes God a material cause. Again, in opposition to the mediaevals, as we shall see subsequently, Spinoza
unmakes God as the final cause. God then to him, if he were
to retain the Aristotelian terminology, would be a material,
formal, and efficient cause. But this terminology even in
Aristotle was not unalterably fixed. The final and efficient
causes are identified by him with the formal cause, and thus

[1] *Moreh Nebukim*, I, 69.

the only real contrast between causes is that of the material and formal.[1] This identification of the three causes is found also in Maimonides. "Aristotle has already explained that in natural things the efficient, formal, and final causes are identical."[2] We can readily see how in Spinoza's reasoning, with his discarding of the old Aristotelian terms matter and form, the old designation of causes as material and formal likewise disappears. "In creation," he says, "no other causes concur except the efficient one."[3] God is therefore spoken of by him as the efficient cause, for even as a material and formal cause, it is only through the active properties of extension and thought that God is conceived as cause. Efficient cause is thus to him the most applicable description of God, efficient in the most general sense of active and as the sum of all conditions that make for causality. There is a suggestion of this kind of reasoning in Spinoza's statement that "since substance is the principle of all its modes, it may with greater right be called active than passive."[4] But in order to show the difference between his conception of God as efficient cause and that of the mediaevals, he analyzes their conception of efficient cause and tries to show in what respect he departs from them.

In the *Short Treatise*, where an entire chapter is devoted to the explanation "that God is a cause of all things,"[5] Spinoza borrows a current eightfold classification of the Aristotelian efficient cause, which has been traced to the work of a Dutch philosopher by the name of Burgersdijck,[6]

---

[1] Zeller, *Philosophie der Griechen*, II, 2, pp. 327–330 (3rd edition). English translation, *Aristotle*, I, pp. 355–358.

[2] *Moreh Nebukim*, III, 13.

[3] *Cogitata Metaphysica*, II, 10 (*Opera*, I, p. 268, ll. 25–26).

[4] *Short Treatise*, I, 2, § 25 (*Opera*, I, p. 26, ll. 29–31).

[5] *Short Treatise*, I, 3.

[6] *Institutiones Logicae*, Lib. I, Cap. XVII. Cf. A. Trendelenburg, *Historische*

to show "how and in what sense God is a cause." This eight-fold classification, with the exception of the eighth, which appears later in the Scholium of Proposition XXVIII, is embodied in Propositions XVI–XVIII of *Ethics*, I. The correspondence between them, preliminary to our discussion of the meaning of these seven kinds of efficient cause, is herewith given:[1]

Ethics, I		*Short Treatise*, I, 3
Prop. XVI	7.	Universal cause
Prop. XVI Corol. 1	1.	Emanative, productive, active, efficient cause[2]
Prop. XVI Corol. 2	4.	Cause through himself (essential)
Prop. XVI Corol. 3...	6.	First, initial cause
Prop. XVII Corol. 1...	5.	Principal cause
Prop. XVII Corol. 2...	3.	Free cause
Prop. XVIII	2.	Immanent cause

However, while Spinoza has borrowed the scheme and terminology of the classification from Burgersdijck, he has made free use of it for his own purpose. The causes enumerated in this list are what the mediaevals themselves would have ascribed to God, but when used by Spinoza there is an implication that these causes are more truly applicable to his own conception of God's causality than to theirs.

But let us follow out this implied contention of Propositions XVI–XVIII that only God as conceived by Spinoza is in the true sense a *universal, efficient, essential, first, principal, free*, and *immanent* cause.

Beiträge zur Philosophie, Vol. III, p. 317 (Berlin, 1867); Ch. Sigwart, *Benedict de Spinoza's kurzer Tractat* (2nd ed.), p. 171; A. Wolf, *Spinoza's Short Treatise*, pp. 190 ff.

[1] Cf. Sigwart, *op. cit.*, p. 172. Sigwart seems to have overlooked the correspondence of Prop. 16 and Corollary 1 of Prop. 16 in the *Ethics* to the 7th and 1st classifications in the *Short Treatise*.

[2] *uytvloeiende, daarstellende, doende, werkende*.

To the mediaevals, from the principle that God is a pure simple form and that "a simple element can produce only a simple thing" it appeared as an inevitable conclusion that, if necessary emanation was to be the theory explaining the origin of the world, the direct emanation from God must be one simple Intelligence and that matter must therefore emerge subsequently in the process.[1] According to this view, while God may indeed be considered as indirectly the cause of all the variety of material things, He is directly only the cause of one simple thing. In this sense, then, God is really what was called a *particular* cause as contrasted with a *universal* cause, for the latter kind of cause meant the ability to produce various things.[2] Thus while the mediaevals would undoubtedly insist upon calling God a universal cause,[3] they could not really call Him a universal cause in the strict sense of the term. But to Spinoza, since God is the direct cause of both extended modes and thinking modes, God can truthfully be called a universal cause.

Furthermore, Spinoza's God can be called a universal cause with more right than the God of the mediaevals for still another reason. Though the mediaevals believed like Spinoza that God is infinite, still they did not believe, for reasons we shall discuss later, that God ever did or ever will create all the infinite things which He has in His mind and which might be created.[4] The world is finite as contrasted with God who is infinite. Their God therefore was a *particular* and not a *universal* cause, since He did not create everything that was in His mind. But to Spinoza, just as from the two known attributes arise the known modes of the world, so also from the infinite attributes, which are unknown to us but which

---

[1] *Moreh Nebukim*, I, 22.   [2] *Short Treatise*, I, 3, § 2 (7).

[3] Cf. quotation from Thomas Aquinas, above, p. 254, n. 2.

[4] Cf. below, pp. 314 ff. and 411 ff.

exist and are conceived as an idea in the infinite intellect of God, arise an infinite number of modes unknown to us.[1] The world is as infinite as God, though only two of its modes are known to us, and God therefore is a universal cause in the true sense of the term. This is what lies behind Proposition XVI. It is a denial of the mediaeval view that the world is finite and not the fullest expression of God's being. If the world were finite, he argues, then God could be called only a particular cause and not a universal cause. But the world is not finite, for "from the necessity of the divine nature infinite numbers of things in infinite ways (that is to say, all things which can be conceived by the infinite intellect) must follow" (Prop. XVI). Hence God can be truly called a universal cause.

But in what manner do the modes follow from God? In the Middle Ages it was said that they follow from God by the process of emanation, and emanation was defined as a special kind of efficient causation which applies exclusively to the action of an immaterial agent upon a material object.[2] "Inasmuch as it has been demonstrated that God is incorporeal and has also been established that the universe is His work and that He is its efficient cause . . . we say that the universe has been created by divine emanation and that God is the emanative cause of everything that comes into being within it."[3] God then is called by the mediaevals the efficient cause only in a restricted sense, in the sense of emanative cause. But to Spinoza, that distinction between the act of a corporeal agent and the act of an incorporeal agent does not exist. He therefore declares unqualifiedly that "God is the efficient cause,"[4] that is to say, the efficient cause in its general unrestricted sense. In the *Short Treatise*

---

[1] Cf. Epistolae 63, 64, and 66.

[3] *Ibid.*

[2] *Moreh Nebukim*, II, 12.

[4] *Ethics*, I, Prop. 16, Corol. 1.

he makes his point still clearer when he says that God can be called indifferently the "emanative," "productive," "active," or "efficient" cause, all of which "we regard as one and the same, because they involve each other." [1]

Probably the mediaevals themselves would subscribe to Spinoza's next statement that "God is cause through himself (*per se*, essentially), and not through that which is accidental (*per accidens*)." [2] But still, since the world of which they maintain God is the cause is unlike God in nature, God being immaterial and the world being material, then, despite their protestations, God must be considered not as an essential cause but as an accidental cause, for one of the meanings of essential cause, and the one which Spinoza has found in Bergersdijck and Heereboord, is that the cause produces something of its own kind. When the cause produces something which is not of its own kind, it is called accidental cause. [3] Consequently, since according to the mediaevals the world which was produced by God is not of His kind, for God is immaterial and the world is material, God then is only an accidental cause.

Similarly the mediaevals would whole-heartedly subscribe to Spinoza's fourth characterization of divine causality contained in his declaration that "God is absolutely the first cause." [4] In fact, God has been called the first cause ever since Aristotle. But behind this statement of Spinoza's that God is the "absolutely" first cause there is an unexpressed argument that the mediaevals could not with full right call

---

[1] *Short Treatise*, I, 3, § 2 (1).

[2] *Ethics*, I, Prop. 16, Corol. 2.

[3] Cf. Burgersdijck, *Institutiones Logicae*, Lib. I, Cap. XVII, Theor. XV–XVI; Heereboord, *Hermeneia Logica*, Lib. I, Cap. XVII, Quaest. XVI: "Similiter, cum animal sibi simile generat, dicitur causa per se generati animalis; cum generat monstrum, dicitur causa per accidens."

[4] *Ethics*, I, Prop. 16, Corol. 3.

their God an absolutely first cause. In the source used by
Spinoza, a distinction is made between two kinds of first
causes. One is called the absolutely first cause (*causa absolute prima*) and the other is called a first cause in its own kind
(*causa prima suo genere*). An absolutely first cause is described not only as a cause which is the first in a series of
causes, but also as one which is in no way dependent upon
anything else.[1] In fact, absolute independence of anything
else, whether external to God or within Him, is what the
mediaevals themselves insist upon when they describe God
as the first cause and as necessary existence.[2] It is with this
in mind that Spinoza argues here against the emanationists.
He seems to say: Inasmuch as according to the emanationists
God could not produce matter directly by himself but only
through His emanations, i.e., the Intelligences, God is dependent, as it were, on his own emanations. He is therefore
not an absolutely first cause. It is only Spinoza's God who
produces everything directly by the necessity of His own
nature and is in no way whatsoever dependent upon anything
else that can be rightfully called an absolutely first cause.

II. God as Free Cause

Besides *universal, efficient, essential,* and *first,* God is also a
principal and *free* cause.[3] With these Spinoza introduces
another one of his fundamental departures from mediaeval
philosophy. On the whole, Spinoza's views on the problem
of freedom may be treated under three headings: 1. The
definition of the terms "free" and "necessary." 2. How

[1] Cf. Burgersdijck, *Institutiones Logicae,* Lib. I, Cap. XVII, Theor. XXIX,
§§ 1–2; Heereboord, *Hermeneia Logica,* Lib. I, Cap. XVII, Quaest. XXVI; *idem.
Meletemata Philosophica, Disputationes ex Philosophia Selectae,* Vol. II, Disp. XVII.

[2] Cf. *Maḳaṣid al-Falasifah,* II, ii, 5–6 (pp. 139–140): "He [who is described as
having necessary existence] does not depend upon anything else." Cf. also *Emunah
Ramah,* II, 1 (p. 47), quoted below, Vol. II, p. 40.

[3] *Ethics,* I, Prop. 17 and Corol. 1–2; *Short Treatise,* I, 3, § 2 (3–5).

God is free. 3. How man is not free. Here in our interpretation of Proposition XVII we shall deal only with the first two topics, leaving the third topic to be discussed in our interpretation of the next group of propositions.

His own understanding of the terms free and necessary is made quite clear by Spinoza himself: "That thing is called free which exists from the necessity of its own nature alone, and is determined to action by itself alone. That thing, on the other hand, is called necessary, or rather compelled, which by another is determined to existence and action in a fixed and prescribed manner." [1] But how did Spinoza come to this definition? We shall try briefly and simply to explain the metaphysical and philological reasoning which had led Spinoza to formulate this definition.

The problem of freedom is sometimes discussed by the mediaevals as a problem of possibility. The question whether anything is absolutely free is thus stated as a question whether anything is absolutely possible. In Crescas, for instance, the headings over the chapters on freedom read: "An exposition of the view of him who believes that the nature of possibility exists," "An exposition of the view of him who believes that the nature of possibility does not exist." [2] There is a suggestion of this method of formulating the problem of freedom in the *Short Treatise* where in the chapter on "Divine Predestination" Spinoza raises the question "whether there are in nature any accidental things, that is to say, whether there are any things which may happen and may also not happen." [3] The phraseology used here by Spinoza reflects the Aristotelian definitions of the accidental and the possible. The former is reproduced by Crescas as that which "has in itself the possibility of being and of

---

[1] *Ethics*, I, Def. 7.   [2] *Or Adonai*, II, v, 1-2.
[3] *Short Treatise*, I, 6, § 2.

not being"; [1] the latter is given by Aristotle himself as that which "may either be or not be." [2]

We have already called attention on several occasions to the mediaeval threefold division of possibility and necessity, namely, (1) possible *per se*, (2) possible *per se* but necessary in consideration of its cause, and (3) necessary *per se*. We have also called attention to the fact that Spinoza has made use of this threefold classification and that he has designated the possible *per se* by the term contingent and the possible *per se* but necessary in consideration of its cause by the general term possible.[3] Now, the question raised by the mediaevals through Crescas whether the nature of the possible exists really means whether pure possibility, i.e., possibility *per se*, exists. Crescas' answer is in the negative. There is nothing in nature which can be described as pure possibility, for for everything a cause can be found. So actually nothing in nature is possible *per se*; everything which is possible *per se* is necessary in consideration of its cause. Possible *per se* does not represent an actual thing in nature; it is only a logical distinction *secundum quid*.[4] It is this conception of the possible *per se* as merely a logical distinction *secundum quid* that must have led Spinoza to designate it by the term contingent, which, in Spinoza's definition of it, appears also as purely a logical distinction in things. According to this view, then, actually existent things fall only under two divisions, those which are necessary by their cause and those which are necessary by their own nature. These two meanings of necessary, in fact, correspond to two out of the five meanings that Aristotle attaches to the term. That which

---

[1] *Or Adonai*, I, i, 8. Cf. my *Crescas' Critique of Aristotle*, p. 249 and p. 551, n. 2; *Physics*, VIII, 5, 256b, 9–10.

[2] *Metaphysics*, IX, 8, 1050b, 11–12. Cf. *Crescas' Critique of Aristotle*, p. 551, n. 3.

[3] *Cogitata Metaphysica*, I, 3; *Ethics*, IV, Defs. 3–4. Cf. above, pp. 188 ff.

[4] Cf. *Or Adonai*, II, v, 3: . . . בצד מה . . . בבחינת.

is necessary by its cause corresponds to necessary in the sense which Aristotle describes as compulsory,[1] and that which is necessary by its own nature corresponds to necessary in the sense which Aristotle describes as that which cannot be otherwise.[2] What Spinoza does, then, in his definition of freedom in the *Ethics* is to simplify the terminology and to call that which is necessary by its own nature free and to call that which is necessary by its cause necessary or compelled. "True freedom," says Spinoza elsewhere, "is only, or no other than [the status of being] the first cause."[3] This on the whole corresponds to the mediaeval definition of freedom. "Free will," says Judah ha-Levi, "*qua* free will, has no compulsory cause."[4] Similarly Crescas defines free will as the ability "to will and not to will without an external cause."[5]

This definition of freedom is applied by Spinoza to God in Proposition XVII and its two Corollaries. Starting out in the proposition itself with the statement that God's action flows from His own nature and is without compulsion, he further explains in the first corollary that the compulsion comes neither from without nor from within Him, that is to say, God is what is generally called a *principal* cause, and concludes in the second corollary that only God is a *free* cause. All these would on their positive side seem to be merely a reassertion of views commonly held by mediaevals. But as elsewhere, Spinoza's statements here have also a negative side and are intended to emphasize something in opposition to the mediaevals. Fortunately, in this case, we do not have to guess what it is that he wants to emphasize and negate. He makes it clear for us in his Scholium.

---

[1] *Metaphysics*, V, 5, 1015a, 26.
[2] *Ibid.*, 34.
[3] *Short Treatise*, I, 4, § 5.
[4] *Cuzari*, V, 20.
[5] *Or Adonai*, II, v, 3 (p. 48b).

On the whole, the mediaevals would have subscribed to Spinoza's proposition that "God acts from the laws of His own nature only, and is compelled by no one." [1] In fact, in the Hymn of Unity, which is incorporated in the Jewish liturgy, we find a statement that reads almost like it: "Thou wast not compelled to perform Thy work, nor wast Thou in need of any help." [2] But still the mediaevals considered God's causality as an act of will, power, or intelligence. Will, power, and intelligence are the three terms which are generally used by mediaevals in connection with creation,[3] with the proviso, of course, that all the three are identical in God.[4] It is by means of will or power or intelligence that the mediaevals find themselves able to resolve all the difficulties about divine causality. The mediaeval philosophers, for instance, admit that God cannot "produce a square the diagonal of which is equal to its side, or similar other impossibilities." [5] Still when the question is raised that "to say of God that He can produce a thing from nothing is . . . the same as if we were to say that He could . . . produce a square the diagonal of which is equal to its side, or similar impossibilities," [6] or "what has made God create at one time rather than at another," [7] they answer to this question that "He willed it so; or, His wisdom decided so." [8]

As against this, Spinoza opposes his own view of causality, and in the process of unfolding it he emphasizes, allusively, to be sure, the distinction between his view and theirs. The

---

[1] *Ethics*, I, Prop. 17.

[2] *Shir ha-Yiḥud*, V.

[3] *Emunot we-De'ot*, II, 4; *Cuzari*, V, 18, 7–10; *Moreh Nebukim*, II, 18, Second Method. Cf. above, p. 204.

[4] *Moreh Nebukim*, II, 53. Cf. above, p. 155.

[5] *Ibid.*, II, 13, and cf. I, 75, 1; I, 75, 5; III, 15; *Emunot we-De'ot*, II, 13.

[6] *Moreh Nebukim*, II, 13, Second Theory.

[7] *Ibid.*, II, 14. Cf. above, p. 100.

[8] *Ibid.*, II, 25. Cf. above, pp. 100 f.

fundamental difference, out of which all others arise, is his elimination of will and design from the causality of God. This is what he means when he says in the first corollary of Proposition XVII that "there is no cause, either external to God or within Him, which can excite Him to act." By a cause within God he means will and design. With the elimination of will and design from the nature of God, creation *ex nihilo* becomes an impossible act, as impossible as any of the things which the mediaevals themselves considered impossible, such, for instance, as the assumption that "God could bring about that it should not follow from the nature of a triangle that its three angles should be equal to two right angles." [1]

Then Spinoza takes up another point.

One of the reasons that led the mediaevals to attribute to God intelligence and will was the utter absurdity of the opposite alternative, for to deny them of Him would imply an imperfection in His nature. God, according to them, must be "free from imperfections," [2] and as a result of this, "we must remove from God anything that looks like an imperfection in Him." [3] Abraham Herrera, in his unpublished *Puerta del Cielo*, of which a printed Hebrew version has existed since 1655, puts the matter in the following way: "The eternal and omnipotent God, whom we call the First Cause, acts not from the necessity of His nature but by the counsel of His intellect, which is of the highest order, and by the choice of His free will," [4] for "to an Agent who is first and most perfect we must attribute that kind of action which on account of its superiority and priority excels any other kind of action, and that is the voluntary kind of action, for it is

---

[1] *Ethics*, I, Prop. 17, Schol.   [2] *'Ikkarim*, I, 15; *Moreh Nebukim*, I, 35.
[3] *'Ikkarim*, II, 7.
[4] *Sha'ar ha-Shamayim*, III, 6, beginning.

more perfect than all the natural and necessary actions and does in fact constitute their entelechy and the realization of their perfection." [1] It is undoubtedly to Herrera that Spinoza refers when he says: "I know, indeed, that there are many who think themselves able to demonstrate that intellect of the highest order and freedom of will both pertain to the nature of God, for they say that they know nothing more perfect which they can attribute to Him than that which is the chief perfection in ourselves." [2]

But Spinoza goes still further in his criticism of Herrera.

Herrera touches upon a question which had been constantly raised in the Cabala, namely, whether God could create the infinite number of things which are in His intellect or whether His power of creation was limited to that which He has created. The question is stated by Moses Cordovero as follows: "We shall raise a question by which some of the adepts in Cabala have been perplexed, namely, whether the Infinite, the King of Kings, the Holy One, blessed be He, has it in His power to emanate more than these Ten Sefirot or not, if we may express ourselves in this way. The question is a legitimate one, for inasmuch as it is of the nature of His benevolence to overflow outside himself, and inasmuch as it is not beyond His power, it may be properly asked why He has not produced thousands of millions of emanations. It should indeed be possible for Him to produce many times Ten Sefirot in the same way as He has produced this world." [3] In the discussion of this question by Herrera two points are made: First, that "if God had acted from His own nature and by necessity, He would have inevitably produced everything that is in His power, which would be infinite." [4] Sec-

---

[1] *Ibid.*, Argument IV.   [2] *Ethics*, I, Prop. 17, Schol.
[3] *Pardes Rimmonim*, II, 7.
[4] *Sha'ar ha-Shamayim*, III, 6, Argument III.

ond, since God has created by will and design, He has purposely created only a part of that which is in His intellect,
in order to be able to create other and more perfect things.
"We shall say briefly, that it is because He does not act by
the necessity of His infinite nature that the Infinite, blessed
be He, even though He is infinite, has not brought into existence or created an infinite number of things in an infinite
time, which He comprehends and includes in His immovable
eternity, nor has He produced them in infinite superficies,
positions, and places, into which His infinite power and
magnitude extend. He acts only by the freedom of His will
and purpose, and it is because of this that He has brought
into existence and created finite things in finite times and
in finite places, and to these things and into these things only
has He extended himself, so that He might be superior to
His creatures not only in an infinite degree of perfection but
also in infinite power, and if He ever wills He may create
other things more excellent and greater and in more suitable,
wider, and longer places and positions, all of which He comprehends and includes most perfectly in His eternity and
greatness. This view offers more easily [than any other view]
a vindication of the infinite power and nature of the First
Cause, namely, the view we have maintained that for every
one of the created things, however excellent it may be, He
is able to produce something more excellent." [1] A similar
argument is reproduced by Spinoza in the *Cogitata Metaphysica*. "If God acts from necessity, He must have created
a duration than which no greater can be conceived." [2]

That Spinoza had in mind the statements we have just reproduced from Herrera is evident from his following summary
of the views of his opponents: "But although they conceive

[1] *Ibid.*, III, 7.
[2] *Cogitata Metaphysica*, II, 10.

God as actually possessing the highest intellect, they nevertheless do not believe that He can bring about that all those
things should exist which are actually in His intellect, for
they think that by such a supposition they would destroy
His power. If He had created, they say, all things which are
in His intellect, He could have created nothing more, and this,
they believe, does not accord with God's omnipotence; so
then they prefer to consider God as indifferent to all things,
and creating nothing excepting that which He has decreed
to create by a certain absolute will." [1] Spinoza's own criticism of this solution of the problem is that it virtually sacri-
fices God's power in order to retain His perfection. "Therefore, in order to make a perfect God, they are compelled to
make Him incapable of doing all those things to which His
power extends, and anything more absurd than this, or more
opposed to God's omnipotence, I do not think can be
imagined." [2]

The mediaevals, after having gone to all the trouble of
ascribing to God intelligence and will, explain them away as
homonymous terms. They say "there is nothing in common
between His essence and our essence. . . . There is only
a resemblance between them in name, but in essence they
are different." [3] Similarly of will they say that "the term will
is homonymously used of man's will and of the will of God,
there being no comparison between God's will and that of
man." [4] Spinoza restates this view in great detail in the
Scholium to Proposition XVII, in the course of which he
explains the homonymous use of terms by the illustration of
the term "dog," which is used for "the celestial constellation
of the Dog and the animal which barks." [5] This illustration

---

[1] *Ethics*, I, Prop. 17, Schol.   [2] *Ibid*. Cf. below, pp. 411 ff.
[3] *Moreh Nebukim*, III, 20.   [4] *Ibid.*, II, 18, Second Method.
[5] A similar illustration is mentioned in *Cogitata Metaphysica*, II, 11.

is found in Philo [1] and in Maimonides and Averroes.[2] The introduction here on the part of Spinoza of the discussion about the homonymity of will and intellect when applied to God, which, as we have seen, is nothing but a restatement of the common mediaeval view, would seem to be entirely superfluous unless we assume that he wanted to make use of it afterwards as a refutation of the mediaevals in their attribution of will and intellect to God. However, no such refutation occurs in the Scholium. Probably what Spinoza meant to convey to the reader, though he does not definitely say so, is that since intellect and will are to be applied to God only homonymously, they are meaningless terms, and consequently God's activity might as well be described as following from the necessity of His nature. This in fact is what he argues in one of his letters: "Since . . . it is admitted universally and unanimously, that the will of God is eternal and has never been different, therefore they must also admit (mark this well) that the world is the necessary effect of the divine nature. . . . For if you ask them whether the divine will does not differ from the human will, they will reply that the former has nothing in common with the latter except in name; moreover they mostly admit that God's will, understanding, essence or nature are one and the same thing." [3] Spinoza's contention in this passage that if the will of God is eternal then the world must be admitted to be the necessary effect of the divine nature reflects Maimonides' elaborate arguments on the incompatibility of the assumption of an eternal will of God and the belief in creation by design.[4]

---

[1] *De Plantatione Noe*, XXXVII, 155.

[2] Maimonides, *Millot ha-Higgayon*, Ch. 13; Averroes, *Epitome of the Isagoge* (*Mabo* in *Kol Meleket Higgayon*, p. 2b). Cf. note in Klatzkin's Hebrew translation of the *Ethics* (*Torat ha-Middot*), p. 348.

[3] Epistola 54.   [4] *Moreh Nebukim*, II, 21.

The opposite of will and design, in the Middle Ages, is not only necessity but also chance. Thus Maimonides, in classifying the various theories of creation, mentions in opposition to intelligent creation not only the Aristotelian theory of necessity but also the Epicurean view of accident and chance.[1] The difference between chance on the one hand, and will and necessity on the other, is that chance denies the existence of a cause at all in creation, whereas will and necessity both assume the existence of a cause, though each conceives the cause to act in a different way. "But it would be quite useless to mention the opinions of those who do not recognize the existence of God, but believe that the existing state of things is the result of accidental combination and separation of the elements and that there is none that rules or determines the order of the existing things."[2] Spinoza similarly tries to differentiate between chance and necessity in one of his letters and makes the interesting observation that if God is assumed to act by a will whose laws are unknown to us, His activity really amounts to chance: "This already impels me . . . briefly to explain my opinion on the question whether the world was created by chance. My answer is that, as it is certain that Fortuitous and Necessary are two contrary terms, it is also clear that he who asserts that the world is the necessary effect of the divine nature also absolutely denies that the world was made by chance; he, however, who asserts that God could have refrained from creating the world is affirming, albeit in other words, that it was made by chance."[3] So also in another letter Spinoza asks his correspondent: "Tell me, I pray, whether you have seen or read any philosophers who hold the opinion that the

---

[1] *Ibid.*, II, 13 and 20; cf. *Emunot we-De'ot*, I, 3, Ninth Theory; *Cuzari*, V, 20.
[2] *Moreh Nebukim*, II, 13.
[3] Epistola 54.

world was made by chance, that is, in the sense in which you understand it, namely, that God, in creating the world, had set himself a definite aim, and yet transgressed His own decree." [1] The implication of these statements is, as is quite evident, that the attribution of will to God really amounts to the denial of causality and to the explanation of the rise of things by chance.

III. The Meaning of Immanent Cause

His denial of chance or of causelessness is reaffirmed by Spinoza on several occasions in a positive way, as, for instance, when he says that "of every existing thing there is some certain cause by reason of which it exists." [2] He furthermore defines the cause of a thing by the statement that "if this [cause] did not exist it were impossible that the thing should exist," [3] which is reminiscent of Crescas' statement in his definition of a cause that "should the cause be conceived not to exist the effect could not be conceived to exist." [4] Now, causes, according to Aristotle, are either external (ἐκτός) to the thing [5] or present (ἐνυπάρχοντα) within the thing. [6] So also Spinoza on several occasions asserts that "we must look for this cause in the thing or outside the thing," [7] and on several other occasions he speaks of external and internal causes. [8]

What these internal and external causes are needs some explanation. Aristotle himself designates the material and formal causes as internal, whereas the efficient cause is de-

---

[1] Epistola 56.
[2] Ethics, I, Prop. 8, Schol.; cf. Epistola 34; Short Treatise, I, 6, § 2.
[3] Short Treatise, I, 6, § 4.
[4] Or Adonai, I, i, 3. Cf. my Crescas' Critique of Aristotle, p. 221.
[5] Metaphysics, XII, 4, 1070b, 23.   [6] Ibid., 22.
[7] Ethics, I, Prop. 8, Schol. 2; Short Treatise, I, 6, § 4; Epistola 34.
[8] Ethics, I, Prop. 11, Schol.; III, Prop. 30, Schol.; Ethics, III, Affectuum Definitiones, 24, Expl.; Epistolae 34 and 60.

scribed by him as external.[1] But inasmuch as the efficient cause is said by Aristotle to be sometimes the same as the formal cause,[2] the efficient cause may thus according to him be both an internal and external cause. Although Aristotle does not give any concrete examples of what he means by external and internal causes, such examples may be gathered from his own writings as well as from the writings of his followers.

Of an external cause the following are two examples:

First, a physical object which is spatially external to another physical object. Thus Maimonides, drawing upon Aristotle, says that "everything must needs have a mover, which mover may be either outside the object moved, as, e.g., the case of a stone set in motion by the hand, or within the object moved, as, e.g., the body of a living being," which is moved by its soul.[3] In a passage corresponding to this Aristotle says that "of those things which are moved essentially, some are moved by themselves (ὑφ' αὑτοῦ, i.e., by an internal cause) and others by something else";[4] and later, in explanation of things which are moved by something else, he says: "Thus, a staff moves a stone, and is moved by a hand, which is moved by a man."[5]

Second, an incorporeal being, like God, causing motion in a corporeal object. In this case, says Maimonides, the term "external"[6] is to be taken in the sense of "separate,"[7] that is to say, separate from body (χωριστὸς τοῦ σώματος) or incorporeal.

Similarly of an internal cause two examples may be found.

---

[1] *Metaphysics*, XII, 4, 1070b, 22 ff.   [2] *Physics*, II, 7, 198a, 24–26.
[3] *Moreh Nebukim*, II, Introduction, Prop. 17.
[4] *Physics*, VIII, 4, 254b, 12–14.   [5] *Ibid.*, VIII, 5, 256a, 6–8.
[6] חוץ, خارج = ἐκτός.
[7] *Moreh Nebukim*, II, 1: נבדל, مفارق = χωριστός[2].

First, the soul which exists in the body and is inseparable from the body and is the cause of its motion. We have already quoted above a statement from Maimonides where the soul is called an internal cause of motion. In a corresponding passage Aristotle similarly illustrates those things which contain in themselves the principle of motion by the example of the motion of an animal.[1]

Second, universal concepts such as genus with reference to species and both of them with reference to the individual essence. Genus and species combined make up a definition and are therefore related to the essence defined as cause to effect, for a good definition, according to Aristotle, must not only set forth the fact but it should also contain (ἐνυπάρχειν) and present the cause.[2] This Aristotelian view is implied in Maimonides' contention that God cannot be defined by genus and species on the ground that "there are no previous causes to His existence by which He could be defined."[3] Furthermore, since a definition according to Aristotle is of the form,[4] it may be called a formal or internal cause. It is to be noted that Aristotle uses the same term ἐνυπάρχειν in describing both the nature of the causality of the definition and the nature of the cause which he calls internal (ἐνυπάρχων). It is evident then that by internal cause he does not mean only a cause which inheres in the effect, but also a cause in which the effect inheres. The essential characteristic of an internal cause therefore is the fact that it is inseparable from its effect, either as the soul is inseparable from the body or as the definition is inseparable from the definiendum, for, as says Aristotle, the whole is in its

[1] *Physics*, VIII, 4, 254b, 15-16.
[2] *De Anima*, II, 2, 413a, 15. Cf. *Analytica Posteriora*, II, 10, 93b, 38 ff.
[3] *Moreh Nebukim*, I, 52. Cf. Munk, *Guide des Égarés*, I, p. 190, n. 3; Friedländer, *Guide of the Perplexed*, I, p. 178, n. 2.
[4] *Metaphysics*, VII, 11, 1036a, 28-29.

parts and the genus is in the species just as the parts are in
the whole and the species is in the genus.[1]

Now, in the Middle Ages we meet with a contrast between
the terms *transiens* and *immanens* in such expressions as
actio transiens and *actio immanens* or *causa transiens* and
causa immanens.[2] These two terms reflect Aristotle's external (ἐκτός) cause and internal (ἐνυπάρχων) cause. That
this is so we have the testimony of Spinoza himself, who
says: "immanent (*inblyvende*) or internal (*innerlyke*) cause
(which is all the same to me)."[3] The term *immanens*, therefore, by analogy with Aristotle's term ἐνυπάρχων, describes
not only a cause which resides in the effect but also a cause
in which the effect resides, for the essential meaning of an
immanent cause, as we have said, is its inseparability from
its effect. The term *transcendens*, however, does not mean
in the Middle Ages the same as *transiens*. It means to be
logically greater or more general, especially to be logically
greater and more general than the ten categories so as not
to be contained under them.[4] In this sense it is used in the
enumeration of the so-called *transcendentales* which are referred to by Spinoza.[5] The term *transcendens* is thus neither
the synonym of *transiens* nor the opposite of *immanens*. In
fact, in the case of an immanent cause of the second kind
we have mentioned, i.e., immanent in the sense in which
the genus is the immanent cause of the species, the cause,
though immanent, may also be called transcendent in so far
as it is more general than its effect. The conception of a

---

[1] Cf. *Physics*, IV, 3, 210a, 17 and 19.

[2] Cf. R. Eucken, *Geschichte der philosophischen Terminologie*, p. 204.

[3] *Short Treatise*, II, 26, § 7 (*Opera*, I, p. 110, ll. 22–23).

[4] Cf. W. Hamilton, *Lectures on Logic*, I, p. 198 (ed. 1866); C. Prantl, *Geschichte der Logik*, III, p. 245; R. Eucken, *Geschichte und Kritik der Grundbegriffe der Gegenwart*, pp. 79–80.

[5] *Ethics*, II, Prop. 40, Schol. 1; *Cogitata Metaphysica*, I, 6. Cf. below, Vol. II, pp. 123 f.

transcendent immanent cause is thus not a contradiction in terms.

In the light of this discussion, when Spinoza says here in Proposition XVIII that "God is the *causa immanens* and not *transiens* of all things," we may ask ourselves in which of their two senses does he use the terms *immanens* and *transiens*. It is quite clear that when he denies that God is a *causa transiens* of all things he means to say that God is neither a spatially external cause of all things nor a separate immaterial cause of all things. It is equally clear that when he affirms that God is the *causa immanens* of all things he does not mean that God is in all things after the analogy of the soul in the body in the Aristotelian manner of expression,[1] though among the Stoics God's immanence in the world is expressed in terms of His being the soul, the mind, or the reason of the world, and hence of His being in the world only as a part of it.[2] Proposition XIV of *Ethics*, I, where Spinoza says that all things are in God, and similarly the two Dialogues in the *Short Treatise*, where he likewise says that all things are in God as parts are in the whole, make it quite clear that the immanence of God does not mean that God is in all things as the soul is in the body, but rather that all things are in God as the less universal is in the more universal or, to use Spinoza's own expression, as the parts are in the

[1] The general misunderstanding of Spinoza's description of God as an immanent cause by taking it in the sense that God is a cause who resides in His effects after the analogy of the soul in the body occurs already in John Colerus' biography of Spinoza, published in Dutch in 1705: "In order to understand him, we must consider that . . . the immanent cause acts inwardly, and is confined without acting outwardly. Thus when a man's soul thinks of, or desires something, it is or remains in that thought or desire, without going out of it, and is the immanent cause thereof. In the same manner, the God of Spinoza is the cause of the universe wherein He is, and He is not beyond it." (English translation: *The Life of Benedict de Spinoza*, London, 1706, reprinted at The Hague, 1906, pp. 67–68.)

[2] Cf. Zeller, *Die Philosophie der Griechen*, III, 1, pp. 140–142; p. 151 (4th edition).

whole.[1] Spinoza's statement that God is the immanent cause of all things is thus not an assertion that God is identical with the aggregate totality of all things; it is only a denial that God is the external and separable and hence immaterial cause of all things. Inseparability from the effect, as we have seen, is the essential characteristic of Aristotle's internal cause. Spinoza makes the meaning of this term clear when he defines the immanent cause negatively as that "which by no means produces anything outside itself" [2] and as that in which "the effect remains united with its cause in such a way that together they constitute a whole." [3] When Spinoza therefore says that all things are in God he means exactly the same thing as when Aristotle says that man exists in animal as a species in a genus.[4] And when he further says that all things are in God as parts are in the whole he means again exactly the same thing as when Aristotle says that the "part is in the whole" [5] and as when Burgersdijck says that "animal is a whole *per se* in respect to man and beast," [6] that is to say, the species man and beast exist in the genus animal as parts in a whole. It is in this sense that God is the immanent cause of all things; He is their internal cause as the genus is the internal cause of the species or the species of the particulars and as the whole is the internal cause of its parts. Now the universal, even though it does not exist separately from the particulars, is not logically identical with the sum of the particulars, for to Spinoza the universal is an *ens rationis*, which means that it has a certain kind of conceptual existence, even though conceptual in the sense that it

---

[1] Cf. above, pp. 74 ff. Cf. also Epistola 32 to Oldenburg.

[2] *Short Treatise*, I, First Dialogue, § 12 (*Opera*, I, p. 30, ll. 24–25).

[3] *Ibid.*, Second Dialogue, § 3 (p. 31, ll. 20–22).

[4] *Physics*, IV, 3, 210a, 17–18.   [5] *Ibid.*, 16.

[6] *Institutiones Logicae*, Lib. I, Cap. XIV, p. 52 (ed. Cambridge, 1680): "Animal est totum [per se] respectu hominis et bestiae."

is *invented* by the mind, as we have shown in our discussion of his definition of attribute.[1] Consequently there is to be a corresponding conceptual distinction between God and the aggregate totality of modes. Being thus the immanent cause of all things in the sense that He is inseparable from them but still logically distinct from them, God may also be said to transcend them according to the old meaning of the term "transcendence," namely, that of being logically distinct and more general. With the totality of modes or what Spinoza calls the *facies totius universi* God is not identical; He is identical only with himself. With reference to the totality of modes God is therefore called an immanent cause, but with reference to himself He is called *causa sui*, which, as we have already shown,[2] means the denial of any kind of cause whatsoever, whether external or internal. This distinction implied in Spinoza's thought between one kind of whole, God, which transcends its parts and is their cause, and another kind of whole, the *facies totius universi*, which is the sum of its parts, is clearly stated by Proclus: "Every wholeness (ὁλότης) is either prior to parts or consists of parts. . . . A whole according to subsistence (καθ' ὕπαρξιν), therefore, is that which consists of parts, but a whole according to cause (κατ' αἰτίαν) is that which is prior to parts."[3]

But here a question may be raised. If God is related to the totality of modes as the universal to particulars or as the whole to the parts, then inasmuch as the universal as well as the whole has only conceptual existence, the existence of God which Spinoza has sought to establish is only a conceptual kind of existence, conceptual, presumably, in the sense of being *invented* by the mind. God is thus an *ens rationis*

[1] Cf. above, pp. 146 ff.   [2] Cf. above, p. 127.
[3] *Institutio Theologica*, LXVII (in *Plotini Enneades*, ed. Creuzer et Moser, Paris, 1855).

and not an *ens reale*. But this would seem to be contrary to the whole trend of Spinoza's proofs for the existence of God, which was to establish God as an *ens reale*.[1]

This question is raised by Spinoza himself in the First Dialogue in the *Short Treatise*. He puts it in the mouth of Desire. "Methinks," says Desire, "I see a very great confusion in this argument of yours; for, it seems you will have it that the whole must be something outside of or apart from its parts, which is truly absurd. For all philosophers are unanimous in saying that the whole is a second intention (*tweede kundigheid*), and that it is nothing in nature apart from human conception (*begrip*)."[2] The "second intention" is the scholastic *intentio secunda* which is applied to such universals as genus and species,[3] and what Desire is arguing is that God, who is said by Spinoza to be the whole, is nothing but an *ens rationis* or *intentio secunda* like a universal and God cannot therefore be, as Desire erroneously assumes Spinoza to say, "outside of or apart from its parts."

In his answer in the First Dialogue, speaking through the character of Reason, Spinoza first disclaims the imputation that he considers God as a whole "outside of or apart from its parts" by pointing out the difference between a transeunt and an immanent cause and by insisting that an immanent cause "by no means produces anything outside itself."

Then in the Second Dialogue, speaking through the character of Theophilus in answer to another question raised by Erasmus, he states that though the whole like the universal is an *ens rationis* there are two differences between them. First, "the universal (*algemeen*) results from various disconnected individuals, the whole, from various united in-

[1] Cf. above, pp. 161 ff.

[2] *Short Treatise*, First Dialogue, § 10.

[3] Cf. R. P. M. Fernandez Garcia, *Lexicon Scholasticum Philosophico-Theologicum*, p. 361. Cf. below, Vol. II, p. 122.

dividuals." [1] Second, "the universal only comprises parts of the same kind, but the whole, parts both the same and different in kind." [2] These two differences, it may be remarked incidentally, reflect two of the several senses of the term whole discussed by Aristotle. Corresponding to Spinoza's description of the whole in the first difference, there is the following passage in Aristotle: "A whole (ὅλον) means . . . that which so contains the things it contains that they form a unity," in the sense of "making up the unity between them," as "the continuous and limited is a whole, when there is a unity consisting of several parts present in it." [3] Corresponding to Spinoza's description of the universal in the second difference, there is Aristotle's statement to the effect that the whole in the sense of the universal is said of a thing which comprises parts which are of the same kind and have common characteristics, "for universal (καθόλου), and, in short, that which is denominated as being a certain whole, are universal and a whole because they contain many things, are predicated of particulars, and are all one according to the predicate. Thus man, horse, and God are all of them one, because they are all living things." [4] Inasmuch as the whole and the universal despite their being both *entia rationis* are admitted by Spinoza to differ from one another on two points, we may also argue on behalf of Spinoza that this particular whole, namely God, though it may be called an *ens rationis* like any universal, differs from universals on still a third point, namely, that it is called an *ens rationis* only in the sense that its real existence can be *discovered* only by the mind, by the ontological proofs based upon the adequacy of the idea of God in our mind. In truth,

---

[1] *Short Treatise*, I, Second Dialogue, § 9.
[2] *Ibid.*
[3] *Metaphysics*, V, 26, 1023b, 27–28, 28–29, 32–33.
[4] *Ibid.*, 29–32.

however, God is an *ens reale*. Attributes, on the other hand, have no reality apart from God; they are said to be perceived by the intellect or the mind in the sense that they are *invented* by the mind.[1] Or, to make use of a modern distinction, God or substance or the whole is according to Spinoza a concrete or real universal, whereas attributes are according to him only abstract universals.

IV. GOD AS CONSCIOUS CAUSE

Among the different terms describing God's causality which Spinoza has discussed, accepting some of them and rejecting others, the term "conscious" is not mentioned by him. We shall try to show that though Spinoza explicitly denies that God acts by will and design, insisting that He acts by the necessity of His own nature, he still admits that God is a conscious cause. In Aristotle as well as among the mediaeval philosophers, conscious causality by itself did not imply will and design, nor did it exclude necessity. Thus Aristotle's necessary activity of God, which was without design, was still a conscious sort of activity. The contemplation of himself is the activity which Aristotle ascribes to God.[2] This self-consciousness of God is furthermore described by Aristotle as an act of pleasure, for "the act of contemplation is what is most pleasant and best."[3] Still this conscious activity is a necessary sort of activity and is unaccompanied by will and design. Maimonides explains the difference between unconscious necessary activity and conscious necessary activity as follows: A cause is said to act by necessity and unconsciously when the effect follows from it "in the same manner as the shadow is caused by a body, or heat by fire, or light by the sun." A cause is said to act

---

[1] Cf. above, pp. 146 ff.   [2] *Metaphysics*, XII, 9, 1074b, 33–35.
[3] *Ibid.*, XII, 7, 1072b, 24.

by necessity but consciously when the effect is said to follow from it in the same way as "when we say that the existence of the intellect necessarily implies the existence of
the intelligible object, for the former is the efficient cause of
the latter in so far as it is an intelligible object." But
Maimonides goes further and explains that although Aristotle
admitted consciousness on the part of God, and ascribed to
Him a certain self-satisfaction with His activity, "we do not
call this design and it has nothing in common with design,"
inasmuch as "it is impossible for Him that He should wish
to be different." "For example, man is pleased, satisfied,
and delighted that he is endowed with eyes and hands, and
it is impossible that he should desire it to be otherwise, and
yet the eyes and hands which a man has are not the result of
his design, and it is not by his own determination that he
has certain properties and is able to perform certain actions."[1]

This would seem to be also the position of Spinoza. God
is a necessary cause acting without will and design but still
a conscious cause. Not only does Spinoza's theory of the
attribute of thought and his belief in the unity of nature
point to that conclusion,[2] but his description of the function
of that infinite mode of thinking as producing invariably
"an infinite or most perfect satisfaction"[3] is almost a verbal
reproduction of Aristotle's or Maimonides' characterization
of the consciousness of the activity of God. Indeed Spinoza
denies of God the emotions of joy and sorrow when he says
that "God is free from passions, nor is He affected with any
affect of joy or sorrow,"[4] but this merely means that the consciousness he ascribes to God must be unlike our own consciousness — a view which was commonly held by the
mediaevals. Indeed in the *Cogitata Metaphysica* he refers

---

[1] *Moreh Nebukim*, II, 20.   [2] Cf. below, Vol. II, pp. 13 ff. and p. 337.
[3] *Short Treatise*, I, 9, § 3.   [4] *Ethics*, V, Prop. 17. Cf. below, Vol. II, pp. 283 ff.

to "personality" (*personalitas*) as a term which theologians
apply to God and dismisses it as something of which he is unable to form a clear and distinct concept. Still he makes it
quite clear that God knows himself and that His understanding by which He knows himself does not differ from His will
and power by which He created the world,[1] that is to say,
God is conscious of himself, but His consciousness of himself
does not imply design and purpose.

[1] *Cogitata Metaphysica*, II, 8. In connection with this attempt to solve the problem of the consciousness of Spinoza's God, compare the discussions in the following
works: A. Trendelenburg, *Historische Beiträge zur Philosophie* (1855), II, pp. 59 ff.;
C. Sigwart, *Spinoza's neuendeckter Tractat von Gott, dem Menschen und desen Glück-
seligkeit* (1866), pp. 94–95; M. Joël, *Zur Genesis der Lehre Spinoza's* (1871), pp. 13–17;
G. Busolt, *Die Grundzüge der Erkenntnisztheorie und Metaphysik Spinozas* (1875), pp.
117 ff.; F. Pollock, *Spinoza* (1880), pp. 352 ff.; J. Martineau, *A Study of Spinoza*
(1882), pp. 334 ff.; E. E. Powell, *Spinoza and Religion* (1906), pp. 47 ff.; E. Lasbax,
La Hiérarchie dans l'Univers chez Spinoza (1919), pp. 187 ff.; H. Höffding, *Spinoza
Ethica* (1924), pp. 49–50.

CHAPTER X

DURATION, TIME, AND ETERNITY

THE next group of propositions of Part I and the subsequent parts of the *Ethics* are strewn with references to eternity and duration. By way of general introduction we shall discuss here Spinoza's definitions of these two terms, and with them also his definition of time.

I. THE STORY OF DURATION

When Spinoza's contemporary Locke discovered that there is some reason in the general impression that duration, time, and eternity "have something very abstruse in their nature," he suggested a way out of the difficulty by tracing them right to "their originals," by which he meant, as he proceeded to explain, "sensation and reflection," which to him were the original sources of all our knowledge.[1] An equal abstruseness confronts one in reading the variety of statements in which Spinoza contrasts the terms duration, time, and eternity. In our attempt to clear up this abstruseness, we may perhaps equally follow Locke's advice to turn right to the originals of these terms — not indeed to the originals in the sense of what Spinoza considered as the sources of our knowledge, but rather to the originals in the sense of the literary sources on which Spinoza drew in his discussions of the meaning of these terms. Here no less than in the other problems which we have already examined Spinoza operated with terms and ideas which had been long in vogue in the philosophic literature with which he was acquainted, modi-

[1] Locke, *Essay Concerning Human Understanding*, II, 14, § 2.

fying them whenever he had reason to do so and turning
them to new uses in his own particular scheme of reasoning.
The task which we have set ourselves in this chapter, therefore, is to analyze briefly the historical background of the
meaning of duration, time, and eternity, to show that there
are certain common principles underlying all the mediaeval
discussions on the meaning of these terms, however differently expressed they may be in language and phraseology,
to collect all the historical strands, and out of them to weave
together Spinoza's conception of duration, time, and eternity.

In Plotinus' elaborate discussion on time there is a historical survey of all the views that make time dependent
upon motion. Among these he reproduces Aristotle's view on
time which in his paraphrase reads that "time is the number
or measure of motion."[1] The original definition of time by
Aristotle, in its *locus classicus*, reads in full that "time is
this, the number of motion according to prior and posterior."[2]
The addition of the term "measure" by Plotinus may be explained on the ground that the term number in the definition
is, according to Aristotle himself, not to be taken in its ordinary meaning,[3] and that the term measure is sometimes substituted by Aristotle for the term number.[4] Rejecting the
Aristotelian definition of time, Plotinus defines it as something independent of motion. Perhaps it will help us to
understand how time is conceived by him apart from motion if we recall that motion does not appear in the first
two of Plotinus' emanated stages of being, which in order of
priority are: (1) the Intelligence ($\nu o\hat{v}s$), (2) the universal
soul ($\psi v\chi\grave{\eta}\ \tau o\hat{v}\ \kappa\acute{o}\sigma\mu o v$), and (3) the all-encircling celestial
sphere ($\pi\epsilon\rho\iota\phi o\rho\acute{a}$). Motion appears only in the sphere, but

---

[1] *Enneads*, III, vii, 8 (ed. Creuzer et Moser, Paris, 1855). For ed. Volkmann
(Leipzig, 1883) raise chapter numbers by one in all subsequent references to *Enneads*.
[2] *Physics*, IV, 11, 219b, 1–2.   [3] *Ibid.*, 4–9.   [4] *Ibid.*, IV, 12, 221b, 7.

time appears, according to Plotinus, in the universal soul.
Repeating Plato's statement, which appears also in a modified form in Philo, that time is the image of eternity,[1] Plotinus identifies time with the life of the universal soul [2] in
contradistinction to eternity, which is identified by him with
the life of the Intelligence.[3] Now, the life of the universal
soul has a certain kind of extension (διάστασις)[4] and succession (ἐφεξῆς).[5] It is varied (ἄλλη)[6] in its nature. It is a process
of transition from one act of thought (διάνοια) to another,[7]
the unity of which exists only by virtue of a certain kind of
continuity (συνέχεια).[8] It is a continuous acquisition of existence (προσκτώμενον . . . ἐν τῷ εἶναι).[9] All these character-
izations of the life of the universal soul are true also of time,
which is identical with that life. It is "the life (ζωή) of the
soul consisting in the movement by which she passes from
one state of life (βίος) to another," [10] or, it is "the length of
the life" of the soul, "proceeding in equal and similar changes
advancing noiselessly," and "possessing a continuity of
energy" (συνεχὲς τὸ τῆς ἐνεργείας ἔχον).[11]

But this kind of time which proceeds "in equal and similar
changes advancing noiselessly" cannot by itself become fixed
and definite; it cannot be measured and divided into definite
portions.[12] For time to be measured and divided there must
be an external standard of measurement, which external
standard is the movement of the all-encircling sphere. "So
that if some one should say that the movement of the sphere,

---

[1] *Timaeus* 37D; *Enneads*, III, vii, Procemium; Philo, *De Eo, Quis Rerum Divinarum Heres Sit*, XXXIV, 165, and *De Mutatione Nominum*, XLVII, 267.

[2] *Enneads*, III, vii, 10.   [3] *Ibid.*, III, vii, 2, end.

[4] *Ibid.*, III, vii, 10 (p. 177, l. 29).

[5] *Ibid.* (l. 25).   [6] *Ibid.* (l. 28).

[7] *Ibid.* (l. 27).   [8] *Ibid.* (l. 42).

[9] *Ibid.* (l. 47).   [10] *Ibid.* (ll. 32–33).

[11] *Ibid.*, III, vii, 11 (p. 178, ll. 3–4).

[12] *Ibid.* (ll. 30–31).

after a certain manner, measures time as much as possible, by its quantity indicating the corresponding quantity of time, which cannot in any other way be grasped or conceived, he indeed will not adduce an absurd explanation of time." [1] The time which we use, then, in our daily course of life is essentially the same as the time which is an image of eternity; it differs from it not in kind but only in degree, in that it is a certain definite portion of it, measured off by the movement of the sphere. Thus, in opposition to Aristotle, Plotinus maintains that time, i.e., the time which we use in our daily course of life, is only measured or made manifest by motion, but it is not generated by motion. [2] And in still another respect Plotinus differs from Aristotle. According to Aristotle, time is primarily defined as the measure of motion, though he declares that in a secondary sense it may also be said that time is measured by motion. [3] But according to Plotinus, time is primarily measured by motion. "Hence some philosophers have been induced to say that time is the measure of motion instead of saying that it is measured by motion." [4] Finally, it is Plotinus' contention that inasmuch as time is within the universal soul, the universe, which is said to move within the universal soul, may on that account also be said to move and to have its being within time. [5]

What we get out of this analysis of Plotinus' discussion of time is that there are two kinds of time. One is indefinite time; the other is definite time. Both of these kinds of time are genetically independent of motion. They are essentially the same: the life of the world soul and an image of eternity. But definite time has some connection with motion in so

[1] *Ibid.* (ll. 48–52).
[2] *Ibid.* (ll. 52–54).
[3] *Physics*, IV, 12, 220b, 14–16. Cf. *Crescas' Critique of Aristotle*, p. 646, n. 22.
[4] *Enneads*, III, vii, 12 (p. 179, ll. 21–23).
[5] *Ibid.*, III, vii, 10 (p. 177, ll. 21–23); 11 (p. 178, l. 26).

far as it is measured by it. The main contrasts between the Aristotelian and the Plotinian definitions of definite time are thus twofold: (1) according to Aristotle time is generated by motion; according to Plotinus, time is only made manifest by motion; (2) according to Aristotle, time is the measure of motion; according to Plotinus, time is measured by motion.

Plotinus, as will have been noticed, uses the same term time for both definite time and indefinite time. But an enigmatic passage in the Encyclopaedia of the Iḫwan al-Ṣafa,[1] which we are going to show to contain a formulation of Plotinus' definition of time, supplies us with a special term for indefinite time.

The Iḫwan al-Ṣafa enumerate four definitions of time. Two of them, the second and third in their enumeration, read as follows: "It is also said that time is the number of the motions of the celestial sphere; or, it is said that time is a duration which is numbered by the motions of the celestial sphere."[2] The first of these definitions is clearly the Aristotelian definition reproduced only in part, as in Plotinus, and with the use only of the original term number. The second definition, it will be noticed, is just the reverse of the first. In the first, it is time which numbers motion; in the second, it is motion which numbers time. The contrast, then, is just

[1] The development of the conception of duration in Arabic and Hebrew philosophic texts presented in the succeeding pages has already been discussed by me on several occasions in the following places: "Note on Crescas' Definition of Time" in the *Jewish Quarterly Review*, n. s., X (1919), pp. 1–17. This was revised, amplified, and incorporated in the notes to Prop. XV in *Crescas' Critique of Aristotle*, especially in note 9 on pp. 636–640 and in note 23 on pp. 651–658, and in the Introduction on pp. 93–98. It was also used by me in "Solomon Pappenheim on Time and Space and His Relation to Locke and Kant" in *Jewish Studies in Memory of Israel Abraham* (1927), pp. 426–440. The subject is presented here in revised, enlarged, and new form.

[2] Fr. Dieterici, *Die Naturanschauung und Naturphilosophie der Araber*, pp. 14–15; Arabic text: *Die Abhandlungen der Ichwân Es-Safâ*, p. 35.

like the one made by Plotinus between his definition and that
of Aristotle. Again, like Plotinus this definition also implies
that there are two kinds of time, one indefinite and the other
definite, and that the indefinite time becomes definite by
the motion of the sphere. But more than Plotinus, this definition gives a special name to the indefinite time. It calls
it duration. If we assume then, as we are certainly justified
in doing, that the Iḥwan al-Ṣafa's definition is a brief formulation of Plotinus' lengthy discussion on time, then we may
restate Plotinus' conception of time as follows: The essence
of time is duration, which is independent of motion and
exists within the universal soul. Time is only a definite and
fixed portion of duration determined by motion.

If this is true, then we may consider Plotinus as the source
of a variety of definitions of time which occur alike in mediaeval Arabic, Hebrew, and Latin sources as well as in modern
philosophy and in which the term duration, sometimes under
the guise of other terms, appears as something independent
of motion. Such definitions, of course, do not always reproduce Plotinus accurately or even follow him completely.
They are changed, modified, become combined with other
definitions, and completely lose their original form. But
they can always be traced, I believe, to Plotinus, and with a
little effort their variations from the original Plotinian definition can always be accounted for. I shall try to reproduce a
few examples of the variety of forms which this Plotinian
definition of time has assumed in Arabic, Hebrew, Latin, and
other philosophic writings down to the time of Spinoza.

We shall first deal with Arabic and Hebrew texts, and then
with texts in Latin and other languages.

In surveying the Arabic and Hebrew philosophic texts we
may discover three sets of definitions in which the influence
of Plotinus is recognizable or the term duration is made use

of. In the first set, the Plotinian conception of time, either
with the mention of the term duration or without it, is used,
as in the Iḫwan al-Ṣafa, in opposition to the Aristotelian definition. In the second set, the Plotinian conception of time,
again either with the mention of the term duration or without it, is used in combination with the Aristotelian definition, and as supplementary to it. In the third set, the
term duration is embodied within the phraseology of a current definition of time which, not unlike that of Aristotle,
made time dependent upon notion.

Of the first set of definitions we have an example in
Saadia's reference to one who "imagines that time is external
to the sphere and that the world is within it." [1] From the
context it is unmistakably clear that the contention of this
definition is that time is by its nature independent of motion
and that it has been put forward in opposition to the definition of Aristotle. The statement that "time is external
to the sphere and the world is within it" is reminiscent of
similar statements made by Plotinus, namely, that "the
sphere exists and is moved within time" ($\dot{\epsilon}\nu$ $\chi\rho\acute{o}\nu\omega$ $\gamma\acute{a}\rho$ $\kappa\alpha\grave{\iota}$
$\alpha\ddot{\upsilon}\tau\eta$ $\kappa\alpha\grave{\iota}$ $\ddot{\epsilon}\sigma\tau\iota$ $\kappa\alpha\grave{\iota}$ $\kappa\iota\nu\epsilon\hat{\iota}\tau\alpha\iota$)[2] or that the activity of the soul
constitutes time and "the universe is within time" ($\dot{o}$ $\delta\grave{\epsilon}$ $\dot{\epsilon}\nu$
$\chi\rho\acute{o}\nu\omega$).[3]

A similar allusion to the Plotinian conception of time as
opposed to that of Aristotle is found in Altabrizi. He enumerates four definitions of time. Three of these either identify
time with motion or make it belong to motion. But one of
these, the fourth one, states that time is neither a body nor
anything belonging to a body.[4] This, it seems to me, is

---

[1] *Emunot we-De'ot*, I, 4.

[2] *Enneads*, III, vii, 11 (p. 178, ll. 17–18).

[3] *Ibid*. (l. 26).

[4] Commentary on Maimonides' Twenty-five Propositions, Prop. 15. Cf. my
Crescas' Critique of Aristotle, pp. 635–636, 656.

merely another way of saying that time is neither motion
nor anything belonging to motion, for body is that which
alone has motion. To deny that time is dependent upon
motion is, therefore, merely to repeat Plotinus' contention
against Aristotle.

An echo of the Plotinian conception of time may be also
found in Crescas. Openly rejecting the Aristotelian definition, he defines time as "the measure of the duration of
motion or rest between two instants." [1] He furthermore
indicates the significance of this definition as an attempt to
free time from motion when he says, again in opposition to
Aristotle, that as a result of his new definition, time exists
only in the soul. It may be remarked here that by "soul"
Crescas does not mean the universal soul of Plotinus, but
rather the human soul. But when Crescas further argues, as
a consequence of his definition of time, that there had existed time prior to the creation of the world,[2] the implication is that prior to the creation of the world time, or rather
duration, existed in the mind of God as did eternity according to the views of Philo and Plotinus. Time in the created
world, however, is essentially not different from time or
duration before the creation of the world. It is not generated
by motion, but only measured by motion. Crescas could
thus repeat with Philo and Plotinus that time is an image of
eternity.

Of the second set of definitions we have a good example in
Maimonides. Though following Aristotle in saying that time
is an accident of motion [3] and hence could not have existed
prior to the creation of the world, Maimonides states that we
may have in our mind an idea of a certain duration which

---

[1] *Or Adonai*, I, ii, 11. Cf. my *Crescas' Critique of Aristotle*, pp. 289, 651–
658, 93–98.   [2] *Ibid.*
[3] *Moreh Nebukim*, II, Introduction, Prop. 15.

existed prior to the creation of the world. He calls that duration a "supposition or imagination of time but not the reality
of time." [1] Maimonides' "supposition or imagination of
time" seems to be the same as Plotinus' "image of eternity,"
i.e., a duration which is independent of motion. But whereas
Plotinus' "image of eternity" is time itself and is essentially
of the same nature as eternity in so far as both are independent of motion, Maimonides' "imagination of time" is
essentially different from time; it is only a pseudo-time, inasmuch as it is independent of motion, whereas time, properly so called, is generated by motion. The Plotinian time is
thus combined by Maimonides with the Aristotelian time and
made to supplement it.

The view of Maimonides is adopted by Albo, and is restated by him in a new way. He says there are two kinds of
time. One is "unmeasured duration which is conceived only
in thought and which existed prior to the creation of the
world and will continue to exist after its passing away."
This he calls "absolute time," in which there is no distinction
of equal and unequal or of before and after, and which he
identifies with what Maimonides has described as an "imagination of time." The other kind of time is that which is
"numbered and measured by the motion of the sphere, to
which are applicable the distinctions of before and after,
of equal and unequal." [2] These two kinds of time, as I have
said in the case of Maimonides, are undoubtedly the result
of a combination of the Aristotelian time and the Plotinian
time.

Examples of the third set of definitions are to be found in
the works of several authors. Saadia has two versions of a
definition which belongs to this type: (1) "Time is nothing

[1] *Ibid.*, II, 13.
[2] '*Ikkarim*, II, 18. Cf. my *Crescas' Critique of Aristotle*, p. 658.

but the extension of the duration of bodies." [1] (2) "The essence of time is the duration of these existent things." [2] Abraham bar Ḥiyya, in whose text there is a doubtful reading of one word, gives a definition of time which like the definitions of Saadia reads either (1) "that time is nothing but the extension of existent things" or (2) "that time is nothing but a term signifying the duration of existent things." [3] Similarly Algazali gives a definition, evidently meant by him to be a paraphrase of Aristotle's definition, which reads that "time is a term signifying the duration of motion, that is to say, the extension of motion." [4] It will be noticed that the common element in all these definitions is the use of the terms extension and duration and that these terms extension and duration are used in connection with "bodies," or "existent things," or "motion," all of which means the same thing, for by "existent things" here is meant "bodies," and "bodies" have "motion." All these definitions, despite their use of the term duration, or extension, imply the dependence of time upon motion, and may be traced, I believe, to a definition the phrasing of which reads that time is the extension (διάστημα) of motion, and which is attributed by Plutarch and Stobaeus to Plato and by Simplicius to Zeno and is included by Plotinus among the definitions which make time dependent upon motion. [5]

Throughout my discussion of Arabic and Hebrew texts I have used the term duration. Now, this term, derived from the Latin *durare*, literally, "to be hardened," and hence, "to continue, to last, to remain," has been used in the Middle

[1] *Emunot we-De'ot*, II, 11.   [2] *Ibid.*, I, 4.
[3] *Hegyon ha-Nefesh*, I, p. 2a.
[4] *Maḳaṣid al-Falasifah*, II, iii (p. 192).
[5] Cf. *De Placitis*, I, 21, and *Eclogae*, I, 8, in Diels, *Doxographi Graeci*, p. 318; Simplicius on *Categories* in Zeller, *Philosophie der Griechen*, III, 1, p. 184, n. 6 (4th edition); *Enneads*, III, vii, 6.

Ages in a certain technical sense in connection with time. In
Arabic and in Hebrew, no more than in Greek, however, is
there any term of the same derivative technical meaning
which is etymologically of the same origin. But the texts
which I have discussed contain three Arabic and eight Hebrew terms which, though etymologically unconnected with
the Latin *duratio*, can be shown from their context and implications to have the same technical meaning as the Latin
duratio. These three Arabic and eight Hebrew terms can be
arranged etymologically in three groups.[1] (1) The terms in
the first group all go back to a root meaning "to stretch, to
extend," and are used in philosophic Arabic and Hebrew as
some of the equivalents of the Greek διάστασις, "extension,"
which, as we have seen, occurs in Plotinus as one of the characteristics of indefinite time. (2) The term in the second
group comes from a root meaning "to join, to keep together,"
and is the equivalent of the Greek συνέχεια, "continuity,"
which, again as we have seen, occurs in Plotinus as one of the
characteristics of indefinite time. (3) The terms in the third
group go back to roots meaning "to remain, to survive, to
exist," and are the equivalents, though not etymologically
of the same origin, of the Greek συνέχεια, and reflect the expressions of continuity and existence used by Plotinus in
connection with indefinite time. The importance of this
philological digression will come out in our discussion of
Latin texts which we now begin.

---

[1] The three groups of terms are as follows:

I. منّة (Iḥwan al-Ṣafa and Algazali), מדה, עת (Hebrew translations of Algazali).
امتداد (Maimonides), המשך (Samuel Ibn Tibbon's translation of Maimonides
and Albo), איכות (Ḥarizi's translation of Maimonides).

II. بقاء (Saadia), קיום, השארות (Judah Ibn Tibbon's translation of Saadia),
עמדה (Abraham bar Ḥiyya).

III. התדבקות (Crescas).

Cf. my *Crescas' Critique of Aristotle*, pp. 638, 639, 655, 656.

In Latin philosophic texts, as far as I have been able to examine them, we find on the whole the conception of duration combined in a variety of manners with the Aristotelian definition of time. A good example of it is to be found in Augustine's treatment of time.

Augustine starts out by saying that time is that "by which we measure the motion of bodies." [1] In this he is certainly following the phraseology of Aristotle. But he does not stop with this. He soon asks himself what time is in itself. [2] In this again he is repeating a question raised by Aristotle. [3] He then proceeds to show that time cannot be identical with the motion of a body, [4] in which again Aristotle himself would agree with him, for to Aristotle time is only an accident of motion but is not motion itself. [5] But still it would seem that Augustine means to deny by his statement more than the identification of motion and time. It would seem that he means to make time more independent of motion than was done by Aristotle, though still not altogether independent of motion as was done by Plotinus. That time was not according to Augustine altogether independent of motion and hence purely subjective in its nature is evidenced by the fact that when he suggests that time is a certain kind of "stretching out" (*distentio*) he immediately adds that he does not know of what it is a stretching out and marvels "if it be not of the mind itself." [6] His answer to this is in the negative. It is not of the mind itself, he says in effect, but it is rather *in* the mind. "In thee it is, O my mind, that I measure my times." [7] Time indeed is the measure of motion, as said Aristotle, but it is not motion itself but

<hr>

[1] *Confessions*, XI, 23.
[3] *Physics*, IV, 10, 217b, 32.
[5] *Physics*, IV, 10, 218b, 9–18.
[7] *Ibid.*, XI, 27.

[2] *Ibid.*, XI, 23 and 26.
[4] *Confessions*, XI, 24.
[6] *Confessions*, XI, 26.

only the memory of motion that time measures. "In thee,
I say, do I measure times. The impression which things make
in thee as they pass by doth still remain, even when the things
themselves are gone, and this impression it is which, being
still present, I measure." [1] Thus a connection of time with
motion is assumed by Augustine, but a connection not with
motion that is still present, but with the image of motion
which exists in the mind after the motion itself is gone. This
is far from the purely ideal conception of time which interpreters of Augustine generally attribute to him. It is certainly unlike the purely ideal conception of time which we
find in Plotinus and Crescas and in the pseudo-time or duration which according to Maimonides and Albo existed prior
to the creation of the world. It is nothing but a modification
of Aristotle's definition of time which must have been suggested to Augustine by Aristotle's own contention that in
some respect time exists only in the soul. [2]

For our immediate purpose, however, the chief importance
of Augustine's discussion of time consists in the term *distentio*
which he uses on several occasions in describing the nature
of time. [3] In this word *distentio*, it seems to me, we may
discern a technical term used as the equivalent of *duratio*.
The term *distentio* is the equivalent of the Greek διάστασις,
and it will be recalled that terms meaning "stretching out"
traceable to the Greek διάστασις were used in Arabic and
Hebrew texts for duration and that the term διάστασις
itself is used by Plotinus as one of the characteristics of his
indefinite time or duration.

The use of the concept of duration in connection with the
Aristotelian definition of time is to be found in the writings

---

[1] *Ibid.*
[2] *Physics*, IV, 14, 223a, 16–23.
[3] *Confessions*, XI, 23, end, and 26.

of almost all the leading scholastics. Confining ourselves
only to what is common to all of them, we may discern in
them the following general characteristics. Duration is assumed by them as a genus of which time is a species, for they
speak of duration as being of three kinds, (a) eternity, (b)
aevum, and (c) time.[1] While time is generally defined after
Aristotle as being the measure of motion, duration is conceived as something independent of motion. Two definitions
of duration may be discerned in their writings. One reads
that duration is the permanence or perseverance or continuation of existence.[2] The other reads that it connotes a certain
succession.[3] Both these expressions, "permanence or perseverance or continuation of existence" and "succession," as
will be recalled, are used by Plotinus among his characteriza-
tions of his indefinite time, and the first of these expressions
is the underlying meaning of some of the terms used by Arabic and Hebrew authors for the concept of duration. One

[1] Cf. Suarez, *Disputationes Metaphysicae*, Disp. L, Sec. III, 1: "Primo, ac praeci-
pue dividitur duratio in creatam et increatam. Duratio increata est aeternitas
simpliciter dicta." . . . Sec. V, 1: "Duratio igitur creata dividi potest primo in permanentem et successivam. . . . Dividitur ergo ulterius duratio creata permanens
in durationem immutabiliter natura sua permanentem, quae aevum appellatur, et
in eam quae licet permanens sit." . . . Sec. VIII, 1: "Agimus ergo de duratione
habente continuam successionem, de qua Philosophi disputant cum Aristotele in
4. Phys. eo quod tempus, Physicum motum consequi videatur." Cf. also Marc.
Anton. Galitius, *Summa Totius Philosophiae Aristotelicae ad mentem S. Bonaven-
turae*, Pars I, Lib. IV, Tract. II, Quaest. III: "Tres durationes communiter a Doc-
toribus assignari solere, omnibus in scholis versatis patentissimum esse opinor."

[2] Cf. Suarez, *op. cit.*, Disp. L, Sec. I, 1: "Dicitur enim durare res, quae in sua
existentia perseverat: unde duratio idem esse censetur, quod permanentia in
esse." Bonaventura, *Commentaria in Quatuor Libros Sententiarum*, Lib. II, Dist.
XXXVII, Art. I, Quaest. II: "Continuatio in esse non est aliud quam duratio."

[3] Cf. Suarez, *op. cit.*, Disp. L, Sec. II, 1: "Est ergo prima opinio Ochami, et Ga-
brielis supra dicentium, durationem distingui ab existentia, quia existentia significat
absolute, et simpliciter rem esse extra suas causas: duratio vero dicit existentiam
connotando successionem, cui vel coexistat, vel possit coexistere res, quae durare
dicitur: vel aliter, quod duratio dicat existentiam, quatenus apta est ad coexisten-
dum successioni." Cf. also Léon Mahieu, *François Suarez*, p. 374.

gets, however, the impression that these typical scholastics did not consider duration as something purely subjective, any more than Augustine did. Whatever they believed the relation of duration to its object to be, they seem to have attached to it some kind of objectivity. All their discussions on that point would seem to be attempts at different interpretations of Aristotle's statement that time, in so far as it is the number of motion and not motion itself, is in the soul.[1]

The scholastic distinction between duration and time appears also in the discussions of Descartes and Locke. Duration is defined by Descartes as a mode of consideration of the perseverance in the existence of a thing.[2] Whether the thing is moved or unmoved it has duration, and duration of the same kind. Time, however, applies only to things in motion, and is defined by him as the measure of motion.[3] Locke follows on the whole the same tradition, but instead of defining duration, like Descartes, as the perseverance in existence, he defines it as the distance (= extension, διά-στασις) between any parts of that succession furnished to us by the train of ideas which constantly succeed one another in the understanding.[4] It will have been noticed that the two characteristic expressions used by Descartes and Locke in their definitions of duration, namely, "perseverance in existence" and "succession," correspond exactly to the two definitions of duration which we find among the scholastics and which can be traced to Plotinus. Furthermore, if we substitute Plotinus' "soul" for Locke's "understanding," we shall find that Locke's characterization of duration is reminiscent of Plotinus' characterization of indefinite time.

[1] *Physics*, IV, 14, 223a, 16–23.
[2] *Principia Philosophiae*, I, 55.
[3] *Ibid.*, and I, 57.
[4] *Essay Concerning Human Understanding*, II, 14, §§ 1–3.

This idea of succession which constitutes duration, continues Locke, is not derived from motion.[1] Time, however, is connected with motion, and is defined by him as duration measured by motion.[2]

The cumulative effect of all these definitions of time in the Greek, Arabic, Hebrew, and Latin philosophic traditions, from Plotinus down to Locke, stands out clearly in its main outline. There is duration. This duration is not generated by motion. It is something generated in the mind. In Plotinus it is said to be in the universal soul. In Augustine it is identified with memory or the impression of things gone that remains in the mind. In Maimonides and Albo, who call it either an imagination of time or absolute time, it is also said to be something which is formed in our mind. In Crescas, time is similarly said to be in the soul. In Locke it is said to be in the human understanding, consisting of the train of ideas within it. Furthermore, this duration exists apart from the physical world. In Saadia it is said to be external to, that is to say apart from, the sphere. In Altabrizi, it is said not to belong to anything corporeal. In Maimonides, Crescas, and Albo it is said to have existed prior to the creation of the world. In Descartes and Locke it is said to apply to things which have no motion. Finally, this duration is considered as something indefinite and indeterminate. Time is generally taken to differ from duration. Though there is no general agreement as to whether time is generated by motion or not, it is generally agreed that time applies to things which have motion. It is considered as a definite portion of motion, and this definiteness, it is generally admitted, is attained by its being measured by motion.

[1] *Ibid.*, § 6.   [2] *Ibid.*, §§ 17 and 19.

II. DURATION AND TIME IN SPINOZA

It is in this mould of thought that we must cast Spinoza's expressions on duration and time. In presenting the subject, we shall first deal with those aspects of duration in which it is contrasted with time, leaving for subsequent discussions all the other aspects of it in which it is contrasted with eternity.

The fullest definition of duration is given by Spinoza in the *Cogitata Metaphysica*.[1] "Duration," it reads, "is the attribute under which we conceive the existence of created things, in so far as they persevere in their own actuality." Substantially it reëchoes one of the two types of definitions of duration which we have reproduced above from scholastic authors and in which *continuatio in esse*, *permanentia in esse*, and *in sua existentia perseverat* are the expressions indiscriminately used.

The immediate literary source of Spinoza, however, would seem to be found in the following statement of Descartes: "We merely think that the duration of each thing is a mode under which we shall conceive this thing, in so far as it perseveres to exist."[2]

Still when we compare closely Spinoza's definition with that of Descartes we shall notice three differences. First, Descartes calls duration a "mode," whereas Spinoza calls it an "attribute." Second, Descartes only says in so far as it perseveres to "exist," whereas Spinoza uses first the term "existence" like Descartes, but then adds the term "actuality" in the statement "in so far as they persevere in their own actuality." Third, Descartes simply says "thing," whereas Spinoza speaks of "created" things. The question

[1] *Cogitata Metaphysica*, I, 4.
[2] *Principia Philosophiae*, I, 55.

before us is whether it was merely as a matter of free para-
phrasing that Spinoza happened to make these three verbal
changes or whether there was some well thought out reason
which led him to introduce them.

With respect to the substitution of the term attribute for
mode, we shall try to show that it was done by Spinoza at
the suggestion of Descartes himself.

While in his formal definition Descartes calls duration a
mode, elsewhere he refers to it indiscriminately as belonging
either to "modes of things" (rerum modos) or to "affections
of things" (rerum affectiones).[1] Modes and affections are used
by Descartes as interchangeable terms, both of them in contrast, on the one hand, to "things" and, on the other hand,
to "eternal truths which have no existence outside our
thought."[2] Now, according to Descartes, while the terms
modes, qualities (or affections), and attributes are on the
whole analogous in meaning, still they are used in different
senses when they are considered with reference to their application to substance.[3] Consequently, though in his formal
definition of duration, as we have seen, he uses the term
"mode" and elsewhere he also refers to it as an "affection,"
he insists that the most proper term to be used in connection with it is "attribute." "And even in created things
that which never exists in them in any diverse way, like
existence and duration in the existing and enduring thing,
should be called not qualities or modes, but attributes."[4]

[1] My statement is based upon the following consideration. In Principia Philosophiae, I, 48, Descartes divides all objects into A (1), things, or (2), affections of
things, and B, eternal truths having no existence outside our thought. Then he
proceeds to say: "Of the things we consider as real, the most general are substance,
duration, order, number." I take it that of these four examples, the first, substance,
is an illustration of A (1), things, whereas the other three, duration, order, number,
are illustrations of A (2), affections of things. Later in 50, instead of "things and
affections of things," he uses the expression "things or modes of things."

[2] Ibid., I, 48.   [3] Ibid., I, 56.   [4] Ibid.

Spinoza thus had very good reason for substituting the term "attribute" for "mode" in the definition of duration. Still occasionally he slips back to the use of the term "affection," which to him as to Descartes is synonymous with "mode."[1] Thus in the following passage he says: "For, as was noted in the first Part of the discussion, duration is an affection (*affectio*) of existence."[2]

Similarly, Spinoza had a very good reason for introducing the term "actuality" to explain the term "existence." The term "existence," when used by Spinoza or his predecessors in the definition of duration, was meant to emphasize two things. In the first place, it was meant to emphasize that it was *existence* and not *motion* that was required for the conception of duration, inasmuch as duration was independent of motion. This, as we have seen, is the common characteristic of duration throughout the history of that term. Descartes makes himself explicit on that point when he says, "For we do not indeed apprehend that the duration of things which are moved is different from that of things which are not moved."[3] In the second place, it was meant to emphasize that there is no duration in beings which have no existence, as, for instance, fictitious beings and beings of reason. Suarez definitely excludes from duration "ficta" and "entia rationes."[4] Now, the word "existence" by itself would perhaps have been sufficient as an emphasis of the second point. Still, in order not to leave any room for doubt, Spinoza adds the phrase "in so far as they persevere in their own *actuality*," that is to say, the existence must be an actual existence and not one which is only in thought. It is not impossible that in phrasing this definition Spinoza was

[1] Cf. below, Vol. II, pp. 193–194.
[2] *Cogitata Metaphysica*, II, 1 (*Opera*, I, p. 250, ll. 13–14).
[3] *Principia Philosophiae*, I, 57.
[4] Suarez, *op. cit.*, Disp. L, Sec. I, 1.

directly influenced by Suarez, who insists that duration is to be attributed to a thing which exists in actuality.[1] The same idea that duration requires an actually existent object is expressed by Spinoza also in the following manner: "Duration is an affection of existence, not of the essence of things."[2] By "essence" he means the concept of a thing which may or may not have existence outside our mind. In the same vein he also says: "The duration of our body does not depend upon its essence . . . nor upon the absolute nature of God . . . but . . . the body is determined to existence and action by causes. . . . The duration, therefore, of our body depends upon the common order of nature and the constitution of things."[3] The dependence of duration upon actually existing things is clearly expressed in the following passage: "Before creation no time and duration can be imagined by us. . . . Hence duration presupposes that things either have been created before it or at least exist with it."[4] It may be recalled that Plotinus gives as one of the characteristics of his indefinite time or duration that it is "a continuity of energy."[5] "Energy" may mean there "actuality" as well as "activity."

By the same token, the introduction by Spinoza of the qualifying term "created" in the expression "of the existence of *created* things" had a certain definite purpose. Indeed Suarez uses it also in connection with duration.[6] But Spinoza means by it something different. By the term "created" Spinoza does not mean here the traditional conception of

---

[1] *Ibid.*: "Igitur in universum *durare* solum tribuitur rei actu existenti, et prout existens est." Cf. Galitius, *op. cit.*, Pars I, Lib. IV, Tract. II, Quaest. 1, § 2: "Duratio est permanentia rei in suo esse actuali, quieto, et perfecto."

[2] *Cogitata Metaphysica*, II, 1.

[3] *Ethics*, II, Prop. 30, Demonst. On essence and existence, see also below, p. 383.

[4] *Cogitata Metaphysica*, II, 10.

[5] See above, p. 333.

[6] See quotation above, p. 344, n. 1.

creation with its inevitable implication of coming into being in time *ex nihilo*. What he means by it is that the things conceived as having duration must have their existence dependent upon a cause, irrespective of the question whether they had a beginning in time or not. Or, as Spinoza himself says, duration is to be attributed to things "only in so far as their essence is to be distinguished from their existence," [1] that is to say, in so far as their existence is not necessary by their own nature but must be brought about by a cause. If this is the meaning of Spinoza's statement, we can find a historical background for it. It corresponds to the contention of Suarez that even if the angels or the heavens were assumed to have been created by God from eternity, they would still have duration, inasmuch as they would still have been called created beings in so far as their existence is conditioned by a cause. [2]

Spinoza's definition of duration as an attribute, or mode, or affection of existence may bring up the question of the relation of duration to existence. Are they identical, or is there some difference between them? and if the latter, what is the difference? To be sure, Spinoza does not raise this question explicitly. But the question had been raised by the scholastics, and Spinoza must have been conscious of it, for some statements in his writings, as we shall try to show, seem to aim at it. The question as to "how duration is related to existence," as stated by Suarez, reads: "whether it is something distinct from the thing itself, or whether it is completely identical with it." [3] Three views are reported.

---

[1] *Cogitata Metaphysica*, II, 1. Cf. use of "created" below, p. 383, n. 5.

[2] *Op. cit.*, Disp. L, Sec. III, v: "Unde si Deus creasset angelum, ut coelum ab aeterno, non esset in eo durationis principium, et nihilominus duratio eius creata esset, et essentialiter differens ab aeternitate."

[3] *Op. cit.*, Disp. L, Sec. I, 1: "Hinc ergo nascitur difficultas, quomodo duratio ad existentiam comparetur; an scilicet, sit aliquid distinctum ab ipsa re, aut prorsus idem sit." Cf. Galitius, *op. cit.*, Pars I, Lib. IV, Tract. II, Quaest. II: "An duratio realiter differat ab existentia?"

According to some, duration and existence differ from each other *in re* and *realiter*, that is to say, they are separable and each of them can be conceived without the other.[1] Others, as Bonaventura, Bañez, and other Thomists, consider the difference between them as a *modal* difference, like that which exists between a substance and a mode or between two modes.[2] Suarez, Scotus, Occam, and Biel, however, consider duration and existence as being *inseparable* though *distinct* from each other, the distinction between them being one of reason.[3] Similarly Descartes, after discussing the three kinds of distinction, the real, the modal, and that of reason (*ratione*), the last of which he defines as that "between substance and some one of its attributes without which it is not possible that we should have a distinct knowledge of it," [4] concludes that "because there is no substance which does not cease to exist when it ceases to endure, duration is only distinct from substance by reason." [5] Evidently drawing upon these discussions, Spinoza likewise says: "From which it clearly follows that duration is distinguished from the whole existence of a thing only *by reason*. For, however much duration you take away from any thing, so much of its existence you detract from it." [6]

In the light of this statement, when Spinoza chose to define duration as an "attribute" of existence, he used the term attribute in the strictly technical sense in which he defines it in the *Ethics*, namely, as a purely subjective aspect of the thing of which it is used. This is an indirect corroboration of our interpretation of Spinoza's attribute as something purely subjective.

[1] Suarez, *op. cit.*, Disp. L, Sec. II.
[2] Cf. Léon Mahieu, *François Suarez*, pp. 372 f.; Galitius, *loc. cit.*
[3] Cf. Léon Mahieu, pp. 373 f.
[4] *Principia Philosophiae*, I, 60 and 62.
[5] *Ibid.*, I, 62.   [6] *Cogitata Metaphysica*, I, 4.

In the passage just quoted, Spinoza, as will have been noticed, uses the expression "the whole existence of a thing" when he wishes to prove that duration differs from existence only by reason. The expression "the whole of existence" implies, of course, that there may be a part of existence and hence a part of duration. This leads Spinoza in the passage quoted to introduce his definition of time. It is possible, he says, to take off a certain portion of the duration of a thing. But "in order to determine this we compare it with the duration of those things which have a fixed and determinate motion, and this comparison is called time." [1] Or as he says in another place: "No one doubts, too, that we imagine time because we imagine some bodies to move with a velocity less, or greater than, or equal to that of others." [2] Here then we have a definition of time in terms of duration the like of which we have already met in Plotinus, in the Arabic Iḫwan al-Ṣafa, in the Jewish Crescas, and in many scholastics. Spinoza's contemporary Locke, as we have seen, restates it. His immediate source, however, must again have been Descartes in the following passage: "But in order to comprehend the duration of all things under the same measure, we usually compare their duration with the duration of the greatest and most regular motions, which are those that create years and days, and these we term time." [3]

Essentially, thus, time and duration, according to Spinoza, are the same. Time is not a new attribute of things, it is not different from the attribute of duration, nor does it add anything to duration. It is only a definite portion of duration measured by motion. Thus Descartes: "Hence this [time] adds nothing to the notion of duration, generally taken, but a mode of thinking." [4] And so also Spinoza:

[1] *Ibid.*
[2] *Ethics*, II, Prop. 44, Schol.
[3] *Principia Philosophiae*, I, 57.
[4] *Ibid.*

"Therefore, time is not an affection of things but only a mode of thought or, as we have said, a being of reason; it is a mode of thought serving to explain duration." [1]

Thus duration is a mode of existence, and time is a mode of duration. It is analogous to the successive relations between time, motion, and body in Aristotle. Motion, according to the mediaeval Aristotelian phraseology, is an accident of body and time is an accident of motion.[2] Substitute the terms duration and existence respectively for motion and body and the term mode for accident and you get a perfect analogy.

The upshot of all this discussion is this. Everything which may be conceived of as existing or as not existing, depending upon some cause for its existence, has existence superadded to its essence. Such a thing is called by Spinoza a created thing. Now, existence of a thing merely means the fact that the concept which we form in our mind of a thing has an object outside our mind to correspond to it. The concept is the essence of the thing; the outside reality is the existence of the thing. Now the mind in which the concept is formed does not create the existence. The existence is given. But when the mind comprehends that given existence, it comprehends it as something enduring, as something persevering in its actuality, and it cannot perceive it otherwise. Existence does not appear to the mind as a point, but as some sort of extension. This conception of the mind of the external existing object as something persevering in its own actuality, or, in other words, this attribute under which we conceive existence, is that which is called duration. Duration thus refers only to things which have existence, and then only to the existence of such things and not to their essence. "It

---

[1] *Cogitata Metaphysica*, I, 4.
[2] *Moreh Nebukim*, II, 13, First Theory.

should be noted under duration, as it will be of use when below we are discussing eternity, that it is conceived as greater and less and *as if it were* composed of parts, and then only as an attribute of existence and not of essence." [1] Note the expression "*as if it were* composed of parts," for duration according to Spinoza is a continuous quantity and does not consist of discrete parts such as moments.[2] Or, again, Spinoza speaks of duration as "existence considered in the abstract, as if it were a certain kind of quantity." [3]

If we were now to compare Spinoza's and Aristotle's conceptions of time with respect to the problem of their subjectivity and objectivity, we should find that there is little difference. Both assume time to be partly real and partly ideal. In so far as Aristotle's motion and Spinoza's existence are outside the mind, the former's time and the latter's duration are real. In so far as the measure of time of Aristotle and the duration of Spinoza are conceptions of the mind, they are both ideal. In fact the same dual nature of time we shall find throughout the mediaeval definitions, despite the controversies among their various proponents on that point. None of the mediaevals believed in the absolute ideality of time. Not even Augustine went as far as that. The only place where we find a conception of absolutely ideal time is where time can be conceived to exist in a mind which has existence without a body and without a physical world to draw its thoughts from, such as God and Plotinus' universal soul. Of such a nature is the time of Plotinus, the time of Crescas, in its existence prior to the creation of the world, the imagination of time of Maimonides, and the absolute time of Albo.

---

[1] *Cogitata Metaphysica*, I, 4.
[2] *Epistola* 12.
[3] *Ethics*, II, Prop. 45, Schol.

Exactly the same definitions of duration and time which
have been found in the *Cogitata Metaphysica* are to be found
in Spinoza's letter to Meyer.[1] Using there the term "modes"
as the equivalent of the expression "created things" in the
Cogitata Metaphysica, meaning thereby something whose essence does not necessarily involve existence, he says that
duration is that by means of which " we can only explain
the existence of modes." He then goes on to say that from
the fact that we can determine duration, there arises time
for the purpose of determining duration, concluding that
time is merely a mode "of thinking or, rather, of imagining."[2]
The additional phrase "or, rather, of imagining" is of no
special significance here. It is probably nothing but a reminiscent expression of Hobbes' statement that "time is a phantasm of motion." [3] Hobbes himself meant by phantasm not
"imagination" as opposed to "thought," but rather imagination in the general sense of not being "the accident or
affection of any body" and of not being "in the things without us, but only in the thought of the mind."[4] This is exactly
what Spinoza meant by suggesting "imagining" as an alternative for "thinking." It is not impossible, too, that the
use of the term "imagining" by Spinoza is a faint reminiscence of the Platonic and Plotinian saying that time is the
"image" of eternity.

Duration is thus assumed by Spinoza to have two characteristics. First, the existence of an object which is said
to be conceived under the attribute of duration must be only
a possible existence, depending upon God as its efficient
cause,[5] which he describes in the *Cogitata Metaphysica* by
the term "created things" and in his letter to Meyer by the

[1] Epistola 12.
[2] *Ibid.* (*Opera*, IV, p. 57, ll. 7–8): "cogitandi, seu potius imaginandi Modos."
[3] *Elementa Philosophiae*, Pars II, Cap. VII, § 3.
[4] *Ibid.*   [5] See below, Vol. II, pp. 80 ff.

term "mode." This differentiates duration from eternity, which we shall discuss later. Second, duration is to be conceived as unlimited, unmeasured, and undetermined. This differentiates duration from time. These two characteristics of duration are contained in the term "indefinite" which Spinoza uses in his definition of duration in the *Ethics*. "Duration," he says, "is the indefinite continuation of existence." [1] Note incidentally his use of the term "continuation," which, as will be recalled, like the terms "permanence" and "perseverance," is used by the scholastics in their definition of duration. In the explanation to this definition in the *Ethics* Spinoza, it seems to me, is trying to bring out the double meaning of the term "indefinite" as corresponding to the two characteristics of duration. In so far as duration applies to existence which is not necessary by its own nature, Spinoza says, "I call it indefinite because it cannot be determined by the nature itself of the existing thing." In so far as duration is unlimited and unmeasured and is, as we have seen above, "the whole existence of a thing" and not merely a portion of it, Spinoza says that he calls it indefinite "because it cannot be determined . . . by the efficient cause, which necessarily posits the existence of the thing but does not take it away." By the "efficient cause" he means here God, who is described by him as "the efficient cause of all things which can fall under the infinite intellect." [2] The implication of the statement here that if duration were not indefinite God would have been taking away (*tollit*) the existence of the thing can be explained by the statement in the *Cogitata Metaphysica* that "however much of duration you take away (*detrahis*), so much of its existence do you take away from it." [3]

[1] *Ethics*, II, Def. 5.   [2] *Ethics*, I, Prop. 16, Corol. 1.
[3] *Cogitata Metaphysica*, I, 4.

Time, as we have seen, does not differ essentially from duration; it is only a limited portion of duration. Spinoza thus sometimes speaks of duration as "indefinite time" (*tempus indefinitum*), and contrasts it with "finite time" (*tempus finitum*), "limited time" (*tempus limitatum*), and "definite time" (*tempus definitum*).[1] And, *vice versa*, he speaks also of time as "determinate duration" (*duratio determinata*).[2] It is for this reason that Spinoza sometimes speaks of "duration or time"[3] as if the two terms meant to him the same thing. In this indeed Spinoza is really reverting to Plotinus' use of the term time and also to those Jewish philosophers who used the term time for that motion-free time which, as we have been trying to show, is known in scholasticism under the name of duration.

III. ETERNITY

The term eternity started on its career in the history of philosophy with two meanings. Like the twofold meanings with which so many of our other philosophic terms have started their historical careers, they may be designated the Platonic and the Aristotelian. Briefly stated, the difference between these two meanings is as follows. To Plato eternity is the antithesis of time and it means the exclusion of any kind of temporal relations. To Aristotle eternity is only endless time. The question before us is, how did it happen that eternity, which prior to Plato, for all we know, had meant simply endless time, came to mean with Plato the exclusion of time?

The answer to this question seems to be that the term eternity has acquired its new meaning in Plato from the nature of the eternal beings to which it was exclusively ap-

---

[1] *Ethics*, III, Prop. 8 and Demonst.   [2] *Ethics*, I, Prop. 21, Demonst.
[3] *Ethics*, I, Def. 8.

plied by him. Beginning as an adjective of those eternal beings, designating only one of their characteristics, namely, that of ceaseless existence, it came to be used, as it so often happens with terms, as a surrogate for those beings. Those "eternal beings" became simply "the eternals" by the same process that "port wine" became simply "port." The adjective eternal thus became with Plato a substantive, the eternals. In this capacity of a substantive, the term eternal was used by Plato not only in the sense of ceaseless existence but as inclusive of all the other properties which characterized those beings for which the term eternal substituted. The new and enlarged concept formed out of the term eternity as a surrogate became in fact a sort of epitome of all the characteristics by which the ceaseless existing beings were differentiated from the other kinds of beings. In other words, it epitomized to Plato all the essential differences between his world of ideas and his world of sense.

This process of investing the term eternity with all the connotations of the eternal beings to which it happened to be exclusively applied went on, as we shall try to show, throughout the history of philosophy, and it is the tracing of this process that constitutes the history of the term.

To Plato the differences between the world of ideas and the world of sense may be summed up, for our present purpose, under two headings. In the first place, the world of ideas is beginningless, whereas the world of sense had a beginning in an act of creation. In the second place, the world of ideas is immovable, immutable, and indivisible, whereas the world of sense is subject to motion, change, and division. The ideas, therefore, which alone in the opinion of Plato were eternal in the original sense of beginningless became the Eternals, and the term eternity, because of its exclusive application to the ideas, came to include in its meaning all the other characteristics of the ideas. Eternity thus came to stand in Plato for permanence, unity, immutability, identity, and indivisibility. It was no longer infinite time, but rather freedom from any sort of temporal relations, for time to Plato, as later to Aristotle, was connected with motion. The relation of time to eternity was conceived by him as that of the world of sense to the world of ideas. Time was thus described by him as the moving image of eternity.[1]

To Aristotle, however, there was more than one kind of beginningless being. The universe as a whole, the celestial spheres, motion, the immaterial Intelligences, and the Immovable Mover were all eternal in the sense of having no beginning and no end. Eternity, therefore, had with him as many meanings as the number of beings to which it was applied. When applied to the universe or to the movable spheres, eternity meant nothing but infinite time, and this was inseparable from motion. For while indeed, argues Aristotle, the object which has infinite motion cannot truly be described as being *in* time, which in the strict technical sense of the term means to be comprehended by time and transcended by it, it is still described by him as being *in* time in the less technical sense of being *with* time, that is to say, of being when time is.[2] When, however, eternity is applied to immovable beings, as God or the Intelligence, it of necessity means a negation of temporal relation, for there can be no time when there is no motion. While Aristotle himself does not say anything on this subject beyond the statements that the universe, circular motion, the spheres, and God are all eternal, this inference is certainly to be derived from his statements.[3]

---

[1] *Timaeus*, 37 D.   [2] *Physics*, IV, 12, 221a, 9–11.
[3] Cf. my *Crescas' Critique of Aristotle*, pp. 287, 646, n. 21. Cf. also Aristotle's discussion of the meaning of αἰών in *De Caelo*, I, 9, 279a, 22–33.

To Plotinus as to Aristotle there is more than one kind of being which has a beginningless existence, for the process of emanation is continuous and therefore the sphere is as eternal, in the sense of having no beginning, as the universal soul, as the intelligible world, as the Intelligence, and as the One or God. But unlike Aristotle he does not apply the term eternity to all of these types of being. Rather like Plato he applies it exclusively to what in his system corresponds to the world of ideas in the system of Plato, to the intelligible world, to the Intelligence and the One. Eternity according to him is identical with God.[1] It is the life of the Intelligence. It is "life consisting in rest, identity, uniformity, and infinity."[2] The universal soul, however, has no eternity but time, or, as we have preferred to call it, indefinite time or duration, whereas the sphere and everything that is moved with it and through it has definite time. Though time is endless to Plotinus, still it is not eternity, for eternity, as in Plato, is essentially of a different nature than time and is an exclusion of any kind of temporal relation.

Among Jewish and Arabic philosophers, the Aristotelian and Plotinian Intelligences as well as the Plotinian universal soul became the Intelligences, the number of which were determined by the number of the celestial spheres and which were identified with the angels of the Bible and functioned as the cause of the motion of the celestial spheres.[3] But with their rejection of the Plotinian emanation and their acceptance in its place of the theory of creation, God became the only being who had endless existence and thereby He also became the exclusive possessor of the attribute of eternity. Eternity could then have been used by them as a

---

[1] *Enneads*, III, vii, 4 (ed. Creuzer et Moser, Paris, 1855).

[2] *Ibid.*, 10 (p. 177, ll. 34–35).

[3] Cf. above, p. 218.

surrogate to God and as an epitome of all His attributes.
Still the problem of creation was for them a vital subject of
discussion and in the course of that discussion they had to
deal with Aristotle's theory of the eternity of the world and
of motion, and this called for the use of the term eternal in
its Aristotelian sense of infinite time. Thus the term eternity
had to be used by them both with reference to God and with
reference to other beings which were supposed by Aristotle
to be of endless existence. The result was that the term
eternity had for them two meanings, again the Platonic
and the Aristotelian. On the one hand, it meant the exclusion of time; on the other, it meant infinite time. Owing to
this double meaning of the term, Jewish philosophers always
took great pains to explain that when eternity is applied to
God it does not mean infinite time but rather freedom from
temporal relations.

We may illustrate this generalization by a brief analysis
of the discussion of the attribute of eternity which occurs
in the writings of some of the leading Jewish philosophers.
It usually takes the form of an explanation of the terms
"first" and "last," the use of which is the Biblical way of
expressing the eternity of God,[1] that is to say, eternity *a parte
ante* and *a parte post*. In their explanation of these Biblical
terms, Jewish philosophers endeavor to emphasize that these
two terms should not be taken literally to mean beginningless
and endless time but should be taken rather as implying
God's exclusion from any kind of temporal relation.

Both Baḥya and Maimonides insist upon this point and
suggest that the term "first" should be taken as a negation
either of God's having anything prior to Him, as Baḥya
expresses himself,[2] or of His having been created, as Mai-

---

[1] Cf. Isaiah 44, 6.   [2] *Ḥobot ha-Lebabot*, I, 6.

monides puts it.[1] Similarly, Judah ha-Levi speaks of God as
transcending all relations of time and explains the terms
"first" and "last" not as affirmations of literal priority and
posteriority but rather as negations of God's having been
preceded by anything and of His ever coming to an end.[2]
A most interesting passage for our purpose is that of Abraham Ibn Daud where eternity is directly identified with
immovability and immutability. "When we ascribe to God
the attribute 'eternal,' we only mean thereby that He was
immovable, that He is immovable, and that He will be immovable. You already know that by motion we mean change
from one state to another."[3] Crescas, though on account of
his defining time as duration independent of motion he has
no objection to the use of divine attributes which imply duration,[4] follows Maimonides in interpreting the term "first" in
the sense of being "uncreated."[5]

The most interesting passage for our purpose, however, is
that of Albo. "First" and "last," he says, mean absolute
independence of any temporal relations.[6] Albo, as we have
already seen, distinguishes between two kinds of time: one,
absolute time or duration, which is infinite, and the other,
definite time, which is finite. Eternity as applied to God,
according to him, excludes duration as well as definite time.[7]
The reason given by him why God alone of all beings is described as eternal is that God alone of all beings has necessary existence by virtue of His own nature, whereas all other
beings have only possible existence by their own nature.[8]

---

[1] *Moreh Nebukim*, I, 57.   [2] *Cuzari*, II, 2.

[3] *Emunah Ramah*, II, iii (pp. 54–55).

[4] *Or Adonai*, I, iii, 3 (p. 23b). Cf. my "Crescas on the Problem of Divine
Attributes" in the *Jewish Quarterly Review*, New Series, VII (1916), pp. 181–182.

[5] *Or Adonai*, I, iii, 3 (p. 24b). Cf. my "Crescas on the Problem of Divine Attributes," p. 207, n. 111.   [6] *'Ikkarim*, II, 18.

[7] *Ibid.*   [8] *Ibid.*

Or to put it in other words, eternity is applied to God, according to Albo, because in God essence and existence are identical.[1] Eternity is, therefore, defined by Albo as identity, uniformity, and immutability,[2] terms which remind us of those used by Plotinus as well as Plato in his characterization of eternity.

The use of eternity as a description of necessary existence *per se*, i.e., of the identity of essence and existence, may be also found in Altabrizi. Among the four definitions of time which he adduces there is one which reads that "time exists in itself, is neither a body nor anything belonging to a body, but is something which has necessary existence by virtue of itself."[3] I have suggested elsewhere that the last statement was taken from the Plotinian definition of eternity and was misapplied by Altabrizi to time.[4]

In exactly the same sense is the term eternity used in mediaeval Latin philosophic texts. It is applied exclusively to God and it is defined as the exclusion from any temporal relations. If other beings are assumed to have an endless existence, they are not described as eternal but by some other term. If the same term eternal is applied also to other beings, then the term when applied to God is said to have a special meaning. In either way, eternal as applied to God means more than the mere negation of beginning and end. It means immovability and necessity of existence.

The contrast between eternity and time as that between permanence and motion is suggested by Augustine when he speaks of eternity as the "ever-fixed" (*semper stantis*) and of time as the "never-fixed" (*numquam stantis*),[5] or when he says that "time does not exist without some kind of

[1] *Ibid.*   [2] *Ibid.*
[3] Altabrizi, Commentary on Maimonides' Twenty-five Propositions, Prop. 15.
[4] Cf. my *Crescas' Critique of Aristotle*, p. 662, n. 29.
[5] *Confessions*, XI, 11.

change caused by motion, while in eternity there is no change." [1] Boethius expresses the distinction between eternity and infinite time in the following statement: "Philosophers say that ever (*semper*) may be applied to the life of the heavens and other immortal bodies. But as applied to God it has a different meaning." [2] Though the world, according to Aristotle, "never began nor were ever to end, and its life did endure with infinite time, yet it is not such that it ought to be called eternal." [3] In order not to confuse eternity with infinite time he suggests two different terms for them. "Wherefore, if we will give things their right names, following Plato, let us say that God is eternal and the world perpetual." [4]

The views of Augustine and Boethius are re-echoed throughout the history of mediaeval philosophic writers. Eternity and time are considered to be of essentially different natures, and in order to take care of the duration of beings which can be described by neither eternity nor time, the term *aevum* is generally used. A list of scholastic views on eternity is given by Suarez. [5] But for our present purpose Suarez' own view on eternity is of significance, for, like Albo, he identifies it with necessary existence *per se*. He argues that eternity is not only a negation of God's having been created, or of His having a beginning and end, or of His being subject to motion and change, but that it has a positive meaning in so far as it expresses the necessity of the existence of God by His own essence, i.e., the identity of His essence and existence. [6]

---

[1] *De Civitate Dei*, XI, 6.
[2] *De Trinitate*, IV, ed. Stewart and Rand, pp. 20–21.
[3] *Consolatio Philosophiae*, V, 6, ed. Stewart and Rand, pp. 400–401.
[4] *Ibid.*, pp. 402–403.
[5] *Disputationes Metaphysicae*, Disp. L, Sec. III.
[6] *Ibid.*, Disp. L, Sec. III, x.

A similar definition also occurs in Abraham Herrera's cabalistic work *Puerta del Cielo*. The author quotes Plato, Plotinus, Boethius, Torquato Tasso, and Ficino on the meaning of eternity. He himself defines it as his contemporary Suarez and as Albo do, as meaning existence which is necessary by its own nature, or the identity of essence and existence, for, as he says, "every essence that is necessary and *per se* is eternal." [1]

Whatever sources Spinoza had consulted about eternity he must have received the following general impression. Eternity as applied to God does not mean merely endless time. It is used as an epitome of the main distinguishing characteristics by which God is differentiated from other beings. These distinguishing characteristics are summed up under two headings, both going back to Aristotle. First, God is immovable, whereas everything else is movable, and hence eternity is said to mean immovability, immutability, permanence, indivisibility, and all the other negations that go with it. Second, God has necessary existence, whereas other beings have only possible existence. Accordingly eternity is also said to mean, as in Albo, Suarez, and Herrera, the necessary existence of God or, which is the same thing, the identity of essence and existence in Him. Following these traditional views on eternity, Spinoza gives his own definition of the term.

To begin with, eternity is not merely beginningless and endless time or duration. "It cannot therefore be explained by duration and time, even if duration be conceived without beginning or end." [2] Indeed, in common speech, we speak of the eternity of the world when we mean its eternal duration in time, but this is an erroneous use of the term. It is

[1] *Sha'ar ha-Shamayim*, III, 4.
[2] *Ethics*, I, Def. 8, Expl.

only because of a defective terminology that "we say that the world has existed from eternity."[1] As we have seen, Boethius has already tried to remedy this defect by introducing the use of the term perpetual. An equally defective use of the term eternity, says Spinoza, is when it is used with reference to things which do not exist, as when we say "that the essence of things is eternal, although we do not think of the things as ever existing."[2] The reference in this passage is undoubtedly to the use of the term eternal with reference to the axiomatic truths which exist only as concepts of the mind, as, for instance, in the expression "eternal truths" used by Descartes. The particular Cartesian passage which Spinoza had in mind is probably the following: "When we apprehend that it is impossible that anything can be formed of nothing, the proposition *ex nihilo nihil fit* is not to be considered as an existing thing, or the mode of a thing, but as a certain eternal truth which has its seat in our mind, and is a common notion or axiom."[3]

Thus eternity, like duration and time, refers only to things which exist, or, as Spinoza would call them, real beings. But inasmuch as real beings are divided, according to Spinoza, into those "whose essence involves existence," i.e., God or Substance, and those "whose essence involves only a possible existence,"[4] eternity, says Spinoza, applies only to the first kind of real being. Accordingly Spinoza reverts to a definition of eternity the like of which we have found in Albo, Suarez, and Herrera. Now, in Spinoza's terminology the expression essence involving existence has the same meaning as *causa sui* or being causeless or infinite — infinite in the sense of undetermined by a cause.[5] Hence Spinoza defines eternity as an "attribute under which we conceive the in-

---

[1] *Cogitata Metaphysica*, II, 1.   [2] *Ibid.*   [3] *Principia Philosophiae*, I, 49.
[4] *Cogitata Metaphysica*, I, 1.   [5] Cf. above, pp. 127, 138.

finite existence of God." [1] "Infinite" is used here in the
sense of causeless, in contrast to "created," which, as we have
seen, is used by him in his definition of duration in the sense
of "caused." [2] Similarly in a letter to Meyer he says that
eternity is the only term which explains the existence of
substance, and hence it means "the infinite enjoyment of
existence, or (in awkward Latin) essendi." [3] Here, too, by infinite existence he means existence undetermined by a cause.
The expression *existendi* or *essendi fruitio* undoubtedly reflects the expression *plentitudo essendi* which is used by
Suarez in his definition of eternity. [4] The same implication
is also to be found in his formal definition of eternity in the
Ethics, which reads as follows: "By eternity I understand
existence itself (*ipsam existentiam*), so far as it is conceived
necessarily to follow from the definition alone of the eternal
thing." [5] I take the *ipsam* in *ipsam existentiam* not only as
a reflexive and emphatic pronoun but in the sense of *existentiam per se* or *per essentiam*, the equivalent of the expression
ipsius esse per essentiam which occurs in Suarez' definition
of eternity. [6]

The existence of God to which alone, then, eternity applies differs from the existence of all other beings, according
to Spinoza, not only in that it is identical with His essence
but also in that it is known and demonstrated in a different
manner from that of the existence of other beings. There
are three ways in which the existence of a thing may be
known, according to Spinoza: the way of perception, the

[1] *Cogitata Metaphysica*, I, 4.   [2] Cf. above, p. 351.
[3] Epistola 12: "hoc est, infinitam existendi, sive, invita latinitate, essendi
fruitionem."
[4] Suarez, *Disputationes Metaphysicae*, Disp. L. Sec. III, x: "Est enim aeternitas
duratio ipsius esse per essentiam: unde sicut ille esse est ipsa plentitudo essendi,
ita aeternitas est (ut ita dicam) ipsa plentitudo durandi."
[5] *Ethics*, I, Def. 8.
[6] Cf. quotation in note 4 above.

way of reason, and the way of intuition — his well-known three stages of knowledge. Now, in the case of all other beings, their existence is known by the first two kinds of knowledge, either by direct perception or by indirect proof *a posteriori*. The existence of eternal truths, the axioms and common notions, are perceived directly as intuitions, or what Descartes would call innate ideas.[1] Spinoza thus says: "By eternity I understand existence itself, so far as it is conceived necessarily to follow from the definition alone of the eternal thing, for such existence, like the essence of the thing, is conceived as an eternal truth."[2] The comparison with eternal truths is meant to bring out the fact that the existence of God which is identical with His essence is intuitively known as the essence of the eternal truths. But there is a difference between the eternal God and the eternal truths. In the eternal God there are both essence and existence, though the two are identical. In the eternal truths there is only essence; there is no existence in them.[3]

In Albo's discussion of the eternity of God, we have seen, not only time but also duration is excluded as an admissible attribute of God. In scholastic philosophy, however, the admissibility of duration as a fitting attribute of God was a mooted point. Suarez quotes Aureolus as being opposed to the attribution of duration to God. He himself is in favor of it.[4] Spinoza likewise raises the question in *Cogitata Metaphysica*, II, 1, and like Albo and Aureolus he denies the applicability of duration to God. The passage in which the discussion is contained, however, seems to refer to certain definite texts which at the present writing I am unable to identify.

[1] Cf. below, Vol. II, pp. 155 ff.
[2] *Ethics*, I, Def. 8, and Expl.
[3] Cf. above, p. 367, notes 2 and 3.
[4] Suarez, *op. cit.*, Disp. L, Sec. III, 11.

CHAPTER XI

MODES

PROPOSITIONS XIX to XXXVI, despite their external appearance of disjointedness and incongruity, have in reality, like all the other groups of propositions we have already treated, a logical order of sequence. They fall into six groups, dealing with the following topics: I. Eternity of God (Props. XIX–XX). II. Infinite and Eternal Modes (Props. XXI–XXIII). III. The Nature of Modes in General (Props. XXIV–XXVII). IV. Finite Modes (Props. XXVIII–XXIX). V. Intellect, Will, and Power (Props. XXX–XXXV). VI. Purposelessness (Prop. XXXVI and Appendix). All these six topics may be subsumed under one general topic which, like that of the preceding group of propositions (Props. XV–XVIII), is the causality of God, Propositions XIX–XXIX dealing with the effects of God's causality, that is to say, modes, and Propositions XXX–XXXVI and Appendix dealing with the necessary and purposeless nature of God's causality. Furthermore, not only are the propositions under each of these topics logically coherent in themselves, but there is also a logical transition from one topic to another.

The subject of Propositions XIX–XXIX is the description of the modal system of the universe. Having already dealt with the nature of God and His attributes, His existence and His causality, Spinoza now undertakes to present a complete and systematic view of his conception of the modes. If we may use here Spinoza's own expressions which we have already discussed previously but which in the *Ethics* are not

introduced by Spinoza until later in the course of the propositions under consideration, we may say that the *Ethics* so
far has dealt with *natura naturans*; from now on it will deal
with *natura naturata*. In our chapter on Extension and
Thought we have already discussed quite fully Spinoza's
system of modes as they are treated by him in his writings
outside the *Ethics*. That chapter may serve us now as a
general introduction to the subject. In this chapter we shall
draw upon it only in so far as it will be necessary for us to
explain the order and the meaning of the propositions before
us, but we shall give fuller consideration to those phases
of the problem which appear for the first time in these
propositions.

To describe the modal system of the universe or, in simpler
language, the world as it is seen, perceived, and thought
of by us, the most natural method for Spinoza would have
been to start with that which we ordinarily think of as directly
known to us, namely, individual things, and work up gradually to that which we ordinarily think of as known to us only
indirectly. He could have done so without the sacrifice of
the use of his own terminology. He could have started with
an enumeration and classification of individual things or
finite modes and then reduced them to two classes, extended
things and thinking things. He could have then considered
the totality of these individual things as constituting the
infinite physical universe and called it by his own expression
"the face of the whole universe" and described it in his own
way as a mediate infinite and eternal mode. He could have
then explained the behavior of the finite modes within the
totality of the universe on the basis of two principles, motion-
and-rest, on the one hand, and understanding, on the other,
and described these again in his own way as immediate infinite and eternal modes. Then he could have gone further

and shown how these two activities are the expressions of
two aspects of a single self-subsistent whole transcending the
aggregate totality of the individual modes and called that
transcendent whole substance and the two aspects, of which
motion-and-rest and understanding are expressions, the
attributes of extension and thought. To have done so
Spinoza would have followed the *a posteriori* method used by
Aristotle and by his adherents in the Middle Ages. But
Spinoza considered himself bound by the self-imposed *a
priori* reasoning of his geometrical method. Substance is
more immediately known to us, according to him, than the
individual things, and the source of knowledge by which it
is known to us is the most reliable. From the definition of
substance the nature of the entire universe follows by necessity as the properties of a triangle follow from the definition
of a triangle. Spinoza, therefore, preferred to start with
substance or God and to work gradually downward to individual things. Spinoza is reported to have remarked to
Tschirnhaus that while most philosophers begin with creatures he began with God [1] — a remark which, it must be said,
describes only his method of exposition but not necessarily
the manner in which he has arrived at his scheme.

But departing though he did from most philosophers,
Spinoza was not altogether without a model.

His model is the theory of emanation. This theory of
emanation with its initial monism is not only taken by him
as a model for his own system in preference to the dualism
which is implied in the Aristotelian theory of the eternal
co-existence of the universe with God, but, as we have seen
on several occasions, it is also used by him as the main target

[1] See K. I. Gerhardt, "Leibniz und Spinoza," in *Sitzungsberichte der königlich
preussischen Akademie der Wissenschaften zu Berlin*, 1889, p. 1077. Cf. below,
Vol. II, p. 4.

of his criticism. There are, of course, fundamental differences between the prototype and the copy, chief among
which is the nature of God, which is pure thought according
to the emanationists but is both thought and extension
according to Spinoza. Barring this fundamental difference
between them, the respective schemes in both systems are
parallel to each other. There is God as the starting point of
both systems. The two immediate infinite and eternal modes
in Spinoza, namely, the absolutely infinite intellect and motion-and-rest, correspond respectively to the Intelligences and
the circular motion of the spheres in emanation. Spinoza's
"face of the whole universe" corresponds to the outermost
celestial sphere which encloses the totality of the physical
universe according to the emanationists, with the difference
that the former was considered as infinite whereas the latter
was considered as finite. And then, within the universes of
both these systems there are individual things.

Another important element of emanation retained by
Spinoza is its terminology. When choosing his terms carefully, he always speaks of things as following (*sequi*) from the
nature of God or from His attributes. This reflects the terms
"proceeding" [1] and "following by necessity" [2] which are
generally used in Hebrew philosophic literature in connection with the process of emanation. Even when he uses some
other term, such as that God "acts" (*agit*) [3] or "to be produced" (*produci*) by God, [4] it is to be understood in the sense
that it follows by necessity from the nature of God. The
term cause which Spinoza applies to God is likewise to be
understood in the logical and geometrical sense, that is to

---

[1] יצא. Cf. *Emunah Ramah*, II, iv, 3.

[2] יתחייב, يلزم. Cf. *Moreh Nebukim*, II, 22.

[3] *Ethics*, I, Prop. 17; IV, Praef.

[4] *Ibid.*, I, Prop. 28, Schol.

say, in the sense in which the premise of a syllogism is said
to be the cause of its conclusion and the definition of a
triangle is said to be the cause of its properties. The term
"cause" (*causa*) to Spinoza means the same as the term
"reason" (*ratio*), which two terms are sometimes connected
by him by the co-ordinating conjunction "or," [1] so that the
causality he affirms of God is not meant to be understood as
implying temporal sequence. [2] In this respect, indeed, his
conception of God's causality corresponds exactly to that
of the emanationists as it is characterized by Maimonides
in the following passage: "It is clear that when Aristotle
says that the first Intelligence necessarily follows from God,
that the second necessarily follows from the first, and the
third from the second . . . he does not mean that one thing
was first in existence and then out of it came the second as
a necessary result. . . . By the expression 'it necessarily
follows' he merely refers to the causal relation; he means to
say that the first Intelligence is the cause of the existence
of the second, the second of the third, and so on . . .; but
none of these things preceded another, or has been in existence, according to him, without the existence of that other.
It is as if one should say, for example, that from the primary
qualities there follow by necessity roughness, smoothness,
hardness, softness, porosity, and solidity, in which case no
person would doubt that though . . . the secondary qualities follow necessarily from the four primary qualities, it is
impossible that there should exist a body which, having the
primary qualities, should be denuded of the secondary ones." [3]
The same idea, it may be added, is reflected in Spinoza's use

[1] *Ibid.*, I, Prop. 11, Demonst. 2 (*Opera*, II, p. 52, l. 31 *et pass.*); IV, Praef.
(*Opera*, II, p. 206, l. 26).

[2] Cf. Joachim, *A Study of the Ethics of Spinoza*, p. 54, n.

[3] *Moreh Nebukim*, II, 21.

of the expression prior in nature [1] or prior in causality [2] which he applies to God.

But whatever the differences between his God and the God of tradition, Spinoza seems to say at the beginning of this new chapter in the *Ethics* that his God does not differ from the traditional God in the matter of eternity. "God is eternal," or, since God's attributes are nothing but certain aspects of His essence, "all His attributes are eternal." [3] Now, eternity in the history of philosophy, as we have shown, meant three things. In the first place, it meant necessary existence *per se*, or the identity of essence and existence. In the second place, it meant immutability. Then, in the third place, it meant, at least in Spinoza's assertions that the eternal existence of God is an eternal truth, to be immediately known as an intuition. [4] In the first two propositions of this new chapter in the *Ethics*, therefore, Spinoza reiterates these three implications of the term eternity. In the first place, it means necessary existence *per se*, or the identity of essence and existence, "for God is substance, which necessarily exists, that is to say a substance to whose nature it pertains to exist," [5] and furthermore, "the existence of God and His essence are one and the same thing." [6] In the second place, eternity means immutability, hence "it follows that God is immutable, or (which is the same thing) all His attributes are immutable." [7] In the third place, the eternal existence of God may be called an eternal truth in so far as it is immediately known as an intuition, for "the existence of God, like His essence, is an eternal truth." [8] It is in this respect only,

---

[1] *Ethics*, I, Prop. 1. Cf. above, p. 77.

[2] *Ibid.*, I, Prop. 17, Schol. (*Opera*, II, p. 63, l. 7): "prior causalitate."

[3] *Ibid.*, I, Prop. 19. [4] Cf. above, p. 369.

[5] *Ethics*, I, Prop. 19, Demonst.

[6] *Ibid.*, I, Prop. 20. [7] *Ibid.*, Corol. 2.

[8] *Ibid.*, I, Prop. 19, Schol.; Prop. 20, Corol. 1.

and not in respect of lack of reality, that Spinoza calls the existence of God an eternal truth.[1]

Again, preserving the vocabulary of emanation, Spinoza speaks of his modes as things which follow from God. But inasmuch as unlike the emanationists Spinoza does not take God to be pure thought but rather as possessing an infinite number of attributes of which the two known ones are thought and extension, he does not speak of a single mode following from God but rather of various modes following respectively from the various attributes. Still like the emanationists he insists that each mode following from an attribute must be similar to the attribute from which it follows in certain essential characteristics. These essential characteristics he sums up in two terms, eternal and infinite. By the term eternal in its application to modes, however, he does not mean eternity in all the three senses which it has in its application to God. For one thing, it cannot mean necessary existence *per se* or the identity of essence and existence, for the modes have no necessary existence *per se* and their existence is not identical with their essence. For another thing, it cannot mean the immediate perception of the modes as an eternal truth, for they are known only through their cause. "Eternal" in this case means only to be immutable, or to exist forever, as Spinoza directly expresses himself in Proposition XXI, or to have indeterminate existence or duration, as he indirectly expresses himself in the Demonstration of Proposition XXI where he describes the opposite of it to have "determinate existence or duration." Similarly by the term infinite which he applies to this mode he does not mean infinity in the sense of causelessness, for the modes have God as their cause. "Infinite" in this case means to be the most perfect, the most complete and the greatest of its kind, that

[1] Cf. above, pp. 367, 369.

is to say, that which cannot be limited by another thing of the same nature, or what Spinoza elsewhere describes as the "infinite in its own kind." [1] That this is what Spinoza means by the term infinite as applied to modes may be gathered from the first part of the Demonstration of Proposition XXI. It is in the light of these remarks, therefore, that we may understand the full meaning of Proposition XXI: "All things which follow from the absolute nature of any attribute of God must *forever exist*, and must be *infinite*; that is to say, through that same attribute they are *eternal* and *infinite*." What he means to say is this: They are eternal only in the sense of existing forever or of being immutable, and they are also infinite only in the sense of being unlimited by another thing of the same attribute.

It is true, of course, that since by eternal and infinite when applied to the immediate modes Spinoza does not mean the same as when these terms are applied to God, he could just as well have said in Proposition XXI that all things which follow from the absolute nature of any attribute of God *cannot* be eternal and infinite. But he chose to phrase his proposition in positive terms evidently because he wanted to emphasize the ever-existence and the infinite perfection of these immediate modes, for it is in these respects that he will want later to differentiate them from individual things or finite modes. Another plausible reason for his choosing to phrase the proposition in positive terms is that by affirming that the modes are infinite in perfection he indirectly hit at the mediaevals who contended that "the existence of an infinite effect is impossible, for, were it to exist, it would be like its cause." [2]

The Demonstration of Proposition XXI follows Spinoza's favorite method of demonstration by proving the impossibil-

---

[1] *Ibid.*, I, Def. 6, Expl. Cf. above, p. 136.
[2] Abraham Herrera, *Sha'ar ha-Shamayim*, V, 12.

ity of the opposite,[1] namely, the impossibility "that in some attribute of God something which is *finite* and has a *determinate existence or duration* follows from the absolute nature of that attribute." For the purpose of his discussion he takes up the mode of the attribute of thought, which he designates here by the name of the "idea of God" (*idea Dei*) but by which he means the same as by what he describes elsewhere as the "absolutely infinite intellect," [2] and asks the reader to observe that the same reasoning is true of the other immediate modes, such, for instance, as motion-and-rest in the attribute of extension. But note how carefully this demonstration is constructed. It falls into two parts, corresponding to the two terms used in the proposition, namely, infinite and eternal. In the first part he tries to show that the immediate modes cannot be finite. In the second part he tries to show that they cannot have a "determinate duration."

The immediate modes which in Proposition XXI Spinoza has shown to be eternal and infinite are designated by him n Proposition XXII as the modification (*modificatio*) by which attributes are modified, and he tries to show also that the mediate mode, which he elsewhere designates by the name of the "face of the whole universe," [3] must likewise be eternal and infinite, in the particular sense, of course, in which, as we have seen, he uses these terms with reference to modes. But instead of the term eternal which we should expect here he uses now the expression to exist necessarily (*necessario existere*), by which, however, he means the same thing. Evidence that by the expression to exist necessarily in this proposition he means the same as by the term eternal in the preceding proposition may be found in the following passage in the demonstration of the next proposition: "If

[1] Cf. above, pp. 97, 183.   [2] Cf. above, pp. 238 ff.
[3] Cf. above, p. 344.

a mode, therefore, be conceived to exist necessarily and to be infinite, its necessary existence and infinitude must be concluded from some attribute of God or perceived through it, in so far as it is conceived to express infinitude and necessity of existence, that is to say, eternity." [1] In the light of these remarks, we may now read Proposition XXII: "Whatever follows from any attribute of God, in so far as it is modified by a modification which through the same attribute exists necessarily and infinitely, must also exist necessarily and infinitely." What he means to say is this: The modes which follow from the immediate modes must be eternal and infinite like the immediate modes themselves. Thus there are two kinds of eternal and infinite modes, namely, immediate and mediate.

In our discussion of the preceding two propositions, for the sake of clearness and in view of the fact that we have already given a complete discussion of the subject in a previous chapter, we have used the terms immediate modes and mediate modes. Spinoza himself, however, has so far used neither of these terms. In fact, in none of the propositions proper of the *Ethics* has he so far used the term mode. He has always spoken generally of things following from God or from the nature of any of God's attributes, though the term affection (*affectio*) in the sense of mode has been used by him in a proposition.[2] To introduce the term mode and to distinguish among modes which are infinite and eternal between those which are immediate and those which are mediate is the purpose of Proposition XXIII. In this proposition, dealing again with the infinite and eternal modes and using again the term "to exist necessarily" for "eternal," he introduces for the first time the term "mode": "Every mode which exists

---

[1] *Ethics*, I, Prop. 23, Demonst.
[2] *Ibid.*, I, Prop. 1; cf. Prop. 4, Demonst.

necessarily and infinitely must necessarily follow either from
the absolute nature of some attribute of God, or from some
attribute modified by a modification which exists necessarily and infinitely," which the Demonstration explains
to mean "either immediately or mediately" and refers in
connection with the former to Proposition XXI and in connection with the latter to Proposition XXII. These two
references make it clear that Proposition XXI deals with
immediate infinite and eternal modes whereas Proposition
XXII deals with mediate infinite and eternal modes.

Thus in these three propositions we have an outline of
Spinoza's theory of infinite and eternal modes and of their
classification into immediate and mediate. But the names of
these modes are not given by him. He mentions here the
name of only one of these immediate infinite and eternal
modes, and this, too, only indirectly, namely, the idea of God
in thought. Another name for this immediate infinite and
eternal mode as well as all the names of the other infinite
and eternal modes is supplied by Spinoza, as we have already
seen, in one of his letters.[1]

In our statement that the term eternal when applied to
modes does not mean the same as the term eternal when applied to God, especially in so far as in the later case the term
means the necessary existence *per se* or the identity of essence and existence, we have anticipated Propositions
XXIV–XXVII. It is evidently because in the preceding
propositions Spinoza has given no hint of this changed meaning of the term except only, as we have suggested, indirectly
when he speaks in Proposition XXI of existing forever as
an alternative of eternal, or when he speaks in the Demonstration of the same proposition of "determinate existence
or duration" as the opposite of eternity, that he now feels

[1] Cf. above, p. 216. Cf. pp. 238, 242, 244.

that an explanation of the term eternal as applied to modes is due. And so immediately after he has completed his outline of his theory of the infinite and eternal modes he proceeds to say that these modes, though called eternal, have no necessity at all of their own nature but that in everything they are and in everything they do they are to be considered as having been determined by God as their cause. Now, the causality of God, it may be recalled, has been described by Spinoza by seven characteristic terms, among which he mentions the following three, namely, that God is (1) an efficient cause, (2) an immanent cause, and (3) a free cause.[1] As distinguished from God in these three respects the modes are now shown by Spinoza in Propositions XXIV, XXV, and XXVI to be dependent upon Him as their efficient cause, their immanent cause, and their free cause.

In the first place, he says in Proposition XXIV, God is the efficient cause of the modes. But before we go further with the proposition, we must point out the relation between Spinoza's use of the term efficient cause and the use of the same term by the mediaevals. In Maimonides, for instance, the term efficient cause means primarily the cause that brings things into being, and is distinguished by him from the term formal cause which means the cause that preserves the existence of things after their having come into being. God is, however, according to him both the efficient and the formal cause of the universe, inasmuch as God is both the cause of the commencement of the existence of things and the cause of the continuance of the existence of things. Thus arguing against those who maintained that the world could continue to exist even without God once it had been produced by God, he says that "they would be right, if God were only the

[1] Cf. above, pp. 304 ff.

efficient cause and if the continuance of the existence of the produced thing were not dependent upon Him. . . . God, however, is himself the form of the universe, as we have already shown, and it is He who causes its continuance and permanence." [1] The same idea that God is both the cause of the creation and the cause of the permanence of the universe runs throughout scholastic philosophy, though a different terminology is used. In Thomas Aquinas the cause of the permanence of the universe is called *causa essendi*, whereas the cause of the creation of the universe is called *causa fiendi*.[2] In Duns Scotus both these causes, which he calls *causa conservans* and *causa producens* respectively, are said to be subdivisions of the efficient cause.[3] Similarly Descartes speaks of God not only as the cause of the creation of the world but also as the cause of its conservation.[4]

Reflecting this historical background and using, like Duns Scotus, the term efficient cause to include both the cause of creation and the cause of conservation, Spinoza says that modes are dependent upon God as their efficient cause, for inasmuch as "the essence of things produced by God does not involve existence," [5] "God is the cause not only of the commencement of the existence of things, but also of their continuance in existence." [6] In the course of his discussion Spinoza refers to the scholastic expression *causa essendi*, mentioned by us before, as a description of the continuance of the existence of things. *Essendi*, in the scholastic use of the term, means *existendi*, as has been pointed out by Spinoza himself in a letter to Meyer,[7] and is therefore to be translated

---

[1] *Moreh Nebukim*, I, 69.
[2] *Summa Theologica*, Pars I, Quaest. 104, Art. 1, Conclusio and ad 2.
[3] *In Octo Libros Physicorum Aristotelis Quaestiones*, Lib. II, Quaest. 8, No. 5.
[4] *Meditationes*, III (*Oeuvres*, VII, p. 49, ll. 12 ff.).
[5] *Ethics*, I, Prop. 24.   [6] *Ibid.*, Corol.
[7] Epistola 12 (*Opera*, IV, p. 55, l. 3). Cf. above, p. 108, n. 4, and p. 141, n. 4.

by "existence" rather than by "essence," though the latter resembles it more closely etymologically.

In the second place, Spinoza wants to say, the modes are dependent upon God as their immanent cause. He does not, however, say so in these very words. What he says reads that "God is the efficient cause not only of the existence of things, but also of their essence." [1] But we shall try to show how in Spinoza's mind to say that God is the cause of the essence of things was the equivalent of saying that God is the immanent cause of things.

The essence of things in Aristotle and throughout the subsequent history of philosophy meant the concept of things as it is formed by its definition. Thus the essence of man is animality and rationality, inasmuch as man is defined as a rational animal. But animality, which is the genus of man, is considered by Aristotle as the cause of man, and that kind of cause, as we have shown, is called an immanent cause in the sense that the effect resides in it. [2] Consequently, if the Aristotelian theory of definition is followed, namely, that a thing is defined by its genus, it may be said that the genus is the cause of the essence of the species, or, to express it differently, the essence of the species is dependent upon the genus as its immanent cause. Now, Spinoza rejects this Aristotelian theory of definition, "although," he says, "all the logicians admit this," [3] and sets up in its place a new theory according to which modes or things "which do not exist through themselves" [4] or which are "created" [5] are to be defined "only through the attributes whose modes they are, and through which, as their genus, they must be

---

[1] *Ethics*, I, Prop. 25.   [2] Cf. above, pp. 323 ff.
[3] *Short Treatise*, I, 7, § 9.
[4] *Ibid.*, § 10.
[5] *Tractatus de Intellectus Emendatione*, § 96 (*Opera*, II, p. 35, l. 12).   Cf. above, pp. 350–351.

understood," [1] or, as he sometimes says, through their "proximate" [2] or "efficient" [3] cause. According to this theory, man is not defined as a rational animal but rather as a combination of the modes of God's attributes of extension and thought, or, as Spinoza himself says, "the essence of man consists of certain modifications of the attributes of God." [4] Still, while Spinoza differs from his predecessors as to the nature of a definition, he does not differ from them as to the meaning of the term essence. The essence of a thing is still to him the concept of a thing attained by what he considers to be the definition of a thing, namely, the attributes of which the thing is a mode, for "a definition, if it is to be perfect," he says, "must explain the innermost essence of a thing." [5] But the attributes are said by Spinoza himself to be related to the *definiendum* as its genus and consequently as its immanent cause.[6] Spinoza is thus enabled to speak of the attributes or of substance or of God, just as his predecessors speak of the genus, as the cause of the essence of the *definiendum*, or, rather, as the immanent cause of the *definiendum*. But still, unlike the Aristotelian definition which merely states what a thing is but does not affirm that it exists,[7] Spinoza's theory of definition maintains that a definition affirms what a thing is as well as that it exists, for "given the definition of a thing, there should be no possibility of questioning whether it exists." [8] Though he says elsewhere that "the essence of things produced by God does not involve existence," [9] he does not mean that there is a possi-

---

[1] *Short Treatise*, I, 7, § 10.
[2] *Tractatus de Intellectus Emendatione*, § 96 (*Opera*, II, p. 35, l. 13).
[3] Epistola 60 (*Opera*, IV, p. 270, l. 22).
[4] *Ethics*, II, Prop. 10, Corol.
[5] *Tractatus de Intellectus Emendatione*, § 95 (*Opera*, II, p. 34, l. 29).
[6] Cf. above, pp. 324, 328.   [7] Cf. above, p. 124.
[8] *Tractatus de Intellectus Emendatione*, § 97 (*Opera*, II, p. 35, ll. 31-32).
[9] *Ethics*, I, Prop. 24.

bility of questioning whether they exist; he only means that
their existence is not determined by their own nature but by
their cause. Consequently, unlike the genus in the Aristotelian definition, the attributes, or substance, or God, or the
proximate or the efficient cause in Spinoza's definition are the
causes of both the existence and the essence of the thing
defined. Hence in wishing to say that the modes are dependent upon God as their efficient cause Spinoza says in Proposition XXV that "God is the efficient cause not only of the
existence of things, but also of their essence."

In the third place, says Spinoza, modes are dependent
upon God as their only free cause. We already know that
by the term free cause Spinoza means that "which exists
from the necessity of its own nature alone, and is determined
to action by itself alone," [1] and that when he speaks of God
as being the only free cause [2] he means that God alone
"acts from the laws of His own nature only, and is compelled by no one." [3] The modes, on the other hand, not being
free, are determined in their action by some cause. This
conclusion with regard to modes is summed up by Spinoza
in two statements in Proposition XXVI, first, in a positive
statement, "a thing which has been determined to any
action was necessarily so determined by God," and second,
in a negative statement, "that which has not been thus
determined by God cannot determine itself to action."

Now this proposition, both in its positive and in its negative statements, would on the whole have been admitted by
the mediaeval Jewish theologians and philosophers. In the
Talmudic literature there occur such sayings as "everything is in the control of God," [4] "everything is foreseen," [5]

---

[1] *Ibid.*, I, Def. 7.   [2] *Ibid.*, I, Prop. 17, Corol. 2.
[3] *Ibid.*, I, Prop. 17.
[4] *Berakot* 33b, and parallels.
[5] *Abot*, III, 15.

and "no one on earth bruises his finger, unless it is decreed in heaven." [1] In the philosophic literature it is generally maintained that everything has a cause which ultimately goes back to God as the first cause. Thus Judah ha-Levi sums up the position of Jewish philosophers by saying that whatever one may think of freedom of the will, it is generally admitted that nothing happens which does not come either directly or indirectly under the decree or determination of God. [2] Similarly Maimonides maintains "that God is the efficient cause of the particular events that take place in the world, just as He is the efficient cause of the universe as a whole as it now exists." [3] But still, while they would have admitted both these parts of the proposition, they would have insisted that man has freedom of the will. The Talmudic statement that "everything is in the control of God" adds "except the fear of God," [4] and the statement that "everything is foreseen" adds "yet freedom of choice is given." [5] Similarly in the philosophic literature the principle of freedom of the will is maintained. Now this freedom of the will, according to its protagonists, does not exclude the omniscience and hence the foreknowledge of God. How these two can be reconciled constitutes the problem of the freedom of the will. Various solutions of this problem are offered. It is sometimes said that while God has foreknowledge of man's choice it does not determine that choice, for God's knowledge is not causative. [6] Or it is admitted that God has no foreknowledge of man's choice, but it is argued that such a lack of foreknowledge is no defect in God. [7] Sometimes it is argued that while indeed both the principle of man's

[1] *Ḥullin* 7b.   [2] *Cuzari*, V, 20.
[3] *Moreh Nebukim*, I, 69.   [4] *Berakot* 33b.
[5] *Abot*, III, 15.
[6] *Emunot we-De'ot*, IV, 4; *Cuzari*, V, 20.
[7] *Emunah Ramah*, II, vi, 2 (p. 96).

freedom and the principle of God's foreknowledge are to be admitted, there is no contradiction between them, for God's knowledge is a homonymous term and is absolutely unlike human knowledge.[1] Now, all these, Spinoza must have argued in his mind, are a sort of specious reasoning and special pleading which do not really remove the essential difficulty. To say that God's knowledge is not causative or that God has no foreknowledge is to deny God's omnipotence and omniscience, and to say that God's knowledge is different from ours is tantamount to an admission that the problem is unsolvable. If God's omnipotence and omniscience are to be maintained, then God must be the cause of every future event and He must also have foreknowledge of that event. If despite this it is maintained that man has freedom of the will, then it means that man can render indeterminate that which has been determined by God. It is this pointed argument against the mediaeval position on the freedom of the human will that Spinoza had in mind when he said in Proposition XXVII that "a thing which has been determined by God to any action cannot render itself indeterminate."

Spinoza has thus explained the two sets of infinite and eternal modes, those which immediately follow from the attributes of God and those which follow from His attributes in so far as they are modified already by the immediate modes. But the world which Spinoza has undertaken to describe does not consist wholly of infinite and eternal modes. The modes which come directly under our observation are what Spinoza calls individual things (*res singulares*), and these are neither infinite in the perfection of their nature nor eternal in the duration of their existence. They are rather imperfect and transient things. Consequently, after having shown in Proposition XXV that God is the efficient cause not

---

[1] *Moreh Nebukim*, III, 20.

only of the existence of the infinite and eternal modes but also of their essence, he derives therefrom in the Corollary of the same proposition that "individual things are nothing but affections or modes of God's attributes, expressing those attributes in a certain and determinate manner." The implication of this statement is that God is also the cause of the existence and of the essence of finite modes. When in the next proposition he states in a general way that God is the cause of the action of a thing, he similarly means to assert that God is the cause of the action of the infinite and eternal modes as well as of the finite and transient modes. Thus individual things, like the infinite and eternal modes, follow from God and are determined by God in their existence, essence, and action.

But if individual things follow from God, then, since God is infinite, where does their finiteness come from? It will be recalled that both in his criticism of the emanationist explanation of the rise of matter out of an immaterial God [1] and in his own argument for the infinity and eternity of the immediate and mediate modes [2] Spinoza insisted upon strict adherence to the principle of necessary causality, namely, that the effect must be like the cause, so that cause and effect are mutually implicative concepts and one can be known by the other.[3] How then on the basis of this principle can Spinoza assert that finite things follow from the infinite God? Spinoza is thus now confronted with the same problem as the emanationists when these latter found themselves called upon to explain the rise of matter — the problem which Spinoza thought he had solved for good when he endowed God with the attribute of extension. The

---

[1] Cf. above, Chapter IV.
[2] Cf. above, pp. 377–378.
[3] *Ethics*, I, Def. 4. Cf. above, p. 90.

problem now returns to him not in the form of how material things arose from an immaterial cause but rather in the form of how finite things arose from an infinite cause.

That Spinoza was conscious of this problem is quite evident. In the Second Dialogue in the *Short Treatise* he puts it in the mouth of Erasmus, who asks, if "the effect of the inner cause cannot perish so long as its cause lasts; . . . how then can God be the cause of all things, seeing that many things perish?" The same problem is again stated by him, not indeed directly in the form of a question but rather indirectly in the form of a positive statement, in the Demonstration of Proposition XXVIII in *Ethics*, I: "That which is finite and which has a determinate existence could not be produced by the absolute nature of any attribute of God, for whatever follows from the absolute nature of any attribute of God is infinite and eternal." In both these places the same solution for the problem is offered. In the Second Dialogue of the *Short Treatise*, Erasmus, speaking for Spinoza, says that "God is really a cause of the effects which He has produced immediately, without any other conditions except His attributes alone; and that these cannot perish so long as their cause endures; but that you cannot call God an inner cause of the effects whose existence does not depend on Him immediately, but which have come into being through some other thing, except in so far as their causes do not operate, and cannot operate, without God, nor also outside Him, and that for this reason also, since they are not produced immediately by God, they can perish." The same explanation is given by Spinoza himself in *Short Treatise*, I, 8, where he says that the individual things are produced by the "general mode," which expression is used by him there to include both the immediate and mediate infinite modes, though he mentions there only the immediate modes.[1] Similarly in the Scholium to Proposition XXVIII of *Ethics*, I, Spinoza maintains that God is the absolutely proximate cause (*causa absolute proxima*) of the immediate infinite modes, that He is only the proximate cause in its own kind (*causa proxima in suo genere*) of the mediate infinite modes, but that in distinction to these, though not in the literal sense of the term, He is the remote cause (*causa remota*) of the individual things.[2] In addition to all this, he also says in Proposition XXVIII as follows: "An individual thing, or a thing which is finite and which has a determinate existence, cannot exist nor be determined to action unless it be determined to existence and action by another cause which is also finite and has a determinate existence, and again, this cause cannot exist nor be determined to action unless by another cause which is also finite and determined to existence and action, and so on *ad infinitum*." Taking all these passages together we may restate Spinoza's explanation of the rise of finite things as follows: Finite things follow directly from finite causes. These finite causes are infinite in number and form an infinite series of causes and effects. This infinite series of finite causes follows from the mediate infinite mode. This mediate infinite mode follows from the immediate infinite modes, which, in their turn, follow directly from God.

---

[1] Cf. above, pp. 216, 249.

[2] From the reading of the opening lines of the Scholium as given in Gebhardt's edition (*Opera*, II, p. 70, ll. 2–4; cf. editor's discussion on p. 352), it is clear that "quaedam a Deo immediate produci debuerunt" (l. 2) refers to the immediate infinite modes and that "et alia mediantibus his primis" (ll. 3–4) refers to the mediate infinite modes. When, therefore, Spinoza says later "that of things immediately produced by God He is the proximate cause absolutely, and not in their own kind" (ll. 5–7), it may be inferred that of the mediate infinite modes God is the proximate cause in their own kind. The distinction between these two senses of proximate cause is found in Heereboord's *Meletemata Philosophica, Disputationes ex Philosophia Selectae*, Vol. II, Disp. XXII. Cf. also above, p. 308.

The analogy between this explanation of the rise of finite things in the system of Spinoza and the explanation for the rise of material things in the system of emanation is quite complete. Just as the emanationists speak of material things as "proceeding" or as "following by necessity" from God, so also Spinoza speaks of finite things as "following" from God.[1] Just as the emanationists start out with the principle that "the direct emanation from God must be one simple Intelligence, and nothing else,"[2] so also Spinoza starts out with the principle that "whatever follows from the absolute nature of any attribute of God is infinite and eternal."[3] Just as the emanationists account for the rise of material things by interposing immaterial Intelligences between God and matter, so also Spinoza accounts for the rise of finite things by interposing infinite modes between God and finite modes. Finally, just as the emanationists arrange all the material things, from the celestial spheres to the lowest of sublunar existences, in a series of causes and effects, so also Spinoza arranges all the finite modes in a series of causes and effects. The only difference between them is that according to the emanationists, who follow Aristotle in his denial of an infinite series of causes and effects,[4] this series is finite, whereas according to Spinoza, who, by his own statement,[5] admits with Crescas the possibility of an infinite series of causes and effects,[6] this series is infinite. The gist of both these explanations is that material things and finite things which cannot be conceived to follow directly from God can be conceived to follow indirectly from Him if we only inter-

[1] Cf. above, p. 373.   [2] *Moreh Nebukim*, II, 22.
[3] *Ethics*, I, Prop. 28, Demonst.
[4] *Metaphysics*, II, 1, 993a, 30 ff.
[5] Epistola 12. Cf. above, pp. 195 ff.
[6] Cf. my *Crescas' Critique of Aristotle*, pp. 68–69; 225–229; 490, n. 13; 496, n. 21.

pose between these material or finite things and God a buffer of intermediate causes.

But still it is hard to see how a buffer of intermediate causes can solve the problem. For, truly speaking, any explanation offered in solution of the problem of the rise of finitude in Spinoza or of the rise of matter in emanation must not only show that finitude or matter does not come directly from the infinite or the immaterial cause but it must also show how either one of these can come at all, seeing that all things, according to both these systems, must ultimately be traced to the infinite or the immaterial God as their prime cause. This is the very reasoning employed by Maimonides in rejecting necessary emanation,[1] and this is also the very reasoning by which Spinoza was forced to the conclusion that God is material.[2] The absence of any attempt on the part of Spinoza to explain his position on this point, or, as it may be phrased, the absence of any explicit statement of a principle of individuation (*principium individuationis*) in the philosophy of Spinoza, makes one wonder whether this failure of his to offer any explanation was not due to the fact that he did not think it was necessary for him to do so. He may have felt quite justified in dispensing with such an explanation for either one of the following two reasons — either because he relied upon his readers to be able to find among the several solutions evolved in the course of the history of philosophy by the various monistic systems, in explanation of their common difficulty as to how the many arose from the one, a solution which would apply to his own particular problem as to how the finite arose from the infinite, or because he relied upon them to discover for themselves some essential difference between his own particular kind of

[1] *Moreh Nebukim*, II, 22. Cf. above, p. 106.
[2] Cf. above, Chapter IV.

monism and the other kinds of monism by which the former
was rendered immune to the difficulty which required a
special principle of individuation for its solution. We shall,
therefore, first canvass the various solutions of the common
difficulty of monistic systems to see if any of them could be
used by Spinoza, and then, in the event of our failure to
find any solution which could be suitably used by him, we
shall try to see if there is not something about Spinoza's conception of God which disposes of that common difficulty of
monistic systems without any recourse to a special principle
of individuation.

One of the explanations of the origin of the many which
is common to monistic systems in the history of philosophy
is to regard the many as unreal and as having only an illusory
existence. In European philosophy this tendency appears
with the Eleatics and recurs under different forms in the
various idealistic systems. Some interpreters of Spinoza
take his finite modes to be of a similar nature. But passages [1]
in which Spinoza couples "affections" with "substance" as
the two things which exist outside the mind, in contrast to
attributes which he uses as an alternative term for substance,
clearly indicate that he considered the modes as something
having reality outside the mind like substance itself, and as
being unlike the attributes, which he considered only as aspects under which substance appears to our mind. The only
difference that Spinoza finds between the reality of substance
and the reality of modes is that the former is due to the
necessity of its own nature whereas the latter is due to the
existence of substance. The finite modes are no less real to
him than the infinite and eternal modes.

Another explanation which occurs in the history of philosophy in answer to the problem of how the many arose from

[1] *Ethics*, I, Prop. 4, Demonst.; Prop. 28, Demonst.

the one or the individual from the general consists in an attempt to accredit all these to matter. According to this explanation, all that is necessary is to account for the origin of matter, but once matter is accounted for, either by the theory of its co-eternal existence with God or by the process of emanation or by the belief in a special act of creation *ex nihilo*, there is a ready explanation for all the change, corruptibility, divisibility, individuality, and in fact for all the changing phenomena of the visible world. It is thus that mediaeval philosophers speak for Aristotle and for themselves of matter as the principle of individuation. Spinoza, however, could not offer matter as his principle of finitude, for if matter is taken as a principle of individuation it is only because it is considered as something which by its very nature is potential, passive, imperfect, and is consequently the cause of divisibility and corruptibility. But Spinoza's matter, being extension and an infinite attribute of God, is none of these,[1] and cannot therefore out of its own nature become the principle of finitude.

Still another explanation occurs in the history of philosophy which has a direct bearing upon Spinoza's problem here, for the problem which the explanation was meant to solve is formulated as here by Spinoza in terms of the rise of the finite from the infinite. This explanation may be designated by the Cabalistic Hebrew term *Zimzum*,[2] i.e., contraction. The theory of *Zimzum* has a long history and is susceptible of various philosophic rationalizations, but we shall quote here a brief statement of its original and unadulterated meaning from Abraham Herrera's *Puerta del Cielo*. Starting with the statement that "from an infinite power, it would seem, an infinite effect would necessarily have to follow," Herrera proceeds to say with the Cabalists that "in a certain

---

[1] Cf. above pp. 237, 257.   [2] צמצום.

manner God had contracted His active force and power in order to produce finite effects." [1] It must have been with reference to this problem of the rise of the finite from the infinite that Solomon Maimon made in one of his works the cryptic remark that the view of Spinoza "agrees with the opinion of the Cabalists on the subject of *Zimzum*." [2] In his autobiography, Solomon Maimon similarly calls attention to the analogy between Spinoza and the Cabalistic principle of *Zimzum* in the following passage: "In fact, the Cabala is nothing but an expanded Spinozism, in which not only is the origin of the world explained by the contraction (*Einschränkung=Zimzum*) of the divine being, but also the origin of every kind of being, and its relation to the rest, are derived from a special (*besondern*) attribute of God." [3] However, Spinoza could have made no use of this theory of contraction in the solution of his problem of the rise of the finite from the infinite, for *Zimzum* as a solution of the problem implies that the infinite cause is an intelligent agent, and it is in this sense that it is generally used among the Cabalists, but to Spinoza, who insists upon the necessary nature of the divine causality, such an assumption is entirely inadmissible. To quote again from Herrera: "The second reason on account of which it is possible for us to maintain that the Infinite had in some manner contracted and limited himself in order to enable himself to produce finite and limited emanations is that the act of contraction is an act by means of His intelligence and His will." [4]

Finally, among the various formulations of the theory of

---

[1] *Sha'ar ha-Shamayim*, V, 12.

[2] Cf. Solomon Maimon's Hebrew commentary *Gib'at ha-Moreh* on *Moreh Nebukim*, I, 74.

[3] *Salomon Maimon's Lebensgeschichte von ihm selbst beschrieben*, Part I, Ch. XIV (1792), p. 146. English translation by J. C. Murray, Boston, 1888.

[4] *Sha'ar ha-Shamayim*, V, 12.

emanation which are advanced as explanations of the problem of the origin of matter there is one which, by analogy
with one of the present-day solutions of the problem of the
origin of life known as "emergent evolution," we may call
"emergent emanation."[1] It assumes indeed, as do all theories
of emanation, that God is immaterial and that matter does
not therefore arise directly from God. Still it does not arise
from anything external to God. Nor does it arise by the will
of God. It arises because in the process of emanation a new
cause inevitably makes its appearance. This new cause does
not proceed from God nor does it come from without, but
is the necessary concomitant of a new relation which, not
present in God, appears in the first Intelligence by the very
nature of its being an emanation and hence, unlike God,
having only possible existence. This theory says in effect that
matter is not the resultant of spiritual causes, but rather an
emergent, arising as something unpredictable out of a new
relation which makes its appearance in the emanated Intelligence. Now such an unpredictable new relation appears also
in Spinoza's immediate infinite modes, and it appears in them
by the very circumstance that their existence is dependent
upon God as their cause, and hence, unlike God, they have
only possible existence. Out of this new relation or condition,
not present in God but present in the immediate infinite
modes, Spinoza might say, there arise the finite modes.
Logically this would be a tenable explanation. But if we
assume this explanation to have been satisfactory to Spinoza
to account for the rise of finite modes from an infinite God,
why should he not have accepted it also as satisfactory to
account for the rise of material things from an immaterial

---

[1] Cf. my paper "The Problem of the Origin of Matter in Mediaeval Jewish
Philosophy and its Analogy to the Modern Problem of the Origin of Life" in *Proceedings of the Sixth International Congress of Philosophy* (1926), pp. 602 ff.

God? What then becomes of his main argument against the immateriality of God? If Spinoza did refuse to accept this sort of reasoning as an explanation of the rise of matter out of an immaterial cause, we must assume that he would also refuse to accept it as an explanation of the rise of finite modes out of an infinite cause.

Inasmuch as none of these historical solutions could be fittingly used by Spinoza, let us now look for some difference between Spinoza and the emanationists — a difference that would be sufficiently valid to dispose of the difficulty with which we are now contending.

Such a difference can be found if we only free Spinoza from the encumbrance of the traditional terminology which he affects, for, in truth, while he uses emanationist terms he does not mean by them exactly what the emanationists mean. When the emanationists speak of things as "proceeding" from God or as "following by necessity" from God,[1] they really mean that there is an actual egression of something from within God which on its departure from God assumes a nature unlike that of God. Though that departure is not in time nor in space, still logically the world follows from God in some order of succession and is outside of God. The Intelligences are thus conceived as proceeding from God and the spheres as proceeding from the Intelligences, and within the spheres appears matter which is not contained in God. In such a conception of succession, the appearance of matter, indeed, has to be accounted for. When Spinoza, however, describes the modes as following (*sequi*) from God or as being produced (*produci*) by God, or when he speaks of God as acting (*agit*) or as a cause, all these expressions, as we have shown above,[2] mean nothing but that the modes are contained in the substance as the conclusion of a syllogism is

[1] Cf. above, p. 373.   [2] Cf. above, p. 373.

contained in its premises and as the properties of a triangle
are contained in its definition.[1] There is no such thing as
the procession of the finite from the infinite in Spinoza. God
or substance is to him an infinite logical crust which holds
together the crumbs of the infinite number of the finite
modes, and that crust is never broken through to allow the
crumbs to escape or to emanate. Infinite substance by its
very nature contains within itself immediate infinite modes,
and the immediate infinite modes contain within themselves
mediate infinite modes, and the mediate infinite modes contain within themselves the infinite number of finite modes,
which last are arranged as a series of causes and effects. In
such a conception of an all-containing substance there can be
no question as to how the finite came into existence out of an
infinite any more than there can be a question as to how substance came into existence. Substance is *causa sui*, and its
nature is such that it involves within itself three orders of
modes — immediate infinite, mediate infinite, and finite.
The question as to how things come into existence can logically appear only within the finite modes, and the answer to
this, as given by Spinoza, is that each finite mode comes into
existence by another finite mode, and so on to infinity, but
the entire infinite series is ultimately contained in God, who
is *causa sui*, through the mediate and immediate infinite
modes. Things are finite by the very fact that they are parts
of a whole which is infinite.

Spinoza has thus proved that both the infinite modes and
the individual things are determined by God in three respects, viz., in their existence, in their essence, and in their
action. As a result of this he concludes in Proposition XXIX
that "in nature there is nothing contingent, but all things
are determined from the necessity of the divine nature to

[1] Cf. *Ethics*, I, Prop. 17, Schol., and above, p. 90.

exist and act in a certain manner." Three statements are
contained in this proposition. In the first place, it denies
contingency, or, as he calls it elsewhere, the existence of
"accidental things," which are defined by him as those
things which have "no cause"[1] or of which, through "a
deficiency in our knowledge . . . the order of causes is concealed from us."[2] Accidental things are similarly defined
by Aristotle as those things which have no determinate
cause.[3] In the second place, since there are no accidental
things in nature but everything in nature is determined in
its existence and action by a cause, there is no freedom in
nature, if by freedom is meant, as it is defined by Spinoza,
that which exists and acts by its own nature and without
any other cause.[4] In the third place, all the causes in nature
are traceable to one cause, which is the necessity of the divine
nature. This concludes Spinoza's treatment of the modes.
Taking now all the modes together, the finite as well as the
infinite, he contrasts them with substance and attributes,
calling the former *natura naturata* and the latter *natura
naturans*.[5] Similarly in the *Short Treatise* he makes the same
classification at the beginning of his treatment of the modes.[6]
But we have already discussed this matter quite fully in the
chapter on Extension and Thought.[7]

---

[1] *Short Treatise*, I, 6, § 2. Cf. above, p. 318.
[2] *Ethics*, I, Prop. 33, Schol. 1. Cf. *Cogitata Metaphysica*, I, 3, and above, p. 189.
[3] *Metaphysics*, V, 30, 1025a, 24.
[4] Cf. *Ethics*, I, Def. 7.
[5] *Ibid.*, I, Prop. 29, Schol. Cf. above, p. 390, n. 1.
[6] *Short Treatise*, I, 8.
[7] Cf. above, pp. 253 ff.

CHAPTER XII

NECESSITY AND PURPOSELESSNESS

I. Intellect, Will, and Power

THE statement in Proposition XXIX that there is nothing contingent in nature, that everything is determined by a cause, and that the causes are traceable to God reflects on the whole the mediaeval philosophic position. When Crescas raises the question whether pure possibility exists in nature, he sums up the case for the negative by the statement that "in the case of all things that are subject to generation and corruption, their existence is necessarily preceded by four causes . . . and when we inquire again into the existence of these causes, it is also found that they must necessarily be preceded by other causes . . . and when we look for other causes for these causes, the same conclusion follows, until the series of causes terminate at the Prime Being who is necessary of existence." [1] Similarly Maimonides states that "when we have found for any existing thing those four causes which are in immediate connection with it, we find for them again causes, and for these again other causes, and so on until we arrive at the first causes," and then finally at God. [2] But the mediaevals, after having asserted the existence of this causal nexus, try to break the nexus at two points, by introducing a certain kind of design in the causality of God and a certain amount of freedom in the action of man. Spinoza will therefore now try to eliminate both design in God and freedom in man and will insist upon an un-

[1] *Or Adonai*, II, v, 2. Cf. above, p. 309.
[2] *Moreh Nebukim*, I, 69.

interrupted sequence of causal continuity. Here in the last seven propositions and Appendix of the First Part of the *Ethics*, which deals with God, he tries primarily to eliminate design in God; later in the last two propositions of the Second Part, which deals with man, he tries to eliminate freedom in man.

The design in God's actions, especially in the act of creation, is expressed by the mediaevals in terms of certain attributes which they find to be implied in the divine act of creation. Thus Saadia derives from the fact of creation that God has life, power, and knowledge.[1] Judah ha-Levi derives from the same fact that God has knowledge, power, life, and will.[2] Maimonides insists that creation must be an act of will and design,[3] which, according to his own statements, imply also life, knowledge, and power.[4] These four attributes then are what according to the mediaevals raise the actions of God above a mere mechanical process and make His causality the result of will, intelligence, and purpose.

In desiring to show that the causality of God is a necessary process Spinoza subjects these attributes to a critical examination with a view to finding out what they may actually mean when applied to God. He does this in two ways. First, he tries to prove that on the showing of the understanding of the meaning of the attributes of intellect, life, and power by the mediaevals themselves God's action must be a necessary action. This method of attack he has followed above in the Scholium to Proposition XVII. Second, unfolding his own conception of these attributes of intellect, will, and power, he again tries to show that God's action is a necessary action. This is what he is proposing to do now in Propositions XXX–XXXIV before us.

---

[1] *Emunot we-De'ot*, II, 4.   [2] *Cuzari*, V, 18, 7–9.
[3] *Moreh Nebukim*, II, 19 and 21.   [4] *Ibid.*, II, 19; I, 53.

In both these places, it will be noticed, Spinoza deals only with three out of the four attributes enumerated by the mediaevals, mentioning only intellect, will, and power, but leaving out life. The reason for his not mentioning life may perhaps be found in the fact that Spinoza defines life as "the power (*vim*) through which things persevere in their existence," and "moreover, the power by which God perseveres in His existence is nothing else than His essence."[1] Now, the "ability to exist" is defined by Spinoza himself as "power" (*potentia*).[2] Consequently, life (*vita*), according to Spinoza, is power (*potentia*). It may therefore be concluded that the omission of the attribute of life by Spinoza in the propositions before us is due to the fact that he has included it under the attribute of power.

In his first kind of argument in the Scholium to Proposition XVII, as we have already seen, Spinoza has arrived at the conclusion that, from the point of view of those who believe that intellect, will, and power pertain to the nature of God, it would have to follow that "God's intellect, will, and power are one and the same thing." On the whole, this represents exactly the views of Saadia, Maimonides, and the other Jewish philosophers, all of whom maintain that these attributes are one and the same in God. To quote a short passage from Maimonides: "You must know that wisdom [i.e., intellect] and life [and for that matter also will and power] in reference to God are not different from each other."[3] Similar statements as to the identity of intellect, will, and power in God are made by Spinoza in his *Cogitata Metaphysica*,[4] and there, too, he is merely repeating the common mediaeval view. In the Scholium to Proposition XVII,

---

[1] *Cogitata Metaphysica*, II, 6.   [2] *Ethics*, I, Prop. 11, Demonst. 3.
[3] *Moreh Nebukim*, I, 53. Cf. quotations from Saadia and Albo above, p. 155.
[4] *Cogitata Metaphysica*, II, 7, note, and 8.

therefore, he tries to establish the necessity of God's causality by arguing from this commonly accepted mediaeval view and contending that if intellect and will pertain to the essence of God and are one, then these attributes must be homonymous terms, and hence meaningless terms, and consequently to say that God acts by intelligence and will is tantamount to saying that God acts by necessity.[1]

But here in these Propositions XXX–XXXIV Spinoza tries to establish this necessary causality of God not by arguing from the generally accepted mediaeval view but by arguing against it. In the first place, he seems to say, the three attributes by which the mediaevals try to characterize the causality of God are not of the same order. Indeed, "the power of God is His essence itself," [2] but as for intellect and will, they do not pertain to the essence of God. Intellect and will, which are the same,[3] are nothing but modes of God. What kind of mode the intellect, or, rather, the absolutely infinite intellect, is, has already been explained by Spinoza. It is the immediate mode of thought corresponding to motion and rest, which are the immediate mode of extension.[4] So is also will an immediate mode of thought. Consequently, "will and intellect are related to the nature of God as motion and rest," [5] except that will and intellect are the immediate mode of the attribute of thought whereas motion and rest are the immediate mode of the attribute of extension. Now, the attribute of thought in its self-conscious activity has as the direct object of its knowledge the essence of God himself and through God's essence also the modes.[6]

---

[1] Cf. above, p. 317.   Cf. also Bruno, *De l'infinito universo et Mondi*, Dial. I, p. 316, ll. 21–31 (ed. Lagarde).   [2] *Ethics*, I, Prop. 34.   Cf. Prop. 17, Schol.

[3] *Ethics*, II, Prop. 49, Corol.; *Tractatus Theologico-Politicus*, Ch. 4 (*Opera*, III, p. 62, ll. 28–29).   [4] Cf. above, p. 216.

[5] *Ethics*, I, Prop. 32, Corol. 2.

[6] Cf. below, Vol. II, p. 17.

The intellect, however, not pertaining to the essence of God and being only a mode of thought, cannot have the essence of God as the object of its knowledge. But still, the object of its knowledge must be something that exists outside the intellect itself. Since, however, outside the intellect there is nothing but God or (which is the same thing by Def. IV) His attributes and their modes,[1] and since furthermore the intellect cannot comprehend the essence of God himself, the object of its knowledge must be the attributes of God and their affections, not only the attribute of thought, of which it is itself a mode, and the modes of thought, but also the attribute and modes of extension.[2] This is what is meant by Proposition XXX: "The actual intellect, whether finite or infinite," that is to say, whether the human intellect or the absolutely infinite intellect, "must comprehend the attributes of God and the affections of God, and nothing else."

The terms "actual intellect" (*intellectus actu*) and "potential intellect" (*intellectus potentia*) used by Spinoza in this proposition are a mediaeval heritage, and are to be found in Arabic, Hebrew,[3] and Latin philosophy, but ultimately go back to Aristotle's νοῦς ἐνεργείᾳ (or ἐντελεχείᾳ) and νοῦς δυνάμει, and these are to be distinguished from the terms "active intellect" (*intellectus agens*) and "passive intellect" (*intellectus passivus*) which go back to the Greek νοῦς ποιητικός and νοῦς παθητικός.[4] The terms "actual" and "potential" describe two states of the intellect, one before the act of thinking, when the intellect is a mere capacity, and the other

---

[1] *Ethics*, I, Prop. 4, Demonst.   [2] Cf. above, pp. 142 f.

[3] The Hebrew and Arabic terms are: (1) השכל בפועל, العقل بالفعل; (2) השכל בכח, العقل بالقوّة.

[4] The corresponding Hebrew and Arabic terms are: (1) השכל הפועל, العقل المنفعل; (2) השכל הנפעל, العقل الفعال.
Cf. below, Vol. II, p. 14.

in the act of thinking, when the intellect is an actuality. The nature of these two states of the intellect is discussed by Aristotle in *De Anima*, III, 4, the most pregnant passage in which is the following: "The intellect is in a manner potentially all objects of thought, but is actually none of them until it thinks." [1] An elaborate discussion of this distinction is also to be found in Maimonides in a chapter which has been drawn upon by Spinoza on several occasions.[2]   But, as Spinoza himself says, he uses the expression "actual intellect" not because he agrees with Aristotle and the mediaevals that there is a "potential intellect" but rather for the purpose of emphasizing the fact that the intellect is to him always that which Aristotle and the mediaevals would describe as actual, "that is to say, the act of understanding itself (*ipsa scilicet intellectione*)." [3]

Furthermore, says Spinoza, since intellect and will are modes whereas power is identical with the essence of God, intellect and will belong to *natura naturata*, whereas power, by implication, may be said to belong to *natura naturans*. Hence the significance of Proposition XXXI, that "the actual intellect, whether it be finite or infinite, together with will, desire, love, etc., must be referred to the *natura naturata* and not to the *natura naturans*." The mention of desire and love in this proposition together with will and intellect is in accordance with Spinoza's habit of referring to desire and love as modes either of will [4] or of thought.[5] Will and intellect, it may be recalled, are considered by Spinoza as modes of thought and as identical with each other.

Spinoza's denial of will as pertaining to the essence of God and his relegation of it to the realm of modes leads him

---

[1] *De Anima*, III, 4, 429b, 30–31.
[2] *Moreh Nebukim*, I, 68.   Cf. above, pp. 238–239; below, Vol. II. pp. 24, 45.
[3] *Ethics*, I, Prop. 31, Schol.
[4] *Short Treatise*, II, 2, § 4, and 16, § 8.   [5] *Ethics*, II, Ax. 3.

directly to a denial of the mediaeval attribution of freedom
of the will to God. As a prelude to what the mediaevals
meant by attributing freedom of will to God, we may first
make clear what they meant by will and by freedom of the
will in general. The best definition of will for our present
purpose is that given by Maimonides. "The true essence of
the will is the ability to will and not to will." [1] Practically
the same definition is also given by Descartes: "The faculty
of will consists alone in our having the power of choosing to
do a thing or choosing not to do it (that is, to affirm or deny,
to pursue or to shun it)." [2] Spinoza, as we shall show on a
later occasion, reproduces this definition when he says that
"by will I understand a faculty of affirming or denying." [3]
The implication of this definition is that there is no will unless
there is that possibility of choice between willing and not
willing. An eternal and immutable will, therefore, is a contradiction in terms, according to Maimonides.[4] As a result
of this definition, no act of the will can be an eternal and immutable act; it must have a beginning and end or it must
be an intermittent act. Now, proceed the mediaevals, if
the changes which by definition must occur in any act of the
will are brought about by external causes the will is said to
be not free. But if they are brought about without any external causes but by the very nature of the will itself, then
the will is called free. "Free will," says Judah ha-Levi, "*qua*
free will, has no compulsory cause." [5] Similarly Crescas defines absolutely free will as the ability "to will and not to will
without an external cause." [6] These definitions, in fact, cor-

[1] *Moreh Nebukim*, II, 18, Second Method.
[2] *Meditationes*, IV (*Oeuvre*, VII, p. 57, ll. 21–23).
[3] *Ethics*, II, Prop. 48, Schol.; *Short Treatise*, II, 16, § 2. Cf. below, Vol. II,
p. 167.
[4] *Moreh Nebukim*, II, 21.
[5] *Cuzari*, V, 20.
[6] *Or Adonai*, II, v, 3 (p. 48b).

respond to Spinoza's own definition of freedom.[1] But while in nature in general, it is admitted by the mediaevals, there is no such free will, and while in the case of man the question of freedom constitutes one of their major problems of philosophy, with reference to God, they all maintain that He acts from the freedom of His will. Says again Maimonides: "If this will pertained to a material thing, so that the object sought after by means of that will was something outside the thing, there would then be a will which would change according to obstacles and newly arising circumstances. But the will of an immaterial being, which in no sense has for its object any other thing, is unchangeable, and the fact that it now wills one thing and tomorrow it wills another thing does not constitute a change in the essence of the being nor does it lead to the assumption of the existence of another cause [external to it]."[2] As against this the position taken by Spinoza may be summed up as follows: Granted that God is free, that freedom cannot be called freedom of the will; for will, he maintains, cannot pertain to the essence of God.

The argument for the inadmissibility of will in God is given in Proposition XXXII. Will, says Spinoza, cannot pertain to the essence of God. It is only an infinite mode, identical with the infinite intellect, following immediately from the attribute of thought. Being a mode of thought, it is determined by thought as its cause, just as the finite will of any individual being is determined by a series of causes, which series is infinite, according to Spinoza himself, or finite, according to the mediaevals.[3] Having a cause, will can no longer be called free. Hence, "the will cannot be called a free cause, but can only be called necessary."[4]

<hr />

[1] *Ethics*, I, Def. 7. Cf. above, p. 311.   [2] *Moreh Nebukim*, II, 18.
[3] Cf. above, p. 196.
[4] *Ethics*, I, Prop. 32, and Demonst.

Furthermore, it follows "that God does not act from freedom of the will," [1] for will does not pertain to His essence
but is only a mode which by its very nature must have
a cause and cannot therefore be free. To say that God acts
from freedom of will has no more meaning than to say that
God acts from freedom of motion, since both are modes
respectively of the attributes of thought and extension.[2]

One of the implications of the mediaeval view that God
acts from freedom of will is that the world could have been
produced by God in another manner and in another order
than that in which it has been produced. A brief statement
of this view is to be found in Herrera's *Puerta del Cielo*.
In his fourth argument in proof that God acts from freedom
of the will he says that "such free action was the beginning
of all the things which were produced and caused by God
when it was so decreed by His will, and by the same token
God could have omitted to bring them into existence or
He could have brought other things into existence, and
even now after having brought these things into existence,
He can still change them, destroy them, and then bring
them back into existence, all according to His free choice
and will." [3]

But perhaps still more pertinent for our present purpose
are the statements made by Maimonides, in which he contrasts Aristotle's theory of necessity with his own theory of
creation by will and design, for in these statements we shall
find the background not only of the view which Spinoza rejects but also the view which he adopts as his own. Restating Aristotle's view, Maimonides says that "it is the view
of Aristotle that this universe proceeded from the Creator by
way of necessity, that God is the cause and the world is the

---

[1] *Ibid.*, Corol. 1.   [2] *Ibid.*, Corol. 2.
[3] *Sha'ar ha-Shamayim*, III, 6.

effect, and that this effect is a necessary one; and just as it cannot be explained why God exists or how He exists in this particular manner, namely, being one and incorporeal, so it cannot be asked concerning the whole universe why it exists or how it exists in this particular manner. For it is necessary that the whole, i.e., the cause as well as the effect, should exist in this particular manner; it is impossible for them not to exist, or to be different from what they actually are. This leads to the conclusion that the nature of everything remains constant, and that nothing changes its nature in any way." [1] As against this Maimonides maintains as his own view that "we who believe in creation must admit that God could have created the universe in a different manner as regards the causes and effects contained in it." [2] Or again: "We, however, hold that all things in the universe are the result of design, and not merely of necessity. It is possible that He who designed them may change them and conceive another design. Not every design, however, is subject to change, for there are things which are impossible by their nature and cannot be altered, as will be explained." [3] The exceptions referred to here by Maimonides are those things which he himself and other mediaevals consider as impossible on account of their involving a contradiction in their definition, such as, e.g., a square the triangle of which is equal to its side. [4]

With this as his background Spinoza formulates his own view in Proposition XXXIII, aligning himself with Aristotle as against Maimonides: "Things could have been produced by God in no other manner and in no other order than that in which they have been produced." Direct references to controversies on this point are made by him in his *Short*

---

[1] *Moreh Nebukim*, II, 19.
[2] *Ibid.*, III, 13.
[3] *Ibid.*, II, 19. Cf. 17.
[4] Cf. above, p. 312, n, 5.

Treatise.[1] In the *Short Treatise*, furthermore, there is a passage parallel to the demonstration of this proposition.[2] Here in the *Ethics* the most important part of the discussion is given in two Scholia. In the first Scholium Spinoza explains the meaning of the terms "necessary," "impossible," "possible," and "contingent," which we have already discussed on several occasions.[3] But the introduction of these terms right after the proposition, which is undoubtedly directed against the passage we have quoted above from Maimonides, is significant, for in that passage of Maimonides, as we have seen, reference is also made to the nature of the impossible. Spinoza seems to challenge Maimonides as follows: You say that while indeed in nature there are certain things which are impossible, there is nothing in it which is absolutely necessary, but everything in it is possible or contingent, inasmuch as everything in nature, according to you, can be changed or come into existence without any previous cause but by the mere will of God. As against you I say that in nature there are only things impossible and things necessary, but nothing that is absolutely possible or contingent.

The second Scholium falls into three parts, as follows: (1) From the beginning of the Scholium to "Neither is there any need that I should here repeat those things which are said in the Scholium to Proposition XVII" (*Opera*, II, p. 74, l. 20–p. 75, l. 3). (2) From "But for the sake of those who differ from me" to "and hence . . . God's intellect and will . . . must have been different, which is absurd" (*Opera*, II, p. 75, l. 3–p. 76, l. 3). (3) From "Since, therefore, things could have been produced by God in no other manner or order" to the end of the Scholium (*Opera*, II, p. 76, l. 4–l. 34).

---

[1] *Short Treatise*, I, 4, § 3 and § 7 (*Opera*, I, p. 37, ll. 16 ff., p. 38, ll. 30 ff.).
[2] *Ibid.*, § 7 (p. 38, ll. 33 ff.).   [3] Cf. above, pp. 188 ff.

In the first part Spinoza deals with a problem which he has already dealt with before in the Scholium to Proposition XVII, but he restates it here in a different form. On the previous occasion the problem was presented by him in the form of a question as to whether God has produced all the things which are actually in His intellect. Here the problem is presented by him in the form of a question as to whether God has produced all the things in as high a degree of perfection as they are actually in His intellect. In a somewhat similar way the problem is stated in the *Cogitata Metaphysica*: "If God created a duration so great that no greater could be given He necessarily diminished His own power." [1] Both these phases of the problem, however, are combined by him into one in the *Short Treatise* when he says: "But now, again, there is the controversy whether, namely, of *all* that is in His idea, and which He can realize so *perfectly*, whether, I say, He could omit to realize anything, and whether such an omission would be a perfection in Him." [2] In the passage from Herrera, which I have quoted as the literary background of Spinoza's discussion in the Scholium to Proposition XVII,[3] it may also be noticed that the two phases of the problem are combined. Not only does Herrera say that only a limited number of those things which are in the intellect of God have been produced by Him, but he also maintains that this limited number of things produced are not of the highest degree of perfection, for God, according to him, can still produce things of higher perfection. In his argument in the first part of the Scholium here Spinoza repeats in the main the arguments employed by him in the first part of the Scholium to Proposition XVII; he only changes the term omnipotence for perfection. His opponents say, he argues here, that if the

---

[1] *Cogitata Metaphysica*, II, 10.   [2] *Short Treatise*, I, 4, § 3.
[3] Cf. above, pp. 314 ff.

things produced by God are of the highest perfection, then God could no longer produce things which are more perfect, and if He could not do so, it would be an imperfection in Him. As against this Spinoza contends, in effect, that, quite the contrary, it is the perfection of God that must lead one to say that the things already produced by Him are of the highest perfection, for if He could have produced more perfect things and did not produce them, then His failure to produce them would have to be accounted for by some imperfection in His nature, the imperfection either of incompetency or of ill-will. A similar argument is put in the mouth of Aristotle by Maimonides in the following passage: "For, according to this theory, God, whom every thinking person recognizes to be endowed with all the kinds of perfections, is in such a relation to the existing beings that He cannot change in them anything. . . . Aristotle says that God does not try to make any change, and that it is impossible that He should will anything to be otherwise from what it is. If it were possible, it would not constitute in Him greater perfection; it might, on the contrary, from some point of view, be an imperfection." [1]

In the second part of the Scholium here Spinoza takes up again the main proposition, namely, "that things could be created in no other mode or order by Him," and tries to prove it against his opponents from their own admission "that will pertains to God's essence." Now, the main point in this premise admitted by his opponents, if we take Maimonides as its chief exponent, is that while the will of God is co-eternal with God, the world is not eternal, for will by its very nature means the ability to will to do a thing at one time and not to will to do it at another time,[2] and to adopt

---

[1] *Moreh Nebukim*, II, 22.   Cf. Bruno, *De l'infinito universo et Mondi*, Dial. I, p. 317, ll. 1 ff. (ed. Lagarde).   [2] *Ibid.*, II, 18.

one course or the other by an act of decree or decision; but, they contend, inasmuch as in the case of God the decree or decision is entirely independent of anything external to Him, it does not produce any change in His essence. As against this Spinoza raises the following question: This decree (*decretum*)[1] of God to make things in the manner and order in which they are, when did it take place? There are three possible assumptions: (1) It could have taken place shortly *before* the things were produced by God. (2) It could have co-existed with God from eternity, without any possibility of its being changed even by the will of God. (3) It could have co-existed with God from eternity, but with the possibility of its being subject to change by the will of God prior to His having produced the things. Spinoza, in the course of his discussion, examines all these three assumptions and tries to show either that they are untenable or that they prove just the opposite of what his opponents have set out to prove.

To begin with, the first assumption is untenable even according to the mediaevals themselves, for, according to Maimonides and others, prior to creation there was no time; what there was then may be called an "imagination of time" or, if you choose, eternity, in which there is no *before* nor *after*.[2] Spinoza thus says: "But since in eternity there is no *when* nor *before* nor *after*, it follows . . . that . . . God had not existed before His decrees, and could never exist without them." [3]

Then, proceeds Spinoza, if the second assumption be true, it will prove his own contention against his opponents.

---

[1] Hebrew and Arabic equivalent: מזירה قدر‎, قضا‎. (*Cuzari*, V, 19; *Moreh Nebukim*, III, 17).

[2] '*Ikkarim*, II, 18. Cf. above, p. 339.

[3] *Ethics*, I, Prop. 33, Schol. 2 (*Opera*, II, p. 75, ll. 12–15).

If things have come into existence exactly in the manner in which it had been decreed by God from eternity and if God could not have changed that decree, then "things could have been produced by God in no other manner and in no other order than that in which they have been produced." [1] This second assumption, it may be remarked, seems to reflect the following statement in Heereboord: "What God does in time He has decreed from eternity." [2] But Spinoza seems to differ from Heereboord as to the meaning of this statement. According to Heereboord, this statement does not mean that "God accomplishes things in time in the order in which He has decreed them from eternity"; [3] it only means that "God produces in time the things which He has decreed from eternity and He produces them as He has decreed to produce them." [4] According to Spinoza, the order as well as the nature of things has been decreed from eternity. In Proposition XXXIII he speaks of the unchangeability of the manner (*modus*) and order (*ordo*) in which things have been produced, and in Scholium II, evidently in direct opposition to Heereboord, he speaks of both the nature of things (*rerum natura*) and their order (*ordo*) [5] as having been decreed by God from eternity.

There is nothing left therefore for his opponents but to adopt the third assumption, namely, that God himself could have changed His eternal decree prior to the creation of the world so that the world could have been created otherwise than the way it had been decreed from eternity. As

---

[1] *Ibid.*, II, Prop. 33.

[2] *Meletemata Philosophica, Disputationes ex Philosophia Selectae*, Vol. II, Disp. XXIV, IX: "Uti quid Deus facit in tempore, ita ab aeterno decrevit."

[3] *Ibid.*: "Quo ordine res Deus decrevit ab aeterno, eo in tempore exequitur."

[4] *Ibid.*: "Quas res decrevit ab aeterno et quales decrevit facere, eas et tales in tempore facit."

[5] *Opera*, II, p. 75, ll. 16–17, 20.

against this, Spinoza raises four objections, which, it must be said, have not passed unnoticed by the mediaevals themselves.

First, it implies that prior to creation there could have been a change in God's will and hence also in His intellect with which His will is identical. Maimonides himself has discussed this problem and admits that such a change in God's will is possible inasmuch as it is not determined by any external cause.[1]

Second, if such a change in God's will was possible before creation, why should it not be possible now after creation? Here, too, Maimonides would say that if God willed it and if it served any purpose He could change the order of nature even after its creation, except in things which are impossible by their own nature and would involve a contradiction in their definition.[2]

Third, Maimonides as well as all other philosophers agrees "that God is an intellect which always is in action, and that there is in Him no potentiality at all."[3] But to say that God changes His will or intellect implies a change from potentiality to actuality, which is contrary to their own premise. This argument, too, has been discussed by Maimonides, who tries to show that in an incorporeal agent a change from non-action to action does not imply a transition from potentiality to actuality. "The active intellect may be taken as an illustration. . . . It is an evident fact that the active intellect does not act continually . . . and yet Aristotle does not say that the active intellect is changeable, or passes from a state of potentiality to that of actuality, although it produces at one time something which it has not

[1] *Moreh Nebukim*, II, 18. Cf. above, pp. 101 ff.
[2] *Ibid.*, II, 19; III, 25. Cf. above, p. 312.
[3] *Ibid.*, I, 68. Cf. above, p. 239.

produced before." [1] In fact, Spinoza himself makes use of this statement of Maimonides in the *Short Treatise*. "Furthermore, of such an agent who acts in himself it can never be said that he has the imperfection of a patient, because he is not affected by another; such, for instance, is the case with the intellect." [2]

Fourth, Maimonides and all the other mediaevals admit that God's will and intellect are identical with His essence.[3] To say therefore that His will could change would imply that His essence could also change. This, too, is answered by Maimonides. "Similarly it has been shown by us that if a being [like God] acted at one time and did not act at another, this would not involve a change in the being itself." [4]

In the third part of the Scholium Spinoza combines all the three phases of the problem and asserts (1) that "things could have been produced by God in no other manner or order," (2) that God created "all things which are in His intellect," and (3) that the things created were created "with the same perfection as that in which they exist in His intellect." All these three principles are included in what Spinoza calls necessity, by which he means that things cannot be otherwise than what they are, that they cannot be more than they are, and that they cannot be more perfect than they are. The mediaeval views which are in opposition to this conception of necessity are divided by Spinoza into two classes. The first class is characterized by him as the view which makes everything dependent upon "the will of God alone" (*Dei tantum voluntas*) or upon "a certain indifferent God's will" (*indifferens quaedam Dei voluntas*) or upon God's "good pleasure" (*ipsius beneplacitum*). According to this

---

[1] *Ibid.*, II, 18, First Method.
[2] *Short Treatise*, I, 2, § 24 (*Opera*, I, p. 26, ll. 23–26).
[3] *Moreh Nebukim*, I, 53 and 68. Cf. above, pp. 155, 317, 402.
[4] *Ibid.*, II, 18, Second Method.

view not only are things in themselves neither perfect nor imperfect, but they are also neither good nor evil. They are so only by the will of God alone, and therefore if God had willed He could have made them otherwise. The second class is characterized by him as the view of those "who affirm that God does everything for the sake of the good." Spinoza's characterization of these two mediaeval views reflects again Maimonides' discussion of the difference between the view of the Mohammedan Ashariya and his own view. According to the Ashariya everything is the result of God's will alone; according to Maimonides, it is the result of both will and wisdom. The essential difference between these two views is the question whether the things created by God and the commandments revealed by Him are the work of an arbitrary will of whether they are created and revealed for the sake of some purpose.[1] "Purpose" is another word used by Maimonides for what Spinoza calls here "the good," for, as says Maimonides, "we call 'good' that which is in accordance with the object we seek."[2] Similarly Heereboord says that "the good is the formal reason of the final cause."[3] All these go back to Aristotle's definition of the good as "that which all things aim at."[4]

In Maimonides' own words the Asharian view is described as the view of those thinkers "who assume that God does not produce one thing for the sake of another, that there are no causes and effects, but that all His actions are the direct result of the will of God, and no purpose can be found for them, nor can it be asked why He has made this and not that; for He does what pleases Him, and it is not to be considered as the result of some kind of wisdom."[5]

---

[1] *Ibid.*, III, 25 and 26.   [2] *Ibid.*, III, 13.
[3] *Meletemata Philosophica, Disputationes ex Philosophia Selectae*, Vol. II, Disp. XXIII, 11: "Bonitas ergo formalis ratio est causae finalis."
[4] *Nicomachean Ethics*, I, 1, 1094a, 3.   [5] *Moreh Nebukim*, III, 25.

His own view is described by him as follows: "The things which God wills to do are necessarily done; there is nothing that could prevent the realization of His will. God, however, wills only that which is possible; not indeed everything that is possible, but only such things as His wisdom decrees upon." [1] "The only question to be asked," says Maimonides in another place, "is this: What is the cause of this design? The answer to this question is that all this has been made for a purpose which is unknown to us." [2]

In criticizing both these views, Spinoza dismisses the first one by summarizing his previous contention that a change in God's will is unthinkable. Still, though he is opposed to this view, he considers it nevertheless "at a less distance from the truth" than the second view, which he proceeds to refute in the following statement. "For these seem to place something outside of God which is independent of Him, to which He looks while He is at work as to a model, or at which He aims as if at a certain mark. This is indeed nothing else than to subject God to fate, the most absurd thing which can be affirmed of Him. . . . Therefore it is not worth while that I should waste time in refuting this absurdity."

There is more hidden away in this statement than what it seems to convey to the mind of the casual reader. We may try to unfold all its implications by making Spinoza address Maimonides directly and speak out all that was in the back of his mind when he gave utterance to this statement. Spinoza seems to address Maimonides as follows:

You say that things do not depend upon an arbitrary will of God but upon a rational will, which you call wisdom, so that everything created by God has a purpose. God, then, is guided by a purpose or by His Wisdom, the nature of

[1] *Ibid.*   [2] *Ibid.*, II, 19.

which you say is unknown to us, but which you maintain is
not external to Him. It is well for you to seek refuge out of
the difficulties into which your own philosophy so often
leads you by pleading ignorance. But those predecessors of
yours, the rabbis, aye, and the philosophers, too, whose traditional teachings, from which you refuse to depart, are re-
sponsible for all your philosophical difficulties, did confess
to know what that divine Wisdom was and the purpose for
which all things were created. They say that the Wisdom,
which speaks in person in the eight chapter of the Book of
Proverbs, is the Torah, or the Law of Moses, and it is the
Torah which is regarded by them as the purpose for which
the world was created.[1] Furthermore, this Torah, though
not considered in Judaism to be eternal, existed, according to
its beliefs, before the creation of the world, and it is said that
God consulted it as to the creation of the world,[2] and that it
served Him as a sort of model according to which the world
was created; as the rabbis say: "God looked into the Torah
and created the world."[3] Not only your rabbis but also
your philosopher Philo speaks of Wisdom and of the Logos
in the same way as the rabbis speak of the Torah, namely,
as divine instruments of creation.[4] Of course, you yourself
do not take these statements literally. You insist upon
identifying Wisdom with the essence of God. But it is these
traditional utterances about Wisdom in the sense of the
Torah that really lie behind your statements that things
were created for some unknown purpose and by some un-

---

[1] Or Adonai, II, vi, 4, quoting as proof-text the rabbinic dictum אלמלא תורה
לא נתקיימו שמים וארץ (Pesaḥim 68b), which he evidently takes to mean "but for
the Torah, heaven and earth would not have come into existence." The dictum,
however, may mean "but for the Torah, heaven and earth would not continue to
exist."   [2] Pirke de-Rabbi Eliezer, Ch. 3.

[3] Genesis Rabbah, I, 1, and parallels.

[4] De Eo: Quis Rerum Divinarum Heres Sit, XLI, 199; De Cherubim et Flam-
meo Gladio, XXXV, 124 ff. Cf. Drummond, Philo Judaeus, II, pp. 205–206.

known divine wisdom. Stripped of this metaphysical garb
with which you have clothed these ancient utterances, your
own statements "seem to place something outside of God
which is independent of Him, to which He looks while He
is at work as to a model, or at which He aims as if at a
certain mark."

But furthermore, Spinoza seems to say to Maimonides,
if the Torah is that which God consulted and by which God
was guided in creating things, then your God is governed
by a Torah or Wisdom or Logos just as some philosophers,
say the Stoics, maintain that the world is governed by fate
(*fatum*, ἡ εἱμαρμένη). "This indeed is nothing else than
to subject God to fate." This by itself makes Spinoza's
statement intelligible enough. But there may be even more
than that in it. The Stoics speak of fate as the Logos of
the universe.[1] Similarly Philo refers to the Logos as that
"which most men call fortune (τύχη),"[2] fortune probably
being here an interchangeable term with fate.[3] What Spinoza
therefore would seem to say to Maimonides is this: Since
the Stoic and the Philonic Logos, which is sometimes used
as the equivalent of Wisdom or your Torah, is called fate,
when God is said to be ruled by the Torah or Wisdom or the
Logos, He is really said to be ruled by fate. In fact Campanella combines the terms "wisdom" and "fate" when he
speaks of the maintenance of things by the power of God or
necessity, by His wisdom or fate (*fatum*), and finally by His
love or ordinance.[4]

---

[1] Cf. Zeller, *Philosophie der Griechen*, III, 1, p. 161, n. 2 (4th ed.). English
translation: *Stoics, Epicureans, and Sceptics*, p. 161, n. 3.

[2] *Quod Deus Sit Immutabilis*, XXXVI, 176.

[3] Cf. Francis Bacon, *De Augmentis Scientiarum*, III, 4 (*Works*, London, 1857,
Vol. I, p. 569): "quas uno nomine *Fatum* aut *Fortunam* vocabant."

[4] Reproduced by Erdmann, *Grundriss der Geschichte der Philosophie*, I, § 246.
4, based upon Campanella's *Philosophia Universalis*, VI, Proem.

Now Spinoza would not shrink from the use of the term "fate" in its strictly Stoic sense of a universal and inscrutable law that governs all things. In fact in *Short Treatise*, I, 6, he practically uses the term "fate" when he describes the contents of the chapter in which he denies the existence of any accidental things by the title "On Divine Predestination." But what he insists upon saying here is that while all things and all actions, in so far as they follow with inevitable necessity from the nature of God, may be said in a certain sense to have a fatalistic necessity, God himself must be conceived as absolutely free and as not being subject to any fate. This distinction evidently was difficult to be grasped by his correspondents, and on several occasions in letters to Ostens and Oldenburg Spinoza felt called upon to explain himself. To quote a few characteristic passages from these letters: "The basis of his argument is this, that he thinks that I take away God's liberty, and subject Him to fate. This is entirely false. For I assert that all things follow with inevitable necessity from the nature of God, just as all assert that it follows from the nature of God that He understands himself." [1] Again: "I want to explain here briefly in what sense I maintain the fatalistic necessity of all things and of all actions. For I do in no way subject God to fate, but I conceive that everything follows with inevitable necessity from the nature of God, just as all conceive that it follows from the nature of God himself that He should understand himself." [2]

Unlike intellect and will, which do not pertain to God, power, as we have already pointed out, is admitted by Spinoza to pertain to the essence of God and to be identical with His essence. Hence Proposition XXXIV: "The power of God is His essence itself." Power, as we have elsewhere

---

[1] Epistola 43.   [2] Epistola 75.

remarked, means to Spinoza the ability to exist and the ability to bring things into existence.[1] Hence Spinoza defines God's power here in the demonstration of the proposition as that "by which He himself and all things are and act." From this definition of power and from its identity with the essence of God Spinoza tries to solve again the problem which he has discussed in Scholium II to Proposition XVII and in the third part of the Scholium to Proposition XXXIII, namely, whether God created all things which are in His intellect. His answer is in the affirmative. Hence Proposition XXXV: "Whatever we conceive to be in God's power necessarily exists." In the *Short Treatise* he expresses the same view by saying: "We deny that God cannot omit to do what He does."[2]

II. Final Causes

It may be recalled that the mediaevals apply the term "cause" to God in three out of its four Aristotelian senses. God is to them the efficient, formal, and final cause, but not the material cause, of the world.[3] In opposition to them, Spinoza made God also the material cause of the world, and by further reducing the formal to the efficient cause, he has throughout his discussion of the causality of God, from Proposition XV to XXXV, elaborated in great detail his conception of the efficient causation of God. In the course of his discussion he has also refuted the views of those who, having denied the principle of causality altogether, attributed the succession and change of things either to chance[4] or to the direct intervention of God's arbitrary will.[5] The latter view, which is discussed by him in the last part of

[1] Cf. above, pp. 204–205.
[2] *Short Treatise*, I, 4, § 1.
[3] Cf. above, p. 302.
[4] Cf. above, p. 318.
[5] Cf. above, pp. 416 ff.

Scholium II to Proposition XXXIII, led him to touch upon the problem of final causation, without, however, going into a full discussion of the problem. Now, at the conclusion of the first Part of the *Ethics*, Spinoza wanted to come out with a formal denial of the mediaeval view as to the existence of final causes in nature.[1] But following his general custom in the propositions of the *Ethics*, instead of directly opposing the mediaevals, he states his own position in positive terms, but in such a manner as to contain an indirect denial of the commonly accepted belief in final causes.

The oppositional views in the history of philosophy to final causes may be summed up under two headings. First, the view that everything is the result of the arbitrary will of God, which, as we have seen, Maimonides attributes to the Mohammedan Ashariya. Second, the view that everything is the result of chance and accident, which, again, Maimonides attributes to the Epicureans.[2] Spinoza, as we have seen, has discussed both these views and rejected them.[3] The method by which he now tries in Proposition XXXVI to reject final causes altogether is by reducing every final cause to an efficient cause. When two events constantly and repeatedly succeed one another, he seems to say, it is not to be explained in terms of final causes, namely, that the first event aims at, or is made to serve, the second event as its purpose, but it is to be explained rather solely in terms of efficient causes, namely, that the second event follows by necessity from the nature of the first event, for "nothing exists from whose nature an effect does not follow." This method of eliminating final causes by reducing them to

---

[1] On the general problem of final causes in the philosophy of Spinoza, see Peter Brunner, *Probleme der Teleologie bei Maimonides, Thomas von Aquin und Spinoza* (Heidelberg, 1928).

[2] *Moreh Nebukim*, II, 13. Cf. above, p. 318.

[3] Cf. above, pp. 416 ff.

efficient causes is already indicated in the *Cogitata Meta-physica*: "Second, I say that in creation no causes concur except the efficient one. I might have said that creation negates or excludes all causes except the efficient." [1] A still clearer statement to the same effect occurs in the Preface to *Ethics*, IV: "A final cause, as it is called, is nothing, therefore, but human desire. . . . Therefore, having a house to live in, in so far as it is considered a final cause, is merely this particular desire, which is really an efficient cause." [2] This in fact is nothing but a logical corollary from Aristotle's own denial of design and purpose in God's causality, which Spinoza seems to be stressing in this proposition against Aristotle. For Aristotle, though he denies design and purpose in the causality of God, still maintains that there are final causes in nature, a logical inconsistency which Maimonides makes much of in his defence of the belief in creation.[3] Thus both Maimonides and Spinoza see the inconsistency in Aristotle's attempt to uphold the existence of final causes in nature while denying at the same time the existence of design in God, but as they are in disagreement as to which of these two premises is correct, they arrive at two diametrically opposite conclusions. Maimonides starts with the Aristotelian premise that there are final causes in nature and therefore argues, as against Aristotle, that there must be design in the causality of God. Spinoza, on the other hand, starts with the Aristotelian premise that there is no design in the causality of God and therefore argues, also against Aristotle, that there cannot be final causes in nature. This denial of final causes by Spinoza re-echoes, on the whole, Francis Bacon's condemnation of the search of final

---

[1] *Cogitata Metaphysica*, II, 10.
[2] *Opera*, II, p. 207, ll. 2–4 and 9–11.
[3] *Moreh Nebukim*, II, 20 ff.

causes in the realm of physics.[1] But unlike Bacon, who admits that final causes are "true and worthy to be inquired in metaphysical speculations"[2] and that they are perfectly compatible with efficient or physical causes, "except that one declares an intention, the other a consequence only,"[3] Spinoza eliminates them even from metaphysical speculations.

If this is the meaning of the last proposition, then the Appendix to Part I, which deals exclusively with the problem of final causes, is, with the exception of the introductory paragraph, really a scholium to the last proposition of Part I. In the Appendix, Spinoza starts out with a restatement of that "which men commonly suppose" with regard to final causes. The passage which follows falls into two parts and betrays the influence of two different sources. The first part restates the view of those who hold "that all things in nature, like men, work for (*propter*) some end; and indeed it is thought to be certain that God himself directs all things to some sure end (*ad certum aliquem finem*)." The immediate source of this view is the following passage in Heereboord: "All natural things work for (*propter*) some end, or, rather, they work to some end, since they are directed by God to an end pre-determined for each thing (*ad finem singulis praefixum*)." [4] The second part of the passage adds "for it is said that God has made all things for man, and man that he may worship God." The immediate source of this statement seems to be a combination of the following passages in Saadia and Maimonides. Saadia's passage reads as follows: "Should it occur to one to ask for what reason

[1] *De Augmentis Scientiarum*, III, 4.

[2] *Ibid.*, III, 4 (*Works*, London, 1857, Vol. I, p. 570; Vol. IV, p. 364).

[3] *Ibid.*

[4] *Meletemata Philosophica, Disputationes ex Philosophia Selectae*, Vol. II, Disp. XXIV, II, § 1: "Res omnes naturales agunt propter finem, aut potius aguntur ad finem, quatenus a Deo diriguntur ad finem singulis praefixum."

did God create all these things, three answers may be given.
. . . The third answer is that He created the beings for their
own benefit so that He might direct them in that benefit and
they might worship Him." [1]   In another place Saadia states
that "although we observe that the created beings are many
. . . the end of all of them is man." [2] Maimonides' passage,
in which there seems to be an allusion to the statements
quoted from Saadia, reads as follows: "But of those who
accept our theory that the whole universe has been created
from nothing, some hold that the inquiry after the purpose
of creation is necessary, and assume that the universe was
only created for the sake of man's existence, that he might
worship God." [3] It must, however, be remarked that, contrary to what may be inferred from Spinoza's statement
here, neither Saadia nor Maimonides is in the least dogmatic about this view. Maimonides definitely rejects the
view that the universe exists for man's sake and that man
exists for the purpose of worshipping God, and gives as his
own view that "we must in continuing the inquiry as to the
purpose of creation at last arrive at the answer that it was
the will of God or that His wisdom decreed it." [4] Even Saadia
gives as his first answer to the question as to the purpose of
creation the view "that God created things for no purpose at
all . . . for God is above any consideration of external
purpose." [5]

Spinoza's own discussion of the problem is divided by
himself into three parts. First, how man came to the idea
of final causes. Second, arguments against the existence of
final causes. Third, certain erroneous conceptions to which
the idea of final causes gave rise.

---

[1] *Emunot we-De'ot*, I, 4.   [2] *Ibid.*, IV, Introduction.
[3] *Moreh Nebukim*, III, 13.   [4] *Ibid.*
[5] *Emunot we-De'ot*, I, 4.

In his account of the origin of the belief in final causes and his explanation of the question "why all are so naturally inclined to embrace it," Spinoza does nothing more than transform the reasons which his predecessors had used as arguments for the existence of final causes into motives for their belief in final causes. He seems to say to them: Your so-called arguments for the existence of final causes are nothing but the expressions of your desires and wishes which you put in the form of logical arguments. Or to put it in other words, Spinoza tries to show that what the mediaevals call reasons are only different forms of rationalization.

Take the conception of final causes in human actions, Spinoza seems to argue, and you will find that even there, where final causes are generally assumed to exist beyond any shadow of a doubt, their existence may be questioned. For what basis is there for this general belief that man does everything for an end, if not the belief that man is free to choose from two alternatives that which is profitable to him. Let us then consider what is meant by this freedom of choice. The best description, Spinoza would seem to argue, is to be found in Saadia, who says that it is a matter of common observation that "man feels that he can speak or remain silent, seize or set loose, and all this without being conscious of any force that could restrain him from carrying out his desire."[1] Freedom then is that feeling of being able to choose without being conscious of any compulsion to make the choice. This choice, furthermore, is supposed to be made in consideration of a certain end which man has in view, and it is this supposition of an end which is generally taken to establish the existence of final causes in human action. But, says Spinoza, is it not possible that the consciousness of freedom

[1] *Ibid.*, IV, 4.

is only a delusion based upon the ignorance of the true causes that really determine one's action, and therefore the belief that one acts for a certain purpose or final cause is also a delusion based upon an ignorance of the real causes, which are always efficient causes, that really necessitate one's action? "It will be sufficient," says Spinoza, "if I take here as an axiom that which no one ought to dispute, namely, that man is born ignorant of the causes of things, and that he has a desire, of which he is conscious, to seek that which is profitable to him. From this it follows, firstly, that he thinks himself free . . . and, secondly, it follows that man does everything for an end."

It must, however, be remarked that Spinoza had been anticipated by Crescas in the suggestion that the consciousness of freedom may be a delusion. In discussing the argument for freedom from the fact that man is not conscious of any compulsion in making a decision, Crescas says that "though man, in making a choice, is unconscious of any compulsion and restraint, it is quite possible that, were it not for some cause that compels him to choose one of the alternatives, he would desire both alternatives alike." [1]

Spinoza continues with the same method of argument with which he had started. Taking the traditional philosophic evidences for design in nature from which the mediaevals tried to prove creation and the existence of an intelligent deity, he transforms them into psychological motives which have induced man to attribute the delusions of his own freedom and of the purposiveness of his own actions to nature and God. The traditional philosophic view is summed up by Maimonides in the following passage: "Aristotle repeatedly says that nature produces nothing in vain, [2] that is to

[1] *Or Adonai*, II, v, 3.
[2] *De Caelo*, I, 4, 271a, 33; *De Anima*, III, 9, 432b, 21.

say, every natural action must necessarily have a certain object. Thus, Aristotle says that plants were created for the sake of animals; and similarly he shows in the case of some other things that one exists for the sake of the other. This is still more obvious in the case of the organs of animals. Know that the existence of such a final cause in the various parts of nature has compelled philosophers to assume the existence of a primal cause apart from nature, namely, that which Aristotle calls the intelligent or divine principle, which divine principle creates one thing for the purpose of another. And know also that to those who acknowledge the truth, the greatest of all arguments for the creation of the world is that which has been demonstrated with regard to natural things, namely, that every one of them has a certain purpose and that one thing exists for the sake of another." [1] All this, says Spinoza, is simply a projection of man's own purposes into the actions of other human beings and into nature, for "by his own mind he necessarily judges that of another" and thus also "it comes to pass that all natural objects are considered as means for obtaining what is profitable." Furthermore, since man has falsely considered these things as means to some end, he thought "it was impossible to believe that they had created themselves," and so again by an analogy of his own experience he inferred "that some ruler or rulers of nature exist, endowed with human liberty, who have taken care of all things for him, and have made all things for his use." The allusions in this passage to the passages quoted from Maimonides are quite apparent. Spinoza finally concludes his argument with a condemnation of the Aristotelian principle quoted by Maimonides, namely, that "nature does nothing in vain," as an attempt to show "that nature, the gods, and man are alike mad."

[1] *Moreh Nebukim*, III, 13.

One would naturally expect that in discussing design in nature Spinoza would resuscitate the old problem of evil which philosophers before him had found at variance with the assumption of design and providence in nature. Spinoza introduces this problem with an enumeration of the so-called physical evils which are similarly discussed by Maimonides in connection with the problem of final causes and design,[1] and in connection with the problem of divine knowledge.[2] The evils which Spinoza happens to mention, "storms, earthquakes, diseases," are reminiscent of the list of evils mentioned by Gersonides, in which are included evils which arise "from the mixture [i.e., diseases] . . . earthquakes, storm, and lightning."[3] But when Spinoza pretends to reproduce the mediaeval explanation of evil by saying that "it was affirmed that these things happened because the gods were angry either because of wrongs which had been inflicted on them by man, or because of sins committed in the method of worshipping them," he does not do justice to their case. Maimonides, Gersonides, and others had more subtle solutions for the problem of evil.

This explanation that physical evil is a divine retribution for moral evil or sin, which Spinoza rightly or wrongly reproduces as the only or the chief explanation that had been advanced for the problem, leads him to revive the old question, already raised in the Bible, especially in the Book of Job, and repeated throughout the history of Jewish religious literature as well as in the literature of other religions, namely, that our observation does not confirm the belief that physical evil is proportionate to moral evil, for "experience," says Spinoza, "daily contradicted this, and showed

[1] *Ibid.*, III, 12.   [2] *Ibid.*, III, 16, end.
[3] *Milḥamot Adonai*, IV, 3 (pp. 160–161); Introduction to his Commentary on Job.

by an infinity of examples that both the beneficial and the injurious were indiscriminately bestowed on the pious and the impious." Parallel passages in which the problem is stated in similar terms can be picked up at random in almost any mediaeval work dealing with this problem. But I shall quote here only the following passage from Crescas: "The great difficulty which cannot be solved completely . . . is the ill-order which is believed to exist in the world from the fact of our observation that many worthy people are like the dust at the feet of unworthy ones, and, in general, the question why there is a righteous man who fares badly and a wicked man who fares well, a question by which prophets and philosophers have been perplexed unto this day." [1]

Many solutions are offered for this problem. Maimonides, for instance, enumerates four theories, the Aristotelian, the Scriptural or his own, the Mutazilite, and the Asharian, and finds that Job and his three friends, Eliphaz the Temanite, Bildad the Shuite, and Zophar the Naamathite, are respectively the spokesmen of these four views.[2] Spinoza seems to sum up all the solutions of the problem in the following general statement: "Hence it was looked upon as indisputable that the judgments of the gods far surpass our comprehension." It is quite possible that this is all that the various solutions ultimately amount to. Strictly speaking, however, the solution mentioned here by Spinoza as typical of all the solutions would, according to Maimonides, represent only the view of Zophar the Naamathite or of the Ashariya.

In the second part of the Appendix we may discern four arguments against final causes.

---

[1] *Or Adonai*, II, ii, 2 (p. 35b). Cf. *Moreh Nebukim*, III, 19; *Milḥamot Adonai*, IV, 2 (p. 156).

[2] *Moreh Nebukim*, III, 17 and 23.

The first two arguments seem to be directed against two statements made by Heereboord. First, "the end is prior in intention to the means." [1] Second, "God . . . works in a most eminent way for an end, not one which is outside himself . . . God has done all things for His own sake . . . not that He stood in need of those things which He made . . . which view the scholastics explain in the following manner: God has done all things for an end, not of want but of assimilation," that is to say "in order to benefit other things which are outside himself," [2] by assimilating them to himself, i.e., by making them like himself. Now, in the *Cogitata Metaphysica*, where Spinoza does not choose to enter into controversy with those "who ask whether God had not determined for himself beforehand an end for the sake of which He had created the world," he is quite willing to say that "a created object is one which presupposes for its existence nothing except God," and to supplement this statement by the explanation that "if God had predetermined for himself some end, it evidently was not independent of God, for there is nothing apart from God by which He was influenced to action." [3] But here in the *Ethics* he rejects any conception of end, even if it be nothing apart from God himself. Heereboord's first statement which declares the priority of the end to the means is characterized by Spinoza as one which "altogether turns nature upside down," for it makes the things which are im-

---

[1] *Meletemata Philosophica, Disputationes ex Philosophia Selectae*, Vol. II, Disp. XXIV, VIII: "Finis est prior in intentione quam media."

[2] *Ibid.*, Disp. XXIV, VI–VII: "Deus . . . modo eminentissimo agit propter finem, non qui extra se sit. . . . Deus omnia fecit propter se . . . non quod istis, quae fecit, indigeret . . . quod Scholastici enunciarunt hoc modo; Deus omnia fecit propter finem, non indigentiae, sed assimilationis, . . . ut bene aliis faciat, quae sunt extra se, rebus." Cf. Baensch's note to this passage in his translation of the *Ethics*.

[3] *Cogitata Metaphysica*, II, 10.

mediately produced by God to exist for the sake of things produced by Him last. The second statement is simply dismissed by him as a verbal quibble and he insists that "if God works to obtain an end, He necessarily seeks something of which He stands in need," and thus "this doctrine does away with God's perfection."

The third argument deals with the scholastic theory of the concurrence of God (*concursus Dei*), of which there is an elaborate discussion in Heereboord.[1] This theory, which is repeatedly stated by Descartes in several different connections,[2] is explained in Spinoza's restatement of Descartes to mean that "each single moment God continually creates things as if anew," from which it follows "that things in themselves have no power to do anything or to determine themselves to any action." [3] A similar explanation of Descartes' principle is given by Blyenbergh in a letter to Spinoza: "Following your assertion, creation and preservation are one and the same thing, and God makes not things only, but also the motions and modes of things, to continue in their own state, that is, concurs in them." From this Blyenbergh infers "that nothing can happen against the will of God."[4] Here in the *Ethics* he illustrates the theory of concurrence by the following example: "For, by way of example, if a stone has fallen from some roof on somebody's head and killed him, they will demonstrate in this manner that the stone has fallen in order to kill the man. For if it did not fall for that purpose by the will of God, how could so many circumstances concur through chance (and a num-

---

[1] *Meletemata Philosophica, Disputationes ex Philosophia Selectae*, Vol. I, Disps. VII–XII.

[2] *Principia Philosophiae*, II, 36. For other references to Descartes and parallel passages in scholastic authors, see Gilson, *Index Scholastico-Cartésien*, 81, and cf. 110–112.

[3] *Cogitata Metaphysica*, II, 11.   [4] Epistola 20.

ber often simultaneously do concur)?" [1] He concludes by characterizing the exponents of this view in the following words: "And so they all fly to God, the refuge for ignorance." [2] A similar description of the Asharian view that every occurrence is determined by the direct intervention of God's absolute will is given by Maimonides in the following passages: "For example, when a storm or gale blows, it causes undoubtedly some leaves of a tree to drop, breaks off some branches of another tree, tears away a stone from a heap of stones, raises dust over herbs and spoils them, and stirs up the sea so that a ship goes down with the whole or part of her contents." [3] Now the Mohammedan Ashariya "admit that Aristotle is correct in assuming one and the same cause [the wind] for the fall of leaves [from the tree] and for the death of a man [drowned in the sea]. But they hold at the same time that the wind did not blow by chance; it is God that caused it to move; it is not therefore the wind that caused the leaves to fall; each leaf fell according to the divine decree; it is God who caused it to fall at a certain time and in a certain place; it could not have fallen before or after that time or in another place, as this had previously been decreed." [4]

The fourth argument [5] is directed against the alleged evidence of design that may be discerned in the structure of the human body. Cicero makes use of this sort of evidence. "But we may yet more easily comprehend that the world was given by the immortal gods to men, if we examine thoroughly into the structure of the body and the form and perfection of human nature." [6] Among the several examples

---

[1] *Opera*, II, p. 80, l. 35–p. 81, l. 2.   [2] *Ibid.*, p. 81, ll. 10–11.
[3] *Moreh Nebukim*, III, 17, Second Theory.
[4] *Ibid.*, Third Theory.
[5] *Opera*, II, p. 81, ll. 11 ff.
[6] *De Natura Deorum*, II, 54, § 133.

which indicate design in the structure of the human body
he mentions the delicate structure of the eye, which he describes in some detail.[1] The same evidence is used also by
Maimonides. Like Cicero, he illustrates it by a description
of the structure of the eye, and then concludes: "In short,
considering the humor of the eye, its membranes and nerves,
with their well-known functions, and their adaptation to the
purpose of sight, can any intelligent person imagine that all
this is due to chance? Certainly not . . . but is according
to our view the result of the action of an intelligent being." [2]
Spinoza's answer to this alleged evidence of design is that
it is based on ignorance, for "when they behold the structure
of the human body, they are amazed; and because they are
ignorant of the causes of such art, they conclude that the
body was made not by mechanical but by divine or super-
natural art." Note the difference between Maimonides'
passage and Spinoza's passage in the choice of an oppositional
term to "intelligent being" or "divine art." In Maimonides
the oppositional term is "chance," i.e., without any cause;
in Spinoza it is "mechanical art," i.e., necessary efficient
causation. Maimonides, however, was not ignorant of "mechanical art" as a possible alternative for "chance" in opposition to "intelligent being," for between his premise that
the structure of the eye could not be the work of chance and
his conclusion that it must be the work of an intelligent
agent he inserts the statements that "this is an artistic organization" and that "nature has no intelligence and no organiz-
ing faculty, as has been accepted by all philosophers," and
it is in consequence of this that we must assume that it is
the work of an intelligent agent. In short, Maimonides
maintains that the artistic organization of the structure of

[1] *Ibid.*, II, 57, § 142.
[2] *Moreh Nebukim*, III, 19.

the eye eliminates not only the assumption of "chance" but also the assumption of a "mechanical art," and points to a "divine art" as its only possible explanation.

In the third part of the Appendix Spinoza shows how from the conception of final causes and from the belief that all things are made for man there has been formed the conception of good, evil, order, confusion, heat, cold, beauty, and deformity. Here, too, Spinoza is transforming a statement used by those who believe in the existence of final causes into an argument against them. The statement which must have given rise to Spinoza's argument here is found in Heereboord. He says: "The end produces the means; not only does it produce them, but it also endows them with goodness, measure, and order." [1] In his criticism of this statement Spinoza is trying to establish the principle that good and evil in all their variety of forms are only relative to man — "they do not reveal the nature of anything in itself, but only the constitution of the imagination." This is not an especially new view. Maimonides has fully developed it, and the following are a few characteristic expressions used by him: "Evils are evils only in relation to a certain thing. . . . All evils are privations. . . . It cannot be said of God that He directly creates evil. . . . His works are all perfectly good." [2] In letters to Blyenbergh Spinoza uses almost the same expressions as Maimonides: "But I for my part cannot admit that sin and evil are something positive . . . for the evil in it [Adam's disobedience] was no more than a privation of a more perfect state which Adam had to lose through that action." [3] "I think that I have sufficiently shown that that which gives its form to evil, error, or crimes does not con-

---

[1] *Meletemata Philosophica, Disputationes ex Philosophia Selectae*, Vol. II, Disp. XXIII, VII: "Finis causat media, nec causat solummodo, sed dat illis bonitatem, mensuram, et ordinem."   [2] *Moreh Nebukim*, III, 10.
[3] Epistola 19 (*Opera*, IV, p. 88, ll. 10-11; p. 91, ll. 4-6).

sist in anything which expresses essence, and that therefore it cannot be said that God is the cause thereof." [1] Similarly in *Cogitata Metaphysica* he repeats the words of Maimonides in saying that "a thing considered in itself is called
neither good nor evil, but only in respect to another being,
which it helps to acquire what is desired, or the contrary." [2]

The direct influence of Maimonides upon Spinoza's treatment of evil is evident beyond any doubt in *Short Treatise*,
I, 4. Spinoza raises there the question how it is possible for
a perfect God to permit confusion to be seen everywhere in
nature. The term "confusion" reflects the expression "absence of order" used by Maimonides [3] and its similar expression "ill-order" which occurs frequently in Gersonides
and Crescas. [4] Spinoza denies that there is real confusion in
nature. What we call confusion is simply a deviation from
certain general ideas which we have set up as exemplars of
perfection. He then dismisses the existence of general ideas,
referring in the course of his discussion to those who say
that "God has no knowledge of particular and transient
things, but only of the general, which in their opinion are
imperishable," and concludes that "God then is the cause
of, and providence over, particular things only." Now,
Maimonides, in a similar way, after discussing the problem
whether Providence extends only to the species or also to
the individuals, [5] proceeds to say that "species and other
general ideas are only things of reason, whilst everything
that exists outside the mind is an individual object, or an
aggregate of individual objects. This being granted, it must
be further admitted that the divine influence, which exists

---

[1] Epistola 23.   [2] *Cogitata Metaphysica*, I, 6.
[3] *Moreh Nebukim*, III, 19: העדר סדור, ‏عدم انتظام.
[4] *Milḥamot Adonai*, IV, 2 (p. 156); *Or Adonai*, II, ii, 2 (p. 35b): ‏רוע הסדור.
[5] *Moreh Nebukim*, III, 17.

in union with the human species, that is, the human intellect, is that which exists in union with the individual intellects, that is to say, that which emanates in Reuben, Simeon, Levi, and Judah." [1]   More especially, Spinoza's reference to "those who follow Aristotle," who "say that these things are not real things, only things of reason," would seem to draw upon Maimonides' statement "that species and other general ideas are only things of reason."

This conception of the relativity of good and evil is expressed by Spinoza in the *Short Treatise* by the statement that they are "entities of reason" (*entia rationis*) as opposed to "real entities" (*entia realia*), for among the entities of reason, he says, are included all relations, and "good and evil are only relations." [2]   Here in the *Ethics*, however, Spinoza goes still further and calls good and evil "entities (*entia*) not of the reason (*rationis*) but of the imagination (*imaginationis*)."

The Appendix is concluded by Spinoza with the question "'why God has not created all men in such a manner that they might be controlled by the dictates of reason alone." [3]   The question is an old one. Judah ha-Levi, for instance, puts it in this way: "Would it not have been better or more commensurate with divine wisdom, if all mankind had been guided in the true path?" [4]   Descartes, too, has raised it. "And, finally, I must also not complain that God concurs with me in forming the acts of the will, that is the judgment in which I go astray." [5]   But "I nevertheless perceive that God could easily have created me so that I never could err, although I still remained free and endowed with a limited

---

[1] *Ibid.*
[2] *Short Treatise,* I, 10. Cf. above, pp. 161–162.
[3] *Opera,* II, p. 83, ll. 26–27.
[4] *Cuzari,* I, 102.
[5] *Meditationes,* IV (*Oeuvres,* VII, p. 60, ll. 26–28).

knowledge." [1] Spinoza has raised the same question also in the *Short Treatise*: "Against all this others object: how is it possible that God, who is said to be supremely perfect, and the sole cause, disposer, and provider of all, nevertheless permits such confusion to be seen everywhere in nature? Also, why has He not made man so as not to be able to sin?" [2] The question was also addressed to Spinoza in a letter by Blyenbergh.[3]

Two answers to this question given by Descartes are made use of by Spinoza.

First, Descartes denies that acts of error and sin have any positive existence with reference to God, for "these acts are entirely true and good, inasmuch as they depend on God."[4] This answer is followed by Spinoza in the *Short Treatise*, in his letter to Blyenbergh,[5] and in the Second Part of the *Ethics*.[6] To quote the *Short Treatise*: "As regards the other [objection], why God has not made mankind so that they should not sin, to this it may serve [as an answer], that whatever is said about sin is only said with reference to us." [7]

Second, Descartes maintains that error and sin were made possible by God for the special purpose of adding to the perfection of the universe as a whole. "And it is easy for me to understand that, in so far as I consider myself alone, and as if there were only myself in the world, I should have been much more perfect than I am, if God had created me so that I could never err. Nevertheless I cannot deny that in some sense it is a greater perfection in the whole universe that cer-

---

[1] *Ibid.* (p. 61, ll. 9–11).
[2] *Short Treatise*, I, 6, § 6.
[3] Epistola 22 (*Opera*, IV, p. 142, ll. 26 ff.).
[4] *Meditationes*, IV (*Oeuvres*, VII, p. 60, ll. 28–29).
[5] Epistola 23 (*Opera*, IV, p. 147, ll. 1 ff.).
[6] Props. 33 and 35. Cf. below, Vol. II, pp. 111 ff.
[7] *Short Treatise*, I, 6, § 8.

tain parts should not be exempt from error as others are than that all parts should be exactly similar." [1] This answer in the form in which it is given by Descartes is not reproduced by Spinoza, and he did not reproduce it for the self-evident reason that he did not believe that anything was created by God for any purpose, even for the perfection of the universe as a whole. But there is in Spinoza an answer which upon a close examination appears to be only a revised form of this answer of Descartes. Error and sin exist in the world, he argues in effect, not because they are to contribute to the perfection of the whole universe but because their exclusion from the world would be contradictory to the conception of God as infinitely great and powerful. Given a God whose greatness and power are infinite, he seems to argue, such a God must be able to produce by the necessity of His nature everything conceivable, and that includes also sin. This is the meaning of the following concluding passage in the Appendix: "I give but one answer: Because to Him material was not wanting for the creation of everything, from the highest down to the very lowest grade of perfection; or, to speak more properly, because the laws of His nature were so ample that they sufficed for the production of everything which can be conceived by an infinite intellect." [2]

[1] *Meditationes*, IV (*Oeuvres*, VII, p. 61, ll. 17–23).
[2] *Opera*, II, p. 83, ll. 27–32.